Connecting Math Concepts

LEVEL

E

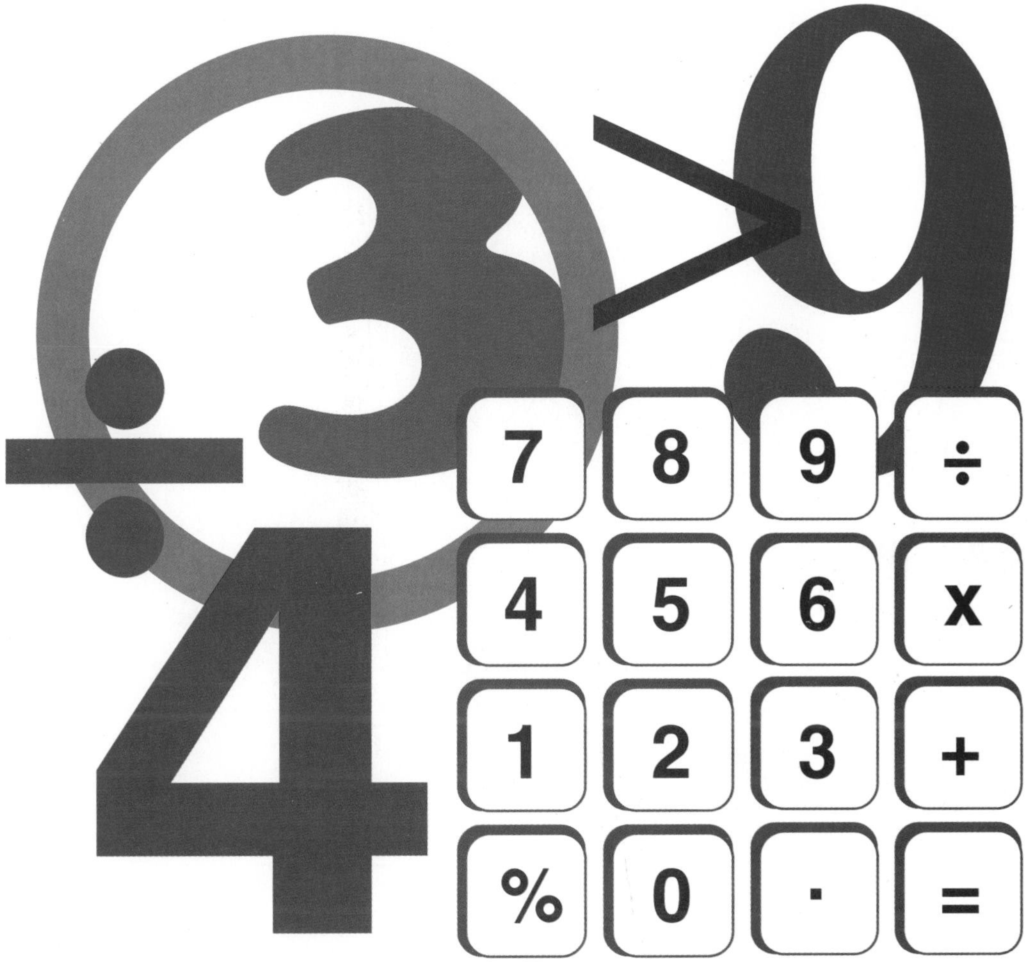

SRA

Columbus, Ohio

The McGraw-Hill Companies

www.sra4kids.com

SRA McGraw-Hill

Send all inquiries to:
SRA/McGraw-Hill
8787 Orion Place
Columbus, OH 43240-4027

Printed in the United States of America.

ISBN 0-02-684693-4

2 3 4 5 6 7 8 9 RRC 07 06 05 04 03

Connecting Math Concepts

Level E

Connecting Math Concepts will teach you a great deal about doing mathematics. When something new is introduced, your teacher will help you work the problems. Very soon, you'll be doing the problems on your own, without help.

Remember, everything that is introduced is something you will learn. It is something that you'll need to work difficult problems that will be introduced later.

Learning is easier when you follow your teacher's directions. Sometimes your teacher will direct you to work part of a problem, sometimes a whole problem, and sometimes a group of problems.

Listen very carefully to the directions and follow them. Work quickly and accurately. Most important of all, work hard. You'll be rewarded with math skills that will surprise you.

Lesson 1

Part 1

- You'll work problems that are presented in the textbook.
- Some are column problems like these:

Part 4

a. 254 − 110	b. 554 − 204

- When you work column problems on lined paper, follow these rules:
  1) **Write the part number. Then write the letter for each problem.**
  2) **Copy the problem carefully.**
  3) **Box your answer.**
  4) **Leave room between your problems. Don't crowd your problems together.**
- When you follow these rules, you'll be able to see what you've written. It's easier to keep your digits lined up. You can also find mistakes more easily.

Part 2

Follow the rules to work these problems.

a. 135 + 217	b. 217 − 206	c. 668 − 128

Part 3

Rewrite each equation.

a. $18 = 10 + 8$ b. $8 = 11 - 3$ c. $32 = 18 + 14$

Part 4

- A lot of problems you'll work are based on number families. A number family is made up of three numbers that always go together to make an addition fact or subtraction fact.
- The family is made up of two small numbers and a big number:

  small number **small number** → big number

  The big number is at the end of the arrow.

- Here's a family with the small numbers shown: The small numbers are 14 and 6.

  14 6 → ■

- To find the **big number,** you **add** the small numbers:

  $$\begin{array}{r} 14 \\ +\ 6 \\ \hline 20 \end{array}$$

  The big number is 20.

  14 6 → 20

- Here's a family with a small number missing:

  ■ 34 → 37

- To find a missing **small number,** you **subtract.** You start with the big number and subtract the small number that is shown:

  $$\begin{array}{r} 37 \\ -34 \\ \hline 3 \end{array}$$

- The subtraction for this family is 37 – 34. The missing small number is 3.

  3 34 → 37

- Here's a family with the other small number missing:

  3 ■ → 37

- The subtraction for this family is:

  $$\begin{array}{r} 37 \\ -\ 3 \\ \hline 34 \end{array}$$

  So the missing small number is 34.

  3 34 → 37

Part 5 Write the problem and the answer for each number family.

a. 16 18 → ■   b. 7 ■ → 47   c. ■ 256 → 421   d. 67 135 → ■

Part 6 Answer each question.

This table shows the number of cars and trucks on two different lots—lot A and lot B.

	Lot A	Lot B	Total for both lots
Cars	13	12	25
Trucks	16	14	30
Total vehicles	29	26	55

Questions

a. How many cars are there for both lots?

b. How many vehicles are on lot B?

c. How many trucks are on lot B?

d. How many trucks are on lot A?

e. How many vehicles are there for both lots?

Part 7

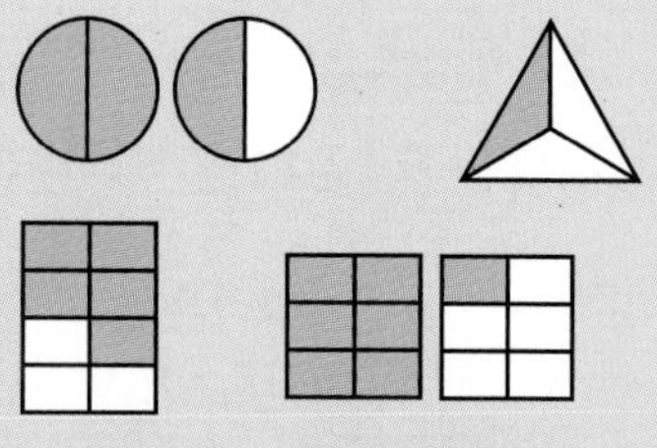

- Some pictures show whole units and shaded parts.
- You can write fractions that tell about these pictures.
- Here are the rules for fractions:

All the parts are the same size.

The bottom number tells the number of equal parts **in each unit.**

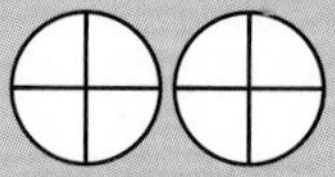

$\frac{}{4}$

The top number tells the number of parts **that are shaded.**

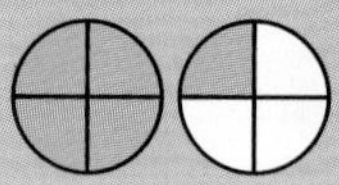

$\frac{5}{4}$

Part 8 Write the fraction for each picture.

a. b. c. d. e.

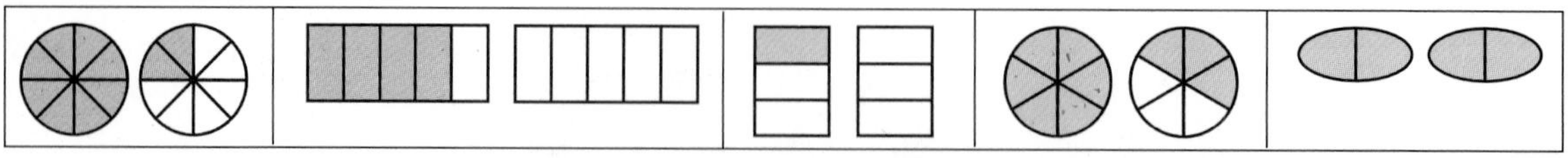

Lesson 2

Part 1 **Write the fraction for each picture.**

a.
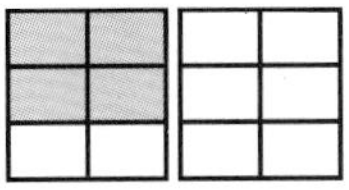

b.
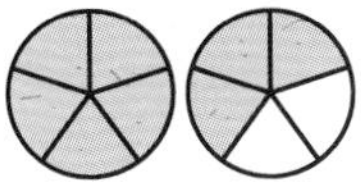

c.
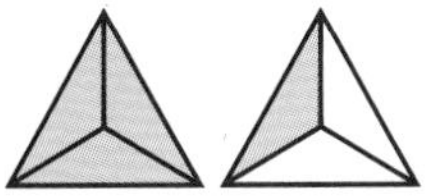

d.
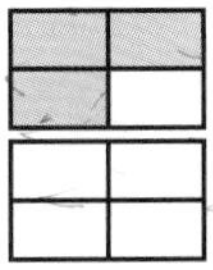

e.
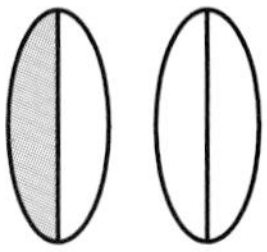

Part 2

This table shows the number of inches of snow that fell in January and February in Hill Park and River Park.

	January	February	Total for both months
Hill Park	35	14	49
River Park	15	18	33
Total for both parks	50	32	82

Questions

a. Which park had more snowfall in February?

b. In which month did River Park have less snowfall?

I see you have a table problem.
There's nothing wrong with this table. This is a math problem!
Town A
Town B
Total
15
17
52
99

Part 3 Answer each question.

This table shows the number of inches of snow that fell in January and February in Hill Park and River Park.

Questions

a. In which month did more snow fall in River Park?

b. In which month did less snow fall in Hill Park?

c. How many inches of snow fell in both parks during January?

d. How many inches of snow fell in both parks during both months?

	January	February	Total for both months
Hill Park	37	24	61
River Park	29	28	57
Total for both parks	66	52	118

e. How many inches of snow fell in Hill Park during February?

f. Which park had more snowfall in February?

Part 4 Write the problem and the answer for each number family.

a. 48 ■ → 71 b. 56 29 → ■ c. ■ 53 → 79 d. 490 130 → ■

Part 5 Rewrite each equation.

a. 15 = 11 + 4 b. 7 = 16 – 9 c. 24 = 4 x 6 d. 36 = 9 x 4

Part 6

- You don't have to look at pictures to figure out if a fraction is more than 1, less than 1 or equal to 1. You can examine the fraction.
- The bottom number tells the number of parts in each unit.
- The top number tells the number of parts shaded.
- Here are the rules for fractions:

  If the top number is less than the bottom number, the fraction is less than 1. $\frac{7}{8}$

  If the top and bottom numbers are the same, the fraction equals 1 unit. $\frac{8}{8}$

  If the top number is more than the bottom number, the fraction is more than 1. $\frac{9}{8}$

Part 7

Copy each fraction that is more than 1.

a. $\frac{4}{5}$ b. $\frac{10}{9}$ c. $\frac{8}{9}$ d. $\frac{7}{6}$ e. $\frac{6}{7}$ f. $\frac{20}{3}$ g. $\frac{12}{4}$

Part 8

- When you multiply by a tens number like 30 or 70 or 90, the last digit of the answer is always zero.
- Here's 34 x 20:
- To work the problem, you write a zero in the ones column.

$$\begin{array}{r} 34 \\ \underline{\times\ 20} \\ 0 \end{array}$$

- Then you work the problem the way you always would. 4 x 2 is 8. 3 x 2 is 6.

$$\begin{array}{r} 34 \\ \underline{\times\ 20} \\ 680 \end{array}$$

Independent Work

Part 9 **Answer each question.**

This table shows the number of red hens and other hens that were on two different farms—Hilary Farm and Fran's Farm.

	Red hens	Hens that were not red	Total hens
Hilary Farm	256	640	896
Fran's Farm	911	12	923
Total for both farms	1167	652	1819

Questions

a. What was the total number of hens on Fran's Farm?

b. How many red hens were on Fran's Farm?

c. How many hens that were not red were there in all?

d. How many red hens were on Hilary Farm?

Part 10 **Copy each problem. Write the answer and box it.**

a. $\begin{array}{r} 411 \\ -\ 306 \\ \hline \end{array}$

b. $\begin{array}{r} 681 \\ -\ \ 90 \\ \hline \end{array}$

c. $\begin{array}{r} 417 \\ +\ \ 68 \\ \hline \end{array}$

d. $\begin{array}{r} 21 \\ 146 \\ +\ \ 83 \\ \hline \end{array}$

I don't think that's the way you're supposed to box your answer.
954
+217
1171
650
-148
502

Lesson 3

Part 1 Working Problems with a Calculator

Make sure your calculator is turned on.

0.

A. $\begin{array}{r} 34 \\ \underline{\times\ 26} \end{array}$ 3 4 x 2 6 =

B. $\begin{array}{r} 340 \\ 12 \\ \underline{+\ 187} \end{array}$ 3 4 0 + 1 2 + 1 8 7 =

Part 2 Work each problem.

a. $\begin{array}{r} 44 \\ \underline{\times\ 13} \end{array}$

b. $\begin{array}{r} 134 \\ 567 \\ \underline{+\ 765} \end{array}$

c. $\begin{array}{r} 427 \\ \underline{-\ 352} \end{array}$

d. $\begin{array}{r} 125 \\ \underline{\times\ \ 40} \end{array}$

e. $\begin{array}{r} 210 \\ 14 \\ \underline{+\ 358} \end{array}$

Part 3 Figure out the missing number for each family.

a. 110 390 → ■

b. 29 ■ → 60

c. ■ 350 → 458

d. 65 28 → ■

Part 4 **Answer each question.**

This table shows the number of redwood and hemlock trees that were planted in Hill Park and River Park.

	Redwoods planted	Hemlocks planted	Total trees planted
Hill Park	22	37	59
River Park	9	12	21
Total for both parks	31	49	80

Questions

a. How many hemlocks were planted in River Park?

b. Were more hemlocks planted in Hill Park or River Park?

c. In which park were more trees planted?

d. What's the total number of hemlocks for both parks?

e. How many redwoods were planted in Hill Park?

Independent Work

Part 5 **Copy and work each problem. Box your answers.**

a. $\begin{array}{r} 114 \\ -\ \ 96 \\ \hline \end{array}$ b. $\begin{array}{r} 314 \\ +\ \ 18 \\ \hline \end{array}$ c. $\begin{array}{r} 5604 \\ -\ \ 302 \\ \hline \end{array}$ d. $\begin{array}{r} 890 \\ +\ 222 \\ \hline \end{array}$

Part 6 **Write the fraction for each picture.**

a. 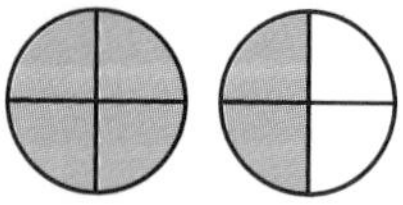

b. 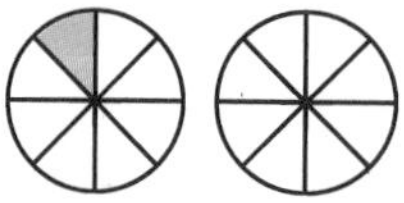

c. 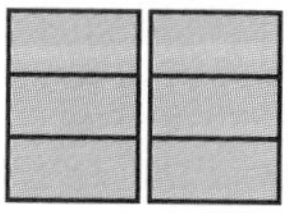

d. 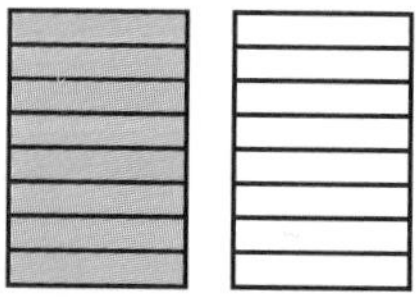

Part 7 **Rewrite each equation so that the underlined number is last.**

a. $\underline{14} = 6 + 8$ b. $\underline{14} = 19 - 5$ c. $\underline{12} = 6 \times 2$ d. $\underline{56} = 8 \times 7$

Lesson 4

Part 1 Answer each question.

This table shows the number of boys and girls that walked across two different bridges—Allen Bridge and Toll Bridge.

	Boys	Girls	Total children
Allen Bridge	42	97	139
Toll Bridge	68	43	111
Total for both bridges	110	140	250

Questions

a. Did more boys go on Allen Bridge or Toll Bridge?

b. How many girls went across Toll Bridge?

c. On Allen Bridge, were there more boys or more girls?

d. What was the total number of children who went across Allen Bridge?

Part 2 Work each problem.

a. $4\overline{)616}$ **6** **1** **6** ÷ **4** =

b. $5\overline{)2615}$

c. $8\overline{)984}$

Part 3

- When you add or subtract fractions, the fractions must have the same bottom number. $\frac{5}{4} + \frac{2}{4} = \frac{7}{4}$
- You can understand why the bottom numbers must be the same by thinking about pictures of fractions.
- Here are pictures of different fractions: The first picture shows fourths. The second picture shows fourths.

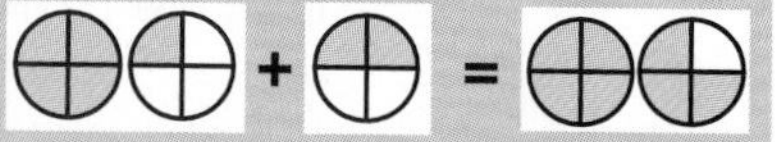

- You can add these fractions. The answer is $\frac{7}{4}$.
- We can do the same thing for subtraction. If we start with $\frac{7}{4}$ and minus $\frac{2}{4}$, we'll end up with $\frac{5}{4}$.

- Here are pictures of two fractions we cannot add or subtract the way they are written:

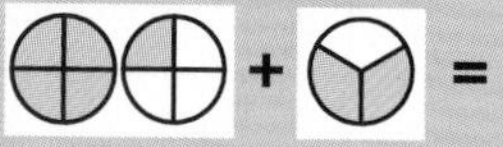

- The answer is not fourths. The answer is not thirds. So we can't add the fractions the way they are written.
- Here are the rules for adding fractions with the same bottom number:

  You copy the bottom number. That tells about the number of parts in each unit. $\frac{5}{4} + \frac{2}{4} = \frac{\ }{4}$

  You add the top numbers. That tells how many shaded parts you'd show in a picture. $\frac{5}{4} + \frac{2}{4} = \frac{7}{4}$

Part 4 Copy the problems you can work the way they are written.

a. $\frac{3}{7} + \frac{3}{3} = ■$

b. $\frac{13}{9} - \frac{3}{9} = ■$

c. $\frac{4}{6} + \frac{7}{3} = ■$

d. $\frac{12}{4} - \frac{10}{5} = ■$

e. $\frac{7}{3} + \frac{7}{3} = ■$

f. $\frac{8}{7} + \frac{2}{7} = ■$

g. $\frac{4}{9} - \frac{2}{5} = ■$

h. $\frac{5}{6} - \frac{5}{6} = ■$

Part 5 Figure out the missing number for each number family.

a. ■ 106 → 324

b. 209 174 → ■

c. 310 ■ → 430

d. ■ 123 → 265

e. 186 248 → ■

Independent Work

Part 6 Write the fraction for each picture.

a. 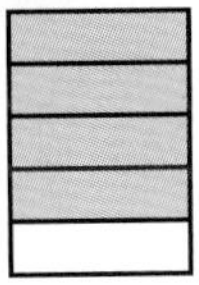

b. 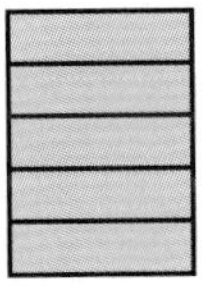

c. 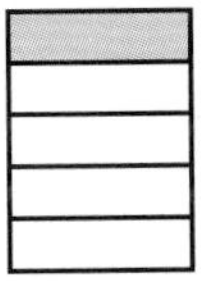

d. 

Lesson 5

Part 1 Write the fraction for each description.

a. The fraction is more than 1. The numbers are 15 and 18.
b. The fraction is less than 1. The numbers are 19 and 20.
c. There are 6 parts shaded. There are 10 parts in each unit.
d. There are 11 parts in each unit. There are 9 parts shaded.
e. The fraction is more than 1. The numbers are 14 and 3.
f. There are 15 parts shaded. There are 14 parts in each unit.

Part 2 Write the place value addition equation for each numeral.

a. 357 b. 932 c. 531 d. 333 e. 38

Part 3 Copy the problems you can work the way they are written. Then work those problems.

a. $\frac{3}{4} - \frac{2}{4} =$ ■

b. $\frac{1}{2} + \frac{3}{4} =$ ■

c. $\frac{7}{3} + \frac{1}{3} =$ ■

d. $\frac{10}{9} + \frac{8}{9} =$ ■

e. $\frac{12}{7} - \frac{12}{8} =$ ■

f. $\frac{15}{2} - \frac{4}{2} =$ ■

g. $\frac{4}{5} + \frac{4}{8} =$ ■

h. $\frac{11}{10} - \frac{5}{9} =$ ■

I can work it the way it's written — I just can't get the right answer.

Part 4

- You've written fractions for pictures like these:

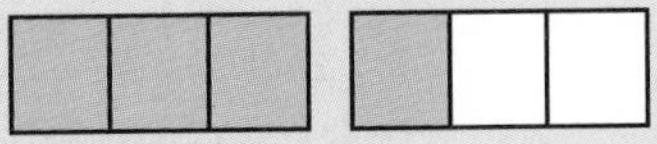

- The number of parts in each unit is the bottom number. The number of shaded parts is the top number. $\frac{4}{3}$
- You can do the same thing with a number line. Number lines are tricky because the end of one unit is the beginning of the next unit.

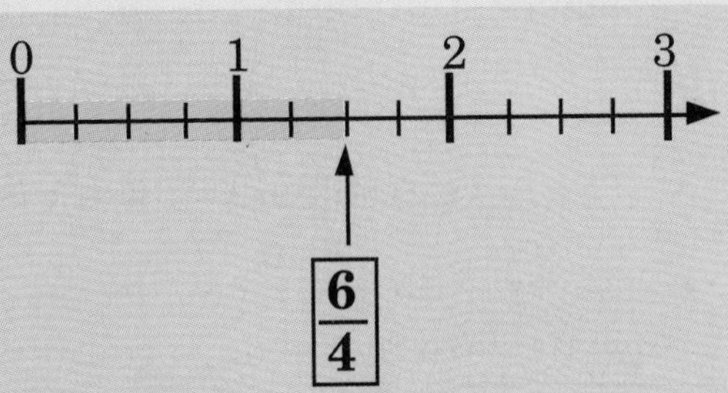

- All the units on the number line have the same number of parts.
- The bottom number of the fraction is the number of parts in each unit. The top number is the number of shaded parts.
- You can also write fractions for any mark on the number line.
- The bottom number tells the number of parts in each unit.
- The top number tells the number of parts **from the beginning of the number line.**

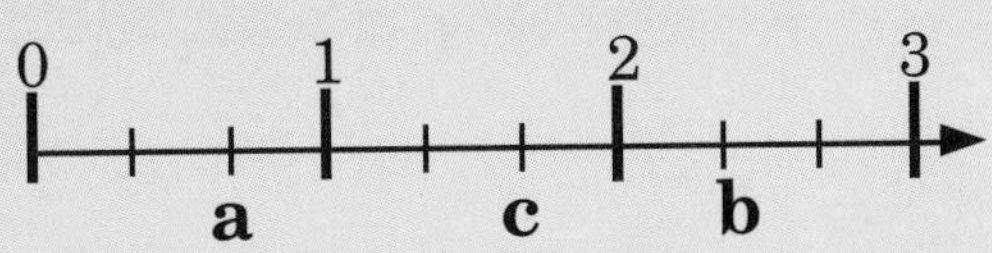

Part 5

Write the fraction for each letter.

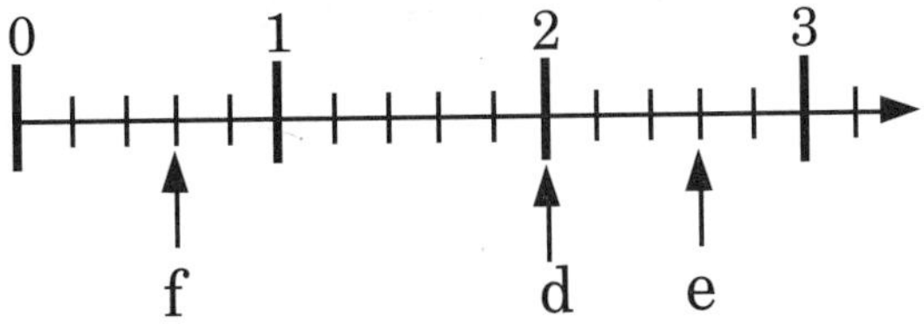

Part 6

- When you multiply by a 2-digit number that does not end in zero, you actually work two problems.
- Here's 53 x 42: → $\begin{array}{r} 53 \\ \underline{\times\ 42} \end{array}$
- The first problem you work is $\begin{array}{r} 53 \\ \underline{\times\ 2} \end{array}$: $\begin{array}{r} 53 \\ \underline{\times\ 42} \end{array}$
- Here's the answer to that problem: → 106
- The next problem you work is $\begin{array}{r} 53 \\ \underline{\times\ 40} \end{array}$. $\begin{array}{r} 53 \\ \underline{\times\ 42} \\ 106 \end{array}$
- You're multiplying by **40,** so you write zero in the ones column: → 0
- The answer to that problem goes right below the other answer: → $\begin{array}{r} {}^{1} \\ 53 \\ \underline{\times\ 42} \\ 106 \\ 2120 \end{array}$
- To find the answer to the **whole** problem, you add. → $\begin{array}{r} 53 \\ \underline{\times\ 42} \\ 106 \\ \underline{+\ 2120} \\ 2226 \end{array}$

Independent Work

Part 7

Figure out the missing number for each number family and box it.

a. 110 ■ → 254

b. ■ 56 → 125

c. 140 63 → ■

d. 28 79 → ■

e. 153 ■ → 280

Lesson 6

Part 1 **Copy the problems you can work the way they are written. Then work those problems.**

a. $\frac{6}{5} - \frac{6}{3} = ■$

b. $\frac{18}{7} + \frac{2}{7} = ■$

c. $\frac{12}{6} - \frac{7}{9} = ■$

d. $\frac{4}{5} - \frac{1}{5} = ■$

e. $\frac{4}{11} + \frac{7}{11} = ■$

f. $\frac{8}{3} + \frac{11}{5} = ■$

g. $\frac{8}{5} + \frac{8}{6} = ■$

h. $\frac{16}{9} - \frac{16}{9} = ■$

Part 2 **For each numeral, write the equation to show the place-value addition.**

a. 16 b. 218 c. 11 d. 112 e. 479

Part 3 **Write the fraction for each description.**

a. The fraction is less than 1. The numbers are 12 and 14.

b. There are 8 parts in each unit. There are 11 parts shaded.

c. There are 4 parts shaded. There are 7 parts in each unit.

d. The fraction is more than 1. The numbers are 10 and 7.

e. There are 5 parts shaded. There are 9 parts in each unit.

f. The fraction is more than 1. The numbers are 8 and 19.

Independent Work

Part 4 Answer each question.

This table shows the number of deer and squirrels that live in Hill Park and River Park.

	Deer	Squirrels	Total for both animals
Hill Park	23	19	42
River Park	40	86	126
Total for both parks	63	105	168

Questions

a. How many of both animals live in Hill Park?

b. Do more deer live in Hill Park or River Park?

c. What's the total number of squirrels for both parks?

d. How many deer live in River Park?

e. In which park do fewer squirrels live?

f. What is the total number for both animals in both parks?

Part 5 Figure out the missing number for each number family.

a. 36 ■ → 88

b. ■ 31 → 123

c. 50 70 → ■

Part 6 Copy and complete each division fact.

a. $7\overline{)56}$ b. $8\overline{)64}$ c. $7\overline{)63}$ d. $6\overline{)54}$ e. $2\overline{)8}$ f. $1\overline{)7}$ g. $4\overline{)28}$

Part J

a. 73 × 92 = 146 + 6570 = 6716

b. 56 × 81 = 56 + 4480 = 4536

c. 42 × 53 = 126 + 2100 = 2226

d. 62 × 34 = 248 + 1860 = 2108

e. 94 × 62 = 188 + 5640 = 5828

Lesson 7

Part 1

Copy the problems you can work the way they are written. Then work those problems.

a. $\frac{35}{8} + \frac{4}{5} =$ ■

b. $\frac{11}{8} - \frac{9}{10} =$ ■

c. $\frac{3}{5} - \frac{3}{5} =$ ■

d. $\frac{15}{3} - \frac{10}{8} =$ ■

e. $\frac{16}{7} + \frac{19}{7} =$ ■

f. $\frac{4}{9} + \frac{12}{3} =$ ■

g. $\frac{12}{8} + \frac{10}{8} =$ ■

h. $\frac{19}{6} - \frac{18}{6} =$ ■

Part 2

- Some fractions equal whole numbers. Pictures for those fractions show whole units with all the parts in each unit shaded.

- Here are pictures of fractions that **do not** equal whole numbers:

- Here are pictures of fractions that **do** equal whole numbers:

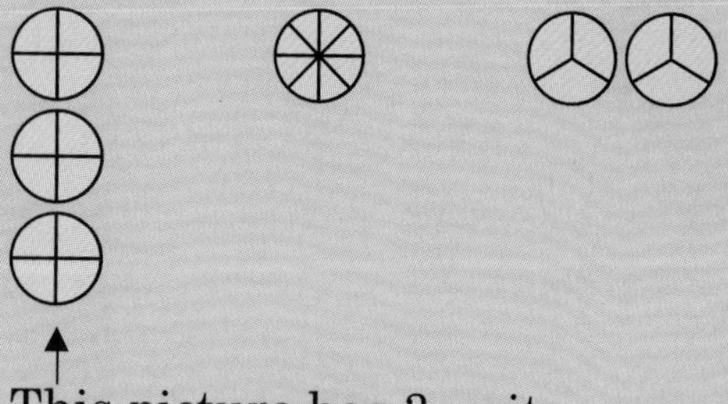

This picture has 3 units shaded. The fraction for this picture equals 3.

- Here's a rule about all fractions that equal whole numbers:

  If the fraction equals a whole number, the top number of the fraction is exactly so many times the bottom number.

- If the fraction equals 2, the top number is 2 times the bottom number.
- If the fraction equals 9, the top number is 9 times the bottom.

Part 3 **Write a fraction for each description.**

Sample problems

The bottom number is 5. The fraction equals 3 whole units.

The bottom number is 8. The fraction equals 4 whole units.

a. The bottom number is 6. The fraction equals 5.

b. The bottom number is 3. The fraction equals 5.

c. The bottom number is 7. The fraction equals 3.

d. The bottom number is 9. The fraction equals 10.

Independent Work

Part 4 **Figure out the missing number in each number family.**

a. 124 13 → ■

b. 90 ■ → 113

c. 24 72 → ■

d. ■ 56 → 64

Part 5 **Write the fraction for each item. Circle each fraction that is more than one whole unit.**

a. 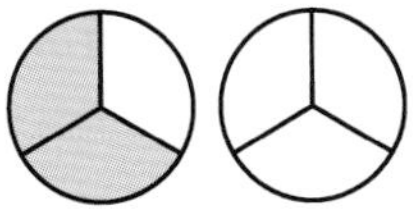

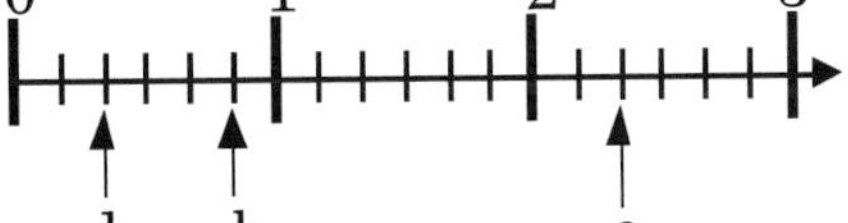

e. 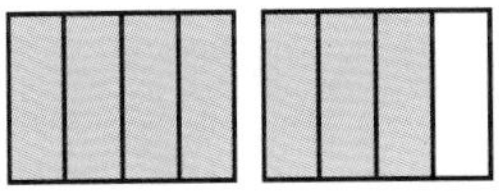

f. The fraction is less than 1. The numbers are 8 and 5.

g. There are 6 parts in each unit. There are 12 parts shaded.

Part 6 **For each numeral, write the equation to show the place-value addition.**

a. 491 b. 12 c. 914 d. 111

Lesson 8

Part 1

- You can read any fraction as a division problem. First you say the top number. Then you say **divided by.** Then you say the bottom number.
  - Here's: $\frac{40}{5}$ That's: $5\overline{)40}$
  - Here's: $\frac{35}{7}$ That's: $7\overline{)35}$
  - Here's: $\frac{42}{9}$ That's: **?**
- When you say the division problem for a fraction, you know what to write.
  - Here's: $\frac{45}{5}$ That's: $5\overline{)45}^{\,9}$

Part 2

Write the division problem and the answer for each fraction.

a. $\frac{14}{7}$ b. $\frac{40}{5}$ c. $\frac{48}{8}$ d. $\frac{32}{4}$ e. $\frac{21}{3}$

Part 3

Figure out the missing number for each number family.

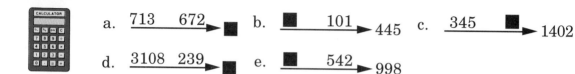

a. 713 672 → ■

b. ■ 101 → 445

c. 345 ■ → 1402

d. 3108 239 → ■

e. ■ 542 → 998

Independent Work

Part 4 **Copy and complete each division fact.**

a. $9\overline{)63}$ b. $6\overline{)54}$ c. $4\overline{)36}$ d. $7\overline{)42}$ e. $1\overline{)5}$

f. $7\overline{)56}$ g. $8\overline{)72}$ h. $5\overline{)35}$ i. $4\overline{)8}$

Part 5 **Answer each question.**

This table shows the number of frogs and fish that lived in Lily Lake and Star Lake in 1969.

	Frogs	Fish	Total
Lily Lake	32	64	96
Star Lake	49	57	106
Total for both lakes	81	121	202

Questions

a. Were there more frogs or more fish in both lakes?

b. In which lake were there fewer fish?

c. What was the total number of both animals in both lakes?

d. Were there fewer of both animals in Lily Lake or Star Lake?

e. How many frogs were in Star Lake?

Part 6 **Copy the problems you can work the way they are written. Work those problems.**

a. $\frac{18}{5} - \frac{18}{4} =$ ■

b. $\frac{9}{8} + \frac{4}{8} =$ ■

c. $\frac{11}{3} - \frac{6}{3} =$ ■

d. $\frac{9}{8} - \frac{8}{9} =$ ■

e. $\frac{14}{5} - \frac{14}{5} =$ ■

f. $\frac{6}{10} + \frac{6}{10} =$ ■

g. $\frac{11}{9} + \frac{3}{9} =$ ■

h. $\frac{15}{21} + \frac{2}{21} =$ ■

Lesson 9

Part 1

Write the division problem and the answer for each fraction.

a. $\frac{6}{3}$ b. $\frac{28}{4}$ c. $\frac{35}{5}$ d. $\frac{21}{7}$ e. $\frac{48}{6}$

Part 2

Figure out the missing number for each number family.

a. ■ 108 → 1240

b. 523 975 → ■

c. 16 ■ → 861

d. 267 593 → ■

Part 3

- When you multiply fractions, you multiply the top numbers and write the answer on top. Then you multiply the bottom numbers and write the answer on the bottom.
- Here's a problem: $\frac{3}{4} \times \frac{2}{5} =$
- The multiplication problem for the top is: 3 x 2. That's 6. You write 6 on top. $\frac{3}{4} \times \frac{2}{5} = \frac{6}{}$
- The multiplication problem for the bottom is: 4 x 5. That's 20. You write 20 on the bottom. $\frac{3}{4} \times \frac{2}{5} = \frac{6}{20}$
- The answer is $\frac{6}{20}$. $\frac{3}{4} \times \frac{2}{5} = \frac{6}{20}$

Part 4

Copy each problem and work it.

a. $\frac{2}{9} \times \frac{4}{2} =$ ■ b. $\frac{1}{3} \times \frac{5}{1} =$ ■ c. $\frac{2}{3} \times \frac{4}{5} =$ ■ d. $\frac{2}{8} \times \frac{6}{5} =$ ■

Part 5

- Some tables have totals at the end of the rows and totals at the bottom of columns. These tables work just like number families for each row and each column.

- Here's a table with four numbers:

			Total
	14	12	
	15	19	
Total			

- Here are the arrows for the rows: The first two numbers are the small numbers. The total is the big number.

			Total
	14	12 →	26
	15	19 →	34
Total			

- Here's the same table with the arrows for the columns: The top two numbers are small numbers. The total at the bottom of each column is the big number.

			Total
	14 ↓	12 ↓	26
	15	19	34
Total	29	31	

- Here's the rule about the rows and columns:

  If there are **two** numbers in a row or column, you can figure out the missing number.

  If there is only **one** number, you **can't** figure out the missing number.

Independent Work

Part 6 **Write the fraction for each description. Circle any fraction that is more than 1 whole unit.**

a. This fraction is more than 1. The numbers are 1 and 28.

b. This fraction is less than 1. The numbers are 34 and 33.

c. This fraction has 5 parts in each whole unit. 11 parts are shaded.

d. This fraction has 11 parts shaded. There are 12 parts in each unit.

e. This fraction has 1 part in each unit. 2 parts are shaded.

Part 7 **Write the fraction for each letter.**

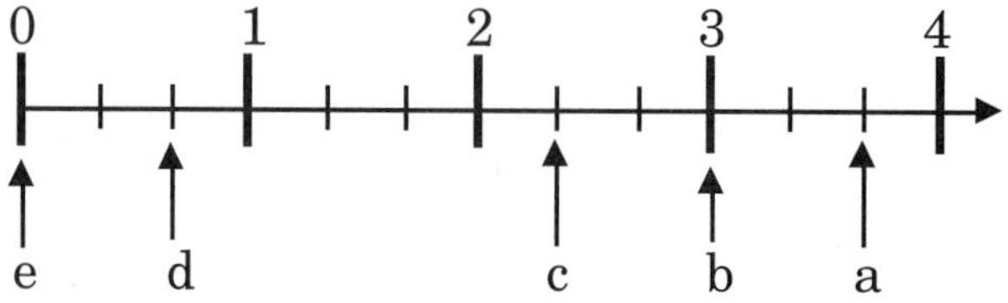

Part 8 **For each numeral, write the equation to show the place-value addition.**

a. 41 b. 14 c. 618

Part 9 **Copy each problem and work it.**

a. $\frac{3}{5} + \frac{9}{5} = \blacksquare$ b. $\frac{17}{20} + \frac{36}{20} = \blacksquare$ c. $\frac{103}{3} - \frac{86}{3} = \blacksquare$ d. $\frac{12}{5} - \frac{11}{5} = \blacksquare$

Lesson 10

Part 1 **Write whether each fraction is more than 1, equals 1 or is less than 1.**

a. $\frac{5}{5}$ b. $\frac{3}{4}$ c. $\frac{5}{4}$ d. $\frac{130}{130}$ e. $\frac{17}{1}$ f. $\frac{1}{2}$

Test 1

Part 1 **Write the fraction for each letter.**

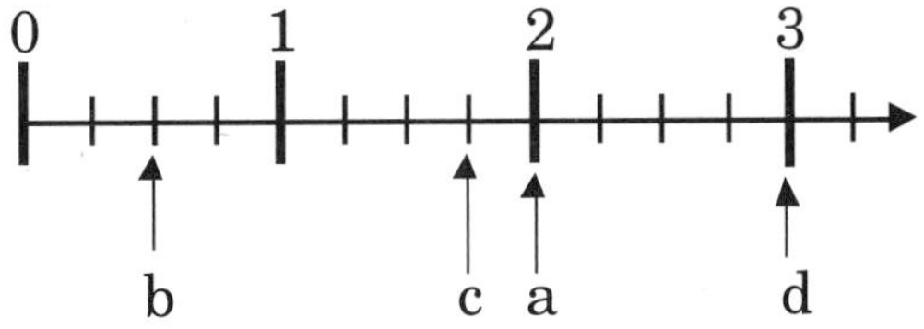

Part 2 **Figure out the missing number for each number family.**

a. 25 382 → ■

b. 257 ■ → 600

c. ■ 145 → 304

d. 625 48 → ■

Part 3 **Copy the problems you can work the way they are written. Then work those problems.**

a. $\frac{14}{5} + \frac{14}{3} =$ ■

b. $\frac{18}{3} - \frac{12}{3} =$ ■

c. $\frac{71}{2} + \frac{3}{3} =$ ■

d. $\frac{24}{7} + \frac{21}{7} =$ ■

e. $\frac{8}{17} - \frac{8}{17} =$ ■

Part 4 Answer each question.

This table shows the number of mice and rabbits counted in Hill Park and River Park.

Questions

a. What is the total number of both animals living in River Park?

b. Do more rabbits live in Hill Park or River Park?

c. What is the total number of mice for both parks?

d. How many rabbits live in River Park?

e. In which park do fewer mice live?

f. What is the total number for both animals in both parks?

	Mice	Rabbits	Total for both animals
Hill Park	23	29	52
River Park	60	76	136
Total for both parks	83	105	188

Part 5 For each numeral, write the equation to show the place-value addition.

a. 68

b. 347

Part 6 Copy the table. Write the division problem for each multiplication problem. Figure out the answer. Write the missing number in both problems.

Multiplication	Division
a. 6 x ■ = 126	
b. 4 x ■ = 860	
c. 5 x ■ = 9505	
d. 2 x ■ = 66	

Lesson 11

Part 1 **Copy and work each problem.**

a. $\frac{2}{3} \times \frac{7}{5} =$ [redacted]

b. $\frac{1}{4} \times \frac{6}{3} =$ [redacted]

c. $\frac{10}{3} \times \frac{8}{6} =$ [redacted]

d. $\frac{2}{1} \times \frac{4}{7} =$ [redacted]

e. $\frac{7}{3} \times \frac{4}{9} =$ [redacted]

Part 2 **Write whether each fraction is more than 1, equals 1 or is less than 1.**

a. $\frac{7}{1}$ b. $\frac{21}{21}$ c. $\frac{92}{95}$ d. $\frac{1}{9}$ e. $\frac{19}{10}$ f. $\frac{59}{59}$

Part 3

- You can check addition problems by subtracting.
- Here's a problem: **401 + 38 = 439**
  The student worked it and wrote the answer.
- One way to check whether the answer is correct is to start with the student's answer and **subtract.**
- Here's the subtraction problem: 439 − 38 = ☐
- If 439 is the correct answer to the addition problem, the answer to the subtraction problem should be 401.

Independent Work

Part 4 **Write the place-value addition equation for each numeral.**

a. 342 b. 6118 c. 7219 d. 59

Part 5 Write the fraction for each description. Circle fractions that are more than 1.

a. The fraction has 4 parts shaded. There are 3 parts in each whole unit.

b. The numbers for the fraction are 5 and 19. The fraction is less than 1.

c. The numbers for the fraction are 81 and 18. The fraction is more than 1.

d. 18 parts are shaded. There are 18 parts in each whole unit.

Part 6 Copy the problems you can work the way they are written. Then work those problems.

a. $\frac{6}{21} + \frac{5}{21} =$ ■ b. $\frac{12}{3} - \frac{12}{7} =$ ■ c. $\frac{9}{5} - \frac{8}{5} =$ ■

d. $\frac{14}{7} - \frac{3}{3} =$ ■ e. $\frac{1}{15} + \frac{14}{15} =$ ■

Lesson 12

Part 1 **Copy the problems you can work the way they are written. Then work those problems.**

a. $\frac{2}{5} \times \frac{3}{8} = $ ■

b. $\frac{13}{6} - \frac{10}{6} = $ ■

c. $\frac{9}{4} - \frac{6}{5} = $ ■

d. $\frac{7}{11} + \frac{4}{11} = $ ■

e. $\frac{3}{8} + \frac{4}{3} = $ ■

f. $\frac{5}{6} \times \frac{2}{6} = $ ■

g. $\frac{3}{5} + \frac{3}{7} = $ ■

h. $\frac{1}{7} + \frac{12}{7} = $ ■

Part 2 **Copy each division problem and work it.**

a. $5\overline{)34}$ b. $7\overline{)28}$ c. $4\overline{)25}$ d. $5\overline{)3}$ e. $3\overline{)18}$

Part 3 **Make a number family for each sentence.**

Sample sentence: Ginger has 36 more than Alex.

a. Donna weighs 149 pounds less than Frank.

b. Earl has $6\frac{1}{2}$ more than George.

c. James has 14 fewer than Bonnie.

d. Terry is 71 years older than Wilbur.

e. Train A traveled 501 fewer miles than train B.

Independent Work

Part 4 **Write the fraction for each description. Circle each fraction that is more than 1. Box each fraction that is less than 1.**

a. The numbers for this fraction are 78 and 79. The fraction is less than 1.

b. The numbers for this fraction are 100 and 101. The fraction is more than 1.

c. This fraction has 13 parts in each unit. 13 parts are shaded.

d. This fraction has 1 part in each unit. 4 parts are shaded.

e. This fraction has 1 part shaded. There are 4 parts in each unit.

Part 5 **Answer each question.**

This table shows the inches of rain that fell in Chicago and New York in 1985 and 1986.

	Chicago	New York	Total for both cities
1985	76	23	99
1986	25	39	64
Total for both years	101	62	163

Questions

a. Which city had more rainfall during 1986?

b. How many inches of rain fell in Chicago during both years?

c. In which year did more rain fall in Chicago?

d. What was the total inches of rain for both cities during both years?

e. In which year did more rain fall in both cities?

Do the Independent Work for Lesson 12 of your Workbook.

Lesson 13

Part 1 Make a number family for each sentence.

a. Train A traveled 3 miles farther than train B.

b. Runner C ran 3 miles per hour slower than runner M.

c. Stream A was 14 feet narrower than stream J.

d. The maple tree was 111 feet taller than the redwood.

e. The parent meeting lasted 20 minutes longer than the business meeting.

f. The worm was $13\frac{3}{4}$ inches shorter than the snake.

Part 2 Copy the problems you can work the way they are written. Then work those problems.

a. $\frac{4}{5} + \frac{7}{5} = \blacksquare$ b. $\frac{7}{8} - \frac{5}{9} = \blacksquare$ c. $\frac{2}{3} \times \frac{9}{8} = \blacksquare$ d. $\frac{8}{3} - \frac{4}{3} = \blacksquare$

e. $\frac{2}{5} + \frac{7}{8} = \blacksquare$ f. $\frac{9}{7} - \frac{5}{7} = \blacksquare$ g. $\frac{5}{6} + \frac{8}{6} = \blacksquare$ h. $\frac{3}{9} \times \frac{6}{1} = \blacksquare$

Part 3 Copy each division problem and work it.

a. $6\overline{)42}$ b. $5\overline{)27}$ c. $8\overline{)4}$ d. $7\overline{)26}$ e. $4\overline{)20}$ f. $6\overline{)36}$

Part 4

- You've figured out missing numbers in a table that's shown twice. You did that by first working the rows in one of the tables and the columns in the other table.

- You can figure out all the numbers in a table that is shown only once. First, work all the rows that have two numbers. Then work all the columns that have two numbers.

- Here's a table:
  You can work two rows.

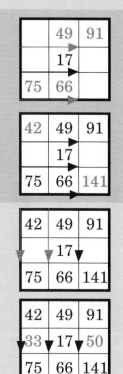

	49	91
	17	
75	66	

- You write the missing numbers for those rows.

42	49	91
	17	
75	66	141

- Then you work the columns. Two of them have two numbers.

42	49	91
	17	
75	66	141

- You write the missing numbers.

42	49	91
33	17	50
75	66	141

Independent Work

Part 5

Write the addition or subtraction problem for each missing number.

a. ■ 46 → 129

b. 157 26 → ■

c. 210 ■ → 482

d. 105 210 → ■

e. 283 174 → ■

f. 26 ■ → 143

Lesson 14

Part 1

- Here are the steps for solving word problems that compare two things.
- You make a number family with two letters and a number. The letters are initials for the things that are compared. The number is the difference number.
- Here's the first sentence of a problem:

  Building A is 20 feet taller than building B.

- The sentence says that building A is taller. So building A is the big number. Building B and 20 are the small numbers.

Dif	B	A
20		→

- After you make the family with two letters and a number, read the rest of the problem and find a number for A or a number for B.
- Here's the sentence that gives a number:

  Building B is 266 feet tall.

- You write that number for B. Now you have two numbers. So you can figure out how tall building A is.

Dif	B	A
20	266	→

- Here's the column problem: Building A is 286 feet tall.

$$\begin{array}{r} 266 \\ +\ 20 \\ \hline \boxed{286} \end{array}$$

Part 2 Make a number family. Add or subtract to answer the question in the problem.

a. Pile A weighs 34 pounds more than pile B. Pile A weighs 98 pounds. How many pounds does pile B weigh?

b. A truck went 231 miles farther than a car went. If the car went 490 miles, how many miles did the truck go?

c. Bob is 14 pounds lighter than his brother Mike. If Bob weighs 87 pounds, how many pounds does Mike weigh?

d. Richard has $95 less than Susan. If Susan has $140, how much does Richard have?

Part 3 For each item, write an equation to show the fractions that are equivalent.

> Equivalent fractions are fractions that are equal. They are equal if they have shaded areas that are exactly the same size. If the shaded areas are not the same size, the fractions are not equal.

a. $\frac{2}{4}$ $\frac{4}{5}$ $\frac{3}{6}$ $\frac{1}{4}$ $\frac{2}{3}$ $\frac{1}{2}$

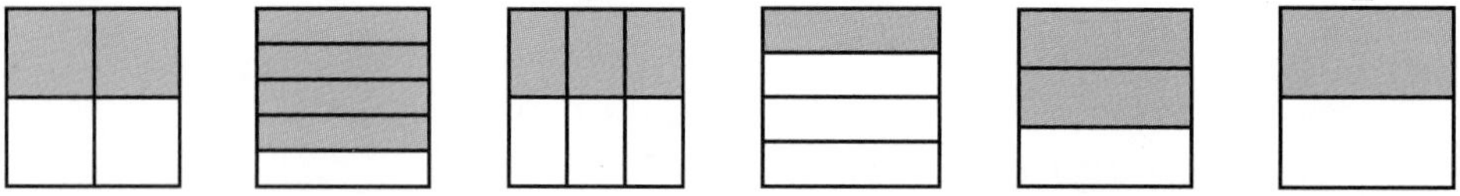

b. $\frac{1}{4}$ $\frac{1}{2}$ $\frac{3}{12}$ $\frac{2}{8}$ $\frac{1}{6}$

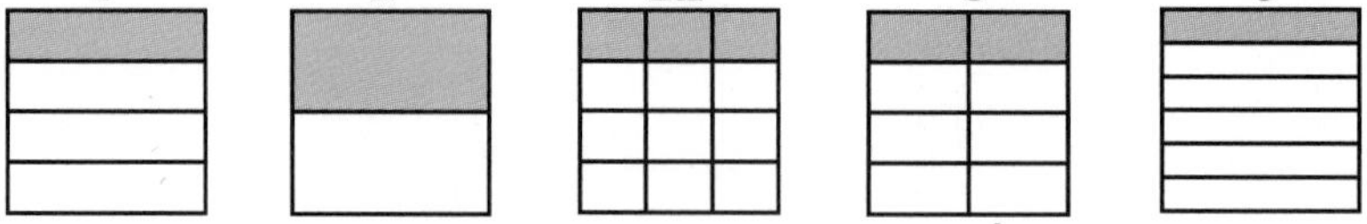

Part 4 Copy and complete each equation.

a. $\frac{\blacksquare}{7} = 6$ b. $\frac{\blacksquare}{5} = 8$ c. $\frac{\blacksquare}{3} = 7$ d. $\frac{\blacksquare}{6} = 4$

Independent Work

Part 5 **Copy the problems you can work the way they are written. Then work those problems.**

a. $\frac{9}{8} - \frac{4}{5} = \blacksquare$ b. $\frac{3}{4} + \frac{2}{4} = \blacksquare$ c. $\frac{9}{3} \times \frac{2}{6} = \blacksquare$ d. $\frac{8}{5} - \frac{7}{5} = \blacksquare$

e. $\frac{1}{2} \times \frac{3}{2} = \blacksquare$ f. $\frac{5}{9} + \frac{7}{7} = \blacksquare$ g. $\frac{2}{6} + \frac{5}{6} = \blacksquare$ h. $\frac{3}{5} - \frac{1}{2} = \blacksquare$

Lesson 15

Part 1 **For each item, write an equation to show the fractions that are equivalent.**

a. 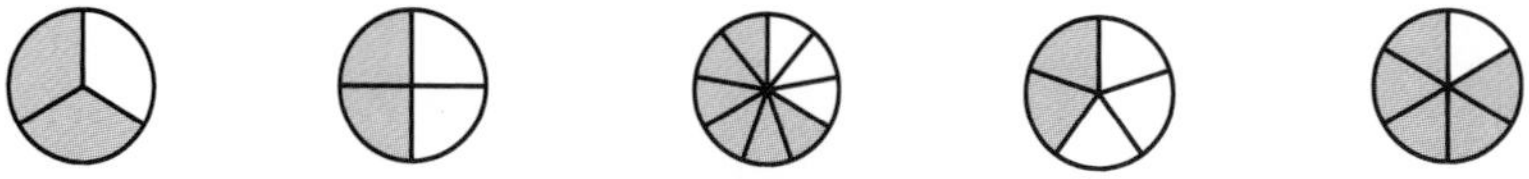

b. 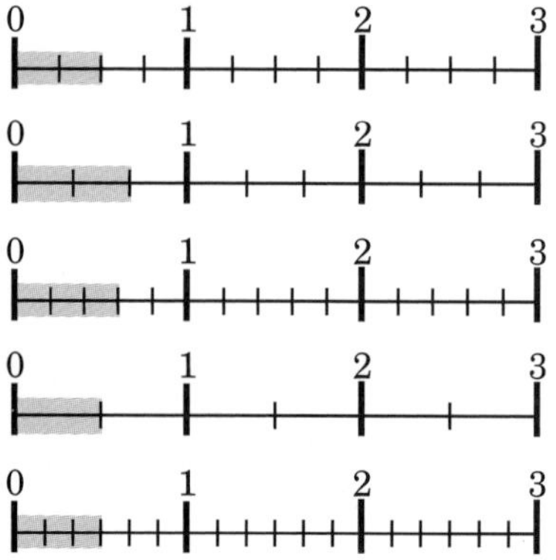

c. 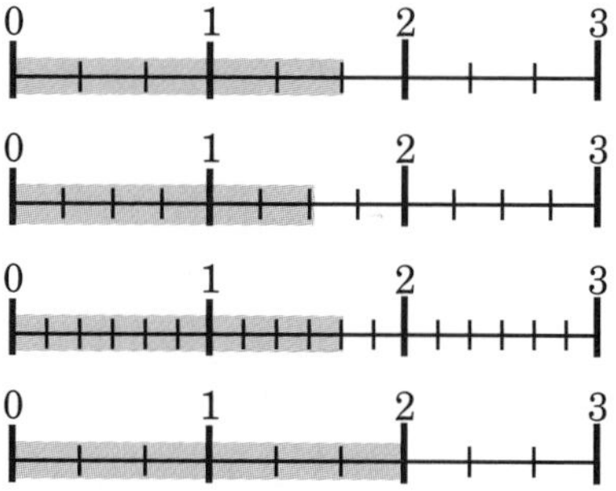

Part 2 **Make a number family. Add or subtract to answer the question in the problem.**

a. Blue Lake is 54 miles longer than Scott Lake. If Scott Lake is 13 miles long, how many miles long is Blue Lake?

b. There are 15 fewer days of vacation in winter than in summer. If there are 91 days of vacation in the summer, how many days of vacation are there in the winter?

c. In February, Sally weighed 22 pounds more than she weighed in November. If she weighed 120 pounds in November, how many pounds did she weigh in February?

d. Simon has 68 more baseball cards in his collection than Peter. If Simon has 195 cards, how many cards does Peter have?

Part 3 **Copy and work each problem.**

a. 2307 x 5

b. 139 x 21

c. 560 x 38

Part 4 Copy the problems you can work the way they are written. Then work those problems.

a. $\frac{3}{4} \times \frac{1}{8} = \blacksquare$

b. $\frac{12}{5} + \frac{2}{2} = \blacksquare$

c. $\frac{18}{4} + \frac{4}{4} = \blacksquare$

d. $\frac{8}{8} - \frac{7}{7} = \blacksquare$

e. $\frac{20}{3} - \frac{9}{3} = \blacksquare$

f. $\frac{56}{2} + \frac{2}{56} = \blacksquare$

Part 5

- Some problems do not have the box for the unknown value after the equal sign.

• Sometimes, the box is the first value or the middle value in the problem.	$\blacksquare - 59 = 310$	$14 + \blacksquare = 158$
• Here's a way to work these problems: ✔ Circle the big number. ✔ Then put the other values in the number family. • If the problem has a minus sign, the first value is the big number. • If the problem has a plus sign, the last value is the big number.	(■) $- 59 = 310$	$14 + \blacksquare =$ (158)
• Once you know which value is the big number, you can make the number family. • You put the **big number** at the end of the arrow.	(■) $- 59 = 310$ 310 59 → (■)	14 ■ → (158)

Sample problems:

$38 + \blacksquare = 93$ $\blacksquare - 53 = 117$

Independent Work

Part 6 Answer each question.

This table shows the number of rangers that were in Hill County and Donner County during July and August.

Questions

a. Which county had more rangers in August?

b. In which month was the total number of rangers greater?

c. What was the total number of rangers in both counties during July?

d. How many rangers were in Hill County during July?

e. In which month were more rangers working in Donner County?

f. Which county had fewer rangers in August?

	Hill County	Donner County	Total for both counties
July	80	62	142
August	71	74	145
Total for both months	151	136	287

Part 7 Copy each problem and write the answer. Below, write the problem with the opposite operation and the answer.

a. 256 – 124 = ■

b. 7001 – 1007 = ■

c. 121 + 393 = ■

d. 96 + 245 = ■

Part J

a. Dif 54, S 13 → B 54
54 + 13 = 67

b. Dif 15, W, S 91 → 16
91 − 15 = 76

c. Dif 22, N 120 → F 22
22 + 120 = 142

d. Dif 68, P, S 195 → 195
195 − 68 = 127

Lesson 16

Part 1

Copy the problems you can work the way they are written. Then work those problems.

a. $\frac{0}{12} + \frac{9}{12} =$ ■   b. $\frac{5}{9} + \frac{5}{3} =$ ■   c. $\frac{4}{8} \times \frac{8}{4} =$ ■

d. $\frac{1}{7} \times \frac{3}{1} =$ ■   e. $\frac{18}{3} - \frac{17}{3} =$ ■   f. $\frac{11}{5} - \frac{7}{4} =$ ■

Part 2

Make a number family. Add or subtract to answer the question in the problem. Box your answer.

a. David is 14 inches shorter than his father. If his father is 72 inches tall, how many inches tall is David?

b. Ardent Hill is 243 feet higher than Jeffrey Hill. If Jeffrey Hill is 943 feet high, how many feet high is Ardent Hill?

c. On Tuesday, the Scouts collected $85 more than they collected on Monday. On Tuesday, they collected $103. How many dollars did they collect on Monday?

d. There were 15 fewer cars parked on Main Street than on Polk Street. If there were 38 cars parked on Main Street, how many cars were parked on Polk Street?

Part 3

Write the fraction for each description.

a. The bottom number of this fraction is 5. The fraction equals 3 whole units.

b. The bottom number of this fraction is 2. The fraction equals 9 whole units.

c. This fraction is more than 1. The numbers are 1 and 15.

d. This fraction is less than 1. The numbers are 2 and 3.

e. This fraction has 5 parts shaded. There are 7 parts in each unit.

Part 4 Check the equations for part 4 in your workbook.

a. $\frac{1}{2} \times \frac{2}{3} = \frac{2}{6}$

b. $\frac{1}{2} \times \frac{3}{3} = \frac{3}{6}$

c. $\frac{1}{2} \times \frac{4}{3} = \frac{4}{6}$

d. $\frac{1}{2} \times \frac{4}{4} = \frac{4}{8}$

Independent Work

Part 5 Answer each question.

This table shows the number of rabbits and kittens in pet shops owned by Ken and Bill.

Questions

a. In which shop are there fewer kittens?

b. In which shop are there more rabbits?

c. How many of both animals are in Bill's shop?

d. How many rabbits are in Ken's shop?

e. What is the total number of both animals in Ken's shop and Bill's shop?

	Rabbits	Kittens	Total for both animals
Ken's shop	27	44	71
Bill's shop	19	58	77
Total for both shops	46	102	148

Part 6 Figure out the missing number for each number family.

a. 19 110 → ■

b. 38 ■ → 212

c. ■ 97 → 148

d. 159 ■ → 182

e. 88 243 → ■

f. 104 476 → ■

Part 7 Copy and work each problem.

a. 43 x 72

b. 359 x 18

c. 537 x 4

Part J

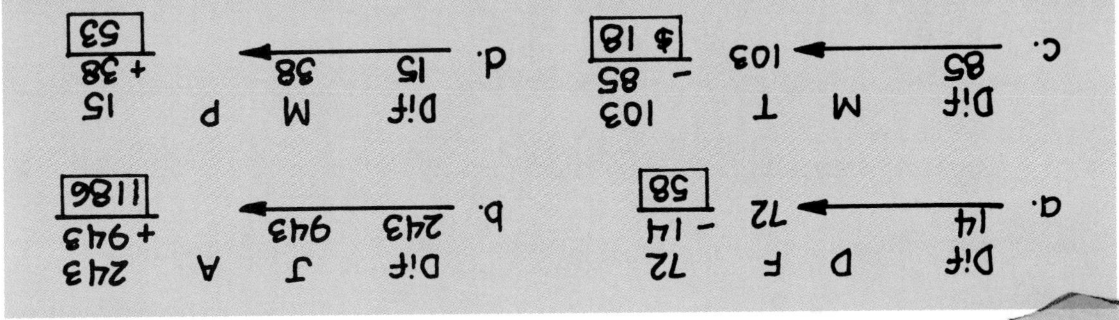

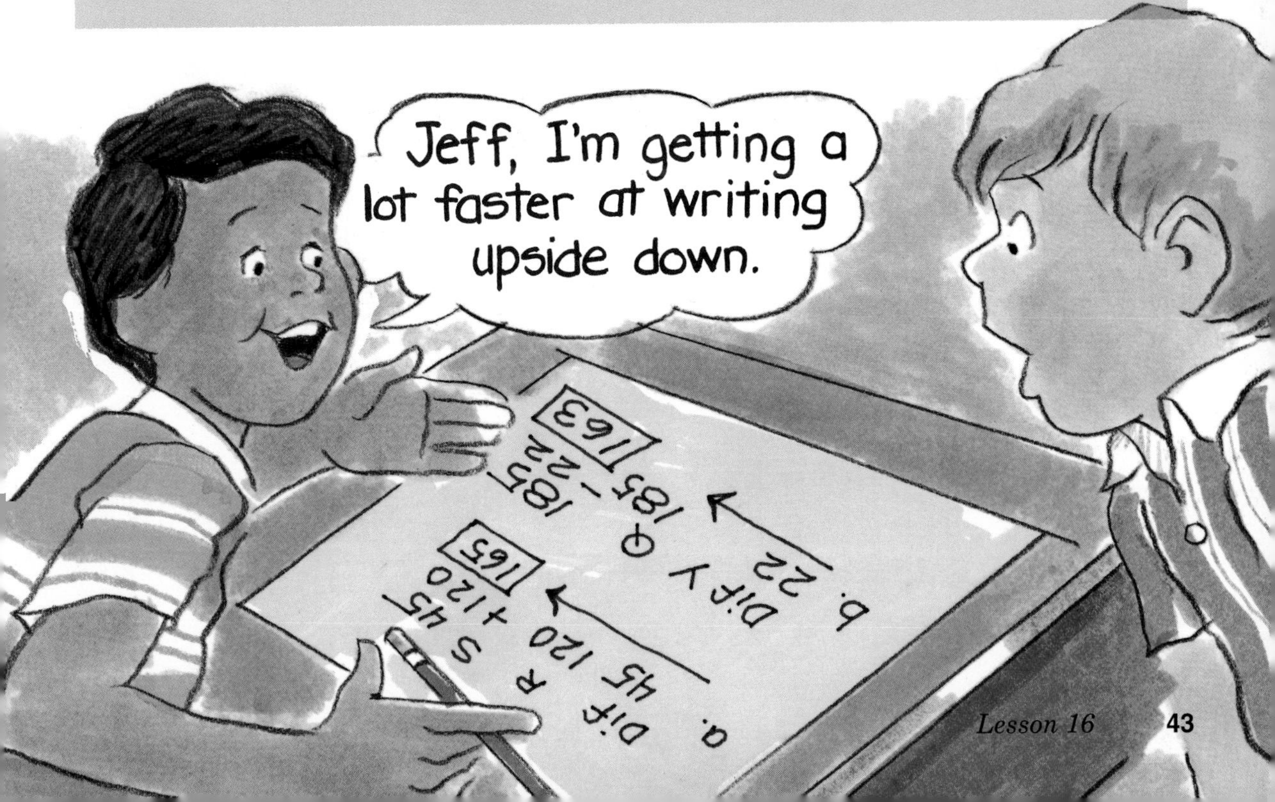

Lesson 17

Part 1

- You know that two fractions are equivalent or equal if the pictures of the fractions have a shaded area that is exactly the same size.

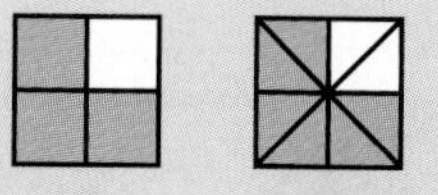

$$\frac{3}{4} = \frac{6}{8}$$

- Here's an important rule: **If fractions are equal, you can multiply by 1 to show that they are equal.**
- Here's how to find the fraction that equals 1: You work the multiplication problem for the top numbers and the problem for the bottom numbers.
- Here's the problem for the top: 3 times some number equals 6. The answer is 2.
- Here's the problem for the bottom: 4 times some number equals 8. The answer is 2.

$$\frac{3}{4} \times \boxed{\frac{\ }{\ }} = \frac{6}{8}$$

- So the fraction that equals 1 is $\frac{2}{2}$.

$$\frac{3}{4} \times \boxed{\frac{2}{2}} = \frac{6}{8}$$

Part 2

Write a multiplication equation for each pair of equivalent fractions.

a. 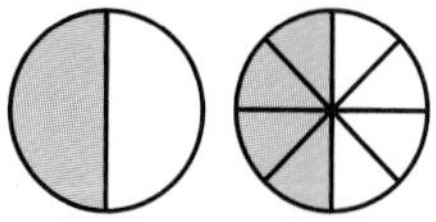

b. 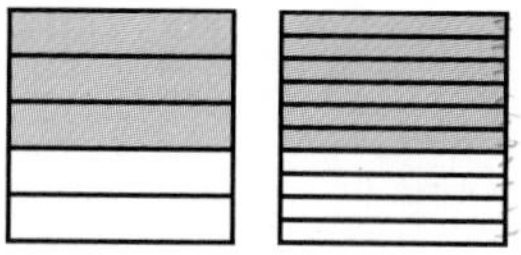

c. 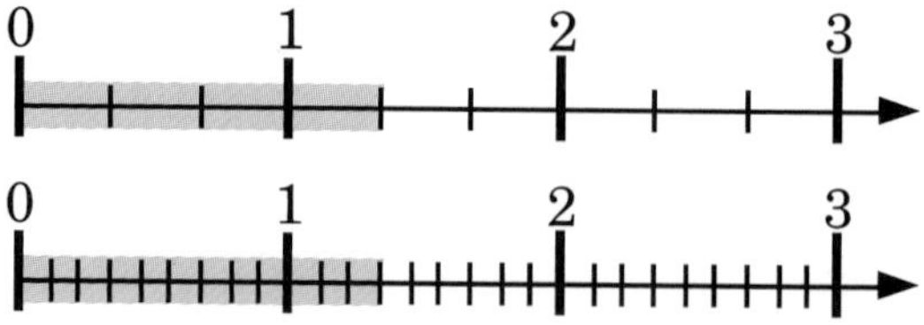

Part 3

- All the values that are written before the decimal point are more than 1.
- All values that come after the decimal point are less than 1.

- You can write a decimal point after any whole number. That's what your calculator does.

  203. 1. 45.

- The columns show how whole numbers and decimals work.
- Whole numbers between 1000 and 9999 have four digits. The first digit is the thousands digit.
- Whole numbers between 100 and 999 have three digits. The first digit is the hundreds digit.
- Whole numbers between 10 and 99 have two digits. The first digit is the tens digit.
- Whole numbers between 1 and 9 have one digit. That digit tells the number of ones.
- If the decimal part ends one place after the decimal point, that part tells about tenths.
- If the decimal part ends two places after the decimal point, that part tells about hundredths.
- If the decimal part ends three places after the decimal point, that part tells about thousandths.

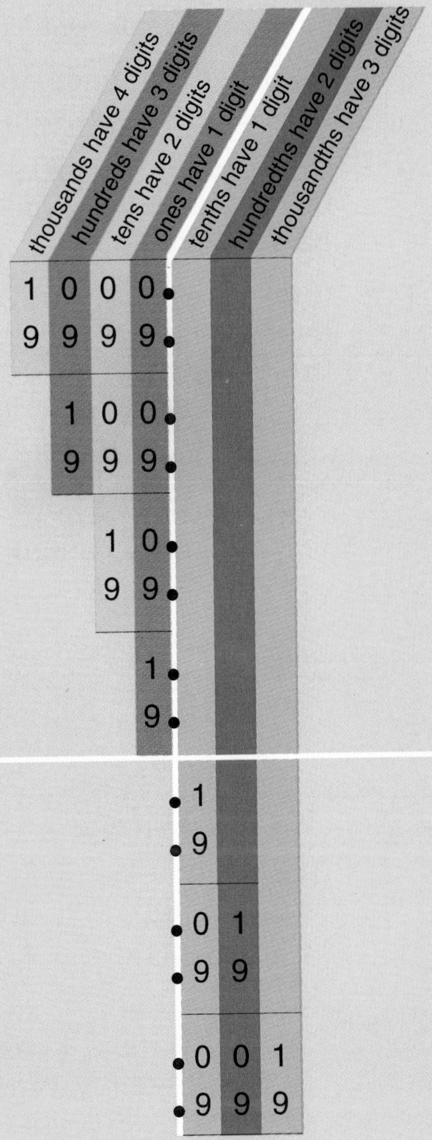

Part 4

Here are rules for reading decimal numbers.

- You read the whole number part. You say **and** for the decimal point. Then you read the decimal part.
- If the number ends **one** place after the decimal point, you say **tenths.**
- If the number ends **two** places after the decimal point, you say **hundredths.**
- If the number ends **three** places after the decimal point, you say **thousandths.**

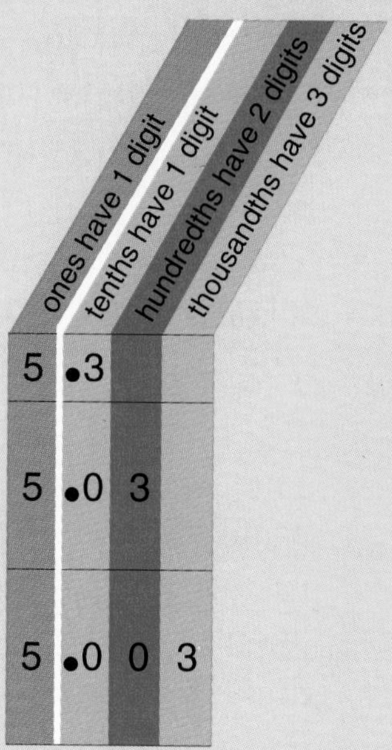

Part 5

Read each decimal number.

a. 6.35
b. 5.13
c. 6.4
d. 5.3
e. 7.41
f. 25.6
g. 3.189
h. 18.502

Part 6

For each fraction, tell which number is the denominator.

a. $\frac{2}{7}$

b. $\frac{9}{3}$

c. $\frac{2}{56}$

Part 7

For each item, write the multiplication problem to figure out the top number of each fraction. Then write the complete equation.

a. $4 = \frac{\blacksquare}{20}$ b. $\frac{\blacksquare}{36} = 8$ c. $5 = \frac{\blacksquare}{27}$

d. $\frac{\blacksquare}{76} = 0$ e. $1 = \frac{\blacksquare}{250}$

Part 8 1. **Check the missing numbers for part 5 in your workbook.**
2. **Answer each question.**

This table shows the number of inches of rain that fell in Bell City and Allen City in 1985 and 1986.

Questions

a. In which year did more rain fall in Allen City?

b. How many inches of rain fell in Bell City in 1986?

c. Which city had more total rainfall during both years?

d. What was the total inches of rain for both cities during both years?

e. In which city did less rain fall in 1985?

	1985	1986	Total for both years
Bell City	18	36	54
Allen City	8	27	35
Total for both cities	26	63	89

Independent Work

Part 9 **Figure out the missing number for each number family.**

a. 48 ■ → 169

b. 317 294 → ■

c. ■ 66 → 212

d. 947 318 → ■

e. 160 38 → ■

f. 418 ■ → 952

Part 10 **Copy and complete each multiplication or division fact.**

a. $4\overline{)0}$

b. $7\overline{)63}$

c. 9 x 0 = ■

d. 7 x 6 = ■

e. $8\overline{)64}$

f. $5\overline{)0}$

g. 1 x 25 = ■

h. $1\overline{)3}$

i. $4\overline{)24}$

Part 11 **Make a number family. Add or subtract to answer the question in the problem.**

a. Audrey has 62 fewer photos in her album than Barbara has. Audrey has 100 photos. How many photos does Barbara have?

b. Mark is 59 years younger than his grandfather. If Mark's grandfather is 72, how old is Mark?

c. Sally collected 97 more comic books than Charles. If Sally has 200 comic books, how many comic books does Charles have?

d. Tennyson City is 181 miles farther away than Jackson City. Jackson City is 255 miles away. How many miles away is Tennyson City?

Lesson 18

Part 1

Copy and complete each equation. Use your calculator to check your answer.

a. $\frac{\blacksquare}{36} = 5$ b. $9 = \frac{\blacksquare}{12}$ c. $\frac{\blacksquare}{4} = 364$ d. $3 = \frac{\blacksquare}{120}$

Part 2

Write an equation for each word problem. Make a number family. Figure out the missing number.

a. In the morning, Jim washed some windows. In the afternoon, he washed 56 more windows. In all, he washed 89 windows. How many windows did he wash in the morning?

b. Tina had 560 stamps. She sold some stamps and ended up with 341 stamps. How many stamps did she sell?

c. The dogs had 478 fleas on them. Then the dogs went into a swamp and some more fleas jumped onto them. The dogs ended up with 1345 fleas on them. How many fleas jumped on while the dogs were in the swamp?

d. The dogs had lots of fleas on them. The dogs went swimming. 1008 fleas jumped off the dogs. The dogs ended up with 309 fleas. How many fleas did the dogs start out with?

Part 3

Write a multiplication equation for each pair of equivalent fractions.

a.

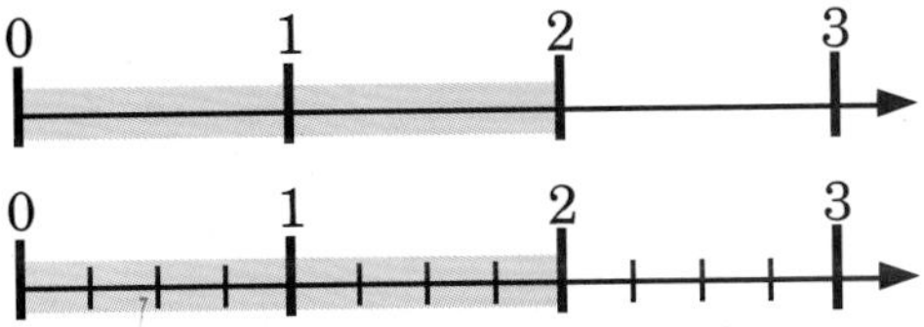

b.

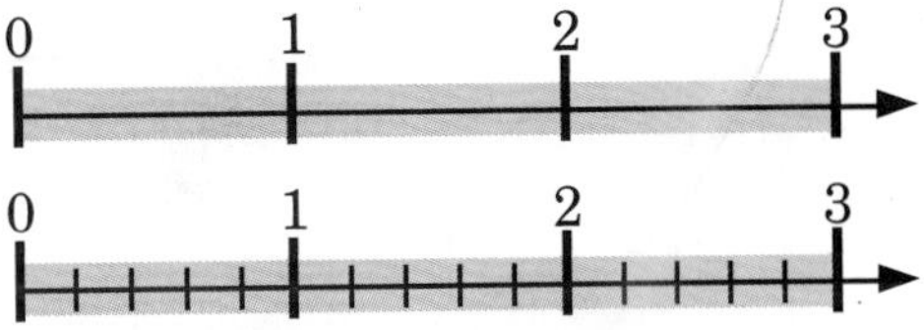

c.

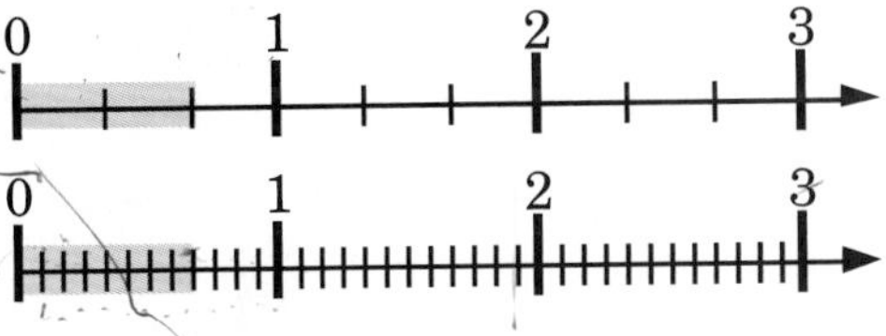

d.

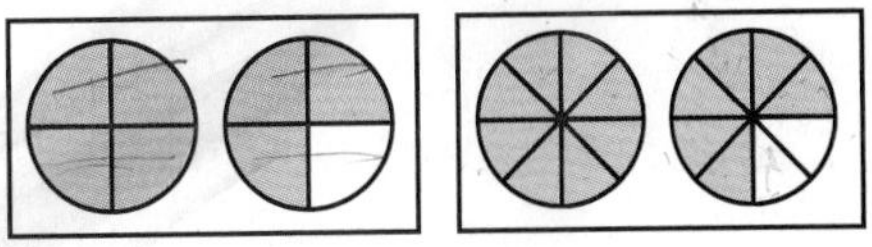

Independent Work

Part 4

Copy and work each problem.

a. 47 x 35

b. 578 x 9

c. 196 x 57

Part 5

Make a number family. Add or subtract to answer the question in the problem.

a. Winston College has 18 fewer trophies than Collier College. Winston College has 56 trophies. How many trophies does Collier College have?

b. Paul has 29 more papers to deliver on his paper route than Martin. Paul delivers 107 papers on his route. How many papers does Martin deliver each day?

c. Susan weighs 118 pounds less than her father. Susan weighs 79 pounds. How many pounds does her father weigh?

Part 6

1. **Check the missing numbers for part 6 in your workbook.**
2. **Answer each question.**

This table shows the number of calves born on two ranches in 1990 and 1991.

Questions

a. On which ranch were more calves born in 1991?

b. What was the total number of calves born on both ranches in 1990?

c. In which year were fewer calves born on Seneca Ranch?

d. How many calves were born on Campbell Ranch in 1991?

e. In which year were more calves born on both ranches?

	Seneca Ranch	Campbell Ranch	Total for both ranches
1990	65	30	95
1991	26	41	67
Total for both years	91	71	162

Part J

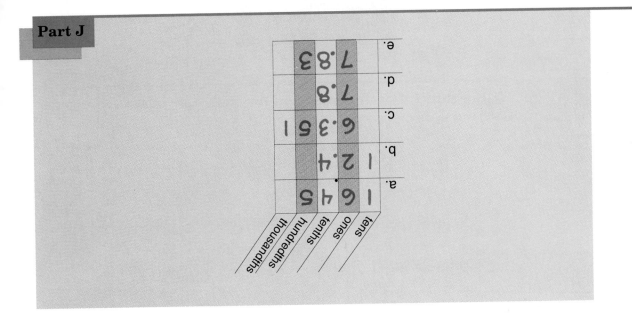

	tens	ones	tenths	hundredths	thousandths
a.	1	6.	4	5	
b.	1	2.	4		
c.		6.	3	5	1
d.		7.	8		
e.		7.	8	3	

Trust me, buddy. You know that 10 is less than 100. So you know I'm giving you a real deal by making your monthly payments $\frac{1}{10}$ of the price, not $\frac{1}{100}$.
Price $48,000

Lesson 19

Part 1 **Write a multiplication equation for each pair of equivalent fractions.**

a. 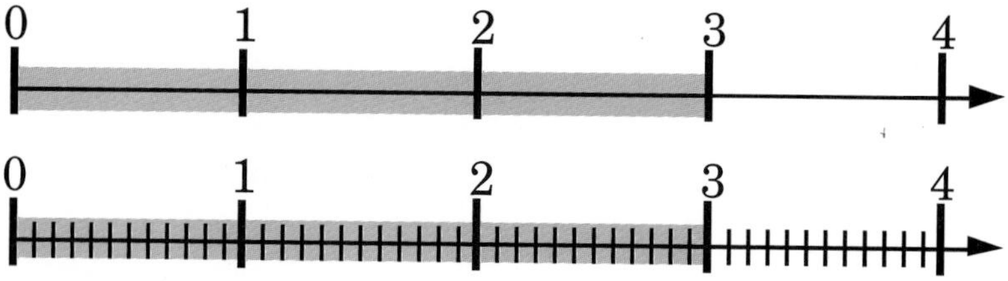

b. 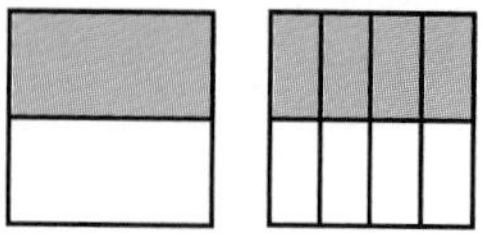

c. 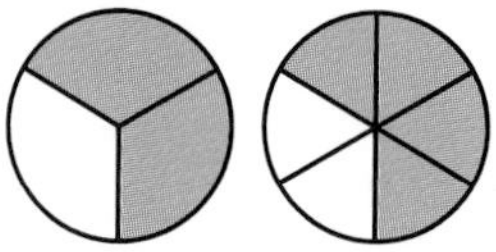

d. 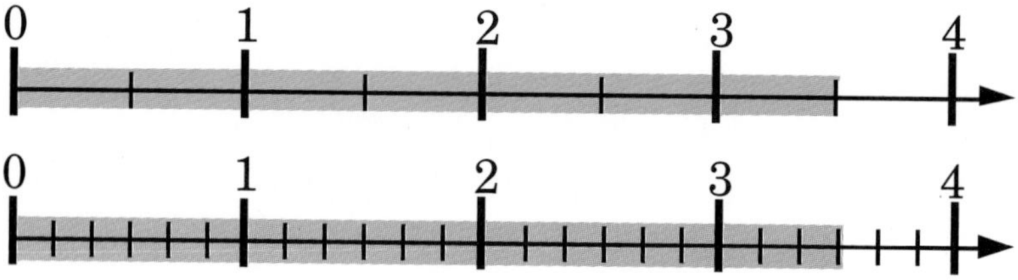

Part 2 **Write the equation for each word problem. Make a number family. Figure out the missing number.**

a. Mary had 620 seashells in her collection. Then some of her seashells got broken. She had 426 seashells left. How many seashells got broken?

b. Sally baked lots of cookies. She gave away 420 cookies. She still had 56 cookies for her family. How many cookies did she bake?

c. Last year, Mike saved 245 nickels in his piggy bank. This year, he has saved 110 more nickels. How many nickels has he saved in all?

d. Billy had 74 baseball cards. He bought some more baseball cards from his neighbor. Now he has 195 baseball cards. How many cards did he buy from his neighbor?

Part 3 Write the fraction for each description.

a. The fraction is more than 1. The numbers are 21 and 22.

b. The fraction equals 7 whole units. The denominator of the fraction is 4.

c. The bottom number of the fraction is 12. The fraction equals 5 whole units.

d. The fraction is less than 1. The numbers are 15 and 16.

e. The fraction is more than 1. The numbers are 15 and 16.

Part 4 Copy and work each problem.

a. $4\overline{)10}$ b. $3\overline{)10}$ c. $3\overline{)20}$ d. $7\overline{)20}$ e. $8\overline{)20}$ f. $7\overline{)31}$

Part 5

- A mixed number is a whole number and a fraction.
- Here are mixed numbers: $5\frac{2}{3}$ $3\frac{5}{8}$ $6\frac{4}{9}$
- You can show mixed numbers on a number line:

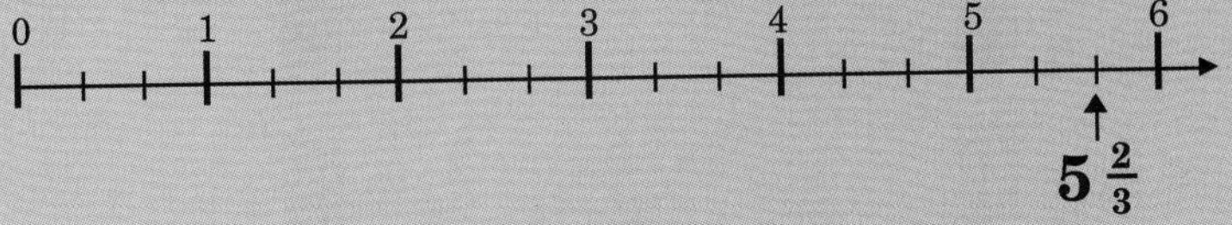

- You can write mixed numbers as fractions.
- First you change the whole number into a fraction.
- Then you add.
- You must make sure the fractions you add have the same denominator.

- Here's: $4\frac{1}{7}$
- That's: $4 + \frac{1}{7}$

- We change 4 into a fraction that equals 4 and has a denominator of 7. That's $\frac{28}{7}$. $\frac{28}{7} + \frac{1}{7}$

- Now we add: $\frac{28}{7} + \frac{1}{7} = \frac{29}{7}$

Part 6

- Decimal numbers such as 3.02 are like mixed numbers. The **part after** the decimal point is the **fraction part** of the mixed number.
- The decimal part may have zeros **before** a digit. $\frac{2}{100}$ must end two digits after the decimal point.
  - This is $\frac{2}{100}$: **.0 2**
  - This is not $\frac{2}{100}$: **.2**
  - This is $\frac{2}{1000}$: **.0 0 2**

Independent Work

Part 7

Copy the problems you can work the way they are written. Then work those problems.

a. $\frac{19}{8} - \frac{14}{5} = \blacksquare$

b. $\frac{8}{5} - \frac{8}{5} = \blacksquare$

c. $\frac{12}{6} + \frac{25}{6} = \blacksquare$

d. $\frac{13}{4} + \frac{2}{4} = \blacksquare$

e. $\frac{1}{2} \times \frac{9}{2} = \blacksquare$

f. $\frac{3}{5} - \frac{1}{2} = \blacksquare$

g. $\frac{9}{3} \times \frac{2}{6} = \blacksquare$

h. $\frac{5}{9} + \frac{24}{7} = \blacksquare$

Part 8

Make a number family. Add or subtract to answer the question in the problem.

a. Amy spotted 27 more birds than Matthew. If Matthew spotted 58 birds, how many birds did Amy spot?

b. The students attending Jefferson Middle School are 152 fewer than the students attending Madison Middle School. There are 356 students at Madison. How many students attend Jefferson?

c. The tennis court is 16 feet shorter than the basketball court. The basketball court is 94 feet long. How many feet long is the tennis court?

Part 9

Copy and work each problem.

a. $\begin{array}{r} 47 \\ \underline{\times\ 98} \end{array}$

b. $\begin{array}{r} 136 \\ \underline{\times\ \ 47} \end{array}$

c. $\begin{array}{r} 4503 \\ \underline{\times\ \ \ \ 3} \end{array}$

d. $\begin{array}{r} 128 \\ \underline{\times\ \ 40} \end{array}$

Part 10

Copy and complete each multiplication or division fact.

a. 9 x 0 = ■

b. 7 x 4 = ■

c. $8\overline{)32}$

d. $5\overline{)35}$

e. 0 x 5 = ■

f. 8 x 3 = ■

g. $4\overline{)0}$

h. 1 x 40 = ■

i. $9\overline{)63}$

Lesson 20

Part 1 **Write each whole number as a fraction with the right denominator. Then add and write the fraction that equals the mixed number.**

a. $1\frac{7}{8}$ b. $5\frac{3}{7}$ c. $2\frac{5}{8}$ d. $3\frac{1}{2}$ e. $4\frac{3}{4}$

Test 2

Part 1 **Write the decimal numbers your teacher describes.**

Part 2 **Copy the problems you can work the way they are written. Then work those problems.**

a. $\frac{14}{3} \times \frac{1}{7} = \blacksquare$

b. $\frac{6}{4} - \frac{0}{4} = \blacksquare$

c. $\frac{19}{7} - \frac{12}{3} = \blacksquare$

d. $\frac{12}{9} + \frac{6}{9} = \blacksquare$

e. $\frac{4}{8} + \frac{4}{7} = \blacksquare$

f. $\frac{9}{6} - \frac{5}{6} = \blacksquare$

g. $\frac{2}{3} - \frac{3}{2} = \blacksquare$

h. $\frac{8}{10} + \frac{5}{10} = \blacksquare$

i. $\frac{4}{8} \times \frac{3}{8} = \blacksquare$

Part 3 **Copy and work each problem.**

a. $\begin{array}{r} 28 \\ \underline{\times\ 43} \end{array}$

b. $\begin{array}{r} 1274 \\ \underline{\times\ \ \ \ 9} \end{array}$

c. $\begin{array}{r} 132 \\ \underline{\times\ \ 70} \end{array}$

Part 4 **For each problem, make a number family. Write and work the column problem to answer the question. Box your answer.**

a. There were 176 more cans in the machine than there were in the box. There were 19 cans in the box. How many cans were in the machine?

b. Mary had 18 more pairs of socks than Andrea had. Mary had 48 pairs of socks. How many pairs of socks did Andrea have?

c. Joe has 457 rocks in his collection. If Joe has 124 more rocks than his brother, how many rocks does his brother have?

Part 5 **For each item, write the pair of equivalent fractions. Figure out the fraction of 1 you multiply by, and complete the equation.**

a. 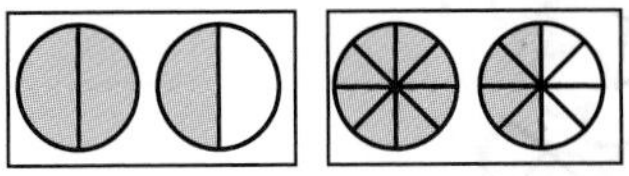

b. 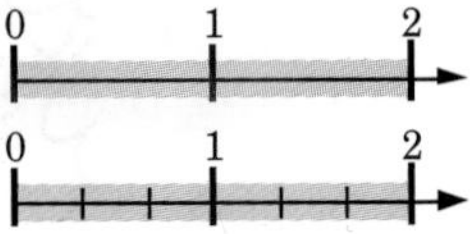

Part 6 **Copy and complete the table.**

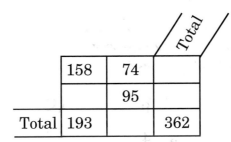

			Total
	158	74	
		95	
Total	193		362

Part 7 **Write the fraction for each description.**

a. The denominator is 7. The fraction equals 2 whole units.

b. The fraction is more than 1. The numbers are 19 and 20.

c. The fraction is less than 1. The numbers are 15 and 16.

d. The denominator is 5. The fraction equals 6 whole units.

Part 8 **Copy and work each problem. Write the answer as a mixed number.**

a. $7\overline{)59}$ b. $5\overline{)22}$ c. $9\overline{)39}$

Part 9 **Answer each question.**

This table shows the number of fish caught in Doe Lake and Arrow Lake in September and October.

Questions

a. In which month were more fish caught in Arrow Lake?

b. How many fish were caught in Doe Lake during October?

c. In which lake were fewer fish caught in September?

d. How many fish were caught in Arrow Lake during both months?

e. In which month was the total greater for the number of fish caught in both lakes?

	Doe Lake	Arrow Lake	Total for both lakes
September	18	56	74
October	34	64	98
Total for both months	52	120	172

Part 10 **Copy and complete the table.**

Fraction equation	Division
a. $\frac{182}{2} =$ ■	
b. $\frac{1435}{7} =$ ■	

Part 11 **Copy and work the problem. Below, check your work by writing a subtraction problem and the answer.**

$1481 + 799 =$ ■

■ − ■ = ■

Lesson 21

Part 1

Any number can be divided by 1 or divided by itself.

Here's 13 divided by 1: $\begin{array}{r}13\\1\overline{)13}\end{array}$

Here's 13 divided by itself: $\begin{array}{r}1\\13\overline{)13}\end{array}$

- For some numbers, you can only divide by are **1** and the number itself. These numbers are **prime numbers.**
- If you can divide by any number other than 1 and the number itself, the number is not a prime number.

- Here are prime numbers: **2, 3, 5, 7, 11, 13**
- Here are numbers that are **not** prime numbers: **4, 6, 8, 9, 10, 12, 14, 15, 16**

- Here's how to test a number to see if it's a prime number. Ask: "Can that number be divided by something other than 1 and the number itself?"

Here's 14: 14

- Can 14 be divided by something other than 1 and 14? Yes.
- 14 can also be divided by 7, and it can be divided by 2. $\begin{array}{r}2\\7\overline{)14}\end{array}$ $\begin{array}{r}7\\2\overline{)14}\end{array}$
- So 14 is not a prime number.

Here's 15: 15

- Can 15 be divided by something other than 1 and 15? Yes.
- 15 can be divided by 3, and it can be divided by 5. $\begin{array}{r}5\\3\overline{)15}\end{array}$ $\begin{array}{r}3\\5\overline{)15}\end{array}$
- So 15 is not a prime number.

Here's 17: 17

- Can 17 be divided by something other than 1 or 17? No. $\begin{array}{r}17\\1\overline{)17}\end{array}$
- So 17 is a prime number.

Part 2

Write the equation for each word problem. Make a number family. Figure out the missing number.

a. On Monday, Donna sold 56 eggs. On Tuesday, she sold some more eggs. She sold a total of 313 eggs on both days. How many eggs did she sell on Tuesday?

b. Sandra picked a lot of cherries. She gave 426 cherries to her friends. She had 183 cherries left. How many cherries did she pick?

c. Carlos collected 345 stones. Then he gave some of them away. He ended up with 123 stones. How many did he give away?

d. In February, it snowed 230 centimeters. Then in March, it snowed another 317 centimeters. How many centimeters did it snow in both months?

Part 3

Write each whole number as a fraction with the right denominator. Then add, and write the fraction that equals the mixed number.

a. $3\frac{4}{7}$ b. $5\frac{1}{2}$ c. $6\frac{2}{9}$ d. $4\frac{5}{6}$ e. $1\frac{3}{8}$

Part 4

- Here are division problems that you can work a digit at a time:

  $3\overline{)963}$ $4\overline{)488}$

- You say the problem for each digit under the division sign. You write the answer above that digit.

- The problem for the first digit is 8 divided by 2: $\begin{array}{r} 4 \\ 2\overline{)806} \end{array}$

- The problem for the next digit is 0 divided by 2: $\begin{array}{r} 40 \\ 2\overline{)806} \end{array}$

- The problem for the last digit is 6 divided by 2: $\begin{array}{r} 403 \\ 2\overline{)806} \end{array}$

Independent Work

Part 5 **Copy each problem and write the answer.**

a. $8\overline{)48}$ b. $6\overline{)50}$ c. $7\overline{)17}$ d. $9\overline{)19}$ e. $3\overline{)20}$ f. $6\overline{)30}$

Part 6 **For each problem, make a number family. Answer the question.**

a. A train went 113 miles farther than a car went. If the train went 209 miles, how many miles did the car go?

b. An oak tree was 211 years older than a maple tree. If the maple was 501 years old, how many years old was the oak?

c. A granite rock was 2988 pounds lighter than a basalt rock. The granite rock was 666 pounds. How many pounds did the basalt rock weigh?

Part 7 **Copy and work each problem.**

a. $\begin{array}{r} 1401 \\ \underline{\times \quad 8} \end{array}$ b. $\begin{array}{r} 149 \\ \underline{\times \ 67} \end{array}$

Part 8 **Write a multiplication equation for each pair of equivalent fractions.**

a.

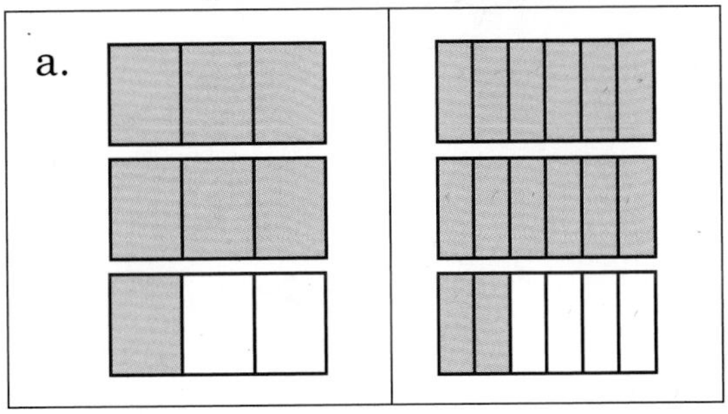

b.

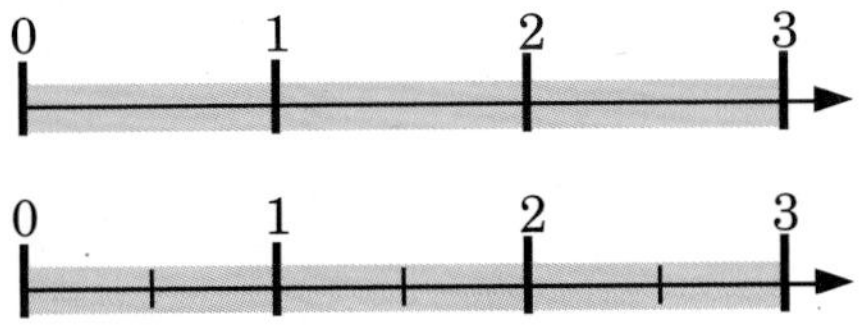

Part 9 **Copy and complete the table.**

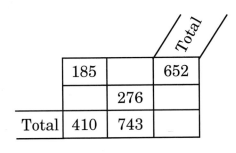

			Total
	185		652
		276	
Total	410	743	

Part J

Multiplication	Fraction equation
a. $5 \times 129 = 645$	$\frac{645}{5} = 129$
b. $6 \times 160 = 960$	$\frac{960}{6} = 160$
c. $8 \times 20 = 160$	$\frac{160}{8} = 20$
d. $9 \times 48 = 432$	$\frac{432}{9} = 48$

I don't know how we can figure out the number of paper clips that go in each box.
Would this give you the right answer?
5×□=645
645

Lesson 22

Part 1 **Write the equation for each word problem. Make a number family. Figure out the missing number.**

a. A truck started out with 624 boxes. The truck delivered lots of boxes. At the end of the day, there were 195 boxes on the truck. How many boxes were delivered?

b. Sarah had 590 buttons. She found some more buttons in a drawer. She now has a total of 626 buttons. How many buttons did she find?

c. A tank was full of water. 240 liters drained out of the tank. There were 172 liters left in the tank. How many liters of water were in the tank to begin with?

d. In the morning, Mark went to the orchard and picked some apples. Later, he picked 128 apples. In all he picked 300 apples. How many apples did Mark pick in the morning?

Part 2

You've learned how to write a mixed number as a fraction.

$$3\frac{4}{5} = \boxed{\frac{}{}}$$

You change the whole number into a fraction with the right denominator: $\frac{15}{5} + \frac{4}{5} =$

Then you add: $\frac{15}{5} + \frac{4}{5} = \boxed{\frac{19}{5}}$

- You can work these problems the fast way by doing the calculation in your head.
- You start with the denominator of the fraction and multiply by the whole number. Then you add the top number of the fraction.

The denominator is 5: $3\frac{4}{5}$

So you multiply 5 x 3: 5 x 3 = 15

Then you add 4: 15 + 4 = 19

Here's the equation: $3\frac{4}{5} = \frac{19}{5}$

Part 3

You've worked problems that have a remainder.

Here's 7 divided by 4: $4\overline{)7}$

You write 1 above the 7: $\begin{array}{r} 1 \\ 4\overline{)7} \end{array}$

Then you write the remainder: $\begin{array}{r} 1\text{ R3} \\ 4\overline{)7}\phantom{\text{ R3}} \end{array}$

- You do the same thing when the number under the division sign has more than one digit.
- The only difference is that you **write the remainder in front of the next digit.**

Here's 72 divided by 4: $4\overline{)72}$

We work the problem for 7 divided by 4. That's 1 with a remainder of 3. $\begin{array}{r} 1 \\ 4\overline{)7{}^{3}2} \end{array}$

Now we combine that 3 with the 2 and work the problem 32 divided by 4. The answer is 8. $\begin{array}{r} 18 \\ 4\overline{)7{}^{3}2} \end{array}$

Independent Work

Part 4

Copy each number. Write the complete equation to show the place-value addition.

a. 364 = [redacted]

b. 123 = [redacted]

c. 86 = [redacted]

d. 914 = [redacted]

Part 5 **Answer each question.**

This table shows the number of fish caught in Doe Lake and Arrow Lake in July and August.

Questions

a. In which month were fewer fish caught in Arrow Lake?

b. How many fish were caught in Arrow Lake during August?

c. In which lake were more fish caught in July?

d. How many fish were caught in Doe Lake during both months?

e. In which month was the total greater for the number of fish caught in both lakes?

	Doe Lake	Arrow Lake	Total for both lakes
July	52	77	129
August	79	101	180
Total for both months	131	178	309

Part 6 **Copy and work each problem.**

a. $\frac{3}{19} - \frac{3}{19} = \blacksquare$

b. $\frac{5}{4} \times \frac{4}{7} = \blacksquare$

c. $\frac{5}{4} + \frac{4}{4} = \blacksquare$

d. $\frac{21}{3} - \frac{18}{3} = \blacksquare$

e. $\frac{5}{9} \times \frac{9}{7} = \blacksquare$

Part 7 **Figure out the missing value in each number family.**

a. ■ 115 → 511

b. 511 115 → ■

c. 87 ■ → 2060

Part 8

Write the fraction for each description.

a. The fraction equals 3. The denominator is 8.

b. The fraction equals 5. The denominator is 2.

c. The numbers for this fraction are 1 and 4. The fraction is more than 1.

d. The numbers for this fraction are 61 and 111. The fraction is less than 1.

e. The numbers for this fraction are 465 and 464. The fraction is less than 1.

Part J

a. 195 □ → 624

624 − □ = 195

624 − 195 = 429

b. 590 □ → 626

590 + □ = 626

626 − 590 = 36

c. 172 240 → □

□ − 240 = 172

172 + 240 = 412

d. □ 128 → 300

□ + 128 = 300

300 − 128 = 172

Part K

Multiplication	Fraction equation
a. 7 x 137 = 959	$\frac{959}{7} = 137$
b. 5 x 33 = 165	$\frac{165}{5} = 33$
c. 2 x 479 = 958	$\frac{958}{2} = 479$
d. 9 x 32 = 288	$\frac{288}{9} = 32$

Lesson 23

Part 1 **Copy each mixed number. Write the fraction it equals.**

a. $3\frac{7}{8}$ b. $1\frac{5}{9}$ c. $6\frac{2}{3}$ d. $5\frac{3}{7}$ e. $10\frac{4}{5}$

Part 2

- The smallest prime numbers are **2, 3, 5, 7, 11.**
  Any number that is not a prime can always be shown as **prime numbers multiplied together.**
- **24** is not a prime number. It can be shown as prime numbers multiplied together: $2 \times 2 \times 2 \times 3 = 24$
- **45** is not a prime number. It can be shown as prime numbers multiplied together: $3 \times 3 \times 5 = 45$
- Any prime numbers that are multiplied together are called **prime factors.**

Part 3 **Multiply the prime factors to find the missing value.**

a. $2 \times 2 \times 3 \times 7 = ■$ b. $2 \times 3 \times 5 = ■$

c. $3 \times 5 \times 5 = ■$ d. $2 \times 2 \times 2 \times 7 = ■$

Part 4 **Copy and complete each equation.**

a. $\frac{560}{5} = ■$ b. $\frac{749}{7} = ■$ c. $\frac{1719}{9} = ■$

d. $\frac{868}{4} = ■$ e. $\frac{972}{3} = ■$

Part 5 **Write the equation for each word problem. Make a number family. Figure out the missing number.**

a. Some students signed up for a weekend trip. Later 48 students dropped out. 152 students ended up going on the trip. How many students signed up at first?

b. There were 184 corn chips on the table. Then some of the corn chips were eaten. If there were 93 corn chips left, how many corn chips were eaten?

c. 47 people were watching a baseball game. Then 105 more people came to watch the game. What's the total number of people who watched the game?

d. Last winter, there were 297 pigs on a farm. Then some pigs were born in the spring. Now there are 423 pigs on the farm. How many pigs were born in the spring?

Independent Work

Part 6 **Make the number family. Answer the question.**

a. The road is 458 centimeters wider than the stream. If the stream is 1111 centimeters wide, how wide is the road?

b. John's dog is 32 years younger than John. If the dog is 2 years old, how many years old is John?

c. There are 70 more students at Hill School than at Edison School. There are 604 students at Hill School. How many students are at Edison?

Part 7

Copy the table and complete it.

Fraction equation	Division
a. $\frac{480}{8} =$	
b. $\frac{198}{9}$	
c. $\frac{270}{5}$	

Part 8

Write the complete equation to show the place-value addition.

a. 38 = [redacted]

b. 151 = [redacted]

c. 693 = [redacted]

Part 9

Copy and work each problem.

a. $\frac{31}{2} + \frac{6}{2} =$ [redacted]

b. $\frac{56}{19} - \frac{5}{19} =$ [redacted]

c. $\frac{2}{4} \times \frac{10}{4} =$ [redacted]

d. $\frac{1}{2} \times \frac{6}{1} =$ [redacted]

Part 10

Test the number for each item. Write P if the number is a prime. Write NP if the number is not a prime.

2	3	5	7	11

a. 101 b. 99 c. 100 d. 39

Part J

a. 48 152 □ ← ; □ − 48 = 152; 48 + 152 = 200

b. □ 93 184 ← ; 184 − □ = 93; 184 − 93 = 91

c. 47 105 □ ← ; 47 + 105 = □; 47 + 105 = 152

d. 297 □ 423 ← ; 297 + □ = 423; 423 − 297 = 126

Lesson 24

Part 1 Write the complete equation for each item.

a. $\frac{414}{3} = \blacksquare$ b. $\frac{138}{6} = \blacksquare$ c. $\frac{356}{4} = \blacksquare$

d. $\frac{2005}{5} = \blacksquare$ e. $\frac{8640}{9} = \blacksquare$

Part 2 Figure out the prime factors for each item.

These are prime numbers: 2 3 5 7 11 13 17 19 23

a. 77
- 7 7 ÷ 2
- 7 7 ÷ 3
- 7 7 ÷ 5
- 7 7 ÷ 7

b. 65 c. 121 d. 221 e. 169

Part 3 Copy each mixed number. Write the fraction it equals.

a. $6\frac{2}{3}$ b. $2\frac{3}{5}$ c. $6\frac{5}{7}$ d. $3\frac{1}{2}$ e. $5\frac{3}{4}$

Part 4

- Another way of writing a multiplication sign is with parentheses.
- Here's another way of writing 4 x 3: $4(3)$
- Here's another way of writing $\frac{1}{2} \times \frac{2}{3}$: $\frac{1}{2}\left(\frac{2}{3}\right)$

Part 5

- Here's an equivalent fraction problem. Part of the second fraction is missing. $\frac{6}{5} = \frac{\blacksquare}{20}$
- You can figure out the missing number. You know that the fractions are equal. So you multiply the first fraction by 1 to get the second fraction. $\frac{6}{5} \times 1 = \frac{\blacksquare}{20}$
- The next thing you do is figure out **the fraction** that equals 1. $\frac{6}{5}\left(\frac{\square}{\square}\right) = \frac{\blacksquare}{20}$
- You can't work the problem on top because there's only one number on top. $\frac{6}{5}\left(\frac{}{}\right) = \frac{\blacksquare}{20}$
- You **can** work the problem on the bottom because there are two numbers.
- The answer is **4.** $\frac{6}{5}\left(\frac{}{4}\right) = \frac{\blacksquare}{20}$
- If you multiply by 4 on the bottom, you have to multiply by 4 on top. The fraction that equals 1 is $\frac{4}{4}$. $\frac{6}{5}\left(\frac{4}{4}\right) = \frac{\blacksquare}{20}$
- Now you multiply on top: 6 x 4. That's **24.** $\frac{6}{5}\left(\frac{4}{4}\right) = \frac{24}{20}$
- Remember the steps for working these problems.
  - ✔ First, find the problem with two numbers.
  - ✔ Then complete the fraction that equals 1.
  - ✔ Then multiply and complete the fraction after the equal sign.

Independent Work

Part 6

Copy and work each problem.

a. $6\overline{)33}$ b. $9\overline{)41}$ c. $9\overline{)59}$

d. $4\overline{)23}$ e. $7\overline{)19}$

Part 7

Copy and work each problem.

a. $\begin{array}{r} 521 \\ \times\ 38 \\ \hline \end{array}$ b. $\begin{array}{r} 24 \\ \times\ 80 \\ \hline \end{array}$

Part 8

Complete each equation. If the fractions are equivalent, write a simple equation below.

a. $\frac{2}{5}\left(\blacksquare\right) = \frac{12}{30}$ b. $\frac{7}{8}\left(\blacksquare\right) = \frac{21}{32}$ c. $\frac{6}{4}\left(\blacksquare\right) = \frac{36}{24}$

Part 9

Write the equation for each word problem. Make a number family. Figure out the missing number.

a. In the morning, a farmer had some watermelons in the barn. After lunch, he put 144 more watermelons in the barn. He ended up with 456 watermelons in the barn. How many were in the barn to begin with?

b. A pile contained 349 tons of sawdust. Then a lot of sawdust was removed from the pile. Now the pile contains 103 tons of sawdust. How many tons were removed?

c. Before the sale, the store had shelves of books. During the sale, 395 books were sold. After the sale, the store still had 174 books. How many books were in the store before the sale?

Part 10

Copy and work each problem.

a. $\frac{12}{7} + \frac{38}{7} = \blacksquare$ b. $\frac{5}{7} \times \frac{2}{9} = \blacksquare$

c. $\frac{1}{12} \times \frac{12}{1} = \blacksquare$ d. $\frac{16}{5} + \frac{7}{5} = \blacksquare$

Part J

Decimal	Mixed number
a. 3.04	$3\frac{4}{100}$
b. 18.7	$18\frac{7}{10}$
c. 2.043	$2\frac{43}{1000}$
d. 10.15	$10\frac{15}{100}$

Lesson 25

Part 1

- If a number is not a prime, you can show the prime factors for that number. The prime factors are the prime numbers that are multiplied together.
- Here's a number that is not a prime: 30
- To show that it isn't a prime, you start with any multiplication fact that ends with 30: 6 x 5 = 30
- Now you check to see if both the factors are prime numbers. **5** is a prime number. **6** is not a prime number. 6 x 5 = 30
- So you show the prime factors for 6: 2 x 3 x 5 = 30

Part 2

Copy each pair of fractions. Below, write the whole number each fraction equals. Circle the fraction that is greater.

a. $\frac{16}{2}$ $\frac{21}{3}$ b. $\frac{15}{3}$ $\frac{30}{5}$ c. $\frac{14}{2}$ $\frac{80}{10}$ d. $\frac{12}{12}$ $\frac{0}{5}$

Part 3

Rewrite each value as prime factors multiplied together.

These are prime numbers: 2 3 5 7 11 13 17 19 23

a. 91 b. 95 c. 187

Independent Work

Part 4

Write the equation for each word problem. Make a number family. Figure out the missing number.

a. A tablet had all its pages. Dan used up 45 pages. Now the tablet has 46 pages. How many pages did the tablet have to begin with?

b. A farmer collected eggs in the morning. In the evening, he collected 572 more eggs. In all, 1204 eggs were collected. How many were collected in the morning?

Part 5

For each item, show the mixed number and the fraction it equals.

a. $7\frac{1}{10} =$ ■ b. $1\frac{8}{9} =$ ■ c. $40\frac{1}{2} =$ ■ d. $6\frac{4}{5} =$ ■

Part 6

Copy the table and complete it.

	Multiplication	Division
a.	6 x ■ = 48	
b.	3 x ■ = 27	

Part 7

Copy and work each problem.

a. 450×6

b. 190×5

c. 614×8

Part 8

Copy the table. Figure out all the missing numbers.

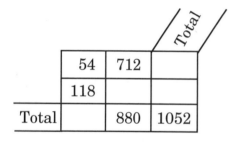

			Total
	54	712	
	118		
Total		880	1052

Part 9

Copy each number. Figure out whether the number is a prime number. Write P or NP after each number.

2 3 5 7 11 13 17 19 23

a. 87 b. 107

c. 91 d. 119

Part J

Decimal	Mixed number
a. 4.14	$4\frac{14}{100}$
b. 6.02	$6\frac{2}{100}$
c. 1.017	$1\frac{17}{1000}$
d. 2.8	$2\frac{8}{10}$
e. 24.31	$24\frac{31}{100}$
f. 14.03	$14\frac{3}{100}$

I guess you could call those mixed numbers, but I don't think they are the type the teacher wants.

Lesson 26

Part 1 **Copy each pair of fractions. Below, write the whole number each fraction equals. If a fraction is greater, circle it.**

a. $\frac{36}{9}$ $\frac{80}{80}$ b. $\frac{35}{5}$ $\frac{20}{2}$ c. $\frac{48}{8}$ $\frac{42}{7}$ d. $\frac{0}{4}$ $\frac{4}{1}$

Part 2 **Copy and complete each pair of equivalent fractions.**

a. $\frac{7}{2}\left(\blacksquare\right) = \frac{\blacksquare}{14}$ b. $\frac{4}{5}\left(\blacksquare\right) = \frac{36}{\blacksquare}$ c. $\frac{9}{10}\left(\blacksquare\right) = \frac{18}{\blacksquare}$

d. $\frac{3}{7}\left(\blacksquare\right) = \frac{\blacksquare}{28}$ e. $\frac{1}{8}\left(\blacksquare\right) = \frac{5}{\blacksquare}$ f. $\frac{9}{3}\left(\blacksquare\right) = \frac{\blacksquare}{24}$

Part 3
1. **Check the missing numbers for part 4 in your workbook.**
2. **Answer each question.**

This table shows the number of red cars and blue cars that were on Hill Street and Valley Street.

Questions

a. What was the total number of both red cars and blue cars on Valley Street?

b. How many blue cars were on Hill Street?

c. Were there more blue cars on Hill Street or on Valley Street?

d. What was the total number of red cars for both streets?

e. Were there more red cars or blue cars on Hill Street?

	Red cars	Blue cars	Total for both colors
Hill Street	48 ✔	33 ✔	81
Valley Street	38	65	103
Total for both streets	86 ✔	98 ✔	184

Independent Work

Part 4 **For each problem, write the equation, make a number family and figure out the answer.**

a. On Monday, Donna spent some money. On Tuesday, she spent $14 more. She ended up spending $34 for both days. How much did she spend on Monday?

b. There were 713 ladybugs in a field. Then some of them left the field. Now there are 104 ladybugs in the field. How many flew away?

c. The bakery made some pies in the morning. Then it made another 145 pies in the afternoon. In all, the bakery made 501 pies during the day. How many pies were made in the morning?

Part 5 **Copy and complete each equation. If the fractions are equivalent, write the simple equation below.**

a. $\frac{4}{7}(\blacksquare) = \frac{24}{42}$ b. $\frac{3}{5}(\blacksquare) = \frac{6}{10}$ c. $\frac{5}{6}(\blacksquare) = \frac{30}{30}$

d. $\frac{10}{4}(\blacksquare) = \frac{20}{16}$ e. $\frac{8}{5}(\blacksquare) = \frac{80}{50}$

Part 6 **Copy each number. Write P if it is a prime number. If it is not a prime number, show the equation with prime factors.**

a. 143 b. 151 c. 161 d. 101

Part 7 **For each problem, make a number family. Figure out the answer to the question.**

a. The stove weighed 120 pounds less than the refrigerator. The stove weighed 175 pounds. How much did the refrigerator weigh?

b. A dove flew 134 meters farther than a hawk flew. The dove flew 2121 meters. How far did the hawk fly?

c. A bus burned 340 more gallons of fuel than a truck burned. The truck burned 640 gallons. How much fuel did the bus burn?

Lesson 27

Part 1 **Copy each item. Circle the value that is larger.**

a. $\frac{1}{3}$ $\frac{1}{8}$ b. $\frac{6}{5}$ $\frac{5}{6}$ c. 4 $\frac{50}{10}$ d. 2 $\frac{1}{2}$ e. $\frac{40}{8}$ $\frac{56}{7}$

Part 2 **Rewrite each equation to show prime factors.**

a. 14 x 9 = 126 b. 5 x 12 = 60 c. 15 x 4 = 60 d. 20 x 6 = 120

Part 3 **Copy and work each item.**

a. $2\overline{)134}$ b. $4\overline{)536}$ c. $8\overline{)424}$ d. $3\overline{)165}$ e. $7\overline{)924}$

Part 4 **1. Check the missing numbers for part 3 in your workbook.**
2. Answer each question.

This table shows the number of meals served in two restaurants on Tuesday and Wednesday.

	Restaurant A	Restaurant B	Total for both restaurants
Tuesday	461	1143	1604
Wednesday	972	1317	2289
Total for both days	1433	2460	3893

Questions

a. How many meals were served in Restaurant B on Wednesday?

b. What was the total number of meals served in Restaurant B?

c. On Tuesday, were more meals served in Restaurant A or Restaurant B?

d. What was the total number of meals served in both restaurants on both days?

e. Did Restaurant A serve fewer meals on Tuesday or Wednesday?

Independent Work

Part 5 **Copy and complete the table.**

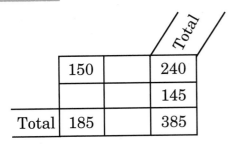

			Total
	150		240
			145
Total	185		385

Part 6 **Write the complete equation for each item. Show the fraction that equals 1. Show the missing number in the last fraction.**

a. $\frac{4}{9}\left(\blacksquare\right) = \frac{20}{\blacksquare}$ b. $\frac{3}{2}\left(\blacksquare\right) = \frac{27}{\blacksquare}$

c. $\frac{1}{5}\left(\blacksquare\right) = \frac{\blacksquare}{35}$ d. $\frac{10}{9}\left(\blacksquare\right) = \frac{\blacksquare}{54}$

Part 7 **Write the fraction for each description.**

a. The fraction equals 45. The denominator is 3.

b. The fraction equals 200. The denominator is 20.

c. The fraction equals 200. The denominator is 1.

d. The fraction equals 200. The denominator is 4.

Part 8 **For each item, show the mixed number and the fraction it equals.**

a. $3\frac{4}{5} = \blacksquare$ b. $9\frac{1}{3} = \blacksquare$ c. $1\frac{4}{5} = \blacksquare$ d. $4\frac{3}{7} = \blacksquare$

Part J

a. 2×7×3×3 = 126 b. 5×2×2×3 = 60

c. 3×5×2×2 = 60 d. 2×2×5×2×3 = 120

Lesson 28

Part 1

- You've learned that the bottom number of a fraction is the **denominator.** $\frac{8}{10}$
- The top number of a fraction is called the **numerator.** $\frac{8}{10}$

a. $\frac{9}{5}$

b. $\frac{7}{11}$

Part 2

You're going to write decimal values that equal fractions.

Here are the rules:

- If you divide a whole number by 10, the answer shows **tenths.**
- If you divide a whole number by 100, the answer shows **hundredths.**
- If you divide a whole number by 1000, the answer shows **thousandths.**

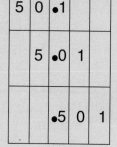

	tens	ones	tenths	hundredths	thousandths
$\frac{501}{10}$	5	0	•1		
$\frac{501}{100}$		5	•0	1	
$\frac{501}{1000}$			•5	0	1

Part 3 Write the decimal value for each fraction.

a. $\frac{375}{10}$ b. $\frac{375}{100}$ c. $\frac{375}{1000}$ d. $\frac{1201}{100}$ e. $\frac{89}{10}$ f. $\frac{52}{100}$

Part 4 Copy and work each item.

a. $8\overline{)956}$ b. $3\overline{)876}$ c. $4\overline{)1261}$ d. $5\overline{)4950}$ e. $7\overline{)4020}$

Part 5

- You can use a sign to show which value is larger.

$5 < 6$
$6 > 5$

- Here's one way to figure out how to make the sign:
  - ✔ Circle the value that is larger.
  - ✔ Then make a sign that has the wide end close to the circle.

- $\frac{1}{2}$ is larger than $\frac{1}{10}$. So you circle $\frac{1}{2}$.
  Then make the wide end of the sign close to $\frac{1}{2}$.

$\frac{1}{2}$ (circled) $\quad \frac{1}{10}$

$\frac{1}{2}$ (circled) $> \frac{1}{10}$

- $\frac{12}{2}$ is larger than $\frac{32}{8}$. So you circle $\frac{12}{2}$.
  The wide end of the sign is close to $\frac{12}{2}$.

$\frac{32}{8} < \frac{12}{2}$ (circled)

Part 6

Copy each item. Circle the larger value. Complete the sign ($<$, $=$, $>$).

a. $\frac{1}{9}$ — $\frac{1}{4}$ b. 3 — $\frac{15}{5}$ c. $\frac{9}{9}$ — $\frac{16}{8}$ d. $\frac{28}{4}$ — $\frac{28}{7}$ e. $\frac{12}{11}$ — $\frac{54}{60}$

Part 7

1. Check the missing numbers for part 3 in your workbook.
2. Answer each question.

This table shows the number of fifth graders and sixth graders at two schools.

Questions

a. In which school are there more fifth graders?

b. What's the total number of sixth graders for both schools?

c. How many sixth graders attend Jefferson School?

d. What's the total number of fifth and sixth graders who attend Madison School?

e. In which school are there fewer sixth graders?

	Fifth graders	Sixth graders	Total for both grades
Jefferson School	✔ 128	✔ 223	351
Madison School	✔ 155	✔ 184	339
Total for both schools	283	407	690

Independent Work

Part 8 **For each item, show the mixed number and the fraction it equals.**

a. $4\frac{7}{8} = \blacksquare$ b. $4\frac{3}{5} = \blacksquare$ c. $4\frac{9}{10} = \blacksquare$ d. $4\frac{1}{9} = \blacksquare$

Part 9 **Write the complete equation for each item.**

a. $8 = \frac{\blacksquare}{1} = \frac{\blacksquare}{2} = \frac{\blacksquare}{3} = \frac{\blacksquare}{8}$

b. $5 = \frac{\blacksquare}{3} = \frac{\blacksquare}{4} = \frac{\blacksquare}{5} = \frac{\blacksquare}{8}$

c. $9 = \frac{\blacksquare}{3} = \frac{\blacksquare}{5} = \frac{\blacksquare}{8} = \frac{\blacksquare}{10}$

Part 10 **For each problem, write the equation, make a number family and figure out the answer.**

a. Before the spring frost, there were 345 plants in the field. Then the frost killed some plants. After the frost, there were 35 plants in the field. How many plants died from the frost?

b. Donna had money in a bank account. She put in another \$38. Now she has \$450 in her account. How much did she have before she put in \$38?

c. There were 370 bees in the field. Then 290 more bees joined them. How many bees ended up in the field?

d. There were some fleas on a dog. Then 111 fleas jumped off the dog. Now there are 12 fleas on the dog. How many fleas were on the dog to begin with?

Part 11 **Write the complete equation for each item. Show the fraction that equals 1. Show the missing number in the last fraction.**

a. $\frac{2}{7}\left(\blacksquare\right) = \frac{\blacksquare}{21}$ b. $\frac{2}{7}\left(\blacksquare\right) = \frac{12}{\blacksquare}$ c. $\frac{2}{7}\left(\blacksquare\right) = \frac{\blacksquare}{70}$

Part 12

Copy and complete the table.

Decimal	Mixed number
a. 6.12	
b.	$4\frac{2}{100}$
c. 3.8	
d.	$4\frac{1}{10}$

Part 13

Write the problem and the answer for each number family.

a. ■ 15 → 147

b. 203 ■ → 999

c. 508 27 → ■

Part 14

Copy and complete each equation. If the fractions are equivalent, write the simple equation below.

a. $\frac{2}{7}(■) = \frac{12}{21}$

b. $\frac{2}{5}(■) = \frac{2}{10}$

c. $\frac{3}{2}(■) = \frac{18}{2}$

d. $\frac{5}{4}(■) = \frac{10}{8}$

Part J

c. 8 × 9 = 72

2×2×2×3×3 = 72

d. 6 × 10 = 60

2×3×2×5 = 60

e. 4 × 8 = 32

2×2×2×2×2 = 32

Lesson 29

Part 1

Copy each item. Circle the larger value. Write the sign (<, =, >).

a. $\frac{16}{8}$ $\frac{7}{8}$ b. $\frac{10}{11}$ $\frac{10}{2}$ c. $\frac{5}{8}$ $\frac{8}{5}$ d. $\frac{15}{3}$ $\frac{15}{5}$ e. $\frac{20}{5}$ $\frac{10}{5}$

Part 2

Write the multiplication fact for each item. Below, rewrite the fact with prime factors.

a. ■ x ■ = 50 b. ■ x ■ = 28 c. ■ x ■ = 56

d. ■ x ■ = 42 e. ■ x ■ = 27

Part 3

For each problem, write the names and the complete equation. Work the problem. Box the answer to the question.

a. There are 5 birds for every 3 cats. How many cats are there if there are 25 birds?

b. There are 7 trucks for every 9 cars. If there are 36 cars, how many trucks are there?

c. There are 8 girls for every 5 boys. If there are 64 girls, how many boys are there?

d. There are 10 cups for every 4 saucers. How many cups are there if there are 28 saucers?

Part 4

Copy each problem and work it.

a. $3\overline{)618}$ b. $4\overline{)832}$ c. $4\overline{)1532}$ d. $2\overline{)6120}$ e. $6\overline{)714}$

Part 5

Write the decimal number for each fraction.

a. $\frac{62}{100}$ b. $\frac{504}{10}$ c. $\frac{2158}{1000}$ d. $\frac{1823}{100}$ e. $\frac{98}{10}$ f. $\frac{709}{100}$

Part 6

Copy the table. Make a number family for each statement. Figure out all the missing numbers in the table.

This table is supposed to show the number of white pelicans and brown pelicans spotted at two wildlife refuges—Peat Island and Fairview Rock.

Facts

a. There are 123 fewer white pelicans than brown pelicans at Peat Island.

b. There are 217 more brown pelicans at Fairview Rock than at Peat Island.

	White pelicans	Brown pelicans	Total for both birds
Peat Island		587	
Fairview Rock			1062
Total for both refuges			

Part 7

- Mixed numbers have a whole number and a fraction. When you figure out the fraction that equals a mixed number, you must change the whole number into a fraction. That fraction must have the same denominator as the other fraction.
- You do the same thing to work addition or subtraction problems that have a whole number and a fraction.

Here's: $\frac{4}{3} + 2$

- You can change 2 into a fraction that has the same denominator as $\frac{4}{3}$. $\frac{4}{3} + 2$
- The fraction that equals 2 is $\frac{6}{3}$.

So you have: $\frac{4}{3} + \frac{6}{3} = \frac{10}{3}$

Independent Work

Part 8

Copy each number. Write P if it is a prime number. If it is not a prime number, show the equation with prime factors.

a. 39 b. 78 c. 79 d. 89 e. 99 f. 109

Part 9

Copy and complete the table.

	Decimal	Mixed number
a.	9.3	
b.		$28\frac{1}{100}$
c.		$4\frac{3}{10}$

Part 10

Copy and complete each equation.

a. $9 = \frac{\blacksquare}{6} = \frac{\blacksquare}{5} = \frac{\blacksquare}{4}$

b. $6 = \frac{\blacksquare}{6} = \frac{\blacksquare}{5} = \frac{\blacksquare}{4}$

Part 11

For each problem, make a number family, figure out the answer and box it.

a. The race car traveled 21 miles per hour slower than the train. The race car went 19 miles per hour. How fast did the train move?

b. Molly was 42 centimeters shorter than Ann. Ann was 187 centimeters tall. How tall was Molly?

Part 12

Copy and work each problem.

a. $\begin{array}{r} 38 \\ \underline{\times\ 50} \end{array}$

b. $\begin{array}{r} 3129 \\ \underline{\times\ \ \ \ 7} \end{array}$

Part 13

Write the complete equation for each item. Show the fraction that equals 1. Show the missing number in the last fraction.

a. $\frac{4}{3}\left(\blacksquare\right) = \frac{\blacksquare}{90}$

b. $\frac{8}{7}\left(\blacksquare\right) = \frac{64}{\blacksquare}$

Part 14

Copy and work each problem.

a. $\frac{2}{5} \times \frac{1}{3} = ■$ b. $\frac{2}{5} + \frac{5}{5} = ■$ c. $\frac{2}{5} \times \frac{5}{5} = ■$

d. $\frac{15}{5} - \frac{13}{5} = ■$ e. $\frac{7}{8} \times \frac{1}{8} = ■$

Part 15

Copy and complete the table.

Multiplication	Division	Fraction equation
a. $8 \times ■ = 560$		
b. $4 \times ■ = 200$		
c. $9 \times ■ = 3600$		

Part 16

Copy each equation. Figure out the missing fraction. If the missing fraction equals 1, write the simple equation below.

a. $\frac{4}{3}(■) = \frac{8}{21}$ b. $\frac{3}{5}(■) = \frac{9}{15}$

Part J

c. $⑧ \times 7 = 56$

$2 \times 2 \times 2 \times 7 = 56$

d. $⑥ \times 7 = 42$

$2 \times 3 \times 7 = 42$

e. $3 \times ⑨ = 27$

$3 \times 3 \times 3 = 27$

Part K

	White pelicans	Brown pelicans	Total for both birds
Peat Island	464	587	1051
Fairview Rock	258	804	1062
Total for both refuges	722	1391	2113

Lesson 30

Part 1

- If the denominator of a fraction is 1, the top number of the fraction tells what the fraction equals. $\frac{4}{1} = 4$ $\frac{13}{1} = 13$
- You can show that these equations are correct by starting with the denominator of the fraction and seeing how many times larger the numerator is.

Part 2

Copy and complete each equation.

a. $\frac{8}{1} = \blacksquare$ b. $\blacksquare = \frac{16}{4}$ c. $\blacksquare = \frac{25}{1}$ d. $\frac{42}{7} = \blacksquare$ e. $\blacksquare = \frac{0}{7}$

Part 3

- Here's one way to tell about a ratio:

  There are 6 cats for every 7 rats. $\frac{\text{cats}}{\text{rats}}\ \frac{6}{7}$
- Here's another way to tell about the same ratio:

  The ratio of cats to rats is 6 to 7. $\frac{\text{cats}}{\text{rats}}\ \frac{6}{7}$
- There are 4 shovels for every 15 workers. **The ratio of...**
- There are 6 frogs for every 9 logs.
- There are 4 moths for every 7 worms.

Part 4 **For each problem, write the names and the complete equation. Box the answer to the question.**

a. The ratio of bats to players is 2 to 11. If there are 16 bats, how many players are there?

b. The ratio of boys to girls is 3 to 4. If there are 24 girls, how many boys are there?

c. The ratio of bottles to cans is 5 to 9. If there are 45 cans, how many bottles are there?

d. The ratio of books to pupils is 8 to 1. If there are 72 books, how many pupils are there?

Part 5 **Write the decimal value for each fraction.**

a. $\frac{628}{1000}$ b. $\frac{525}{10}$ c. $\frac{169}{100}$ d. $\frac{43}{10}$

Test 3

Part 1 **Write the equation for each word problem. Make the number family. Then figure out the missing number.**

a. Doris had some money. Then she earned $35. She ended up with $156. How much did she start out with?

b. There were some frogs in the pond. 112 frogs jumped out of the pond. Now there are 133 frogs in the pond. How many frogs were in the pond to begin with?

Part 2 **Copy each item. Circle the fraction that is larger. Write the sign ($<$, $=$, $>$).**

a. $\frac{9}{9}$ $\frac{9}{10}$ b. $\frac{7}{8}$ $\frac{9}{8}$ c. $\frac{12}{3}$ $\frac{15}{5}$

Part 3 **Copy and complete the table.**

	Decimal	Mixed number
a.	6.08	
b.		$1\frac{5}{10}$
c.		$26\frac{2}{1000}$

Part 4 **Copy the table. For each fact, make a number family and check marks. Figure out all the missing numbers in the table.**

This table is supposed to show the number of yellow pencils and red pencils in two different places.

Facts

a. There are 101 more yellow pencils on the shelf than in the drawer.

b. In the drawer, there are 56 fewer yellow pencils than red pencils.

	Yellow pencils	Red pencils	Total pencils
On the shelf		186	
In the drawer	29		
Total for both places			

Part 5 **Copy and complete each equation.**

a. $7 = \frac{■}{1} = \frac{■}{2} = \frac{■}{3} = \frac{■}{9}$

b. $2 = \frac{■}{1} = \frac{■}{2} = \frac{■}{3} = \frac{■}{9}$

Part 6 **Copy each item. Rewrite each fact to show prime factors.**

a. 6 x 9 = 54

b. 8 x 10 = 80

Part 7 Write the complete equation for each item. Show the equivalent fractions and the fraction that equals one.

a. $\frac{7}{5}\left(\blacksquare\right) = \frac{\blacksquare}{40}$

b. $\frac{3}{5}\left(\blacksquare\right) = \frac{27}{\blacksquare}$

c. $\frac{1}{8}\left(\blacksquare\right) = \frac{\blacksquare}{48}$

Part 8 For each item, show the mixed number and the fraction it equals.

a. $4\frac{2}{3} = \blacksquare$

b. $6\frac{1}{8} = \blacksquare$

c. $1\frac{4}{7} = \blacksquare$

Part 9 Copy and work each problem.

a. $4\overline{)936}$

b. $5\overline{)129}$

Part 10 Copy the table and complete it.

Multiplication	Division	Fraction equation
a. $4 \times \blacksquare = 244$		
b. $9 \times \blacksquare = 828$		
c. $5 \times \blacksquare = 95$		

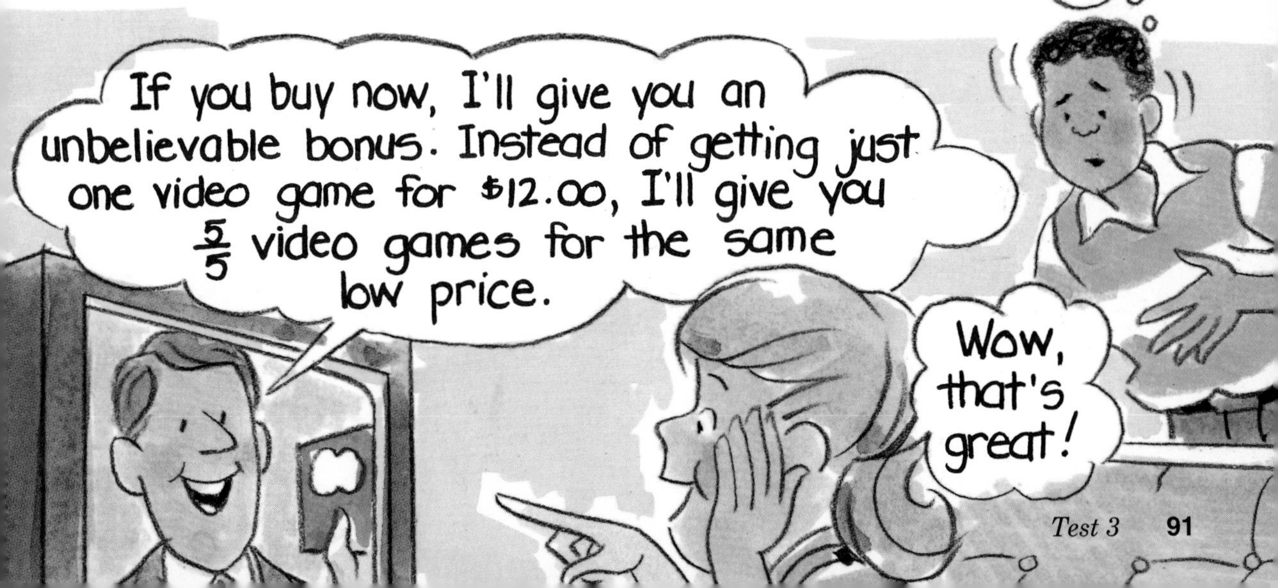
If you buy now, I'll give you an unbelievable bonus. Instead of getting just one video game for $12.00, I'll give you $\frac{5}{5}$ video games for the same low price.
Wow, that's great!
!

Lesson 31

Part 1

- Here's how to work addition and subtraction problems that involve dollar amounts: \$56.55 – \$8.40
- Line up the decimal points:

$$\begin{array}{r} 56.55 \\ -\ \ 8.40 \\ \hline \end{array}$$

- Write \$ in front of the first value and in front of the answer.
- Write the decimal point in the answer.

$$\begin{array}{r} \$\,56.55 \\ -\ \ \ 8.40 \\ \hline \$\,48.15 \end{array}$$

Part 2

Write each problem as a column problem and work it.

a. \$34.20 – \$1.11

b. \$110.56 + \$55.91

c. Bill spent \$13.20. Then he spent \$4.12. How much did he spend in all?

Part 3

Write the decimal number for each fraction. Check your work with a calculator.

a. $\frac{7071}{10}$ b. $\frac{2}{1000}$ c. $\frac{26}{10}$ d. $\frac{5}{100}$ e. $\frac{5024}{100}$

Part 4

Copy each problem and work it.

a. $4\overline{)8206}$ b. $5\overline{)4370}$ c. $6\overline{)7237}$

Part 5

- You know that if you multiply a value by more than 1, you end up with more than you start with.

Here's: $5 \times 2 = 10$

- You're multiplying by more than 1, so you end up with more than you start with.
- The answer is 10. That's more than 5. $5 < 10$
- You also know that if you multiply a value by 1, you end up with exactly the same value you start with.

$5 \times 1 = 5$

$5 = 5$

- Here's a new rule:

If you multiply by less than 1, you end up with less than you start with.

- Here's: $5 \times \frac{1}{2}$.
- The answer is $\frac{5}{2}$. That's **less than 5.** $5 > \frac{5}{2}$

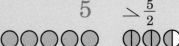

- Remember, if you multiply by less than 1, you end up with less than you start with.

Part 6

For each item, write whether the answer is more than 4 or less than 4.

a. $4 \times \frac{6}{5} =$ [redacted] b. $4 \times \frac{5}{6} =$ [redacted] c. $4 \times 6 =$ [redacted] d. $4 \times \frac{1}{2} =$ [redacted]

Part 7

- Sometimes, you multiply a whole number by a fraction.

  Here's: $5 \times \frac{4}{2}$

- You can change 5 into a **simple fraction that equals 5.** That fraction is $\frac{5}{1}$. $\frac{5}{1} \times \frac{4}{2}$

- The fraction tells you that there's only 1 part in each unit.
  5 parts are shaded. So 5 whole units are shaded.

Here's the picture for $\frac{5}{1}$: 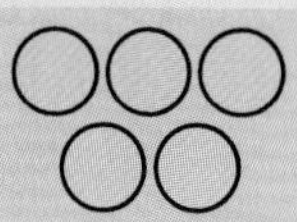

I understand that the ratio of saddles to cowboys is 10 to 3, but I'd like to know why.
LUCKY

Part 8 **For each problem, write the names and the complete equation. Box the answer to the question.**

a. The ratio of men to women is 9 to 5. If there are 50 women, how many men are there?

b. The ratio of calculators to students is 3 to 7. If there are 21 students, how many calculators are there?

c. The ratio of cowboys to saddles is 10 to 3. If there are 36 saddles, how many cowboys are there?

Part 9

- A fraction is **simplified** if it has the smallest numerator and the smallest denominator that is possible.
- Here are the steps:

✔ You start with a fraction that is not simplified. $\frac{28}{21}$

✔ You show the **prime factors** for the numerator and the denominator. $\frac{28}{21} = \frac{2 \times 2 \times 7}{3 \times 7}$

✔ You cross out any **fractions that equal 1.** $\frac{28}{21} = \frac{2 \times 2 \times \cancel{7}}{3 \times \cancel{7}}$

✔ Then you multiply the values that are **not crossed out.**

On top, you have 2 x 2. That's 4.
On the bottom, you have 3. $\frac{28}{21} = \frac{2 \times 2 \times \cancel{7}}{3 \times \cancel{7}} = \frac{4}{3}$

So: $\frac{28}{21} = \frac{4}{3}$

Independent Work

Part 10 Answer each question.

This table shows the number of men and women who live in two different towns.

Questions

a. Which town has more men, Smalltown or Tinyville?

b. Which town has more adults?

c. What's the total number of women for both towns?

d. What's the total number of adults in Tinyville?

e. How many men live in Smalltown?

	Men	Women	Total
Smalltown	156	577	733
Tinyville	142	124	266
Total	298	701	999

Part 11 Copy and complete each equation.

a. $\frac{4}{6}\left(\blacksquare\right) = \frac{36}{\blacksquare}$

b. $\frac{7}{6}\left(\blacksquare\right) = \frac{\blacksquare}{48}$

Part 12 **Copy the table. Make a number family and check marks for the fact. Figure out all the missing numbers in the table.**

This table is supposed to show the number of tacos and hamburgers sold at two different stands.

Fact

The total number of hamburgers sold at both stands is 91 more than the total number of tacos sold at both stands.

	Tacos	Hamburgers	Total
Rosy's Stand	92		186
Al's Stand			
Total	167		

Part 13 **Copy each equation. Figure out the missing fraction. If the missing fraction equals 1, write the simple equation below.**

a. $\frac{4}{3}(\blacksquare) = \frac{12}{12}$

b. $\frac{7}{9}(\blacksquare) = \frac{35}{45}$

c. $\frac{4}{7}(\blacksquare) = \frac{24}{56}$

Lesson 32

Part 1

You have learned to write the remainder for division problems. The remainder can also be written as a fraction. When you write the remainder as a fraction, you show the answer as a mixed number. **You change the remainder into a fraction by dividing.**

- The answer to this problem is 4 with a remainder of 6. $7\overline{)34}$ = 4 R6
- The problem divides by 7. So you can divide the remainder by 7. That's $\frac{6}{7}$. $7\overline{)34}$ = $4\frac{6}{7}$
- The answer to this problem has a remainder of 4. $9\overline{)31}$ = 3 R4
- The problem divides by 9. So you can divide the remainder by 9. That's $\frac{4}{9}$. $9\overline{)31}$ = $3\frac{4}{9}$
- The answer to this problem has a remainder of 1. $5\overline{)16}$ = 3 R1
- The problem divides by 5. So you can divide the remainder by 5. That's $\frac{1}{5}$. $5\overline{)16}$ = $3\frac{1}{5}$

Remember, when you have a remainder, you can write it as a fraction. **The number you divide by tells the denominator for the fraction.**

Part 2

Rewrite the complete answer to each problem as a mixed number.

Sample problem: $7\overline{)25}$ = 3 R4

a. $5\overline{)33}$ = 6 R3

b. $4\overline{)11}$ = 2 R3

c. $3\overline{)22}$ = 7 R1

d. $6\overline{)41}$ = 6 R5

Part 3 For each problem, write the names and the complete equation. Box the answer to the question.

a. There are 2 pounds of sand for every 5 pounds of water. If there are 35 pounds of water, how many pounds of sand are there?

b. The ratio of trucks to cars is 4 to 9. There are 72 cars. How many trucks are there?

c. The ratio of dishes to cups is 5 to 3. There are 50 dishes. How many cups are there?

d. They completed 4 pictures every 3 hours. They completed 24 pictures. How many hours did they work?

Part 4 Copy and work each problem.

a. $3 \times \frac{7}{8} = \blacksquare$ b. $\frac{1}{5} \times 9 = \blacksquare$ c. $\frac{7}{3} \times \frac{4}{5} = \blacksquare$ d. $\frac{20}{5} \times \frac{4}{3} = \blacksquare$

Independent Work

Part 5 Copy each problem and work it.

a. $7\overline{)4242}$ b. $3\overline{)2802}$ c. $9\overline{)1008}$ d. $8\overline{)4320}$

Part 6 Write the fraction for each description.

a. This fraction equals 7. The denominator is 11.

b. This fraction equals 11. The denominator is 5.

c. The numbers for this fraction are 13 and 3. The fraction is less than 1.

d. The fraction is more than 1. The numbers are 12 and 13.

e. This fraction equals 50. The denominator is 2.

Part 7 Work each problem. Show the number family if the problem requires addition or subtraction.

a. There were 166 fewer men than women at the meeting. If there were 77 men, how many women were there?

b. The wheel made 16 revolutions every 3 minutes. If the wheel turned for 15 minutes, how many revolutions did it make?

c. The workers completed 11 houses every 30 days. If the workers completed 33 houses, how many days did they work?

d. The gold coin was 125 grams heavier than the copper coin. If the gold coin weighed 601 grams, how many grams did the copper coin weigh?

Part 8 Copy the table and complete it.

Multiplication	Division	Fraction equation
a. $8 \times ■ = 720$		
b. $7 \times ■ = 427$		
c. $12 \times ■ = 156$		

Part J

a. $\frac{3}{1} \times \frac{7}{8} = \frac{21}{8}$ b. $\frac{1}{5} \times \frac{6}{1} = \frac{6}{5}$ c. $\frac{7}{3} \times \frac{4}{5} = \frac{28}{15}$ d. $\frac{20}{5} \times \frac{4}{3} = \frac{80}{15}$

Lesson 33

Part 1

Copy the table. Figure out all the missing numbers.

			Total
	12		36
		25	
Total	27		

Part 2

The simplest way to solve some problems is to make a table.

There were red cars and black cars on two lots. The lots are Al's lot and Lisa's lot. There were 12 black cars on Lisa's lot. The total number of red cars was 98. Al's lot had 15 red cars. The total number of cars for both lots was 176.

a. How many black cars were on Al's lot?

b. What's the total number of black cars for both lots?

c. Did Lisa's lot have more red cars or black cars?

- The first names in the problem are **column** headings.
- There were red cars and black cars on two lots.
- The column headings are **red cars, black cars,** and **total.**

	Red cars	Black cars	Total

- The next names in the problem are **row** headings.
- The lots are Al's lot and Lisa's lot.
- The row headings are **Al's lot, Lisa's lot,** and **total.**

	Red cars	Black cars	Total
Al's lot			
Lisa's lot			
Total			

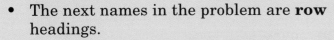

- Now you can read the rest of the problem, fill in the missing numbers, and answer the questions.

Part 3 Make a table for the problem. Answer the questions.

Game wardens put trout and bass in two different lakes. The lakes were Blue Lake and Ross Lake. The wardens put 125 trout in Blue Lake. They put 74 bass in Blue Lake and 128 bass in Ross Lake. They put a total of 231 fish in Ross Lake.

a. How many trout were put in Ross Lake?

b. How many total fish were put in Blue Lake?

c. How many bass were put in both lakes?

Part 4 Rewrite the complete answer to each problem as a mixed number.

a. $\begin{array}{r} 5\text{ R}2 \\ 9\overline{)47} \end{array}$ b. $\begin{array}{r} 4\text{ R}4 \\ 5\overline{)24} \end{array}$ c. $\begin{array}{r} 6\text{ R}2 \\ 3\overline{)20} \end{array}$ d. $\begin{array}{r} 4\text{ R}1 \\ 7\overline{)29} \end{array}$

Part 5 Copy each fraction. Show the prime factors for the numerator and the denominator. Write the simplified fraction.

Sample problem: $\frac{8}{18}$

a. $\frac{15}{25}$ b. $\frac{10}{40}$ c. $\frac{42}{35}$ d. $\frac{8}{16}$

Independent Work

Part 6 Copy the table and complete it.

Multiplication	Division	Fraction equation
a. 6 x ■ = 2352		
b. 5 x ■ = 1300		
c. 9 x ■ = 243		

Part 7 **For each problem, write the names and the complete equation. Box the answer to the question.**

a. The ratio of gears to machines is 10 to 2. If there are 200 machines, how many gears are there?

b. 12 boxes weigh 5 pounds. How many boxes would weigh 45 pounds?

c. The ratio of ducks to geese is 3 to 4. If there are 36 ducks, how many geese are there?

Part 8 **Copy each equation. Figure out the missing fraction. If the missing fraction equals 1, write the simple equation below.**

a. $\frac{2}{7}(\blacksquare) = \frac{12}{21}$

b. $\frac{2}{5}(\blacksquare) = \frac{2}{10}$

c. $\frac{3}{2}(\blacksquare) = \frac{18}{12}$

d. $\frac{5}{4}(\blacksquare) = \frac{10}{8}$

Part 9 **Write the complete equation for each item.**

a. $8 = \frac{\blacksquare}{5} = \frac{\blacksquare}{10} = \frac{\blacksquare}{1} = \frac{\blacksquare}{7}$

b. $9 = \frac{\blacksquare}{5} = \frac{\blacksquare}{10} = \frac{\blacksquare}{1} = \frac{\blacksquare}{7}$

Lesson 34

Part 1 **Rewrite the complete answer to each problem as a mixed number.**

a. $\begin{array}{r} 6\text{ R2} \\ 3\overline{)2\ 0} \end{array}$ b. $\begin{array}{r} 6\text{ R3} \\ 4\overline{)2\ 7} \end{array}$ c. $\begin{array}{r} 5\text{ R3} \\ 7\overline{)3\ 8} \end{array}$

d. $\begin{array}{r} 4\text{ R4} \\ 5\overline{)2\ 4} \end{array}$ e. $\begin{array}{r} 9\text{ R1} \\ 2\overline{)1\ 9} \end{array}$ f. $\begin{array}{r} 3\text{ R5} \\ 6\overline{)2\ 3} \end{array}$

Part 2 **For each equation, make a number family and answer the question.**

> ***Sample problem:*** There were 182 gallons of water in a tank. 97 gallons leaked out. How many gallons ended up in the tank?

a. Molly collected 228 shells. She gave away some shells. She ended up with 49 shells. How many did she give away?

b. A bank account had some money in it. Then \$45.60 was taken out of the account. There was still \$13.90 in the account. How much was in the account to begin with?

c. At the end of the day, there were 95 cartons of milk in the store. Earlier that day, the store sold 118 cartons. How many cartons did the store have at the beginning of the day?

Part 3 **Copy and work each problem. Circle the last value if it's more than the value you start with.**

a. $\frac{2}{3} \times \frac{9}{4} = \blacksquare$ b. $\frac{5}{1} \times \frac{7}{5} = \blacksquare$ c. $\frac{3}{7} \times \frac{6}{1} = \blacksquare$ d. $\frac{2}{5} \times \frac{5}{10} = \blacksquare$

Part 4 Make a table for each problem. Answer the questions.

Problem 1

At two camps there were both boys and girls. The camps were Roger's Camp and Miller's Camp. There were 217 boys at Miller's Camp. There were 149 girls at Miller's Camp. The total number of boys for both camps was 642. The total number of children for both camps was 1109.

a. What was the total number of children at Miller's Camp?
b. Were there more boys or girls at Roger's Camp?
c. Were there fewer children at Miller's Camp or Roger's Camp?

Problem 2

In 1978 and 1979, babies were born in two counties. The counties were Queen County and Prince County. In 1979, 73 babies were born in Queen County. The total number of babies born in 1979 was 141. The total number of babies born in Prince County during both years was 263. In 1978, the total number of babies born in both counties was 237.

a. How many babies were born in Queen County in 1978?
b. In 1979, were more babies born in Queen County or Prince County?
c. In which year were fewer babies born in Prince County?

Independent Work

Don't forget to complete the tables and answer the questions for part 4 of your textbook.

Part 5 Write the complete equation for each item.

a. $7 = \frac{■}{4} = \frac{■}{2} = \frac{■}{9} = \frac{■}{1}$

b. $11 = \frac{■}{1} = \frac{■}{3} = \frac{■}{2} = \frac{■}{5}$

Part 6 For each problem, write the names and the complete equation. Box the answer to the question.

a. A factory completed 3 cars every 4 minutes. How many minutes would it take the factory to complete 24 cars?

b. The ratio of fleas to lions is 29 to 1. If there are 200 lions, how many fleas are there?

c. The ratio of needles to pins is 7 to 12. If there are 49 needles, how many pins are there?

Part 7 Copy the table and complete it.

	Decimal	Mixed number
a.		$4\frac{3}{100}$
b.	1.5	
c.	130.001	
d.		$6\frac{3}{10}$

Lesson 35

Part 1 **Copy and work each problem. Circle the last value if it's more than the value you start with.**

a. $\frac{5}{8} \times \frac{7}{8} =$ [redacted] b. $\frac{5}{8} \times \frac{8}{7} =$ [redacted] c. $6 \times \frac{12}{13} =$ [redacted] d. $\frac{1}{9} \times \frac{13}{2} =$ [redacted]

Part 2 **Make a number family and answer the question.**

a. A man ends up with $6.00. Earlier that day, he spent some money to buy groceries. At the beginning of the day, he had $49.20. How much did he spend?

b. After Walter gave away 52 baseball cards, he had 156 cards left. How many cards did Walter have to begin with?

c. At the end of the trip, there were 162 liters of fuel in the tank of a large truck. At the beginning of the trip, there had been 666 liters in the tank. How many liters of fuel were used up during the trip?

Part 3 **Rewrite the answer to each problem as a mixed number.**

a. $\begin{array}{r} 5\text{ R3} \\ 4\overline{)23} \end{array}$ b. $\begin{array}{r} 8\text{ R4} \\ 7\overline{)60} \end{array}$ c. $\begin{array}{r} 6\text{ R2} \\ 5\overline{)32} \end{array}$ d. $\begin{array}{r} 5\text{ R1} \\ 2\overline{)11} \end{array}$ e. $\begin{array}{r} 6\text{ R2} \\ 3\overline{)20} \end{array}$

Part 4 **Copy each problem and work it. Write the complete answer as a mixed number.**

Sample problem: $\begin{array}{r} 5 \\ 4\overline{)23} \end{array}$

a. $\begin{array}{r} 8 \\ 7\overline{)60} \end{array}$ b. $\begin{array}{r} 4 \\ 2\overline{)9} \end{array}$ c. $\begin{array}{r} 4 \\ 6\overline{)29} \end{array}$ d. $\begin{array}{r} 7 \\ 5\overline{)37} \end{array}$

Part 5 **Copy each fraction. Show the prime factors for the numerator and the denominator. Write the simplified fraction.**

a. $\frac{28}{24}$ b. $\frac{35}{10}$ c. $\frac{5}{50}$ d. $\frac{36}{81}$

Part 6 **Make a table for each problem. Answer the questions.**

Problem 1

Sunshine Farm and Citrus Farm harvested lemons and oranges. Sunshine Farm harvested 829 lemons. The total number of oranges harvested on both farms was 1194. Citrus Farm harvested a total of 1540 pieces of fruit. Citrus Farm harvested 719 oranges.

a. What was the total number of lemons harvested?
b. How many total pieces of fruit were harvested at Sunshine Farm?
c. How many total pieces of fruit were harvested at Citrus Farm?

Problem 2

Sarah and David counted seagulls and ducks at the coast. Sarah counted 128 ducks. David counted 235 seagulls. A total of 345 ducks were counted. Sarah counted 125 seagulls.

a. How many ducks did David count?
b. Who counted more birds, Sarah or David?
c. Were fewer ducks or seagulls counted?

Part 7

- You've learned that if the decimal part of a number is hundredths, it ends two places after the decimal point.
- If the decimal part is thousandths, it ends three places after the decimal point.
- To write those values, you may need zeros **before** the last digit.
- There's a big difference between decimal numbers and whole numbers. If you make zeros **after** the whole number 6, you make numbers that are bigger.
- But if you make zeros after a decimal number, the number **does not get bigger.**
- All these decimal numbers show exactly the same value. They all equal 2.6.
- Remember, zeros after the last digit of a decimal number don't change the value.

					tenths	hundredths	thousandths	ten thousandths
				•	0	6		
				•	0	0	6	
		6	0	•				
	6	0	0	•				
6	0	0	0	•				
			2	•	6			
			2	•	6	0		
			2	•	6	0	0	
			2	•	6	0	0	0

Independent Work

Don't forget to complete the tables and answer the questions for part 6 of your textbook.

Part 8

Figure out the missing value. Then write the complete equation.

a. 3 x 27 = ■

b. 3 x ■ = 210

c. 8 x ■ = 224

d. 18 x 9 = ■

e. 5 x ■ = 380

Part 9 Write the fraction for each description.

a. This fraction equals 7. The denominator is 9.

b. This fraction equals 4. The denominator is 80.

c. The numbers for this fraction are 33 and 44. The fraction is more than 1.

d. This fraction is less than 1. The numbers are 30 and 20.

Part 10 Write each problem with the whole number shown as a fraction. Work the problems.

a. $3 + \frac{4}{7} =$ [redacted]

b. $3 - \frac{4}{7} =$ [redacted]

c. $3 \times \frac{4}{7} =$ [redacted]

d. $8 - \frac{2}{3} =$ [redacted]

e. $\frac{2}{7} \times 12 =$ [redacted]

f. $\frac{2}{7} + 12 =$ [redacted]

Part J

a. 3.400 = 3.4

b. 16.70 = 16.7

c. 4.3700 = 4.37

d. 1.01000 = 1.01

e. 5.000 = 5.

If you open your savings account now at Questionable Security Bank, you won't receive a mere 3.4 percent interest on your savings. You'll receive a whopping 3.4000000 percent!
What a deal.
Not!

Lesson 36

Part 1 **Copy and work each problem. Circle the value you end up with if it's more than the value you start with.**

a. $8 \times \frac{1}{2} = $ ■ b. $\frac{12}{4} \times \frac{2}{3} = $ ■ c. $\frac{20}{5} \times \frac{3}{2} = $ ■ d. $\frac{9}{3} \times 3 = $ ■

Part 2 **Make a table for the problem. Answer the questions.**

Baseball cards and football cards were collected by two people. The people were Milly and George. Milly had 27 baseball cards in her collection. George had 52 football cards. George had a total of 75 cards.

a. How many baseball cards did George have?
b. How many football cards did both people have?
c. Which person had fewer total cards?

Milly had 25 more football cards than George had.

Part 3 **Copy each fraction. Show the prime factors for the numerator and denominator. Write the simplified fraction.**

a. $\frac{10}{25}$ b. $\frac{4}{12}$ c. $\frac{12}{9}$ d. $\frac{24}{28}$

Part 4 For each problem, make a number family and answer the question.

a. 117 people got in an empty train. Some people got off at different stations. Nobody else got in the train. When the train reached the last station, there were 34 people in it. How many people got off before the last station?

b. A train started out with 342 people in it. At the first stop, 201 people got off the train. How many people were still in the train?

c. There were lots of people in a train. At the first stop, 156 people got off. There were still 218 people in the train. How many people were in the train to begin with?

Part 5 Rewrite each decimal value that can be written with fewer zeros.

a. 3.04 b. 3.40 c. 11.003 d. 8.050 e. 11.300 f. 8.5

Independent Work

Don't forget to complete the table and answer the questions for part 2 of your textbook.

Part 6 Copy each problem and work it.

a. $5\overline{)4565}$ b. $3\overline{)3741}$ c. $4\overline{)4820}$ d. $5\overline{)545}$

Part 7 **Work each problem. Box the answer to the question the problem asks.**

a. The ratio of workers to machines is 3 to 8. If there are 30 workers, how many machines are there?

b. The pool is 25 feet wider than the deck. If the deck is 18 feet wide, how many feet wide is the pool?

c. Pile A contains 136 fewer bricks than pile B. Pile B has 1345 bricks. How many bricks are in pile A?

Part 8 **Write each problem with the whole number shown as a fraction. Work the problems.**

a. $\frac{2}{3} + 15 =$ ■ b. $\frac{2}{3} \times 15 =$ ■ c. $12 - \frac{1}{2} =$ ■

d. $12 + \frac{1}{2} =$ ■ e. $12 \times \frac{1}{2} =$ ■

Part 9 **Copy the table and complete it.**

	Decimal	Mixed number
a.		$14 \frac{3}{1000}$
b.	7.25	
c.		$40 \frac{7}{100}$
d.	5.9	

Part J

a. $\frac{10}{25} = \frac{2 \times \cancel{5}}{5 \times \cancel{5}} = \frac{2}{5}$ b. $\frac{4}{12} = \frac{\cancel{2} \times \cancel{2}}{\cancel{2} \times \cancel{2} \times 3} = \frac{1}{3}$

c. $\frac{12}{9} = \frac{2 \times 2 \times \cancel{3}}{3 \times \cancel{3}} = \frac{4}{3}$ d. $\frac{24}{28} = \frac{\cancel{2} \times \cancel{2} \times 2 \times 3}{\cancel{2} \times \cancel{2} \times 7} = \frac{6}{7}$

Lesson 37

Part 1

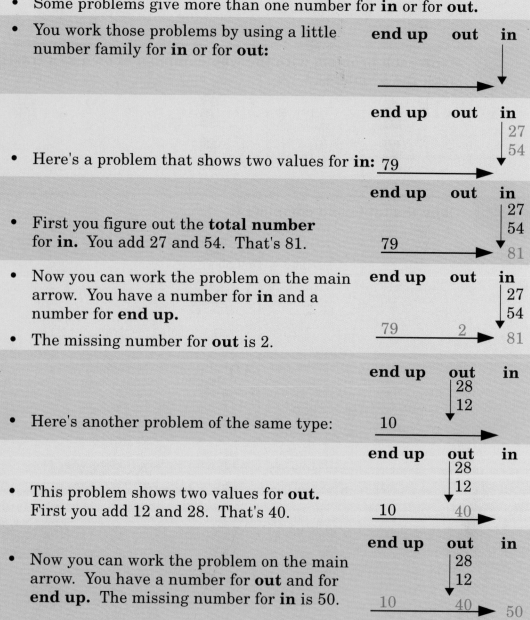

- You've worked problems that tell about the amounts for **in, out** and **end up.**
- Some problems give more than one number for **in** or for **out.**
- You work those problems by using a little number family for **in** or for **out:**

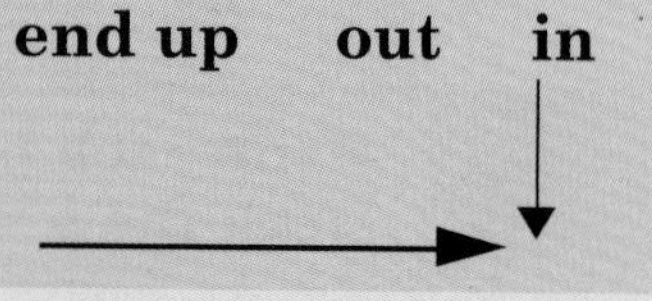

- Here's a problem that shows two values for **in:**

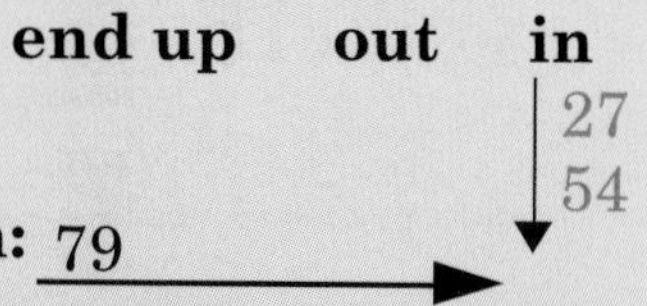

- First you figure out the **total number** for **in.** You add 27 and 54. That's 81.

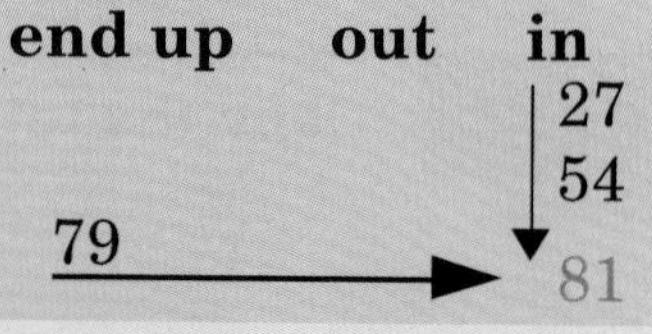

- Now you can work the problem on the main arrow. You have a number for **in** and a number for **end up.**
- The missing number for **out** is 2.

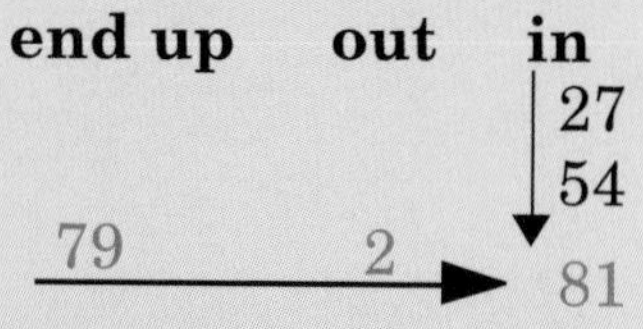

- Here's another problem of the same type:

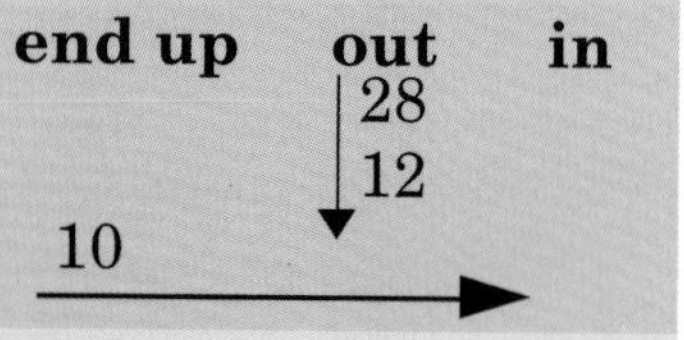

- This problem shows two values for **out.** First you add 12 and 28. That's 40.

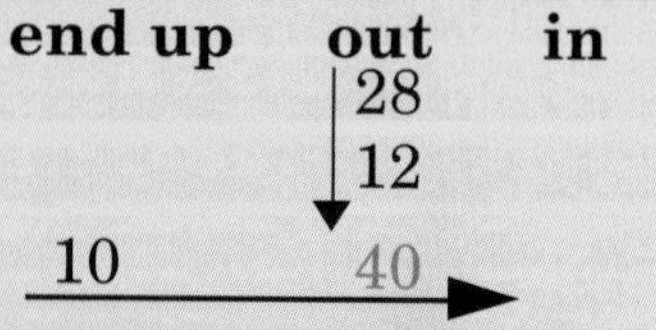

- Now you can work the problem on the main arrow. You have a number for **out** and for **end up.** The missing number for **in** is 50.

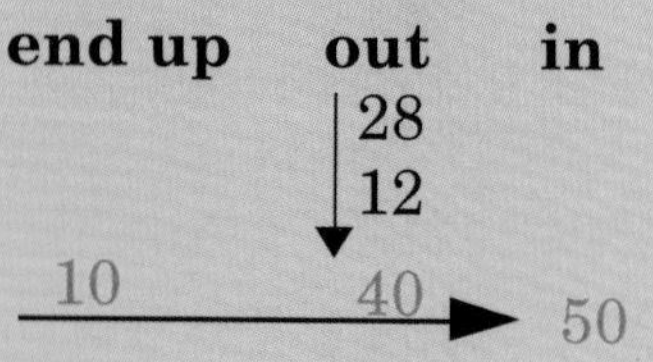

Part 2 Copy each problem. Figure out the totals for the little number families. Then work the problem for the main number family arrow.

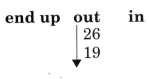

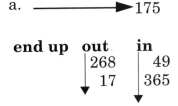

a.

end up	out	in
	26	
	19	
		175

b.

end up	out	in
		163
		57
		9
47		

c.

end up	out	in
	268	49
	17	365

d.

end up	out	in
	17	296
	28	55
	114	

Part 3 Copy each fraction. Show the prime factors for the numerator and denominator. Write the simplified fraction.

a. $\frac{21}{28}$ b. $\frac{12}{8}$ c. $\frac{3}{18}$ d. $\frac{24}{30}$

Part 4 Copy and work each problem. Write the complete answer as a mixed number.

a. $5\overline{)47}$ b. $6\overline{)439}$ c. $7\overline{)446}$ d. $4\overline{)123}$

Part 5 Copy and work each problem. Circle the value you end up with if it's more than the value you start with.

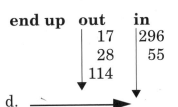

a. $\frac{6}{3} \times \frac{4}{4} = \blacksquare$ b. $\frac{4}{2} \times \frac{3}{1} = \blacksquare$ c. $8 \times \frac{3}{4} = \blacksquare$ d. $\frac{10}{5} \times \frac{5}{2} = \blacksquare$

Part 6 Make a table for the problem. Answer the questions.

Two clinics treated mumps and chicken pox. The clinics were Brewer's Clinic and Park Clinic. 73 cases of mumps were treated at Brewer's Clinic. 195 cases of chicken pox were treated at Park Clinic. A total of 263 cases of chicken pox were treated.

a. How many cases of chicken pox were treated in Brewer's Clinic?
b. Which hospital treated the larger number of cases?
c. What was the total number of all cases?

At Park Clinic, there were 12 fewer cases of mumps than chicken pox.

Independent Work

Don't forget to complete the table and answer the questions for part 6 of your textbook.

Part 7 Rewrite each decimal value that can be written with fewer zeros.

a. 7.008 b. 7.080 c. 7.800 d. 80.01 e. 12.030 f. 5.6

Part 8 Figure out the missing value. Then write the complete equation.

a. 6 x ■ = 264 b. 5 x ■ = 1065 c. 8 x 40 = ■

d. 9 x ■ = 729 e. 10 x ■ = 1200 f. 9 x 73 = ■

Part 9

Copy the table. Figure out the missing numbers and answer the questions.

> This table is supposed to show the number of small boats and large boats on two different lakes—Lake Jane and Lake Long.

Questions

a. What's the total number of boats for both lakes?

b. What's the total number of small boats for both lakes?

c. How many large boats are on Lake Long?

d. On which lake were there fewer small boats?

	Small boats	Large boats	Total
Lake Jane	80	3	
Lake Long			261
Total		49	

Part 10

Copy each problem and work it.

a. $5\overline{)4005}$

b. $5\overline{)6520}$

c. $\begin{array}{r} 7003 \\ \underline{\times \quad 11} \end{array}$

d. $\begin{array}{r} 189 \\ \underline{\times \ 98} \end{array}$

Part J

a. $\frac{21}{28} = \frac{3 \times 7}{2 \times 2 \times 7} = \frac{3}{4}$

b. $\frac{12}{8} = \frac{2 \times 2 \times 3}{2 \times 2 \times 2} = \frac{3}{2}$

c. $\frac{3}{18} = \frac{3}{2 \times 3 \times 3} = \frac{1}{6}$

d. $\frac{24}{30} = \frac{2 \times 2 \times 2 \times 3}{2 \times 3 \times 5} = \frac{4}{5}$

Lesson 38

Part 1

- For these subtraction problems, the answer is less than 10. You can work the problems by using the last digits of the numbers. You pretend that the top digit has a 1 in front of it. Then you just subtract.

Sample problem:

$$\begin{array}{r} 35 \\ -\ 28 \\ \hline \end{array}$$

a. $\begin{array}{r} 35 \\ -\ 27 \\ \hline \end{array}$ [redacted]

b. $\begin{array}{r} 42 \\ -\ 35 \\ \hline \end{array}$ [redacted]

c. $\begin{array}{r} 48 \\ -\ 39 \\ \hline \end{array}$ [redacted]

Part 2

- Some fractions that can be simplified equal whole numbers.

Here's: $\frac{12}{3}$

- You know it equals 4 because the numerator is 4 times the denominator. $\frac{12}{3} = 4$
- By showing the prime factors, you show that $\frac{12}{3}$ equals 4. $\frac{12}{3} = \frac{2 \times 2 \times \cancel{3}}{\cancel{3}} = 4$
- You could write 1 as the denominator of the simplified fraction: $\frac{12}{3} = \frac{2 \times 2 \times \cancel{3}}{\cancel{3}} = \frac{4}{1}$
- When the denominator is 1, you don't have to write it. $\frac{12}{3} = \frac{2 \times 2 \times \cancel{3}}{\cancel{3}} = 4$

Part 3

Copy the fraction. Show the prime factors. Write the simplified fraction.

a. $\frac{42}{6}$ b. $\frac{6}{42}$ c. $\frac{9}{12}$ d. $\frac{45}{9}$ e. $\frac{24}{4}$

Part 4 Make a table for the problem. Answer the questions.

Workers planted fir trees and maples in two parks—Rock Park and Wilson Park. They planted 128 fir trees in Rock Park. The total number of maples planted in both parks was 543. In Rock Park, they planted 17 more maples than firs. A total of 400 trees were planted in Wilson Park.

a. What's the total number of trees that were planted?

b. Were there more maples planted in Rock Park or Wilson Park?

c. How many firs were planted in Wilson Park?

d. In which park were more trees planted?

Part 5 Copy each problem and work it. Circle the starting value or the ending number to show which is larger.

a. $\frac{18}{2} \times \frac{1}{9} = \blacksquare$ b. $\frac{10}{5} \times \frac{4}{2} = \blacksquare$ c. $\frac{6}{2} \times 3 = \blacksquare$ d. $\frac{12}{3} \times \frac{2}{4} = \blacksquare$

Part 6 Copy each problem. Figure out the totals for the little number families. Then work the problem for the main number family arrow.

a. end up / out: 25, 104 / in — main arrow: 84 →

b. end up / out: 58, 107 / in: 92, 110, 75 — main arrow: →

c. end up / out / in: 214, 68 — main arrow: 95 →

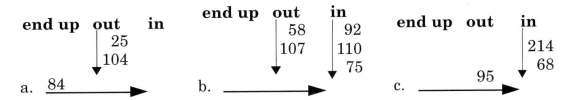

Independent Work

Don't forget to complete the table and answer the questions for part 4 of your textbook.

Part 7 Copy each problem and work it. Write the complete answer as a mixed number.

a. $3\overline{)581}$ b. $4\overline{)3881}$ c. $8\overline{)518}$ d. $9\overline{)455}$

Part 8 **Work each problem. Box the answer to the question the problem asks.**

a. A magazine had 58 fewer pages than a book. The magazine had 199 pages. How many pages did the book have?

b. There are 4 workers for every 3 machines. If there is a total of 36 machines, how many workers are there?

c. The ratio of fish to frogs in a pond is 9 to 8. If there are 72 fish, how many frogs are there?

d. The sand weighed 134 tons more than the gravel. If the sand weighed 456 tons, how many tons did the gravel weigh?

Part 9 **Write each problem with the whole number shown as a fraction. Work the problems.**

a. $\frac{5}{8} + 2 = \blacksquare$ b. $\frac{5}{2} \times 3 = \blacksquare$ c. $7 \times \frac{1}{3} = \blacksquare$

d. $7 - \frac{1}{3} = \blacksquare$ e. $\frac{15}{2} - 6 = \blacksquare$

Part J

c. $\frac{9}{12} = \frac{3 \times 3}{2 \times 2 \times 3} = \frac{3}{4}$ d. $\frac{45}{9} = \frac{3 \times 3 \times 5}{3 \times 3} = 5$ e. $\frac{24}{4} = \frac{2 \times 2 \times 2 \times 3}{2 \times 2} = 6$

Lesson 39

Part 1 **Copy each problem and work it. Circle the starting fraction or the ending fraction to show which is larger.**

a. $\frac{4}{3} \times \frac{2}{3} = \blacksquare$ b. $\frac{6}{5} \times \frac{6}{4} = \blacksquare$ c. $\frac{20}{3} \times \frac{1}{3} = \blacksquare$ d. $\frac{4}{5} \times \frac{5}{4} = \blacksquare$

Part 2

- You've worked word problems that give amounts for **in, out** and **end up.** Some word problems give more than one value for **in** or for **out.** You work these problems by making a little number family for those amounts.

- Here's a problem:

  There were 211 gallons in a tank. Then 92 gallons leaked out of the tank. Then 56 gallons went into the tank. How many gallons ended up in the tank?

- That problem gives more than one value for **in.** Those values go in a little number family.

  end up **out** in
  211
  56

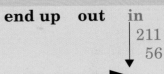

- The value for **out** goes on the main arrow.

  end up out **in**
  211
  56
  92

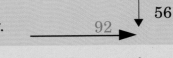

- Now you figure the total for **in** and work the problem on the main number family arrow.

  end up **out** **in**
  211
  56
  92 → 267

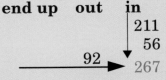

- The tank ends up with 175 gallons in it.

Part 3

For each problem make a number family with a small number family for in or out. Answer the question the problem asks.

Sample problem:	A tank has 459 gallons in it. Then 312 gallons are drained from the tank. Then another 84 gallons are drained from the tank. How many gallons are still in the tank?

a. At the end of the day, a tank has 140 gallons of water in it. The tank started out with 112 gallons in it. Later in the day another 336 gallons were added. Then some water was removed from the tank. How many gallons of water were removed?

b. There's a lot of water in a tank at the beginning of the day. In the morning, 127 gallons were removed from the tank. In the afternoon, another 402 gallons were removed. At the end of the day, there were still 583 gallons in the tank. How many gallons were in the tank at the beginning of the day?

Part 4

- You can write any fraction as a division problem. Sometimes, the answer is a mixed number.

Here's: $\frac{23}{4}$

The division problem is: $4\overline{)23}$

The answer is 5 with a remainder of 3.

$$\begin{array}{r} 5\text{ R3} \\ 4\overline{)23} \end{array}$$

3 divided by 4 is $\frac{3}{4}$.

$$\begin{array}{r} 5\frac{3}{4} \\ 4\overline{)23} \end{array}$$

- Remember these steps:
  - ✓ Read the fraction as a division problem.
  - ✓ Write the division problem.
  - ✓ Figure out the answer and write it as a mixed number.

Part 5

Write each fraction as a division problem and work it. Write each answer as a mixed number.

a. $\frac{36}{5}$ b. $\frac{46}{7}$ c. $\frac{33}{4}$ d. $\frac{52}{9}$

Part 6

Make a table for the problem. Answer the questions.

There were butterflies and cocoons in two laboratories. The laboratories were named AB Lab and Miller's Lab. There were 88 cocoons in AB Lab. There was a total of 100 cocoons for both labs. The total number of butterflies was 56 more than the total number of cocoons. Miller's Lab had 92 butterflies.

a. In Miller's Lab, were there fewer butterflies or cocoons?
b. What was the total number of butterflies and cocoons in AB Lab?
c. How many cocoons were in Miller's Lab?

Independent Work

Don't forget to complete the table and answer the questions for part 6 of your textbook.

Part 7

Figure out the missing number for each number family.

a. 147 165 → ■
b. ■ 263 → 542
c. 49 ■ → 146
d. 197 68 → ■

Part 8

Copy each problem and work it. Write the complete answer as a mixed number.

a. $5\overline{)3093}$ b. $8\overline{)605}$ c. $3\overline{)3334}$

Part 9

Work each problem. Box the answer to the question the problem asks.

a. 3 coins are worth $18. How much are 21 coins worth?

b. Jan is 31 years younger than her mother. Jan is 15 years old. How many years old is her mother?

c. There are 5 tan dogs for every 4 white dogs. If there are 48 white dogs, how many tan dogs are there?

d. The barn is 115 feet longer than it is wide. If the barn is 213 feet long, how many feet wide is it?

Part 10

Copy the table and complete it.

Multiplication	Division	Fraction equation
a. $8 \times \blacksquare = 640$		
b. $5 \times \blacksquare = 995$		
c. $2 \times \blacksquare = 666$		

Part 11

Write the complete equation for each item.

a. $6 = \frac{\blacksquare}{3} = \frac{\blacksquare}{7} = \frac{\blacksquare}{6} = \frac{\blacksquare}{1}$

b. $8 = \frac{\blacksquare}{6} = \frac{\blacksquare}{1} = \frac{\blacksquare}{9} = \frac{\blacksquare}{4}$

c. $3 = \frac{\blacksquare}{5} = \frac{\blacksquare}{3} = \frac{\blacksquare}{10} = \frac{\blacksquare}{9}$

Lesson 40

Part 1

- Here's a fact about your calculator:

  If you enter a decimal value that is less than 1, your calculator will display a zero before the decimal point.

- If the answer to a problem is .3, your calculator will show it as: **0.3**
- You can use your calculator to show the decimal value for any fraction that is less than 1.
- Here's a fraction that is less than 1: $\frac{3}{100}$
- If you read it as a division problem, you say: "3 divided by 100."
- If you work that problem on your calculator, your calculator will show that the answer is: **0.03**

  That's: $\frac{3}{100}$

Part 2

For each item, answer the question with a number and a unit name. Box the answer.

a. There are 3 dogs for every 7 cats. How many dogs are there for 35 cats?

$$\frac{\text{dogs}}{\text{cats}}\ \frac{3}{7}\left(\frac{5}{5}\right) = \frac{\boxed{15}}{35}$$

b. Billy is 28 pounds heavier than Sam. Sam weighs 119 pounds. What does Billy weigh?

Dif S B: 28, 119 →

$$28 + 119 = \boxed{147}$$

c. There were 118 gallons of water in a tank. Some water drained from the tank. There were still 58 gallons in the tank. How much water drained from the tank?

end up out in: 58 → 118

$$118 - 58 = \boxed{60}$$

d. The ratio of buttons to bows is 5 to 2. There are 45 buttons. How many bows are there?

$$\frac{\text{buttons}}{\text{bows}}\ \frac{5}{2}\left(\frac{9}{9}\right) = \frac{45}{\boxed{18}}$$

Test 4

Part 1 **Read the problem. Make a number family that shows in, out and end up. Answer the question with a number and a unit name. Box the answer.**

A train had some people in it. 27 people got off the train at the first station. There were still 134 people in the train. How many people were in the train to begin with?

Part 2 **Write the equation. Answer the question with a number and a unit name. Box the answer.**

The ratio of strings to balloons is 13 to 4. If there are 200 balloons, how many strings are there?

Part 3 **Make the table for this problem. Show the headings and the four numbers the problem tells about. DO NOT FIGURE OUT THE REST OF THE NUMBERS.**

There were men and women at two hotels. The hotels were the Greer Hotel and the Victoria Hotel. There were 36 women at the Greer Hotel. The total number of adults at the Victoria Hotel was 501. The number of men at the Victoria Hotel was 41. There were 500 men at the Greer Hotel.

Part 4 **Copy the table that is shown. Put in the four numbers the problem tells about. DO NOT FIGURE OUT THE REST OF THE NUMBERS.**

This table is supposed to show the number of dogs and cats at Al's Kennel and at Bo's Kennel.

The total number of dogs and cats at Bo's Kennel is 147. Al's Kennel has 68 dogs. There are 29 more dogs at Bo's Kennel than there are at Al's Kennel. The total number of cats for both kennels is 263.

	Dogs	Cats	Total
Al's Kennel			
Bo's Kennel			
Total			

Part 5 **Copy each problem and work it. Circle the value you end up with if it's more than the value you start with.**

a. $\frac{3}{5} \times \frac{4}{3} =$ [redacted] b. $8 \times \frac{3}{4} =$ [redacted] c. $\frac{6}{5} \times \frac{3}{3} =$ [redacted] d. $5 \times \frac{6}{5} =$ [redacted]

Part 6 **Write each problem with the whole number shown as a fraction. Work the problem. Write the answer as a fraction.**

a. $4 \times \frac{2}{3} =$ [redacted] b. $4 + \frac{2}{3} =$ [redacted] c. $\frac{1}{9} \times 6 =$ [redacted] d. $\frac{30}{5} - 3 =$ [redacted]

Part 7 **Copy the number family. Figure out the number for end up.**

end up	out	in
	7	41
	106	181

Part 8 **Copy each problem and work it. Write the complete answer as a mixed number.**

a. $5\overline{)343}$ b. $4\overline{)707}$

Part 9 **Copy each fraction. Show the prime factors for the numerator and the denominator. Write the simplified fraction.**

a. $\frac{6}{42}$ b. $\frac{24}{21}$ c. $\frac{10}{40}$

Lesson 41

Part 1

- Some fractions cannot be simplified. A fraction cannot be simplified unless it has a common factor in the numerator and in the denominator.

Here's: $\frac{14}{15}$

The factors for 14 are 2 and 7.
The factors for 15 are 3 and 5. $\frac{14}{15} = \frac{2 \times 7}{3 \times 5}$

No factor appears in **both** the numerator and denominator. So the fraction cannot be simplified because you cannot cross out a fraction that equals 1.

- Here's another fraction that cannot be simplified: $\frac{21}{10}$

The factors for the numerator are 3 and 7.
The factors for the denominator are 2 and 5. $\frac{21}{10} = \frac{3 \times 7}{2 \times 5}$

No factor appears in **both** the numerator and denominator.

Part 2

Copy each fraction. Write the prime factors for the numerator and the denominator. Cross out any fractions that equal 1. Write the value you get when you multiply.

a. $\frac{8}{15}$ b. $\frac{7}{6}$ c. $\frac{14}{28}$ d. $\frac{36}{12}$

Part 3

Copy each problem and work it. Circle the starting fraction or the ending fraction to show which is the larger value.

a. $\frac{2}{5} \times \frac{7}{8} = \blacksquare$ b. $\frac{2}{3} \times \frac{9}{8} = \blacksquare$ c. $\frac{1}{2} \times \frac{8}{4} = \blacksquare$

Part 4 **For each problem, make a number family with a small number family for in or out. Answer the question with a number and a unit name.**

a. There were lots of flowers in a garden. Mrs. Jones picked 13 flowers. Then Andy picked 48 flowers, and Ginger picked 4 flowers. After all those flowers were picked, the garden still had 101 flowers in it. How many flowers had been in the garden to begin with?

b. An elevator starts out with 11 people in it. At the first stop, 8 more people get in the elevator. At the next stop, 2 more people get in the elevator. At the next stop, some people get out of the elevator. There are still 9 people in the elevator. How many people got out of the elevator?

c. A bus filled up its fuel tank and went on a trip. For the first part of the trip, the bus used up 88 liters of fuel. For the next part of the trip, the bus used up 17 liters of fuel. The fuel tank ended up with 122 liters of fuel. How much fuel was in the tank to begin with?

Part 5

- You've learned that you can use your calculator to find the decimal values for fractions that are less than 1 and for mixed numbers.
- All the fractions you've worked with were tenths, hundredths or thousandths. But you can use your calculator to show the decimal value that equals **any fraction** or **any mixed number.**

Here's: $\frac{4}{8}$

- It's less than 1. So the decimal number that equals $\frac{4}{8}$ is less than 1. To find out what it is, you work the division problem, **4** ÷ **8**.

Here's: $3\frac{6}{8}$

- To work the problem with your calculator, first work the division problem for the fraction, then add the whole number.

Part 6

Copy each fraction or mixed number. Complete the equation to show the decimal value it equals.

a. $\frac{3}{12} = ■$ b. $\frac{14}{8} = ■$ c. $\frac{600}{80} = ■$ d. $7\frac{4}{50} = ■$

Part 7

Copy each problem and work it. Write the answer as a mixed number.

a. $8\overline{)51}$ b. $9\overline{)31}$ c. $7\overline{)33}$ d. $9\overline{)86}$

Part 8

Write each fraction as a division problem and work it. Write each answer as a mixed number.

a. $\frac{19}{2}$ b. $\frac{35}{8}$ c. $\frac{42}{5}$ d. $\frac{23}{3}$

Independent Work

Part 9

Copy each problem. Figure out the value for the box.

a.
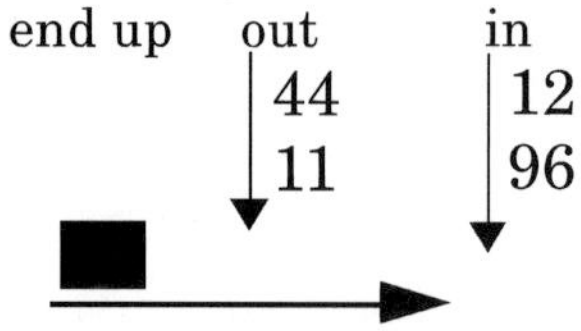

b.
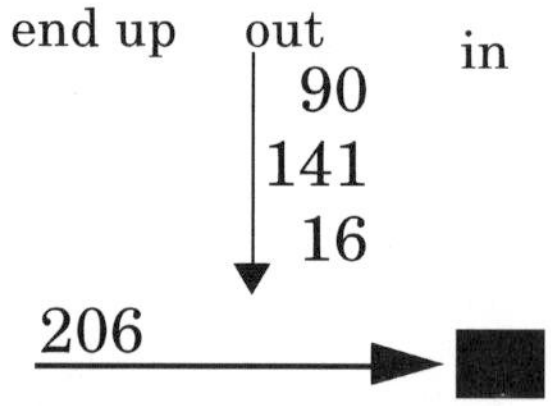

Part 10

Copy and complete each equation.

a. $5 = \frac{■}{3} = \frac{■}{20} = \frac{■}{11} = \frac{■}{1}$ b. $7 = \frac{■}{10} = \frac{■}{1} = \frac{■}{6} = \frac{■}{40}$

Part 11 **Copy the table that is shown. Figure out the number the fact tells about and write it in your table. Figure out the rest of the numbers in the table. Answer the questions.**

This table is supposed to show the number of white roses and red roses at two different weddings. The weddings were for the Donners and the Kellys.

Fact

At the wedding for the Kellys, there were 46 more white roses than red roses.

	White roses	Red roses	Total
Donners			
Kellys		102	
Total	200		400

Questions

a. Which wedding had the most roses?

b. Were there more white roses or red roses at the Donners' wedding?

c. What was the total number of red roses at both weddings?

Part 12 **Copy and work each problem. Write the answer as a mixed number.**

a. $7\overline{)38}$ b. $7\overline{)58}$ c. $7\overline{)69}$ d. $8\overline{)49}$ e. $8\overline{)79}$ f. $8\overline{)12}$

Lesson 42

Part 1 **Copy each fraction. Write the prime factors for the numerator and the denominator. Cross out any fractions that equal 1. Write the value you get when you multiply.**

a. $\frac{40}{50}$ b. $\frac{24}{6}$ c. $\frac{25}{6}$ d. $\frac{1}{14}$

Part 2 **For each problem make a number family with a small number family for in or out. Answer the question the problem asks with a number and a unit name.**

a. Rita collected 16 stamps. Then she collected another 127 stamps. She gave 39 stamps away. How many stamps were left in her collection?

b. A truck's gas tank had 19 liters of gas in it. Then another 41 liters were put in the tank. The truck used up some of the gas on a trip. At the end of the trip, the truck had 17 liters of gas in the tank. How much fuel was used up on the trip?

c. A dog had fleas on it. 12 fleas jumped off the dog. Then another 51 fleas jumped off the dog. After the fleas jumped off, there were 101 fleas left on the dog. How many fleas were on the dog to begin with?

Part 3 **Copy each item. Then complete an equation to show the decimal value it equals.**

a. $2\frac{4}{1000}$ b. $4\frac{5}{8}$ c. $\frac{5}{20}$ d. $\frac{11}{10}$

Part 4

- You've worked ratio problems. The first part of each problem is the rule. That rule tells you how to construct equivalent fractions.
- Here's a rule: **There are 3 girls for every 4 trees.**
- You can use that rule to figure out any number of girls or any number of trees.

$\frac{\text{girls}}{\text{trees}}$ 

- If you have 6 girls, you have to make sure that you have enough trees.
- That's 8.

$\frac{\text{girls}}{\text{trees}}$ 

- You have twice as many girls, and twice as many trees.

$$\frac{\text{girls}}{\text{trees}} \ \frac{3}{4}\left(\frac{2}{2}\right) = \boxed{\frac{6}{8}}$$

- If you have 12 trees, you must have the right number of girls.
- That's 9.

$\frac{\text{girls}}{\text{trees}}$ 

- You have three times as many trees and three times as many girls.

$$\frac{\text{girls}}{\text{trees}} \ \frac{3}{4}\left(\frac{3}{3}\right) = \boxed{\frac{9}{12}}$$

Part 5

For each item, write the equivalent fractions with names and numbers. Figure out the fraction that equals one.

a. 

$\frac{\text{girls}}{\text{trees}}$ $\frac{■}{■}\left(\frac{■}{■}\right) = \frac{■}{■}$

b. 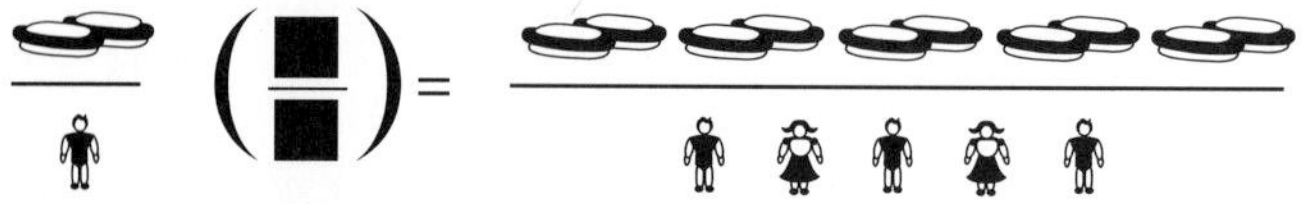

$\frac{\text{hot dogs}}{\text{persons}}$ $\frac{■}{■}\left(\frac{■}{■}\right) = \frac{■}{■}$

c. 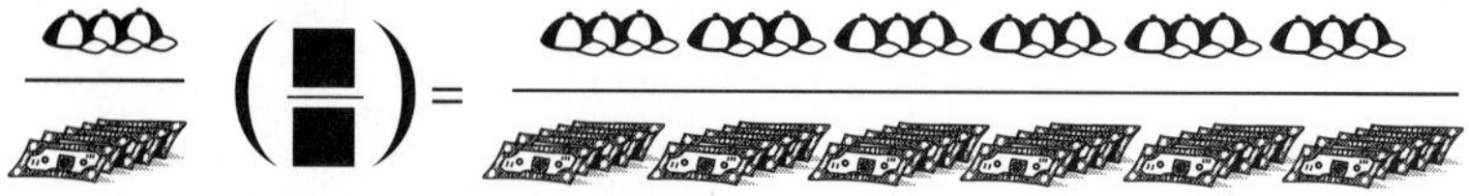

$\frac{\text{caps}}{\text{dollars}}$ $\frac{■}{■}\left(\frac{■}{■}\right) = \frac{■}{■}$

Independent Work

Part 6

Copy and work each item. Circle the starting or ending value to show which is larger.

a. $4 \times \frac{7}{8} = ■$

b. $\frac{5}{6} \times \frac{6}{5} = ■$

c. $\frac{1}{8} \times \frac{1}{8} = ■$

d. $\frac{12}{3} \times \frac{11}{12} = ■$

e. $\frac{1}{8} \times \frac{12}{1} = ■$

Part 7

Copy each problem. Figure out the value for the box.

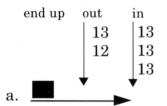

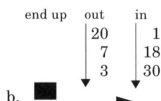

a.

end up	out	in
	13	13
	12	13
		13
■	↓	↓

b.

end up	out	in
	20	1
	7	18
	3	30
■	↓	↓

Part 8 Copy and complete the table.

Multiplication	Division	Fraction equation
a. 4 x ■ = 60		
b. 9 x ■ = 270		

Part 9 For each problem, figure out the answer to the question. Write the answer as a number and a unit name.

a. In Stanley Park, the ratio of elm trees to maple trees is 4 to 5. If there are 20 maple trees, how many elm trees are there?

b. There were 2 workers for every 6 tons of dirt. There were 18 tons of dirt. How many workers were there?

c. A truck uses 5 gallons of fuel every hour. If the truck runs for 560 hours, how much fuel does it use?

d. The temperature on top of Snow Mountain was 16 degrees lower than the temperature on top of Crystal Mountain. If the temperature on top of Crystal Mountain was 67 degrees, what was the temperature on top of Snow Mountain?

e. A truck started on a trip with a full tank. The truck used 45 gallons of fuel. There were still 13 gallons of fuel in the tank. How much fuel does the tank hold?

f. There were 56 people in a bus. Some people got off the bus. There were still 16 people on the bus. How many people got off?

Lesson 43

Part 1 **For each problem, make a number family with a small number family for in or out. Answer the question as a number and a unit name.**

a. There were lots of flowers in the garden. Mrs. Stevens picked 45 flowers. Then her son picked 17 more flowers. There were still 29 flowers in the garden. How many were in the garden to begin with?

b. There were 25 cookies in a box. Yesterday, Mrs. Johnson put 32 more cookies in the box. Today, she put another 48 cookies in the box. Her children ate some of the cookies. Now there are only 18 cookies left in the box. How many cookies did the children eat?

c. At the end of the trip, there are 17 gallons in the gas tank of a bus. In the morning, the bus used up 29 gallons of fuel. In the afternoon, the bus used up 32 gallons of fuel. How many gallons of fuel did the bus start out with?

Part 2

- Here's a problem that is worked:

$$\begin{array}{r} 61\frac{2}{6} \\ 6\overline{)368} \end{array}$$

- To check the work, first multiply the whole number in the answer by the number you divide by.
- Write that answer under the second division sign. →

$$\begin{array}{r} 61 \\ 6\overline{)368} \\ \overline{)366} \end{array} \qquad \begin{array}{r} 61 \\ \times\ \ 6 \\ \hline 366 \end{array}$$

- Now you subtract to find the remainder. →

$$\begin{array}{r} 61 \\ 6\overline{)368} \\ -\overline{)366} \\ \hline 2 \end{array}$$

- You write the remainder as a fraction. The problem divides by 6, so the remainder divides by 6. The fraction is $\frac{2}{6}$.
- If you get the same fraction as the other problem, you know the answer is correct.

$$\begin{array}{r} 61\frac{2}{6} \\ 6\overline{)368} \\ -\overline{)366} \\ \hline 2 \end{array}$$

Part 3 **Copy each fraction. Write the prime factors and the simplified fraction. If the fraction is more than 1, write it as a mixed number.**

Sample problem: $\frac{8}{6}$	a. $\frac{32}{12}$	b. $\frac{15}{40}$	c. $\frac{42}{36}$	d. $\frac{56}{10}$	e. $\frac{14}{56}$

Part 4 **For each item, write the equivalent fractions with names and numbers. Figure out the fraction that equals 1.**

a.

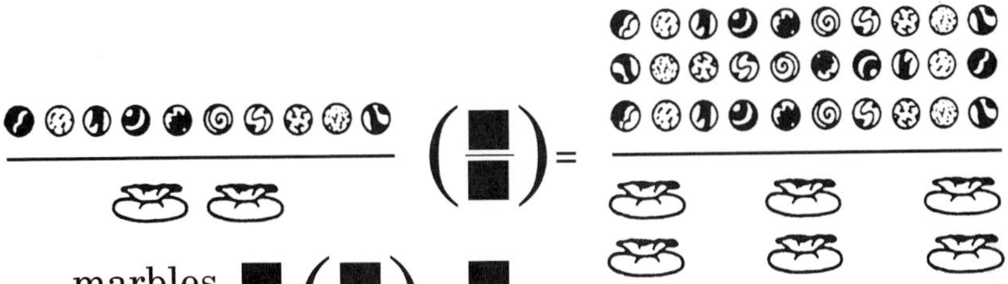

$\frac{\text{marbles}}{\text{bags}}$ $\frac{■}{■}\left(\frac{■}{■}\right) = \frac{■}{■}$

b.

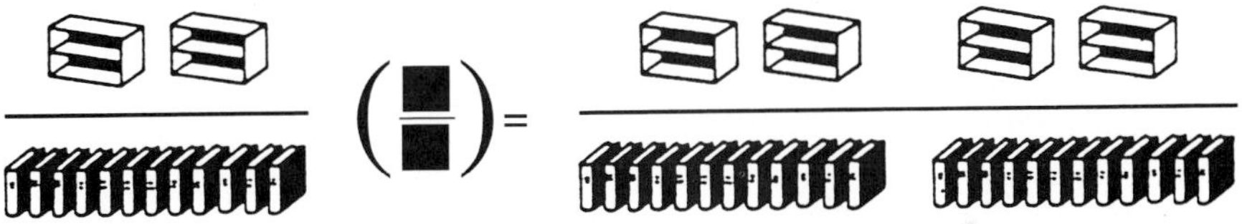

$\frac{\text{shelves}}{\text{books}}$ $\frac{■}{■}\left(\frac{■}{■}\right) = \frac{■}{■}$

Part 5

- You've worked problems that look like multiplication problems but that require division.

$$5(\blacksquare) = 455$$

$$\begin{array}{r} 91 \\ 5\overline{)455} \end{array}$$

- You do the same thing when you work with a pair of equivalent fractions. You work a division problem for the top numbers or a division problem for the bottom numbers.

$$\frac{5}{7} = \frac{185}{259}$$

- Both equivalent fractions are shown. So you can work either the problem on top or the problem on the bottom. For either problem, you'll get the same answer.

$$\frac{5}{7}\left(\frac{\blacksquare}{\blacksquare}\right) = \frac{185}{259}$$

- The problem for the top numbers is $5(\blacksquare) = 185$.

$$\frac{5}{7}\left(\frac{\blacksquare}{\blacksquare}\right) = \frac{185}{259}$$

- The problem for the bottom numbers is $7(\blacksquare) = 259$.

$$\frac{5}{7}\left(\frac{\blacksquare}{\blacksquare}\right) = \frac{185}{259}$$

- The answer to either of those problems is 37. So the fraction that equals 1 is $\frac{37}{37}$.

$$\frac{5}{7}\left(\frac{37}{37}\right) = \frac{185}{259}$$

- Remember, **if fractions are equivalent, you can work a division problem on top or on the bottom.**

Independent Work

Part 6 **Make a table and answer the questions.**

Two bands have drummers and marchers. The bands are in Flint Town and Mill Town. There are 72 drummers in the Flint Town band. The total number of marchers for both the bands is 148. There are 48 marchers in the Mill Town band. There are 56 drummers in the Mill Town band.

a. What's the total number of drummers for both the bands?

b. Are there more marchers in the Flint Town band or in the Mill Town band?

c. Which band has the greater total of marchers and drummers?

Part 7 **Copy and complete each equation to show the decimal value for each mixed number.**

a. $2\frac{6}{8} = \blacksquare$ b. $1\frac{3}{5} = \blacksquare$ c. $2\frac{2}{8} = \blacksquare$ d. $112\frac{1}{4} = \blacksquare$

Part 8 **For each problem, figure out the answer to the question. Write the answer as a number and a unit name.**

a. Tina had money in the bank. On Tuesday, she took out $120. She still had $518 in the bank. How much did she have in the bank before Tuesday?

b. There were 67 students in a train. Some students got off the train at the first stop. There were still 49 students in the train. How many got off at the first stop?

c. In Fran's garden, the ratio of roses to daisies is 7 to 6. If there are 63 roses in her garden, how many daisies are there?

d. The cook used 4 cups of milk for every 5 cups of onions. The cook prepared 45 cups of onions. How many cups of milk did she need?

Part 9 **Copy and work each item. If there is a remainder, write the answer as a mixed number.**

a. $5\overline{)37}$ b. $5\overline{)28}$ c. $5\overline{)24}$ d. $5\overline{)9}$

e. $4\overline{)37}$ f. $4\overline{)28}$ g. $4\overline{)24}$ h. $4\overline{)9}$

Part 10 **Write the complete equation for each item.**

a. $10 = \frac{\blacksquare}{3} = \frac{\blacksquare}{10} = \frac{\blacksquare}{8} = \frac{\blacksquare}{25}$ b. $4 = \frac{\blacksquare}{5} = \frac{\blacksquare}{1} = \frac{\blacksquare}{4} = \frac{\blacksquare}{25}$

Lesson 44

Part 1 **Use your calculator. For each pair of equivalent fractions, write the complete equation showing the fraction that equals 1.**

a. $\frac{27}{38} \quad = \frac{405}{570}$

b. $\frac{8}{9} \quad = \frac{504}{567}$

c. $\frac{3}{4} \quad = \frac{354}{472}$

d. $\frac{15}{11} \quad = \frac{375}{275}$

Part 2 **Rewrite each item as prime factors multiplied together.**

a. $2 \times 3 \times 4 = 24$

b. $3 \times 3 \times 6 = 54$

c. $2 \times 12 \times 3 = 72$

d. $5 \times 18 \times 2 = 180$

Part 3 **For each problem make a number family with a small number family for in or out. Answer the question the problem asks.**

a. A water tank was half filled. Then, 230 gallons were removed from the tank. Then, another 56 gallons were removed. Then, 100 gallons were removed. The tank still had 444 gallons in it. How many gallons were in the tank to begin with?

b. There were 58 passengers in a train. At the next stop, 15 more passengers got in the train. At the next stop, 28 passengers got in the train. Then some passengers got off the train. After those passengers left, there were still 77 passengers in the train. How many passengers got off the train?

c. On Wednesday, Tim had $46 in the bank. On Thursday, he put another $118 in the bank. On Friday, he took $45 out of the bank. On Saturday, he put another $87 in the bank. How much money was now in Tim's bank account?

Part 4 **Copy each pair of fractions. Replace the question mark with the correct sign: = or ≠.**

a. $\frac{3}{4} \; ? \; \frac{33}{48}$

b. $\frac{5}{4} \; ? \; \frac{60}{56}$

c. $\frac{3}{5} \; ? \; \frac{42}{70}$

d. $\frac{9}{10} \; ? \; \frac{180}{220}$

Independent Work

Part 5 **Work each item. Remember to box the answer and write the unit name.**

a. If it takes 3 minutes for a machine to fasten 8 buttons, how many minutes would it take the machine to fasten 72 buttons?

b. Milly runs 16 miles every 3 weeks. How many miles does she run in 9 weeks?

c. The red race car went 46 miles per hour slower than the blue race car. The blue race car went 211 miles per hour. How fast did the red race car go?

d. There were 129 more students in the elementary school than there were in the high school. There were 467 students in the high school. How many students were in the elementary school?

e. There are 10 tapes in 1 case. If there are 22 cases, how many tapes are there?

f. The ratio of clear marbles to colored marbles was 7 to 3. If there were 56 clear marbles, how many colored marbles were there?

Part 6 **Copy each division problem and work it. If there is a remainder, write the answer as a mixed number.**

a. $5\overline{)742}$ b. $4\overline{)146}$ c. $9\overline{)325}$ d. $3\overline{)915}$ e. $6\overline{)329}$ f. $8\overline{)648}$

Part 7 **Copy and work each problem.**

a. $\frac{5}{6} \times \frac{2}{3} = \blacksquare$ b. $\frac{4}{7} + \frac{5}{7} = \blacksquare$ c. $\frac{2}{9} + \frac{7}{9} = \blacksquare$

d. $\frac{6}{7} - \frac{2}{7} = \blacksquare$ e. $\frac{5}{9} \times \frac{12}{9} = \blacksquare$ f. $\frac{11}{5} - \frac{6}{5} = \blacksquare$

Part 8

Simplify each fraction. Then write it as a mixed number.

a. $\frac{51}{18}$ b. $\frac{36}{24}$ c. $\frac{49}{21}$ d. $\frac{55}{40}$

Part J

a. $2 \times 3 \times \boxed{2 \times 2} = 24$

b. $3 \times 3 \times \boxed{2 \times 3} = 54$

c. $2 \times \boxed{2 \times 2 \times 3} \times 3 = 72$

d. $5 \times \boxed{2 \times 3 \times 3} \times 2 = 180$

36/24 = (2+2+3+3)/(2+2+2+3) =
Fran has caught onto part of the idea about how prime factors work. Now all she's got to do is learn what a **factor** is.
Recycle

Lesson 45

Part 1 **Write the fraction for each division problem.**

a. $3\overline{)36}$

b. $6\overline{)144}$

c. $8\overline{)450}$

Part 2

You know how to work multiplication problems that have a missing middle value. You work a division problem to figure out the missing value. You can also write the missing value as a **fraction.**

Here's: $3(\blacksquare) = 369$

That's: $3\left(\frac{369}{3}\right) = 369$

Remember, instead of working a division problem, you can just show the fraction for the division problem.

Part 3 **For each problem, make a number family with the numbers the problem gives. Then figure out the answer to the question.**

a. A plane had 131 people in it. Then 81 more people got in the plane. Then 46 people got off the plane. Then 51 people got in the plane. Then 76 people got off the plane. How many people were still in the plane?

b. A tank had some water in it. In the morning, 113 gallons were removed from the tank. In the afternoon, 450 gallons were removed from the tank. The tank still had 304 gallons in it. How many gallons of water were in the tank at the beginning of the day?

c. There were 125 peanuts in a jar. 12 peanuts were taken out of the jar. Then 15 more peanuts were taken out of the jar. 36 peanuts were put into the jar. 90 peanuts were taken out of the jar. How many peanuts were still in the jar?

Part 4 For each item, make a number family and answer the question.

a. An ant went 117 centimeters. A ladybug went 320 centimeters. What is the difference in distance the insects went?

b. The horse weighed 1420 pounds. The bull weighed 2230 pounds. How much lighter was the horse than the bull?

c. 1834 centimeters of snow fell on Snow Mountain. 400 centimeters of snow fell on Great Mountain. What was the difference in snowfall on the two mountains?

Part 5 For each pair of equivalent fractions, write the complete equation showing the fraction that equals 1.

a. $\frac{19}{15} = \frac{931}{735}$ b. $\frac{7}{8} = \frac{476}{544}$ c. $\frac{20}{21} = \frac{1780}{1869}$

Independent Work

Part 6 Copy the table and complete it.

	Mixed number	Decimal	Fraction
a.	$6\frac{3}{10}$		
b.			$\frac{460}{100}$
c.		2.05	
d.	$12\frac{3}{100}$		

Part 7 Rewrite each equation to show prime factors.

a. 3 x 2 x 8 = 48

b. 5 x 10 x 2 = 100

c. 14 x 4 = 56

d. 20 x 3 = 60

Part 8 Copy and work each problem.

a. $5 \times \frac{19}{20} = \blacksquare$

b. $\frac{1}{9} \times \frac{5}{3} = \blacksquare$

c. $\frac{7}{1} \times \frac{15}{2} = \blacksquare$

d. $\frac{12}{5} \times \frac{7}{7} = \blacksquare$

Part 9 Make a number family for each problem. Show a little number family if you need one. Answer the question.

a. Tina had some money in the bank. She took out $3.40. Later she took out $18.25. She still had $45.70 in her bank account. How much did she have to start out with?

b. The eagle weighed 56 ounces more than owl. The eagle weighed 84 ounces. How much did the owl weigh?

c. A truck weighed 7800 pounds. The trailer weighed 1110 pounds. What was the difference in the weight of these objects?

d. A tank started out empty. 145 gallons of water flowed into the tank. Another 96 gallons flowed into the tank. Then 156 gallons flowed out of the tank. How many gallons of water ended up in the tank?

Part 10 Copy and work each problem. If the fractions shown are equal, write the simple equation below.

a. $\frac{3}{4} \times \blacksquare = \frac{12}{20}$

b. $\frac{7}{8} \times \blacksquare = \frac{49}{64}$

c. $\frac{5}{8} \times \blacksquare = \frac{20}{32}$

d. $\frac{10}{2} \times \blacksquare = \frac{60}{20}$

Lesson 46

Part 1

- You can use number families to show fractions.

  The small numbers are fractions along the arrow.

  The big number is the fraction at the end of the arrow.

  The two small numbers must add up to the big number.

- Some fraction number families have a fraction that equals 1 as the **big number.**

  a. $\frac{2}{3} \quad \frac{1}{3} \rightarrow \frac{3}{3}$ b. $\frac{5}{7} \quad \frac{2}{7} \rightarrow \frac{7}{7}$

- Here are facts about those families:

  All fractions in the number family must have the same denominator. So if you know one of the small numbers, you can figure out the other fractions in the family.

  $\frac{4}{7}$ ■ $\rightarrow 1$

- Here's a family with a small number of $\frac{4}{7}$:

  $\frac{4}{7} \quad \frac{\ }{7} \rightarrow \frac{\ }{7}$

- All the fractions in the family must have the same denominator.
- The big number equals 1, so it is $\frac{7}{7}$:

  $\frac{4}{7} \quad \frac{\ }{7} \rightarrow \frac{7}{7}$

- The missing small number is $\frac{3}{7}$:

  $\frac{4}{7} \quad \frac{3}{7} \rightarrow \frac{7}{7}$

- Remember the steps for completing fraction number families:

  ✓ Change 1 into a fraction with the right denominator.

  ✓ Then figure out the missing small number.

Part 2

Write each number family with 1 shown as a fraction with the right denominator. Figure out the missing fraction and box it.

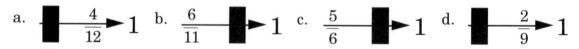

a. ■ $\frac{4}{12} \rightarrow 1$ b. $\frac{6}{11}$ ■ $\rightarrow 1$ c. $\frac{5}{6}$ ■ $\rightarrow 1$ d. ■ $\frac{2}{9} \rightarrow 1$

Part 3 **Copy and complete each pair of equivalent fractions. Show the fraction that equals 1.**

a. $\frac{3}{13} = \frac{591}{\blacksquare}$ b. $\frac{7}{5} = \frac{\blacksquare}{295}$ c. $\frac{8}{12} = \frac{\blacksquare}{300}$

Part 4 **Make a number family with the numbers the problem gives. Then figure out the answer to the question.**

a. Fran earned $145. Then she spent $89. Then she spent $19. Then she earned $123. Then she spent $111. How much did she end up with?

b. 136 ants were in an anthill. Another 450 ants went into the anthill. Some ants left the anthill. There were still 335 ants in the anthill. How many ants left the anthill?

c. There were 12 cars in a parking lot. 16 more cars went into the lot. 22 cars went out of the lot. 49 cars went into the lot. 11 cars went out of the lot. How many cars were left in the lot?

Independent Work

Part 5 **Copy each equation. Figure out the missing fraction. If the missing fraction equals 1, write the simple equation below.**

a. $\frac{2}{3}\left(\blacksquare\right) = \frac{8}{12}$

b. $\frac{4}{9}\left(\blacksquare\right) = \frac{24}{45}$

c. $\frac{2}{11}\left(\blacksquare\right) = \frac{8}{33}$

d. $\frac{7}{6}\left(\blacksquare\right) = \frac{63}{54}$

Part 6 **Copy the table and complete it.**

	Mixed number	Fraction
a.	$1\frac{7}{12}$	
b.	$2\frac{3}{10}$	
c.		$\frac{24}{7}$

Part 7

Work each ratio problem. Write the answer as a number and a unit name.

a. There are 35 gallons of gas in 2 tanks. How many gallons are in 6 tanks?

b. There are 8 books for every 2 children. If there are 72 books, how many children are there?

c. 1 box holds 9 decorations. How many boxes hold 63 decorations?

d. 3 men can make 24 cabinets. How many cabinets can 9 men make?

Part 8

Copy and work each problem.

a. $\frac{4}{5} + \frac{3}{5} = \blacksquare$

b. $\frac{2}{9} \times \frac{3}{7} = \blacksquare$

c. $\frac{10}{9} - \frac{6}{9} = \blacksquare$

d. $\frac{2}{6} \times \frac{7}{6} = \blacksquare$

e. $\frac{9}{12} + \frac{4}{12} = \blacksquare$

Part 9

For each item, make a number family. Answer the question.

a. A lion weighed 1800 pounds less than an elephant. The lion weighed 365 pounds. How much did the elephant weigh?

b. An elevator had 2 people in it. Then 6 people got in the elevator. Then 11 more got in the elevator. Then some got out of the elevator. 10 people ended up in the elevator. How many people got out?

c. The temperature at the top of the mountain was 19 degrees lower than the temperature at the bottom of the mountain. If the temperature at the top was 41 degrees, what was the temperature at the bottom?

d. Ginger had some money in her bank account. She took out $12.30. The she took out $19.50. She ended up with $200.30 in her account. How much did she start out with?

Part 10

Copy and work each problem. If there is a remainder, write the answer as a mixed number.

a. $5\overline{)486}$

b. $7\overline{)188}$

c. $3\overline{)159}$

Lesson 47

Part 1 **Write each number family with 1 shown as a fraction with the right denominator. Figure out the missing fraction and box it.**

a. $\frac{7}{10}$ ——— ■ ⟶ 1

b. ■ ——— $\frac{4}{11}$ ⟶ 1

c. ■ ——— $\frac{19}{20}$ ⟶ 1

Part 2 **Copy and complete each pair of equivalent fractions. Show the fraction that equals 1.**

a. $\frac{21}{6} = \frac{189}{■}$

b. $\frac{7}{12} = \frac{182}{■}$

c. $\frac{3}{15} = \frac{■}{630}$

d. $\frac{13}{8} = \frac{■}{504}$

Part 3 **Make a fraction number family for each word problem. Answer the question the problem asks.**

a. $\frac{3}{5}$ of the children in a class are girls. What fraction of the class are boys?

b. $\frac{2}{9}$ of the trees in a forest are dead. What's the fraction for trees that are not dead?

c. In Rivertown, $\frac{6}{11}$ of the days are rainy. What is the fraction for days that are dry?

d. In Deer City, $\frac{5}{8}$ of the days are not cold. What is the fraction for days that are cold?

Part 4 **Copy each problem. Write the missing value as a fraction. Below, write the equation that shows the fraction as a whole number.**

Sample problem:

$$9\left(\frac{369}{9}\right) = 369$$

a. 3(■) = 243

b. 5(■) = 410

c. 9(■) = 36

d. 7(■) = 525

Part 5

For each problem, make a number family with the numbers the problem gives. Then figure out the answer to the question.

a. Don had lots of spending money when he went on vacation. On Saturday, he spent $11. On Sunday, he spent $36. On Monday, he spent $25. He still had $48 left to spend. How much spending money did he have at the beginning of his vacation?

b. 32 cookies were given to the bake sale. Then 18 cookies were sold. Another 50 cookies and then another 35 cookies were given to the bake sale. Then 60 cookies were sold. How many cookies were left?

c. A tank had 48 gallons of water in it. 56 gallons were added. Then some water was drained from the tank. 17 gallons were left in the tank. How much water was drained from the tank?

Independent Work

Part 6

Copy and complete each equation to show the decimal value for each mixed number.

a. $5\frac{2}{5} =$ ■   b. $7\frac{4}{20} =$ ■   c. $6\frac{8}{10} =$ ■   d. $15\frac{3}{4} =$ ■

Part 7

Write an equation to show each value as prime factors multiplied together.

a. 36 =   b. 42 =   c. 90 =   d. 48 =   e. 20 =

Part 8 **Make a number family for each word problem. Answer the question the problem asks.**

a. There are 540 students at the elementary school. There are 662 students at the high school. How many fewer students attend the elementary school than the high school?

b. There were 645 ants in an anthill. Another 126 ants joined them. An anteater ate some of the ants. There were 370 ants left in the anthill. How many ants were eaten?

c. In an orchard, there are 28 fewer pear trees than apple trees. There are 29 pear trees. How many apple trees are there?

d. Julie is 27 years younger than her mother. If her mother is 41, how old is Julie?

e. 38 passengers got in an airplane at New York. 28 passengers got in at Detroit. At Chicago, 312 more passengers got in and 41 passengers got out. How many passengers were still in the plane when it left Chicago?

Part 9 **Copy each division problem and work it. If there is a remainder, write the answer as a mixed number.**

a. $4\overline{)760}$ b. $6\overline{)437}$ c. $5\overline{)592}$ d. $3\overline{)196}$ e. $7\overline{)742}$

Part J

a. $26\overline{)185}$ = $7\frac{3}{26}$; -182; 3

b. $49\overline{)456}$ = $9\frac{15}{49}$; -441; 15

c. $81\overline{)360}$ = $4\frac{36}{81}$; -324; 36

Lesson 48

Part 1

Copy each problem. Write the missing value as a fraction.

a. $5(\blacksquare) = 3$

b. $8(\blacksquare) = 7$

c. $10(\blacksquare) = 6$

d. $9(\blacksquare) = 10$

Part 2

Make a fraction number family for each word problem. Answer the question the problem asks.

a. $\frac{3}{4}$ of the vehicles are not cars. What fraction of the vehicles are cars?

b. $\frac{3}{10}$ of the animals are horses. What's the fraction for the animals that are not horses?

c. $\frac{2}{5}$ of the fish are trout. What fraction of the fish are not trout?

d. $\frac{1}{9}$ of the cups are not filled. What fraction of the cups are filled?

Part 3

Make a number family for each problem. Answer each question.

a. Fran started out with $60 in her bank account. She took out $11. She put $35 in the account. She took out $56. How much did she end up with?

b. A truck's fuel tank was full. The truck used up 13 gallons. Then the truck used up 34 gallons. Then the truck used up 6 gallons. At the end of the trip, the tank still had 9 gallons in it. How much fuel does the tank hold?

Part 4

Copy and complete each pair of equivalent fractions. Show the fraction that equals 1.

a. $\frac{3}{11} = \frac{561}{\blacksquare}$

b. $\frac{10}{7} = \frac{\blacksquare}{203}$

c. $\frac{15}{14} = \frac{\blacksquare}{70}$

Part 5

Copy each problem. Figure out the missing value. If the fractions are equivalent, write the simple equation below.

a. $\frac{20}{15}(\blacksquare) = \frac{280}{225}$

b. $\frac{9}{7}(\blacksquare) = \frac{504}{392}$

c. $\frac{14}{6}(\blacksquare) = \frac{126}{54}$

d. $\frac{3}{8}(\blacksquare) = \frac{336}{336}$

Independent Work

Part 6

Copy the table. Fill in the missing numbers. Answer the questions.

This table is supposed to show the number of fish caught in Doe Lake and Arrow Lake in September and October.

Facts

1. In September, 18 fish were caught in Doe Lake.
2. In October, a total of 98 fish were caught in both lakes.
3. In Doe Lake, 16 more fish were caught in October than in September.

	Doe Lake	Arrow Lake	Total
September			
October			
Total			172

Questions

a. How many fish were caught in Arrow Lake during October?

b. What is the total number of fish caught in September?

c. Were more fish caught during September or during October?

Part 7 **Rewrite each equation that is wrong. Show the correct decimal number.**

a. $\frac{75}{100} = .075$ b. $\frac{78}{10} = 7.8$ c. $\frac{120}{100} = 12.0$

d. $\frac{3}{1000} = .03$ e. $\frac{565}{100} = 5.65$

Part 8 **Copy and work each problem. If there is a remainder, write the answer as a mixed number.**

a. $3\overline{)579}$ b. $4\overline{)396}$ c. $5\overline{)806}$ d. $2\overline{)601}$

Part 9 **Copy and work each problem.**

a. $\frac{2}{3} \times \frac{5}{4} =$ [redacted] b. $\frac{9}{5} \times \frac{4}{8} =$ [redacted]

c. $\frac{5}{4} \times \frac{7}{9} =$ [redacted] d. $\frac{8}{9} \times \frac{8}{7} =$ [redacted]

Part 10 **Copy and complete the table.**

	Fraction	Mixed number
a.	$\frac{13}{10}$	
b.		$5\frac{6}{7}$
c.	$\frac{28}{25}$	
d.		$1\frac{3}{8}$

Part J

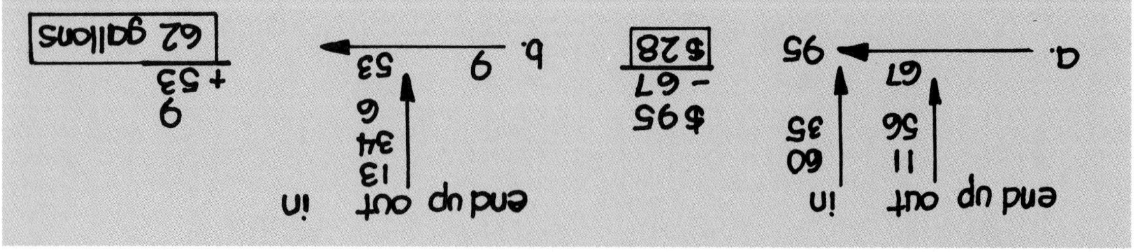

Lesson 49

Part 1 **Make a fraction number family for each word problem. Answer the question the problem asks.**

a. $\frac{5}{7}$ of the trees are large. What's the fraction for the trees that are not large?

b. $\frac{8}{12}$ of the people in the office are women. What fraction of the people are men?

c. $\frac{5}{7}$ of the food the cow ate was not hay. What fraction of the food was hay?

d. Jim scored $\frac{1}{3}$ of the team's points. What fraction of the points did his teammates score?

Part 2 **Copy and complete each equation.**

a. $15(\blacksquare) = 1$

b. $12(\blacksquare) = 42$

c. $94(\blacksquare) = 7$

d. $8(\blacksquare) = 7$

I figured out what fraction of the trees are not large. It's the top 1/3.
I don't think that's what they wanted you to figure out.
6/7 of the trees are large. What's the fraction for the trees that are not large?

Part 3

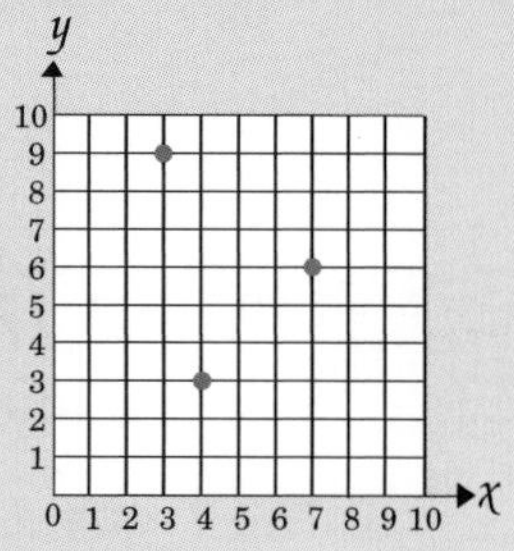

- This kind of grid is a coordinate system.

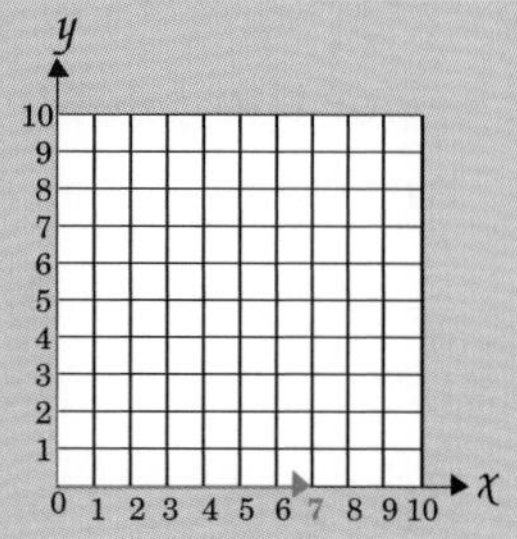

$x = 7$

- The points on a coordinate system can be identified by their x value and their y value.
- The x value is the distance from zero this way: ⟶
- Here the x value is 7.

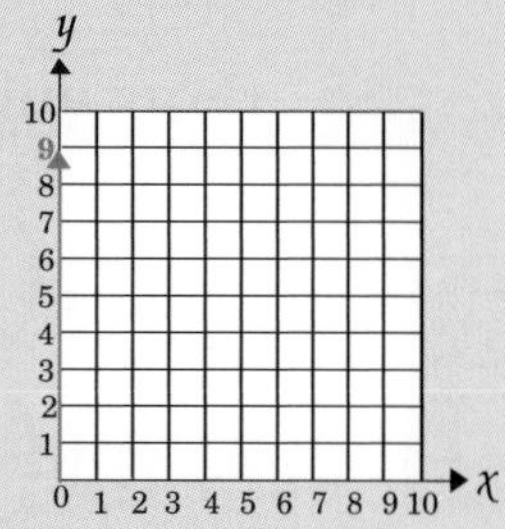

- The y value is the distance from zero this way: ↑
- Here the y value is 9:

$y = 9$

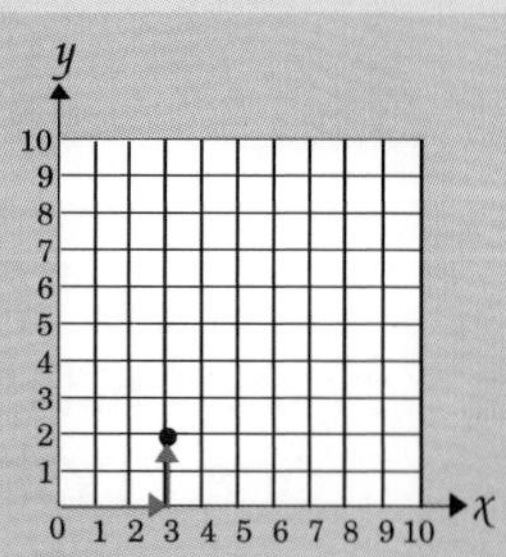

- You can tell about any point on the coordinate system by telling first about x and then about y.

$x = 3,\ y = 2$

- The point is 3 places in the x direction: ⟶ and 2 places in the y direction: ↑

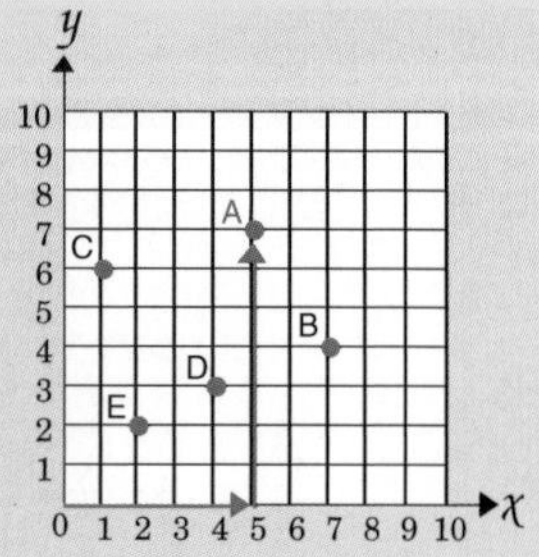

- Here is the x value and the y value for the point at A: $x = 5,\ y = 7$.
- To get to point A, you go 5 places in the x direction and then 7 places up for y.

Part 4

Copy each problem. Figure out the missing value. If the fractions are equivalent, write the simple equation below.

a. $\frac{8}{7}\left(\blacksquare\right) = \frac{464}{406}$ b. $\frac{3}{5}\left(\blacksquare\right) = \frac{108}{175}$ c. $\frac{9}{15}\left(\blacksquare\right) = \frac{477}{795}$

Part 5

For each item, make a ratio equation. Write the answer as a number and a unit name.

a. The ratio of boys to girls is 5 to 4. There are 300 boys. How many girls are there?

b. In Zemo's factory, it takes 11 minutes to make 4 dresses. How many minutes does it take to make 780 dresses?

c. A cook uses 5 potatoes for every 2 meals. How many potatoes does the cook need for 50 meals?

Independent Work

Part 6

Rewrite each equation that is wrong. Show the correct decimal number.

a. $\frac{3}{4} = .5$ b. $\frac{7}{10} = .07$ c. $\frac{356}{10} = 35.6$

d. $\frac{14}{1000} = .014$ e. $\frac{12}{8} = .15$

Part 7

Copy and work each problem.

a. $\frac{5}{3} \times \frac{7}{5} = \blacksquare$ b. $\frac{26}{3} + \frac{5}{3} = \blacksquare$

c. $\frac{12}{7} - \frac{5}{7} = \blacksquare$ d. $\frac{4}{9} \times \frac{9}{4} = \blacksquare$

Part 8

Copy and work each problem.

a. $\begin{array}{r} 356 \\ \underline{\times\ 21} \end{array}$ b. $\begin{array}{r} 199 \\ \underline{\times\ 24} \end{array}$ c. $\begin{array}{r} 56 \\ \underline{\times\ 78} \end{array}$

Part 9 Copy and complete the table. Answer the questions.

This table is supposed to show the number of men and women who worked at two different mills, Johnson Mill and Howard Mill.

Facts

1. There were 123 men at Johnson Mill.
2. There were 122 more women than men at Johnson Mill.
3. The total number of women for both mills was 888.
4. The total number of men at both mills was 666.

	Men	Women	Total
Johnson Mill			
Howard Mill			
Total			

Questions

a. How many women worked at Johnson Mill?

b. How many men worked at Howard Mill?

c. How many workers were at Howard Mill?

d. Were there more workers at Johnson Mill or Howard Mill?

Part 10 Copy and complete each equation to show the decimal value for each mixed number.

a. $3\frac{6}{8} = ■$ b. $10\frac{1}{4} = ■$ c. $4\frac{1}{10} = ■$ d. $12\frac{10}{25} = ■$

Part 11 Copy and complete each equation.

a. $5 = \frac{■}{7} = \frac{■}{10} = \frac{■}{1} = \frac{■}{5}$

b. $8 = \frac{■}{6} = \frac{■}{1} = \frac{■}{4} = \frac{■}{3}$

Lesson 50

Part 1 **Copy and complete each equation.**

a. $26(\blacksquare) = 7$

b. $19(\blacksquare) = 32$

c. $6(\blacksquare) = 27$

d. $20(\blacksquare) = 5$

Part 2 **For each item, make a ratio equation. Answer the question.**

a. A machine moves 7 meters every 3 seconds. How many seconds does it take for the machine to move 672 meters?

b. The ratio of leaves to buds on a tree was 13 to 9. There were 387 buds on the tree. How many leaves were on the tree?

Test 5

Part 1 **Copy and complete the table.**

	Mixed number	Fraction	Decimal
a.		$\frac{21}{10}$	
b.			5.65
c.	$2\frac{3}{100}$		

Part 2 **Copy each problem. Multiply, subtract and write the fraction.**

a. $\begin{array}{r} 6 \\ 54\overline{)329} \\ \blacksquare \end{array}$

b. $\begin{array}{r} 7 \\ 15\overline{)116} \\ \blacksquare \end{array}$

Part 3 **Copy and work each item. Circle the value you start with or the value you end up with to show which is larger.**

a. $\frac{3}{8} \times \frac{2}{3} = \blacksquare$ b. $\frac{9}{4} \times \frac{16}{15} = \blacksquare$ c. $4 \times \frac{7}{6} = \blacksquare$

Part 4 **For each item, make a number family. Answer the question.**

a. An elevator started out with some people in it. At the second floor, 2 people got off. At the third floor, 7 people got off. At the fourth floor, 2 people got off. At the sixth floor, 5 people got off. There were still 2 people in the elevator. How many people were in the elevator when it started out?

b. A tank started out with 400 gallons of water. 18 gallons leaked out of the tank. Then 41 gallons were put in the tank. Then 90 gallons were put in the tank. Then 56 gallons leaked out of the tank. How much water was still in the tank?

Part 5 **Copy the table and complete it.**

	Mixed number	Fraction
a.		$\frac{28}{3}$
b.	$10\frac{1}{9}$	
c.	$1\frac{7}{8}$	
d.		$\frac{5}{4}$

Part 6 **Copy each equation. Figure out whether the fractions are equal. If they are equal, write the simple equation below.**

a. $\frac{5}{6}\left(\blacksquare\right) = \frac{110}{138}$

b. $\frac{12}{7}\left(\blacksquare\right) = \frac{156}{91}$

c. $\frac{6}{11}\left(\blacksquare\right) = \frac{150}{275}$

Part 7 **Copy and complete each equation to show the decimal value for each mixed number.**

a. $5\frac{3}{8} = \blacksquare$ b. $8\frac{4}{5} = \blacksquare$

Lesson 51

Part 1 **Make a fraction number family for each word problem. Box the answers to the questions the problem asks.**

Sample problem:	7 berries are not ripe. 2 berries are ripe. What's the fraction for the berries that are ripe? What's the fraction for the berries that are not ripe?

a. There were 14 cars. 9 were painted. The rest were not painted. What's the fraction for the cars that were painted? What's the fraction for the cars that were not painted?

b. 12 cars are painted. 7 cars are not painted. What's the fraction for cars that are not painted? What's the fraction for cars that are painted?

c. There are 13 girls. There are 7 boys. What fraction of children are girls? What fraction of the children are boys?

d. There are 14 children. 9 are girls. What fraction of the children are boys? What fraction of the children are girls?

Part 2 **Copy each problem with the missing value shown as a fraction.**

a. $14(\blacksquare) = 80$

b. $24(\blacksquare) = 4$

c. $6(\blacksquare) = 55$

d. $39(\blacksquare) = 18$

Part 3

Use lined paper. Write the x and y values for points A through E.

A $x =$ ■, $y =$ ■

B $x =$ ■, $y =$ ■

C $x =$ ■, $y =$ ■

D $x =$ ■, $y =$ ■

E $x =$ ■, $y =$ ■

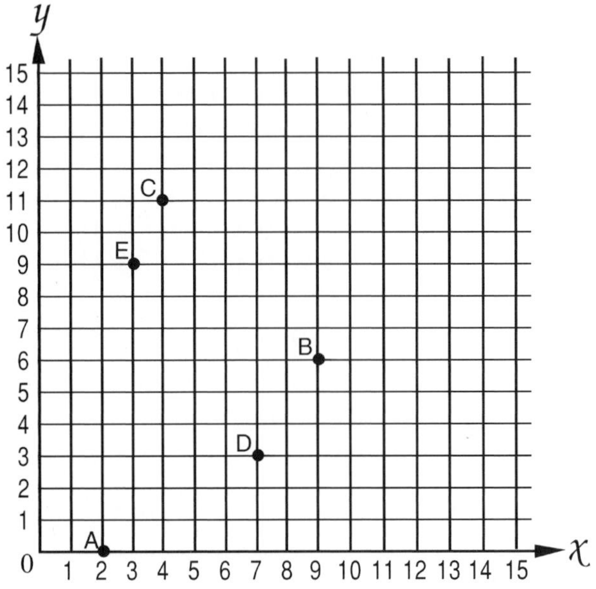

Part 4

For each item, make a ratio equation and answer the question.

a. If 4 cows eat 87 pounds of grass, how much do 24 cows eat?

b. The ratio of new stamps to old stamps is 2 to 9. If there are 450 new stamps, how many old stamps are there?

c. If there are 19 bolts on 1 machine, how many bolts would be needed for 12 machines?

Independent Work

Part 5

Copy each fraction. If the fraction can be simplified, simplify it. If the fraction is more than 1, write it as a mixed number.

a. $\frac{42}{36}$ b. $\frac{9}{15}$ c. $\frac{19}{5}$ d. $\frac{25}{9}$

Part 6

For each problem, make a number family. Answer the question with a number and unit name.

a. Tim is 16 years old. His grandfather is 71 years old. How much older than Tim is his grandfather?

b. Tim's sister Sue is 18 years old. An oak tree is 78 years older than Sue. How old is the oak tree?

Part 7

Copy and complete the table.

	Fraction	Mixed number
a.	$\frac{12}{7}$	
b.	$\frac{26}{3}$	
c.		$1\frac{5}{8}$
d.		$15\frac{2}{9}$

Part 8

Copy and work each problem.

a. $6\overline{)4748}$

b. $7\overline{)3002}$

c. $5\overline{)6604}$

d. $8\overline{)5631}$

Part 9

Make a number family with the headings in, out and end up. Answer the question.

a. John had $4. Then he earned $13. Then he bought school supplies for $7. Then he spent $3 on a gift. Then he earned $11. How much money did he end up with?

b. A bus starts out with 12 people on it. At the first stop, 3 people get on the bus and 1 person gets off the bus. At the next stop, 12 people get on the bus and 2 people get off the bus. At the next stop, 7 people get off the bus. How many people are still on the bus?

c. Donna has 18 apples. She picks 37 apples. Then she buys another 40 apples. She uses some apples to make apple pies. She ends up with 11 apples. How many apples did she use in her pies?

Part J

c. $30\overline{)239}$ 8 -240

$30\overline{)239}$ $7\frac{29}{30}$ -210 29

d. $72\overline{)584}$ $8\frac{8}{72}$ -576 8

$72\overline{)584}$

Part K

a. $\frac{\text{cows}}{\text{pounds}} \quad \frac{4}{87}\left(\frac{6}{6}\right) = \frac{24}{522}$ **522 pounds**

b. $\frac{\text{new stamps}}{\text{old stamps}} \quad \frac{2}{9}\left(\frac{225}{225}\right) = \frac{450}{2025}$ **2025 old stamps**

c. $\frac{\text{bolts}}{\text{machines}} \quad \frac{19}{1}\left(\frac{12}{12}\right) = \frac{228}{12}$ **228 bolts**

Lesson 52

There are 3 clean dogs for every 8 dogs in the kennel.

Part 1

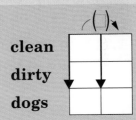

- You've worked ratio problems that have two names. Later, you're going to work ratio problems that have three names.
- You'll use this kind of table to work ratio problems with three names:
- The arrow on top of the table shows that you have to multiply all the numbers in the first column by the same value to get the numbers in the second column.
- The arrows pointing down each column show that the columns work just like number families.

clean		
dirty		
dogs		

- If you have two numbers in a column, you can figure out the third number:
- You find the missing number in the first column by working the problem: 8 – 3.
- You find the missing number in the second column by working the problem: 12 + 20.

clean	3	12
dirty	■	20
dogs	8	■

- Here's a table with the values for men, women and adults:
- You can figure out all the missing numbers in the table.
- To find the missing number in the first column, you work the problem: 5 – 2.
- You can't figure out the missing number in the second column by adding or subtracting. **But you can make a ratio equation.**

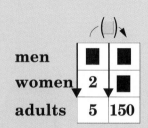

men	■	■
women	2	■
adults	5	150

- Here's the ratio equation for women to adults:
- The numerators are the values from the **women** row.
- The denominators are the values from the **adult** row.
- There are 60 women.

$$\frac{\textbf{women}}{\textbf{adults}}\ \frac{2}{5}\left(\frac{\ }{\ }\right) = \frac{■}{150}$$

$$\frac{\textbf{women}}{\textbf{adults}}\ \frac{2}{5}\left(\frac{30}{30}\right) = \frac{60}{150}$$

- You write 60 in the **women** row of the table.
- You can figure out the missing number for men by subtracting: 150 – 60.
- There are 90 men.

men	3	■
women	2	60
adults	5	150

Part 2 **Make a fraction number family for each word problem. Box the answers to the questions the problem asks.**

a. There were 24 people. 19 of the people were wealthy. The rest were not wealthy. What fraction of the people were wealthy? What fraction of the people were not wealthy?

b. At Joe's Market, there are 2 watermelons that are rotten and 94 watermelons that are good. What fraction of the melons are rotten? What fraction of the melons are good?

c. There was a total of 15 bottles. 13 of those bottles were broken. What fraction of the bottles were broken? What fraction of the bottles were not broken?

d. 17 of the drivers wore glasses. 88 drivers did not wear glasses. What fraction of the drivers wore glasses? What fraction of the drivers did not wear glasses?

Independent Work

Part 3 **For each problem, write the whole number as a fraction and work the problem.**

a. $4 - \frac{7}{8} = $ ■

b. $\frac{3}{4} + 8 = $ ■

c. $\frac{3}{4} \times 8 = $ ■

Part 4 **For each item, make a ratio equation and answer the question.**

a. The ratio of posts to beams is 3 to 8. There are 72 beams. How many posts are there?

b. The shadow grows 7 inches every 3 minutes. If the shadow grows 56 inches, how many minutes have passed?

c. A machine uses 6 tons of fuel every 5 days. How many days would it take the machine to use 300 tons of fuel?

Part 5 **For each item, make a number family. Answer the question.**

a. Mr. Jones had lots of eggs. He delivered 144 eggs to Joe's Market. He delivered 84 eggs to Fran's Market. He delivered 66 eggs to AC Market. Mr. Jones still had 300 eggs. How many eggs did he start out with?

b. A large balloon had 11 pounds of air in it. Then 4 pounds more were pumped into the balloon. Then some air leaked out of the balloon. The balloon ended up with 3 pounds of air in it. How many pounds leaked out?

c. A hat store had 280 hats in stock. On Monday, the store sold 45 hats. The store also received a shipment of 60 hats. On Tuesday, the store sold 115 hats. On Wednesday, the store sold 57 hats. The store also received 103 hats. How many hats did the store have at the end of the day on Wednesday?

Part 6 **Copy and work each problem.**

a. $6\overline{)1100}$ b. $3\overline{)2103}$ c. $8\overline{)1591}$ d. $5\overline{)703}$

Part 7 **Copy and complete each equation. If the fractions are equal, write the simple equation below.**

a. $\frac{4}{7}\left(\blacksquare\right) = \frac{40}{63}$ b. $\frac{2}{9}\left(\blacksquare\right) = \frac{420}{1890}$ c. $\frac{1}{15}\left(\blacksquare\right) = \frac{40}{675}$

Part J

a. $24\overline{)175}$ $24\overline{)175}$

b. $65\overline{)623}$ $65\overline{)623}$

c. $49\overline{)250}$ $49\overline{)250}$

d. $78\overline{)498}$ $78\overline{)498}$

Lesson 53

Part 1 **Make a fraction number family for each problem. Box the answer to the question the problem asks.**

a. $\frac{1}{7}$ of the people were thirsty. What fraction of the people were not thirsty?

b. 32 bottles were not broken. 3 bottles were broken. What fraction of the bottles were broken?

c. James got 4 of the items wrong. He got 21 of the items correct. What fraction of the items did he get correct?

d. $\frac{5}{8}$ of the students were boys. What fraction of the students were girls?

e. There were 18 members on the team. 6 members had blue eyes. What fraction of the team did not have blue eyes?

Independent Work

Part 2 **Copy and work each problem. If the answer can be simplified, simplify it. If the simplified fraction is more than 1, write it as a mixed number.**

a. $2 \times \frac{5}{4} = \blacksquare$

b. $\frac{1}{2} \times \frac{3}{4} = \blacksquare$

c. $18 \times \frac{1}{2} = \blacksquare$

d. $\frac{12}{2} \times \frac{13}{10} = \blacksquare$

Part 3 **Make a table. Answer the questions.**

Sam and Ann counted ducks and geese. Sam counted 52 geese. Ann counted a total of 183 birds. The number of birds counted by both people was 482. Ann counted 100 geese.

a. How many ducks did Ann count?

b. Who counted more birds?

c. Did Sam count fewer ducks or fewer geese?

d. What was the total number of geese counted?

Part 4

For each problem, write the whole number as a fraction and work the problem.

a. $9 + \frac{4}{5} = \blacksquare$ b. $\frac{2}{5} \times 9 = \blacksquare$

c. $5 - \frac{8}{3} = \blacksquare$ d. $3 \times \frac{12}{5} = \blacksquare$

Part 5

For each item, make a ratio equation and answer the question.

CALCULATOR

a. There are 56 horseshoes for every 14 horses. How many horseshoes are needed for 98 horses?

b. A recipe uses 3 eggs for every 10 ounces of milk. How many ounces of milk are needed for 57 eggs?

c. In a garden, the ratio of weeds to flowers is 17 to 2. If there are 450 flowers, how many weeds are there?

Part 6

Copy and complete each equation. If the fractions are equivalent, write the simple equation below.

CALCULATOR

a. $\frac{2}{3}(\blacksquare) = \frac{450}{360}$ b. $\frac{7}{8}(\blacksquare) = \frac{490}{720}$ c. $\frac{3}{2}(\blacksquare) = \frac{900}{600}$

Part J

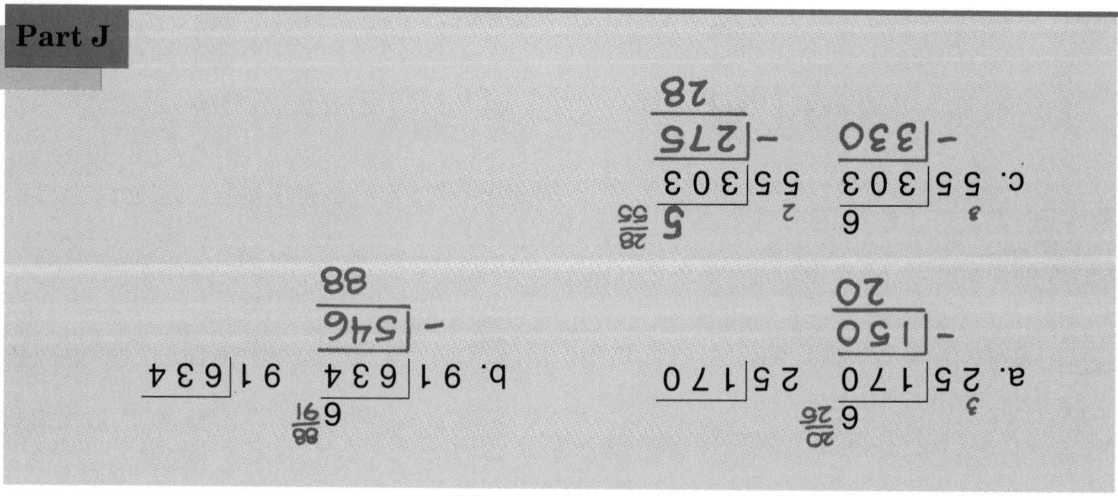

Lesson 54

Part 1

- If two fractions are equivalent, the first fraction is multiplied by 1. $\frac{2}{3}\left(\frac{7}{7}\right) = \frac{14}{21}$
- If the first fraction is **not** multiplied by 1, the fractions are **not** equivalent. $\frac{2}{3}\left(\frac{6}{7}\right) = \frac{12}{21}$
- When fractions are not equivalent, you can figure out which fraction is greater.
- If the middle fraction is **more than 1,** the **last fraction is more** than the first fraction. $\frac{5}{9}\left(\frac{3}{2}\right) = \frac{15}{18}$
- If the middle fraction is **less than 1,** the **last fraction is less** than the first fraction. $\frac{5}{9}\left(\frac{2}{3}\right) = \frac{10}{27}$

Part 2

Copy and complete each equation. If the fractions are not equal, circle the larger fraction. If the fractions are equal, circle the equal sign.

a. $\frac{3}{4}\left(\blacksquare\right) = \frac{24}{28}$ b. $\frac{10}{9}\left(\blacksquare\right) = \frac{80}{72}$ c. $\frac{1}{7}\left(\blacksquare\right) = \frac{18}{126}$

d. $\frac{2}{3}\left(\blacksquare\right) = \frac{24}{39}$ e. $\frac{5}{3}\left(\blacksquare\right) = \frac{55}{30}$

Part 3

Copy each problem and write the missing fraction.

a. $16\left(\blacksquare\right) = 7$ b. $8\left(\blacksquare\right) = 259$

c. $4\left(\blacksquare\right) = 1$ d. $30\left(\blacksquare\right) = 19$

Part 4 Make a fraction number family for each problem. Figure out the answers to the questions the problem asks.

a. There were vehicles on a lot. $\frac{7}{13}$ of those vehicles were not cars. What fraction of the vehicles were cars? What's the fraction for all the vehicles?

b. 9 of the students went to music class. The other 19 students went to art class. What fraction of the students went to music class? What fraction of the students went to art class?

c. There are 45 workers. 35 of these workers wore gloves. The rest of the workers did not wear gloves. What fraction of the workers wore gloves? What fraction of the workers did not wear gloves?

d. $\frac{9}{20}$ of the cars parked on a lot are white. What fraction of the cars on the lot are not white? What's the fraction for all cars on the lot?

Independent Work

Part 5 Copy and work each problem.

a. $8\overline{)476}$ b. $3\overline{)476}$ c. $2\overline{)1218}$ d. $7\overline{)1208}$

Part 6 For each item, make a ratio equation and answer the question.

a. If 27 eggs are needed to make 12 omelettes, how many eggs are needed for 108 omelettes?

b. There are 6 ounces of water in every 7 pounds of sand. If there are 980 pounds of sand, how many ounces of water are there?

c. The ratio of dry days to rainy days was 29 to 2. If there were 68 rainy days, how many dry days were there?

Part 7 Copy the table and complete it.

	Fraction	Decimal	Mixed number
a.			$3\frac{4}{10}$
b.		1.561	
c.	$\frac{760}{100}$		
d.			$1\frac{1}{10}$

Part 8 For each item, make a number family. Answer the question.

a. Ginger had $210 in her bank account. On Monday, she put in another $306. On Tuesday, she put in another $111. On Wednesday, she took out $400. On Friday, she put in $35. How much money was in her account at the end of Friday?

b. The truck started out with a full tank of fuel. On the first part of the trip, the truck used up 91 liters of fuel. On the next part of the trip, the truck used up 211 liters of fuel. On the last part of the trip, the truck used up 38 liters of fuel. The tank still had 49 liters of fuel in it. How much did the tank start out with?

c. A bus started out with 11 passengers. At the first stop, 13 passengers got in. At the next stop, 3 passengers got off. 14 passengers got in. At the next stop, 4 passengers got off. 16 passengers got in. At the next stop, 26 passengers got off. How many passengers were still in the bus?

Part 9 Write each value as prime factors multiplied together.

a. 42 b. 60 c. 36 d. 32

Part J

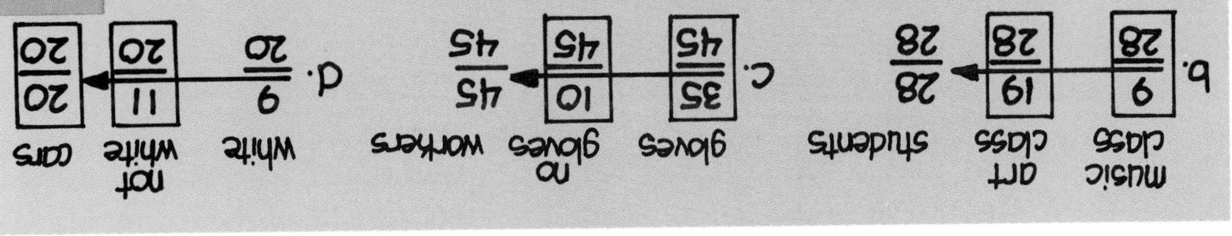

Lesson 55

Part 1 **Copy and complete each equation. If the fractions are not equivalent, circle the larger fraction. If the fractions are equivalent, circle the equal sign.**

a. $\frac{3}{1}\left(\blacksquare\right) = \frac{54}{17}$

b. $\frac{8}{7}\left(\blacksquare\right) = \frac{160}{175}$

c. $\frac{9}{5}\left(\blacksquare\right) = \frac{90}{55}$

d. $\frac{8}{7}\left(\blacksquare\right) = \frac{96}{84}$

Part 2

- Some lines intersect. Those are lines that touch each other or cross each other.
- Each of these pairs of lines intersect:

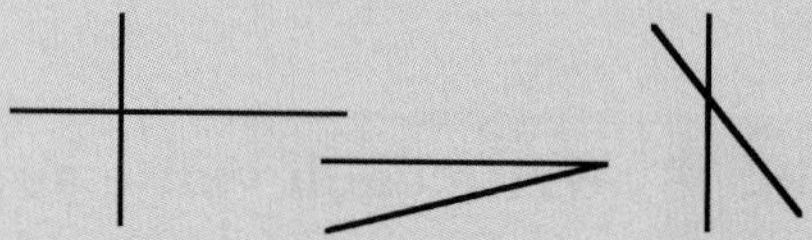

- Some lines never intersect. Those lines are **parallel.** Parallel lines are always the same distance from each other.
- Each set shows parallel lines. The lines do not intersect.

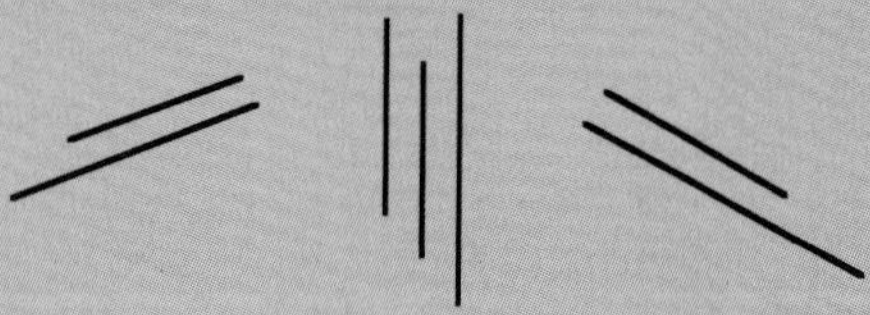

Part 3 **Write whether the lines in each set are parallel or not parallel.**

a. 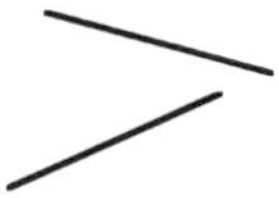

b. 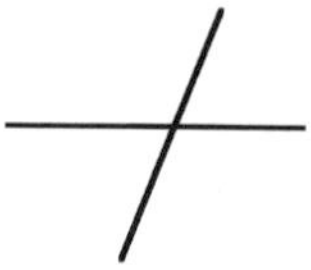

c. 

d. 

e. 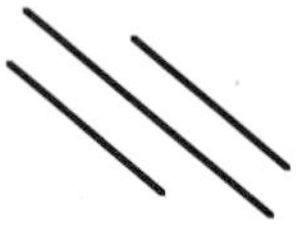

f. 

Part 4

- You know that if the top number and the bottom number of a fraction are the same, the fraction equals 1.
- Here are some fractions that equal 1:

$$\frac{6}{6} = 1 \qquad \frac{3}{3} = 1 \qquad \frac{234}{234} = 1$$

- You can write complicated fractions that equal 1 as long as the top and the bottom show **exactly the same value.**
- On top is the fraction $\frac{14}{100}$:

  On the bottom is the fraction $\frac{14}{100}$:

$$\frac{\frac{14}{100}}{\frac{14}{100}} = 1$$

  The top and the bottom are exactly the same, so the whole fraction equals 1.
- Here are the same fraction values written as decimals: $\frac{.14}{.14} = 1$
- Remember, if the top and the bottom show exactly the same value, the whole fraction equals 1.

Independent Work

Part 5

Copy and work each problem. If the answer is too big, rewrite the problem with an answer that is 1 less and work the problem.

a. $60\overline{)360}$ with answer 6

b. $77\overline{)540}$ with answer 7

c. $87\overline{)689}$ with answer 8

d. $48\overline{)333}$ with answer 7

Part 6 Work each problem. Make a number family or a ratio equation.

a. The ratio of dogs to cats is 11 to 10. If there are 720 cats, how many dogs are there?

b. The temperature was 64 degrees higher in the valley than it was at the top of the mountain. The temperature at the top of the mountain was 4 degrees. What was the temperature in the valley?

c. There were 311 fewer elephants than hippos. There were 567 elephants. How many hippos were there?

d. There are 7 pounds of cement for every 12 pounds of water. How much cement is needed for 168 pounds of water?

e. In March, it rained 51 millimeters less than it rained in July. In July, it rained 89 millimeters. How much did it rain in March?

f. If a tractor travels 13 feet every 3 seconds, how far will the tractor go in 60 seconds?

g. If 1 bus holds 64 people, how many people could 12 buses hold?

Part 7 Copy each fraction. If the fraction can be simplified, simplify it. If the simplified fraction is more than 1, write it as a mixed number.

a. $\frac{24}{30}$ b. $\frac{11}{50}$ c. $\frac{40}{9}$ d. $\frac{40}{6}$ e. $\frac{56}{7}$

Part 8 Copy and complete the table.

	Multiplication	Fraction equation	Division
a.	$6 \times ■ = 372$		
b.	$4 \times ■ = 168$		
c.	$10 \times ■ = 80$		

Part 9 For each problem, write the whole number as a fraction and work the problem.

a. $4 - \frac{2}{7} = ■$

b. $6 + \frac{2}{9} = ■$

c. $\frac{3}{8} \times 7 = ■$

d. $14 \times \frac{6}{5} = ■$

Lesson 56

Part 1 **Write the x and y values for the points that are incorrect.**

	x	y
M	2	1
J	4	2
D	8	4
F	12	6

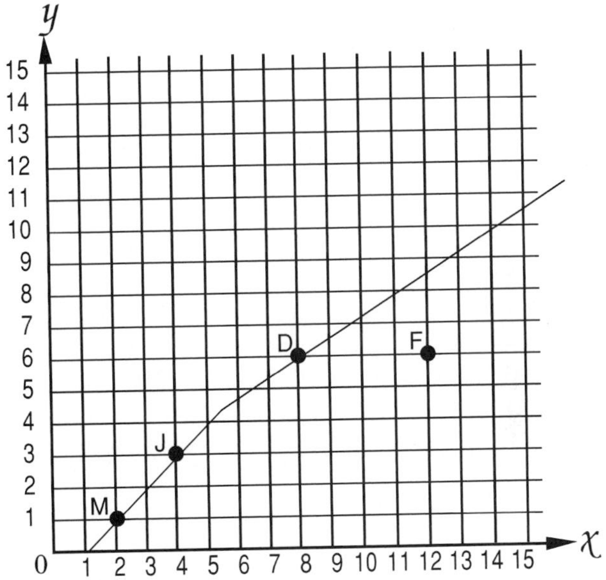

Part 2 **Copy and complete each equation. If the fractions shown are not equivalent, circle the larger fraction. If the fractions are equivalent, circle the equal sign.**

a. $\frac{2}{9}\left(\blacksquare\right) = \frac{22}{99}$

b. $\frac{8}{8}\left(\blacksquare\right) = \frac{96}{104}$

c. $\frac{5}{1}\left(\blacksquare\right) = \frac{35}{8}$

d. $\frac{9}{4}\left(\blacksquare\right) = \frac{360}{360}$

Part 3

- Some figures have opposite sides that are parallel.
- Figure 1 has one pair of parallel sides. Those sides are marked with arrows.

Figure 1

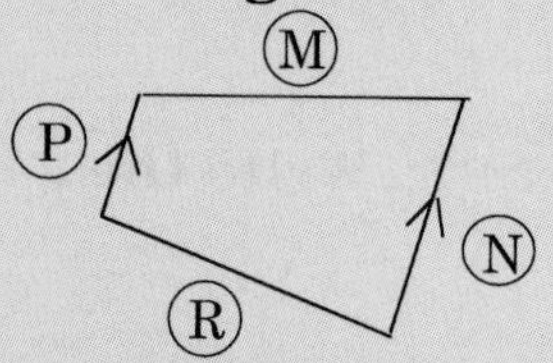

- Figure 2 has one pair of parallel sides.

Figure 2

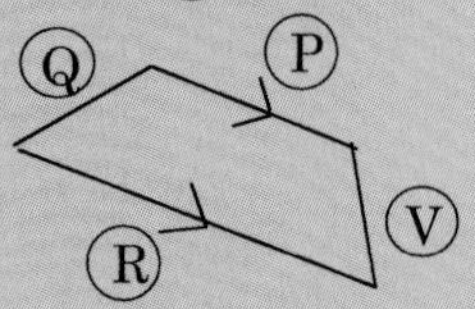

- Figure 3 has **two** pairs of parallel sides.
- Here's a rule about 4-sided figures: If both pairs of opposite sides are parallel, the opposite sides are the same length.

Figure 3

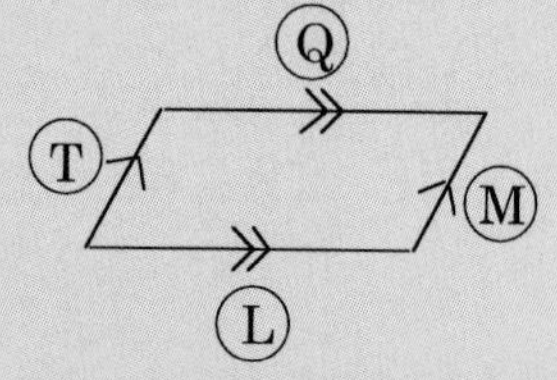

- In figure 4, side P is 9 inches long. So the parallel side is 9 inches long.
- Side T is 5 inches long. So the parallel side is 5 inches long.
- Remember the rule about 4-sided figures. If both pairs of opposite sides are parallel, the opposite sides are the same length.

Figure 4

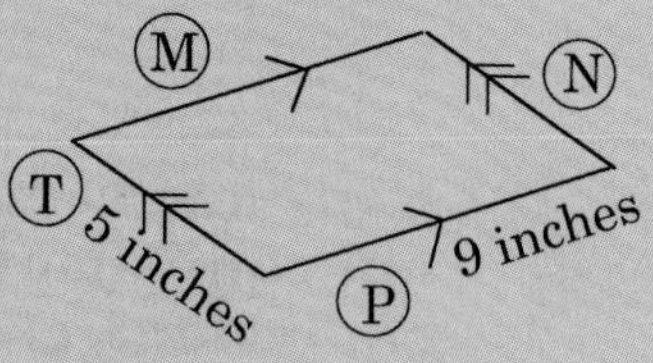

Part 4

- To work some types of word problems, you can make **ratio tables.** Those problems name three different things.

- Here's a problem:

  The ratio of rainy days to dry days is 1 to 8. There were 48 dry days. How many total days were there? How many rainy days were there?

- The problem names three things: **rainy days, dry days** and **total days.** So you make a table, with total days on the bottom.

	Ratio	
rainy		
dry		
days		

- The first sentence of the problem tells the ratio for rainy days to dry days: **The ratio of rainy days to dry days is 1 to 8.** You can get a total for the first column. →

	Ratio	
rainy	1	
dry	8	
days	9	

- The second sentence of the problem gives a number for the second column: **There were 48 dry days.**

	Ratio	
rainy	1	
dry	8	48
days	9	

- You can figure out the number of total days by using a ratio equation:

$$\frac{\text{dry}}{\text{days}} \quad \frac{8}{9}\left(\frac{6}{6}\right)=\frac{48}{\boxed{54}}$$

- There were 54 total days.

- Then you can complete the table and answer the questions.

	Ratio	
rainy	1	6
dry	8	48
days	9	54

Independent Work

Part 5 **For each problem, make a fraction number family and box the answer to the question.**

a. If $\frac{2}{9}$ of the fish were bass, what fraction of the fish were not bass?

b. 12 students wore jackets. The rest did not wear jackets. There were 29 students. What fraction of the students did not wear jackets?

c. $\frac{5}{12}$ of the day was sunny. What fraction of the day was not sunny?

Part 6 **Copy and work each problem. If the answer is too big, rewrite the problem with an answer that is 1 less and work the problem.**

a. $24\overline{)190}$ with 8 above

b. $78\overline{)234}$ with 3 above

c. $96\overline{)475}$ with 5 above

d. $13\overline{)107}$ with 8 above

Part 7 **For each problem, make a number family and answer the question.**

a. A water tank started out with 101 gallons in it. On Monday, 308 gallons were added. On Tuesday, 106 gallons were added. On Wednesday, 400 gallons were removed. How many gallons were still in the tank?

b. A train started out with some people in it. At the first stop, 13 people got off. At the next stop, 16 people got off. The train still had 59 people in it. How many people did the train start out with?

Part 8 Copy and work each problem.

a. $3\overline{)5800}$

b. $5\overline{)5800}$

c. $7\overline{)5800}$

d. $2\overline{)5800}$

Part 9 Copy and complete the table.

	Fraction	Mixed number
a.	$\frac{27}{2}$	
b.		$1\frac{7}{8}$
c.		$2\frac{3}{10}$
d.	$\frac{23}{9}$	

Part 10 Copy and complete the table.

	Decimal	Mixed number	Fraction
a.	3.44		
b.		$1\frac{3}{100}$	
c.			$\frac{705}{10}$

This number shows how much I'll give you for your car. I haven't shown the decimal point in the number, but don't worry about it. What difference can a little old decimal point make?
$ 25000
USED CARS

Lesson 57

Part 1

Make a ratio table. Answer the questions for each item with a number and unit name.

a. There are boys and girls in a school. There are 3 girls for every 5 children. There are 402 boys in the school.
   1. How many children are in the school?
   2. How many girls are in the school?

b. For every 7 students, 4 wear glasses. The rest do not wear glasses. There are 64 students who wear glasses.
   1. How many students do not wear glasses?
   2. What is the total number of students?

c. There are blue balloons and red balloons at a party. The ratio of blue balloons to red balloons is 3 to 5. There is a total of 240 balloons.
   1. How many blue balloons are there?
   2. How many red balloons are there?

Part 2

Write the x and y values for the points that are incorrect.

	x	y
B	3	1
C	6	2
M	9	3

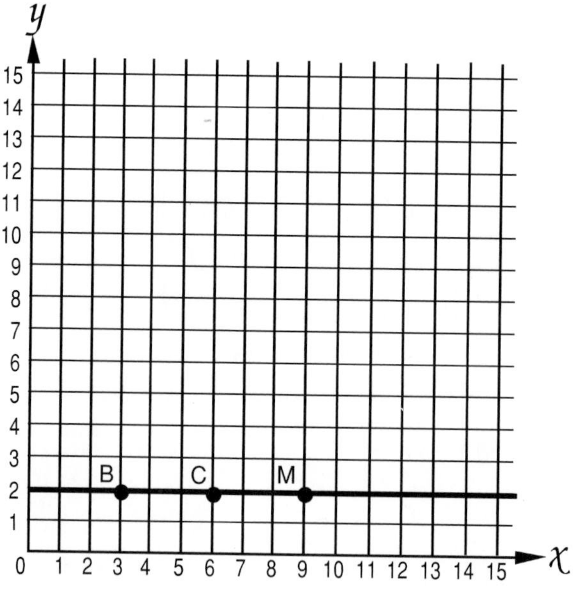

Independent Work

Part 3 **Copy and work each problem.**

a. $4\overline{)7080}$ b. $9\overline{)9401}$ c. $6\overline{)5002}$ d. $6\overline{)3066}$

Part 4 **For each item, make a ratio equation and answer the question.**

a. The recipe called for 2 cups of raisins for every 3 cups of nuts. If there were 120 cups of nuts, how many cups of raisins were there?

b. At Sunnyville, there were 21 sunny days for every 3 cloudy days. How many sunny days would there be for 15 cloudy days?

c. If 3 ounces of paint covered 43 square feet, how many square feet could be covered by 48 ounces?

d. The ratio of hawks to eagles was 7 to 2. There were 420 hawks. How many eagles were there?

Part 5 **Write each value as prime factors multiplied together.**

a. 56 b. 64 c. 72 d. 27

Part 6 **Make a fraction number family for each problem. Box the answers to the questions.**

a. The frost killed $\frac{3}{10}$ of the oranges. What fraction of the oranges did not die?

b. On a car lot, 12 of the cars were yellow and 50 were not yellow. What fraction of the cars were not yellow? What fraction of the cars were yellow?

c. 7 bugs were red. There were 40 bugs in all. What fraction of the bugs were not red? What's the fraction for all the bugs?

Part 7

Copy and complete each equation. If the fractions shown are not equivalent, circle the larger fraction. If the fractions are equivalent, circle the equal sign.

a. $\frac{5}{2}(\blacksquare) = \frac{95}{96}$ b. $\frac{9}{8}(\blacksquare) = \frac{432}{384}$ c. $\frac{3}{7}(\blacksquare) = \frac{48}{105}$

Part J

a. $45\overline{)350}$ 7 $\frac{35}{45}$
−315
35

$45\overline{)350}$

b. $52\overline{)448}$ 9
−468

$52\overline{)448}$ 8 $\frac{32}{52}$
−416
32

c. $38\overline{)210}$ 6
−228

$38\overline{)210}$ 5 $\frac{20}{38}$
−190
20

d. $67\overline{)288}$ 4 $\frac{20}{67}$
−268
20

$67\overline{)288}$

Lesson 58

Part 1

- The perimeter is the distance around a figure. To find the perimeter, you add the length of each side.
- To find the perimeter of this figure, you add:

Figure 1

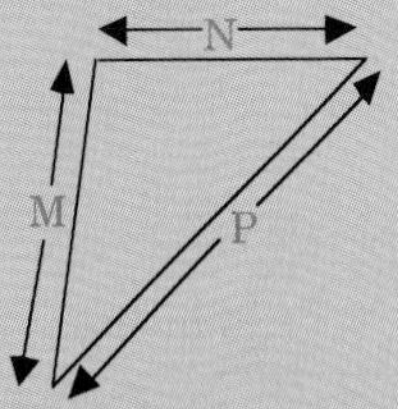

side M
side N
\+ side P

- To find the perimeter of this figure, you add:

Figure 2

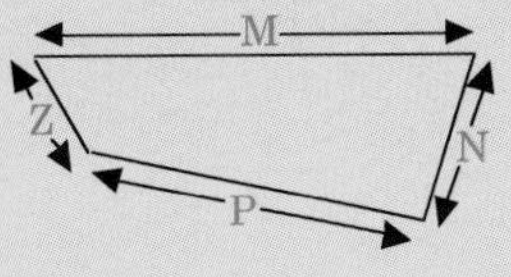

side Z
side M
side N
\+ side P

- Here's a figure with two pairs of opposite sides that are parallel:

Figure 3

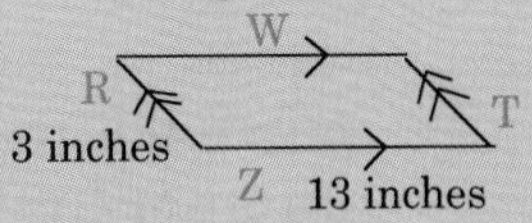

- The lengths of two sides are shown. You can figure out the lengths of the sides that are not shown.
- To figure out the perimeter, you just add the lengths of all sides:
- The perimeter is 32 inches.

$$\begin{array}{r} 3 \\ 3 \\ 13 \\ +\ 13 \\ \hline \boxed{32\text{ inches}} \end{array}$$

Part 2 Find the perimeter of each figure. Remember the unit name.

a.

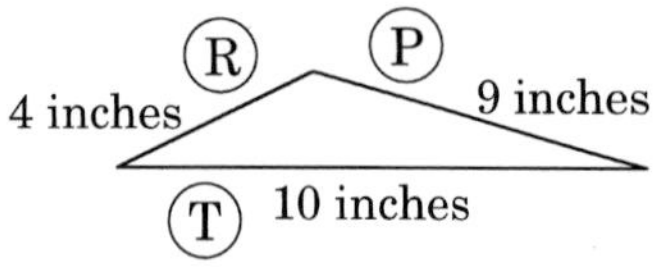

b.

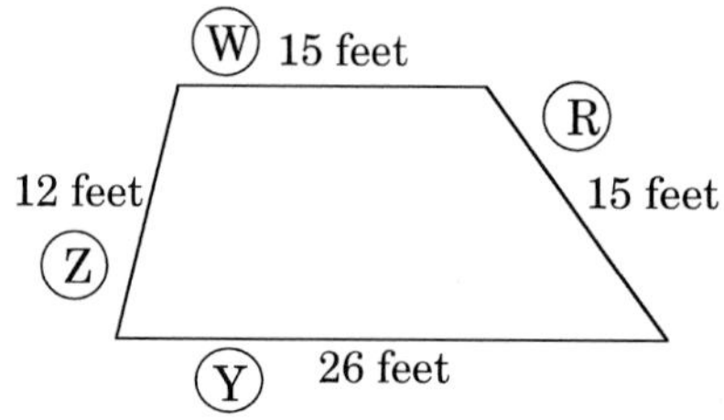

c.

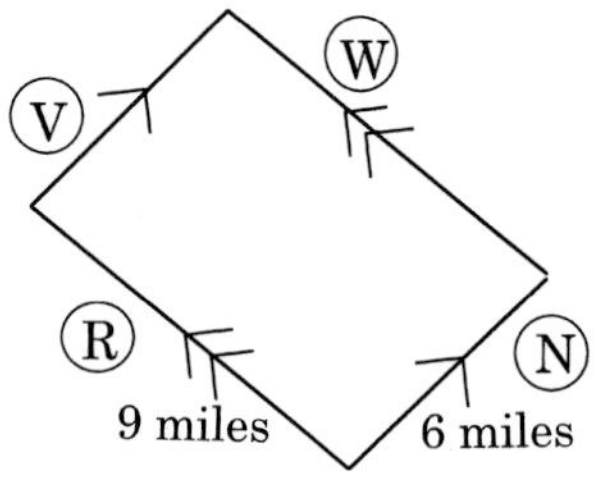

d.

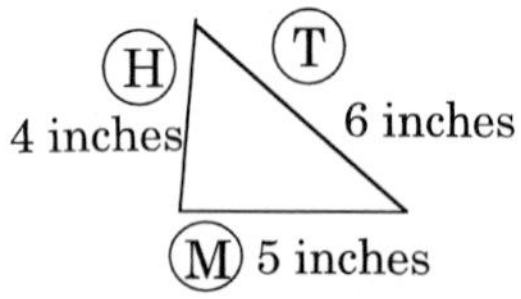

e.

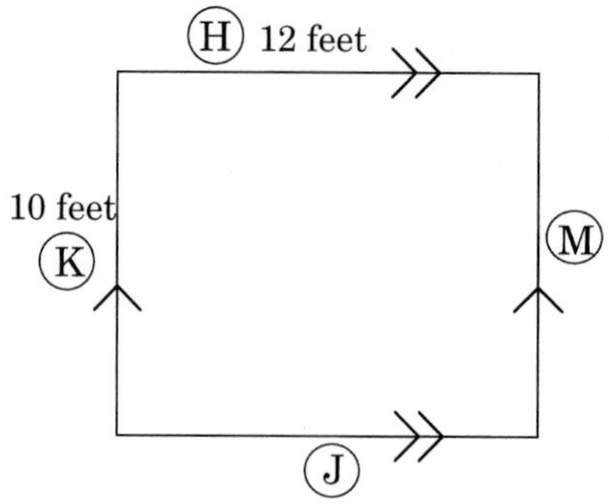

Part 3 For each item, make a ratio table. Answer the questions with a number and unit name.

a. Bernard has 2 U.S. stamps for every 7 foreign stamps. Bernard has 105 foreign stamps.
   1. How many U.S. stamps does he have?
   2. How many stamps does he have in all?

b. In the school library, the ratio of hardback books to paperback books is 5 to 4. There is a total of 7200 books in the library.
   1. How many hardback books are there?
   2. How many paperback books are there?

Part 4 **Write the answer to each question as a whole number or mixed number. Remember the unit name.**

$\frac{\text{pounds}}{\text{dogs}} \quad \frac{\boxed{\frac{145}{3}}}{8}$

a. How many pounds of food did 8 dogs eat?

$\frac{\text{dresses}}{\text{minutes}} \quad \frac{5}{\boxed{\frac{117}{7}}}$

b. How many minutes did it take to make 5 dresses?

$\frac{\text{months}}{\text{houses}} \quad \frac{26}{\boxed{\frac{184}{9}}}$

c. How many houses were built in 26 months?

$\frac{\text{worms}}{\text{cans}} \quad \frac{\boxed{\frac{210}{5}}}{4}$

d. How many worms were in 4 cans?

Part 5 **For each item that is incorrect, copy the problem with an answer 1 more than the whole number shown. Work the problem again.**

a. $25\overline{)190}$ answer $7\frac{15}{25}$; -175; remainder 15

b. $16\overline{)98}$ answer $5\frac{18}{16}$; -80; remainder 18

c. $63\overline{)448}$ answer $6\frac{70}{63}$; -378; remainder 70

d. $35\overline{)297}$ answer $8\frac{17}{35}$; -280; remainder 17

e. $19\overline{)101}$ answer $5\frac{6}{19}$; -95; remainder 6

f. $28\overline{)125}$ answer $3\frac{41}{28}$; -84; remainder 41

Independent Work

Part 6 **Copy and work each problem.**

a. $2\overline{)5036}$ b. $2\overline{)3789}$ c. $8\overline{)1111}$

Part 7 **Write each value as prime factors multiplied together.**

a. 60 b. 50 c. 80 d. 81

Part 8 Copy the table and complete it. Answer the questions.

This table is supposed to show the number of evergreen trees and trees that are not evergreen in two parks.

Facts

1. There are 555 trees that are not evergreen in Glenn Park.
2. In Horace Park, there are 566 evergreen trees.
3. There are 658 trees in Glenn Park.

	Horace Park	Glenn Park	Total
Evergreen			
Not evergreen			
Total			1665

Questions

a. In which park are there more trees?

b. Are there more evergreen trees or trees that are not evergreen?

c. How many trees are in Horace Park?

d. How many evergreen trees are in Glenn Park?

Part 9 Copy and complete the table.

	Fraction	Mixed number
a.		$1\frac{4}{7}$
b.		$3\frac{2}{40}$
c.	$\frac{23}{4}$	
d.	$\frac{16}{13}$	

Part 10 For each problem, make a fraction number family and box the answer to the question.

a. 7 students passed the test. 1 student failed the test. What fraction of the students passed the test?

b. In February, $\frac{3}{28}$ of the days were above freezing. The rest were below freezing. What fraction of the days were below freezing?

Lesson 59

Part 1 **Find the perimeter of each figure. Remember the unit name.**

a.

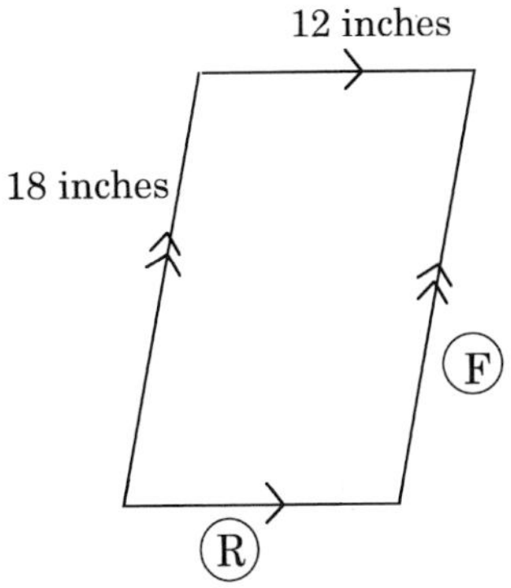

b.

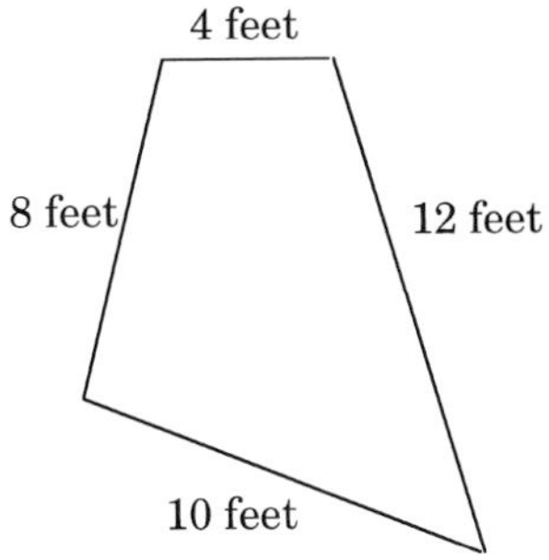

c.

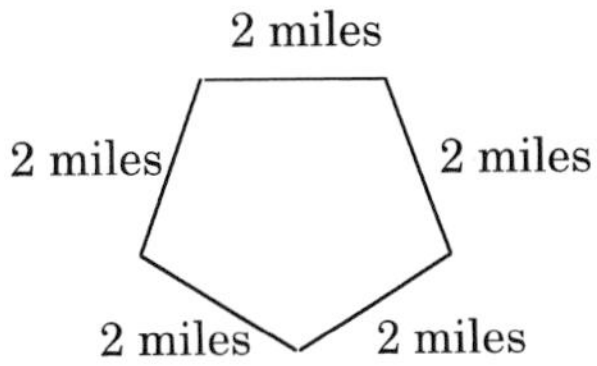

d.

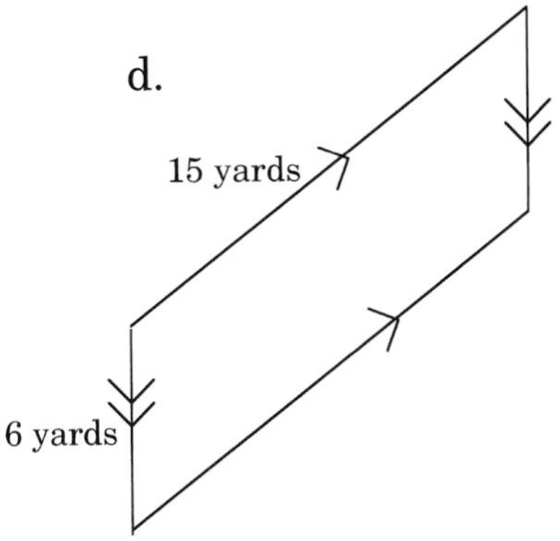

e.

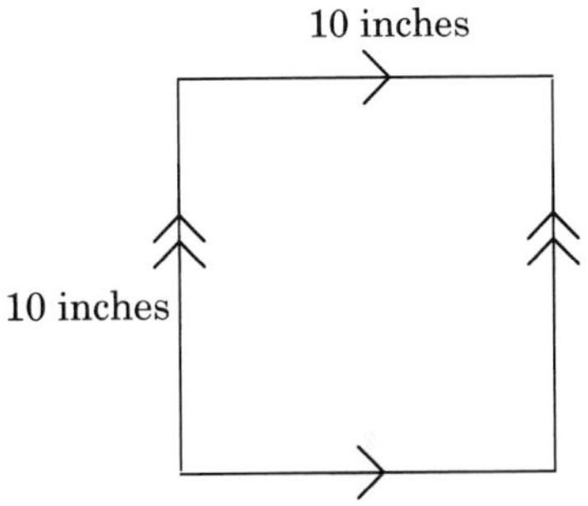

Part 2 **Make a ratio table. Answer the questions in each item.**

a. In Pine Grove, there are pine trees and oak trees. The ratio of pines to oaks is 8 to 3. There are 144 oak trees in the grove.
   1. How many total trees are there?
   2. How many pines are in the grove?

b. Jill collects quarters and dimes. She has 4 quarters for every 3 dimes. She has 96 dimes.
   1. How many quarters does she have?
   2. How many coins does she have in her collection?

Part 3

For each item that is incorrect, copy the problem with an answer 1 more than the whole number shown. Work the problem again.

a. $17\overline{)119}$, answer $6\frac{17}{17}$

$- 102$

17

b. $41\overline{)214}$, answer $4\frac{50}{41}$

$- 164$

50

c. $38\overline{)335}$, answer $8\frac{31}{38}$

$- 304$

31

d. $25\overline{)200}$, answer $7\frac{25}{25}$

$- 175$

25

Part 4

Write the answer to each question as a whole number or mixed number. Remember the unit name.

coins	$\boxed{\frac{612}{3}}$
boxes	9

a. How many coins are in 9 boxes?

buildings	8
windows	$\boxed{\frac{208}{8}}$

b. How many windows are in 8 buildings?

pounds	$\boxed{\frac{627}{5}}$
sacks	1

c. How many pounds are in each sack?

containers	96
gallons	$\boxed{\frac{288}{5}}$

d. How many gallons do 96 containers hold?

Independent Work

Part 5

Make a fraction number family and box the answers to the questions for each item.

a. There are 4 kings in a deck of cards. There are 48 cards that are not kings. What fraction of the cards are kings? What's the fraction for all the cards?

b. There are 32 objects in a bag. 5 of the objects are red. What's the fraction for all the objects in the bag? What's the fraction for the objects that are not red?

c. During an earthquake, 11 people in a building were injured. The rest of the people were not injured. There were 300 people in the building. What fraction of the people were injured? What fraction of people were not injured?

Part 6 Copy and work each problem.

a. $8\overline{)260}$ b. $4\overline{)5430}$ c. $6\overline{)5430}$

Part 7 Make a table to show the x and y values for each point.

	x	y
A	■	■
B	■	■
C	■	■
D	■	■

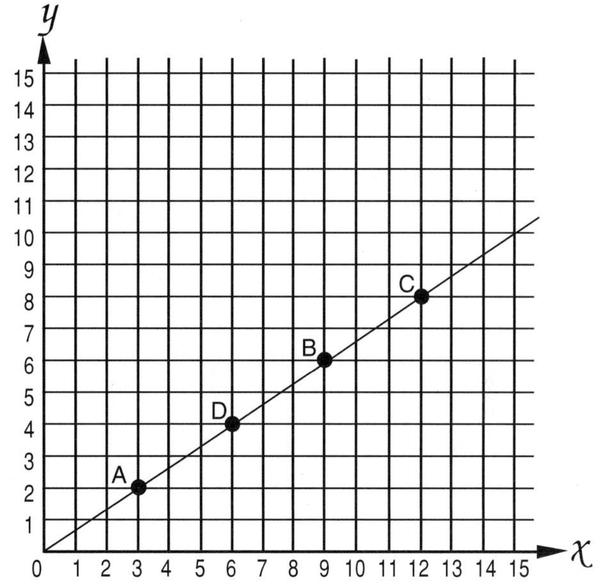

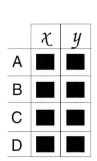

Part 8 For each problem, make a number family and answer the question.

a. The garden had 56 more tomato plants than carrots. There were 96 carrots. How many tomato plants were there?

b. A warehouse had 45 cases of glasses. 126 more cases were delivered to the warehouse. Then 88 cases were removed. Then 18 cases were delivered to the warehouse. How many cases of glasses did the warehouse end up with?

c. Mrs. Monroe was 31 years older than her daughter, Julie. Mrs. Monroe was 47 years old. How old was her daughter?

d. Rita collected stamps. She had 411 fewer U.S. stamps than Canadian stamps. She had 181 U.S. stamps. How many Canadian stamps did she have?

e. An elevator started out with a lot of people in it. At the second floor, 3 people got off. At the third floor, 7 people got off. At the fourth floor, 4 people got off. There were still 5 people on the elevator. How many people did the elevator have to begin with?

Lesson 60

Part 1 **Write the answer to each question as a whole number or a mixed number and unit name.**

$\frac{\text{bottles}}{\text{cartons}}\ \frac{\boxed{\frac{324}{3}}}{9}$ $\qquad$ $\frac{\text{hours}}{\text{feet}}\ \frac{3}{\boxed{\frac{276}{5}}}$ $\qquad$ $\frac{\text{pints}}{\text{containers}}\ \frac{\boxed{\frac{159}{4}}}{7}$

a. How many bottles do 9 cartons hold?

b. How many feet does the snail move in 3 hours?

c. How many pints do 7 containers hold?

Part 2 **Copy and complete each equation. Box the answer.**

a. $\frac{9}{11}\left(\blacksquare\right) = \frac{\blacksquare}{44}$ $\quad$ b. $\frac{5}{6}\left(\blacksquare\right) = \frac{\blacksquare}{7}$ $\quad$ c. $\frac{14}{9}\left(\blacksquare\right) = \frac{\blacksquare}{2}$ $\quad$ d. $\frac{10}{7}\left(\blacksquare\right) = \frac{200}{\blacksquare}$

Test 6

Part 1 **Make a ratio table for each problem. Write complete answers to the questions.**

a. On a ship, there were 6 women for every 5 men. There were 80 men on the ship.
   1. How many adults were on the ship?
   2. How many women were on the ship?

b. The ratio of old buildings to new buildings in a neighborhood was 7 to 4. There were 200 new buildings.
   1. How many total buildings were there in the neighborhood?
   2. How many old buildings were in the neighborhood?

Part 2 **Copy and complete each equation. If the fractions shown are not equivalent, circle the larger fraction. If the fractions are equivalent, circle the equal sign.**

a. $\frac{2}{3}(■) = \frac{18}{33}$ b. $\frac{5}{8}(■) = \frac{55}{88}$ c. $\frac{3}{7}(■) = \frac{75}{168}$

Part 3 **For each item, make a fraction number family and box the answers to the questions.**

a. There were 15 dirty cars and 8 clean cars.
   1. What fraction of the cars were dirty?
   2. What fraction of the cars were clean?

b. $\frac{4}{5}$ of the cars had snow tires.
   1. What fraction of the cars did not have snow tires?
   2. What's the fraction for all the cars?

Part 4 **Copy each problem and multiply. If the answer is too big, rework the problem with the right answer. Write the answer to the division problem as a mixed number.**

a. $13\overline{)98}$ with 7 written above

b. $51\overline{)400}$ with 8 written above

Part 5 **Write the x and y values for each point shown on the coordinate system.**

A $x =$ ■, $y =$ ■

B $x =$ ■, $y =$ ■

C $x =$ ■, $y =$ ■

D $x =$ ■, $y =$ ■

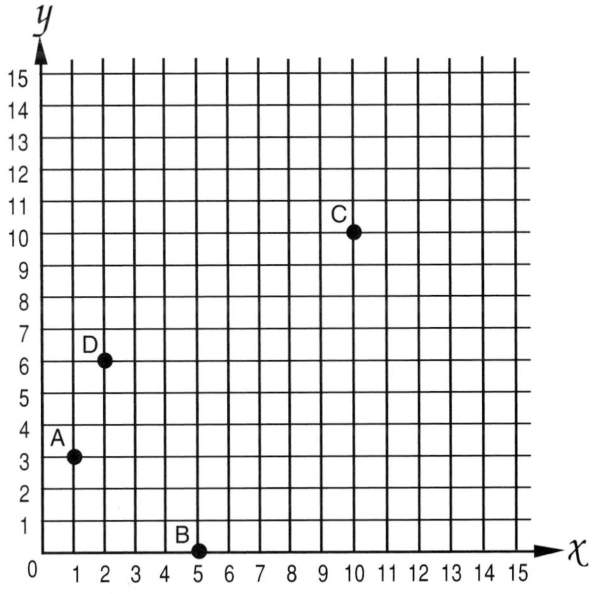

Lesson 61

Part 1

For each item that is incorrect, copy the problem with an answer one more than the whole number shown. Work the problem again.

a. $$\begin{array}{r} 9\frac{25}{26} \\ 26\overline{)259} \\ -\underline{234} \\ 25 \end{array}$$

b. $$\begin{array}{r} 5\frac{17}{17} \\ 17\overline{)102} \\ -\underline{\ \ 85} \\ 17 \end{array}$$

c. $$\begin{array}{r} 7\frac{50}{48} \\ 48\overline{)386} \\ -\underline{336} \\ 50 \end{array}$$

d. $$\begin{array}{r} 7\frac{31}{37} \\ 37\overline{)290} \\ -\underline{259} \\ 31 \end{array}$$

e. $$\begin{array}{r} 5\frac{75}{62} \\ 62\overline{)385} \\ -\underline{310} \\ 75 \end{array}$$

f. $$\begin{array}{r} 8\frac{20}{19} \\ 19\overline{)172} \\ -\underline{152} \\ 20 \end{array}$$

Part 2

Make a ratio table. Answer the questions in each item. Write your answer as a number and a unit name.

a. Andy seals boxes. Andy seals 3 red boxes for every 7 blue boxes. Last week, Andy sealed a total of 650 boxes.
   1. How many red boxes did he seal?
   2. How many blue boxes did he seal?

b. On Maple Street, the ratio of older cars to newer cars is 2 to 7. There were 810 cars on Maple Street.
   1. How many were older cars?
   2. How many were newer cars?

Part 3

Find the perimeter of each figure.

a.
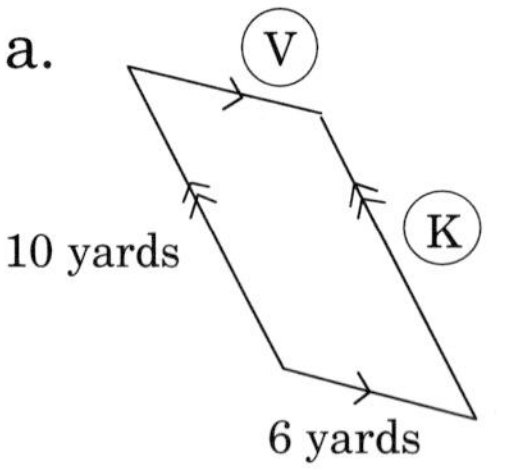

b.
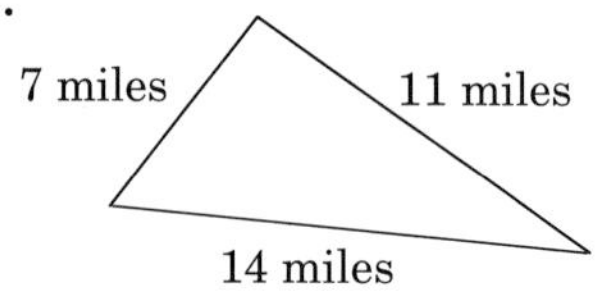

c.
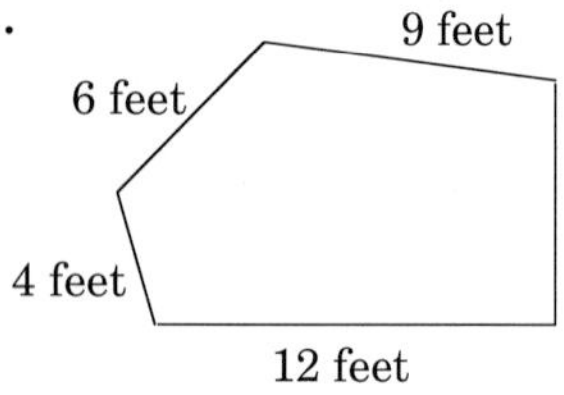

d.
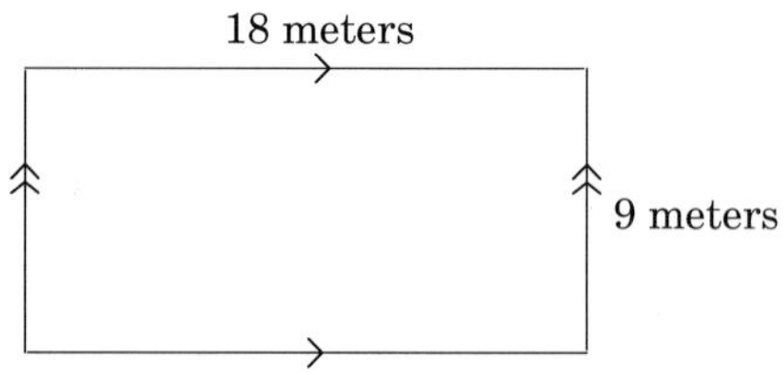

Part 4 For each item, make a ratio equation. Answer the question the problem asks.

a. There were 9 bees for every 2 flowers. There were 20 flowers. How many bees were there?

b. There were 2 wasps for every 14 flowers. There were 9 wasps. How many flowers were there?

c. A recipe uses 3 pints of milk for every 13 eggs. How many pints of milk are needed for 5 eggs?

d. A factory makes 11 gloves every 3 seconds. How many gloves will the factory make in 27 seconds?

Independent Work

Part 5 Copy and work each problem. If the answer can be simplifed, simplify it. If the simplified fraction is more than 1, write it as a mixed number.

a. $\frac{4}{3} \times \frac{1}{3} =$ ■

b. $7 \times \frac{5}{8} =$ ■

c. $\frac{27}{50} + \frac{13}{50} =$ ■

d. $\frac{4}{3} + \frac{1}{3} =$ ■

e. $\frac{4}{5} - \frac{4}{5} =$ ■

f. $\frac{5}{3} \times 20 =$ ■

Part 6 Copy and complete the table.

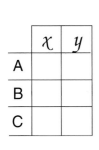

	x	y
A		
B		
C		

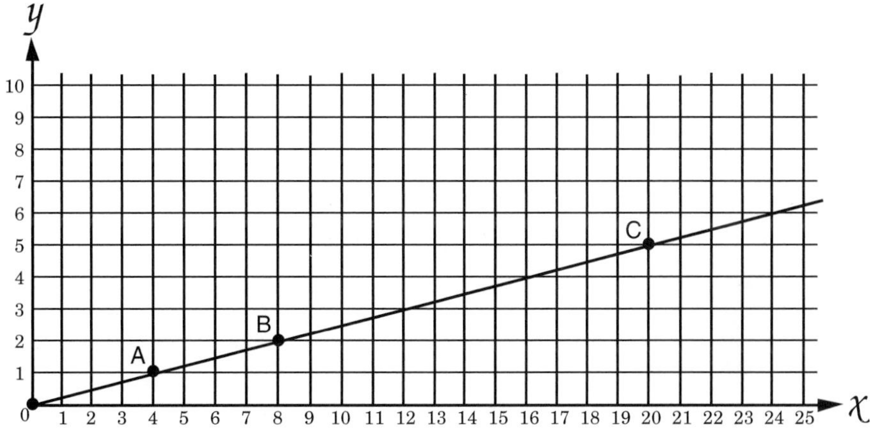

Part 7 **For each problem, make a number family and answer the questions.**

a. There were 8 white hamsters and 71 hamsters that were not white.
   1. What was the fraction of hamsters that were white?
   2. What was the fraction for all the hamsters?

b. $\frac{3}{57}$ of the students in Hays School were twins.
   1. What fraction of the students were not twins?
   2. What was the fraction for all the students?

c. 41 of the people on a boat were passengers. The rest of the people on the boat were crew members. There was a total of 58 people on the boat.
   1. What fraction of the people were crew members?
   2. What fraction of the people were not crew members?

d. Al weighed 41 pounds less than his father weighed. Al's father weighed 210 pounds. How much did Al weigh?

e. A car lot had new cars and used cars. There were 56 more used cars than new cars. There were 45 new cars. How many used cars were on the lot?

f. Jan ran 560 yards farther than Tom ran. Jan ran 3000 yards. How far did Tom run?

Part 8 **Write the complete equation for each item.**

a. $4 = \frac{■}{60}$ b. $8 = \frac{■}{3}$ c. $9 = \frac{■}{9}$ d. $2 = \frac{■}{113}$

Lesson 62

Part 1 **Make a ratio table. Answer the questions in each item. Write your answer as a number and a unit name.**

a. In a mixture, the ratio of sand to water is 3 to 8. The mixture weighs 44 pounds.
   1. How much does the water weigh?
   2. How much does the sand weigh?

b. In Greenville, there are 3 people who wear glasses to every 7 people who do not wear glasses. There are 210 people who wear glasses in Greenville.
   1. How many people are there in Greenville?
   2. How many people do not wear glasses?

Part 2

- You can figure out the number of squares in rectangles on the coordinate system.
- Here's the equation you use: **squares = x x y**

- Here's a rectangle on the the coordinate system:
- The x value is 3. The y value is 6.
- If you multiply 3 x 6, you'll know the number of squares in the rectangle.

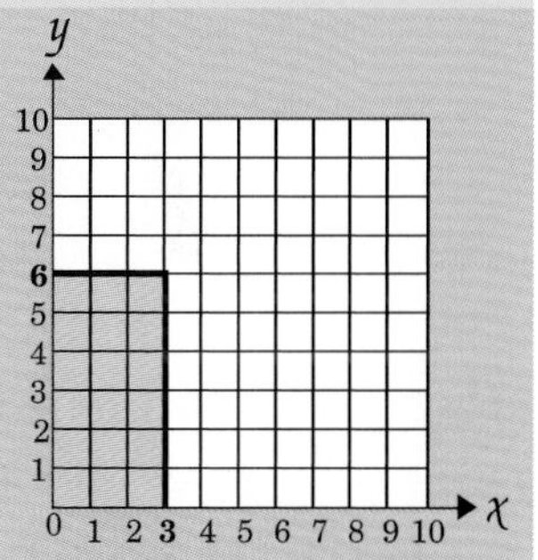

squares = x x y

- Here's another rectangle:
- What's the x value?
- What's the y value?
- What's x x y?

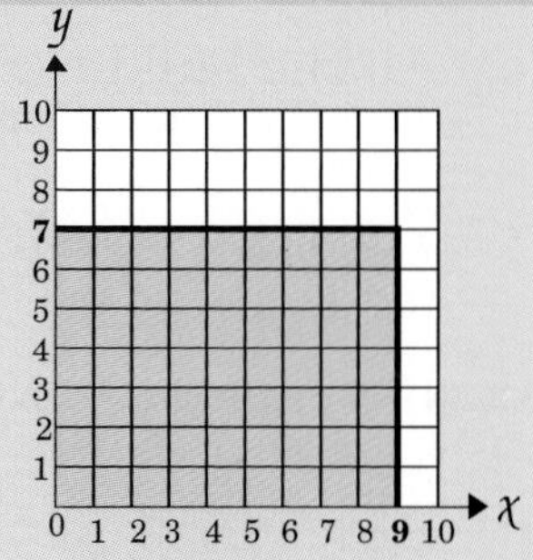

squares = x x y

Part 3

For each item, first write the equation: squares = x x y. Below, write the equation with numbers for x and y. Figure out the number of squares.

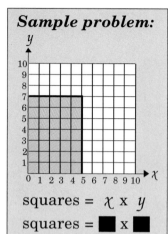

Sample problem:

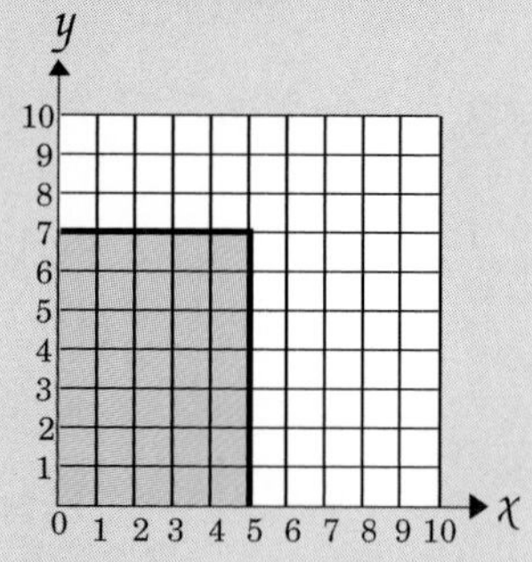

squares = x x y

squares = [redacted] x [redacted]

a.

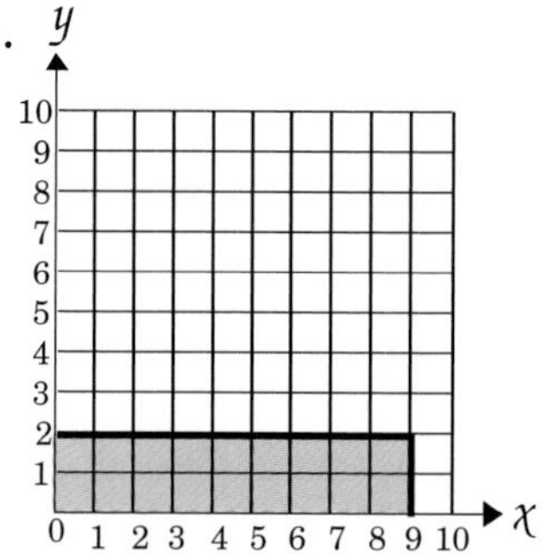

b.

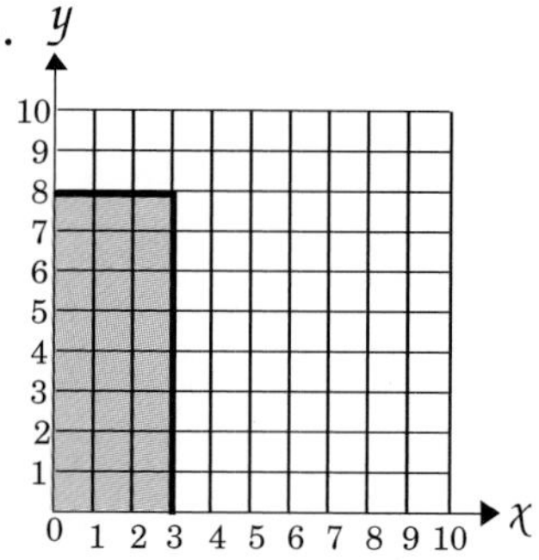

Part 4

Copy and work each problem.

a. $\frac{11}{3} - \frac{6}{3} =$ [redacted]

b. $\frac{5}{9} + \frac{5}{9} =$ [redacted]

c. $\frac{10}{2} - \frac{7}{2} =$ [redacted]

d. $\frac{15}{6} - \frac{10}{6} =$ [redacted]

Part 5

For each item, make a ratio equation. Answer the question the problem asks.

a. If a train travels 12 meters in 5 seconds, how far will the train travel in 3 seconds?

b. All the buildings in Sametown are the same. There are 9 windows in each building. There are 54 buildings. How many windows are there?

c. The ratio of frogs to toads is 7 to 6. If there are 42 frogs, how many toads are there?

d. If 5 cans weigh 3 pounds, how many pounds do 11 cans weigh?

Part 6

- Here are rules for answers to division problems:

- If you can't subtract, the whole number in the answer is too big.

$$\begin{array}{r} \textcircled{7} \\ 24\overline{)155} \\ -168 \end{array} \xrightarrow{\text{Make the number smaller.}} \begin{array}{r} 6 \\ 24\overline{)155} \end{array}$$

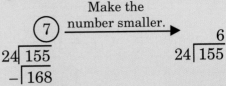

- If you get a fraction that is less than 1, the answer is correct.

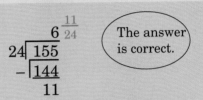

$$\begin{array}{r} 6\frac{11}{24} \\ 24\overline{)155} \\ -\underline{144} \\ 11 \end{array}$$

The answer is correct.

- If you get a fraction that equals 1 or more than 1, make the whole number in the answer bigger.

$$\begin{array}{r} 5\frac{35}{24} \\ 24\overline{)155} \\ -\underline{120} \\ 35 \end{array} \xrightarrow{\text{Make the whole number bigger.}} \begin{array}{r} 6 \\ 24\overline{)155} \end{array}$$

Independent Work

Part 7

Show the prime factors for each number.

a. 88 b. 46 c. 74 d. 30

Part 8

For each problem, make a number family and answer the questions.

a. There were 39 baskets. 7 were red. The rest were not red.
1. What fraction of the baskets were red?
2. What fraction of the baskets were not red?

b. At a club, $\frac{12}{17}$ of the boys were under 6 feet tall.
1. What fraction of the boys were at least 6 feet tall?
2. What is the fraction for all the boys?

Part 9 **Copy and complete the table.**

	Fraction	Mixed number
a.		$2\frac{3}{10}$
b.		$1\frac{7}{8}$
c.		$5\frac{7}{9}$
d.	$\frac{56}{55}$	
e.	$\frac{90}{4}$	
f.	$\frac{100}{3}$	

Part 10 **Copy and work each item.**

a. $6\overline{)568}$

b. $3\overline{)4567}$

c. $4\overline{)4567}$

Part 11 **For each problem, make a number family and answer the question.**

a. On Monday, Gate's Store started with $443 and spent $350. On Tuesday, the store spent $521 and received $482. On Wednesday, the store spent $119 and received $802. How much money did the store have at the end of the three-day period?

b. A mail truck delivered packages and picked up packages. The truck started out with 861 packages. At the first stop, the truck dropped off 68 packages. At the next stop, the truck dropped off 11 packages and picked up 143 packages. At the next stop, the truck dropped off 429 packages and picked up 95 packages. At the last stop, the truck dropped off 511 packages. How many packages did the truck still have?

c. Another mail truck started out with 350 packages and picked up 11 packages at one stop. The truck picked up 49 packages at another stop. The truck dropped off packages at different stops. The truck ended up with 71 packages. How many packages did it drop off?

Part J

a. $\frac{11}{3} - \frac{6}{3} = \frac{5}{3}$

b. $\frac{5}{9} + \frac{5}{9} = \frac{10}{9}$

c. $\frac{10}{2} - \frac{7}{2} = \frac{3}{2}$

d. $\frac{15}{6} - \frac{10}{6} = \frac{5}{6}$

Lesson 63

Part 1 **For each item, make a ratio equation and answer the question.**

a. A recipe uses 2 potatoes for every 3 cups of onions. How many cups of onions are needed for 40 potatoes?

b. If Mary runs at the rate of 11 yards every 5 seconds, how many yards would she travel in 45 seconds?

c. If it takes 4 hours to assemble 3 desks, how many desks could be assembled in 9 hours?

Part 2 **For each rectangle, first write the equation. Then figure out the number of squares.**

a.

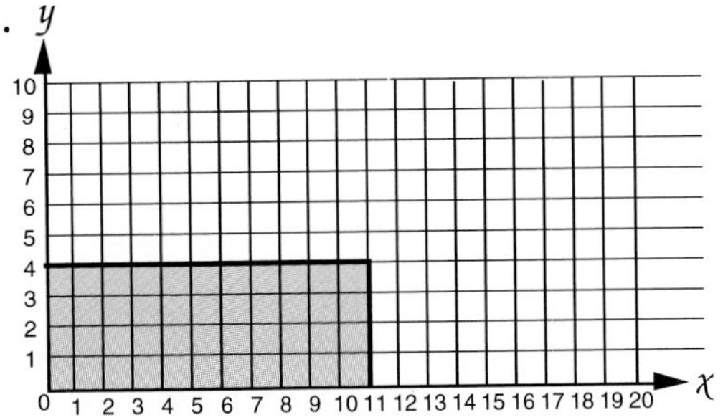

b.

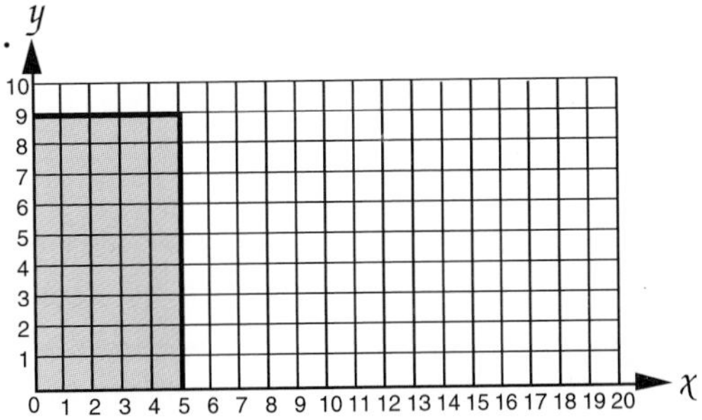

c.

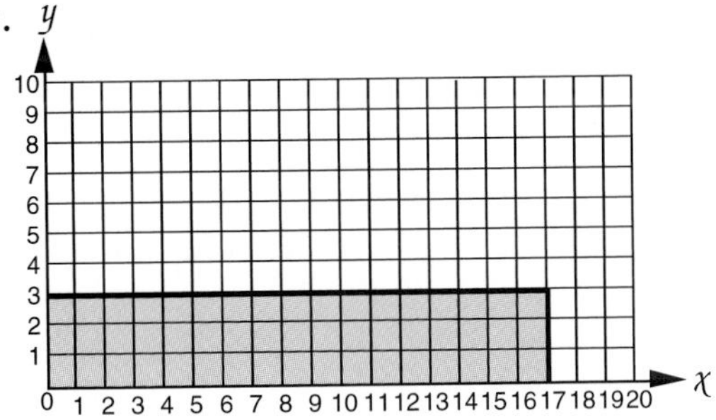

Part 3 **Make a ratio table. Answer the questions. Write your answer as a number and a unit name.**

At Randolph School, the ratio of boys to girls is 4 to 9. There are 728 students in the school.

1. How many girls are there?
2. How many boys are there?

Independent Work

Part 4 **Write the prime factors for each number.**

a. 99 b. 24 c. 54 d. 26 e. 80

Part 5 **Make a table to show the x and y values for each point.**

	x	y
A	■	■
B	■	■
C	■	■
D	■	■

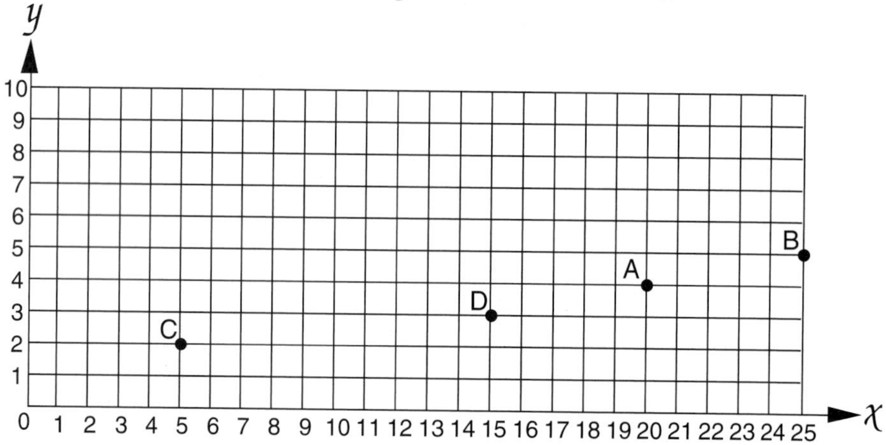

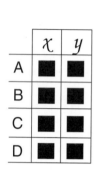

Part 6 **Make a fraction number family for each word problem. Box the answers to the questions the problem asks.**

a. In a park were 27 dogs. 21 dogs had collars. What fraction of the dogs did not have collars? What fraction of the dogs did have collars?

b. A coin store had 26 rare coins that were old and 142 rare coins that were new. What's the fraction for all the coins? What fraction of the coins were new?

c. On the first day of March, $\frac{3}{14}$ of the trees in the park had buds. What fraction of trees did not have buds? What's the fraction for all the trees?

Part 7 **Copy and work each problem.**

a. $3\overline{)8800}$ b. $5\overline{)2300}$ c. $7\overline{)5100}$ d. $2\overline{)5100}$

Part 8 For each problem, make a number family and answer the question.

a. The cost of the dinner was \$4.49 more than the cost of lunch. The cost of lunch was \$3.63. How much was dinner?

b. The rock weighed 508 pounds less than the truck. The truck weighed 5560 pounds. How much did the rock weigh?

c. A plane traveled 817 feet per second faster than a bird traveled. The plane traveled 823 feet per second. How fast did the bird travel?

If that plane was going 817 feet per second faster than I was going, and if my power pack can make me go as fast as that plane, how many feathers will I have left when I stop?

Part J

a. $64\overline{)328}$: 6; −384 — 5; −320; 8; $5\frac{8}{64}$

b. $37\overline{)180}$: 4; −148; 42; $4\frac{42}{37}$ — 5; −185; $5\frac{5}{37}$

c. $42\overline{)243}$: 6; −252 — 5; −210; 33; $5\frac{33}{42}$

d. $16\overline{)130}$: 7; −112; 18; $7\frac{18}{16}$ — 8; −128; 2; $8\frac{2}{16}$

Lesson 64

Part 1

- You've worked with fraction number families that have a big number of 1.
- Here's a fact about those families:

  The numerators of the fractions are ratio numbers.

- Here's a number family with a big number of 1:

  ripe $\frac{6}{11}$ **not ripe** $\frac{5}{11}$ → **berries** $\frac{11}{11}$

- The numerators are 6, 5 and 11. Those are ratio numbers.
- The ratio of ripe berries to not ripe berries is 6 to 5.
- The ratio of ripe berries to total berries is 6 to 11.
- The ratio of not ripe berries to total berries is 5 to 11.

	ratio	
ripe	6	
not ripe	5	
berries	11	

- Here's a ratio problem that tells about a fraction:

  <u>In a factory, $\frac{3}{5}$ of the employees were women. The rest were men.</u> There were 890 employees. How many employees were men?

- For the underlined sentences, we can make a fraction number family. The fraction for women is $\frac{3}{5}$. The big number is all of the employees. That's 1.

  women $\frac{3}{5}$ **men** → **employees** 1

- Here's the family with all the fractions:

  women $\frac{3}{5}$ **men** $\frac{2}{5}$ → **employees** $\frac{5}{5}$

- The numerators show ratio numbers. So you can put them in the first column of a ratio table.
- You put in the number you know for the second column. **There were 890 employees.**
- Now you can figure out the missing numbers in the table.

	ratio	
women	3	
men	2	
employees	5	890

Part 2 Make a fraction number family and ratio table. Answer the questions.

a. There were used cars and new cars on a lot. $\frac{3}{7}$ of the cars were used. There were 64 new cars on the lot.
   1. How many used cars were on the lot?
   2. How many total cars were on the lot?

b. A laboratory made a mixture of sulphur and water. $\frac{4}{5}$ of the mixture was sulphur. The rest was water. The total mixture weighed 180 pounds.
   1. How many pounds of sulphur were in the mixture?
   2. How many pounds of water were in the mixture?

c. $\frac{5}{8}$ of the corn harvest was used for cornmeal. The rest was canned. This year 93 tons of corn was canned.
   1. How much corn was made into cornmeal?
   2. What was the weight of the total corn harvest?

Part 3 For each rectangle, first write the equation. Then figure out the number of squares.

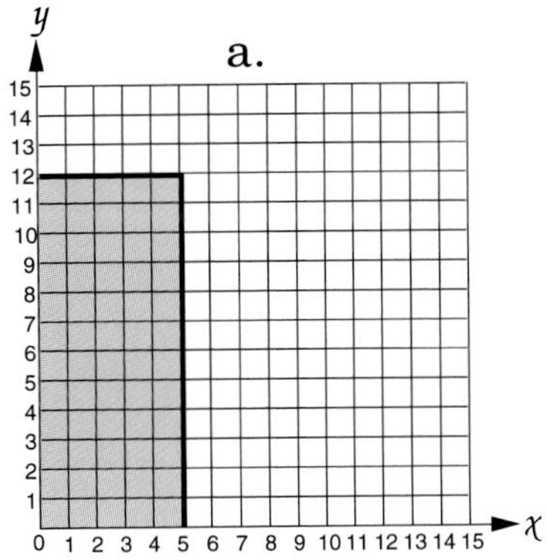

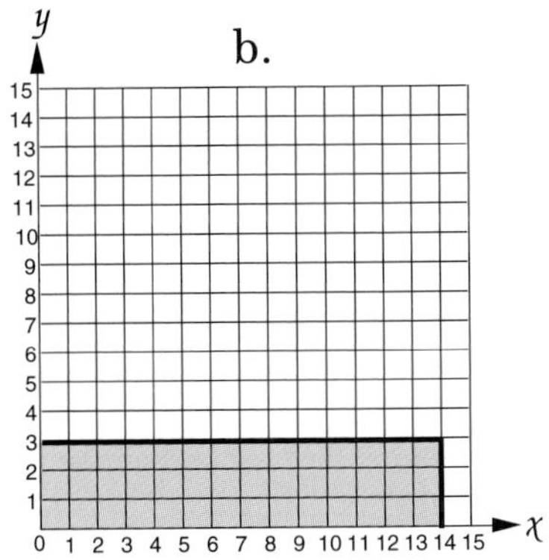

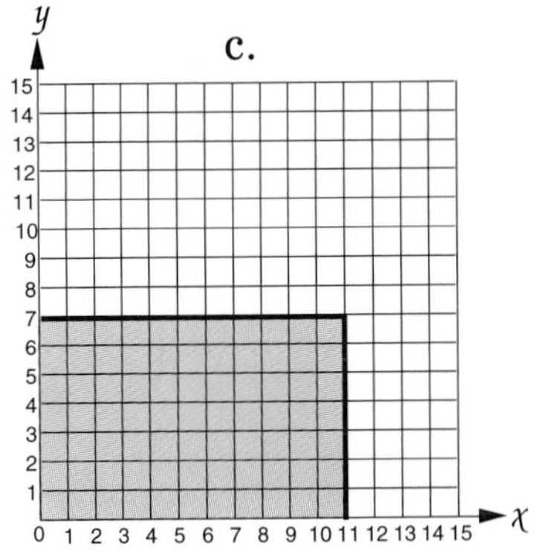

Part 4

Copy each problem. Rewrite each problem with the whole number shown as a fraction and work it.

a. $3 + \frac{5}{9}$

b. $1 - \frac{11}{12}$

c. $\frac{11}{7} + 5$

Independent Work

Part 5

Copy the table and complete it. Answer the questions.

This table is supposed to show the pints of red paint and white paint used in two different camps.

Questions

a. Which camp used more white paint?

b. Were more pints of red paint used in Blaze Camp or in Quiet Camp?

c. What was the total amount of paint used in both the camps?

d. How many total pints of paint were used in Blaze Camp?

	Red	White	Total
Blaze Camp		42	
Quiet Camp	14		219
Total	190		

Part 6

Copy and work each problem.

a. $9\overline{)5099}$ b. $8\overline{)5099}$ c. $6\overline{)5099}$

Part 7

For each item, make a ratio equation and answer the question. Write the answer as a whole number or a mixed number.

a. The ratio of ducks to geese was 7 to 6. If there were 84 ducks, how many geese were there?

b. If a machine made 5 nails in 11 seconds, how many seconds would it take for the machine to make 3 nails?

c. During February, a snow machine covered a ski area at the rate of 6 inches of snow every 5 days. How many inches of snow covered the area in 18 days?

d. In 5 minutes, Jan picked 3 pounds of berries. How long would it take her to pick 20 pounds of berries?

Part 8

Copy and work each problem.

a. 450×18

b. $450 - 18$

c. $4090 - 2111$

Part 9

Copy and complete each equation. If the fractions shown are not equivalent, circle the larger fraction. If the fractions are equivalent, circle the equal sign.

a. $\frac{7}{8}(\blacksquare) = \frac{70}{64}$ b. $\frac{8}{5}(\blacksquare) = \frac{88}{60}$ c. $\frac{4}{7}(\blacksquare) = \frac{80}{140}$

Part J

a. $28\overline{)169}$ — quotient $5\frac{29}{28}$; -140; 29
$28\overline{)169}$ — quotient $6\frac{1}{28}$; -168; 1

b. $42\overline{)345}$ — quotient 9; -378
$42\overline{)345}$ — quotient $8\frac{9}{42}$; -336; 9

c. $37\overline{)140}$ — quotient 4; -148
$37\overline{)140}$ — quotient $3\frac{29}{37}$; -111; 29

Lesson 65

Part 1

Make a fraction number family and ratio table. Answer the questions.

a. $\frac{2}{9}$ of the trees in the park were evergreens. The rest were not evergreens. There were 405 trees in the park.

1. How many trees were evergreens?
2. How many trees were not evergreens?

b. $\frac{1}{8}$ of the men wore suspenders. The rest didn't wear suspenders. There were 126 men who did not wear suspenders.

1. How many men wore suspenders?
2. How many men were there in all?

Part 2

For each item, figure out the first common number. Write it as the answer to both problems. Then complete the problems.

a. 6 x ■ = ■
8 x ■ = ■

b. 4 x ■ = ■
8 x ■ = ■

c. 6 x ■ = ■
4 x ■ = ■

Part 3

Copy and work each problem. Rewrite the problem if you need to.

a. $\frac{7}{5} - \frac{5}{5}$

b. $1 - \frac{3}{8}$

c. $\frac{9}{10} + 4$

d. $\frac{13}{9} + \frac{6}{9}$

Part 4 For each rectangle, first write the equation for figuring out the number of squares. Below, write the equation with numbers for x and y. Figure out the number of squares.

a. 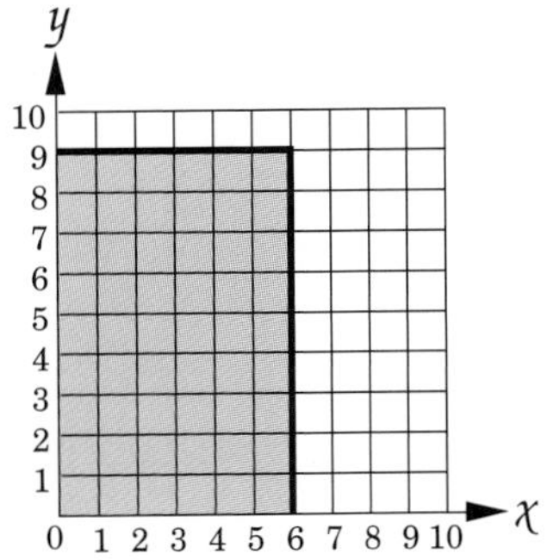

b. 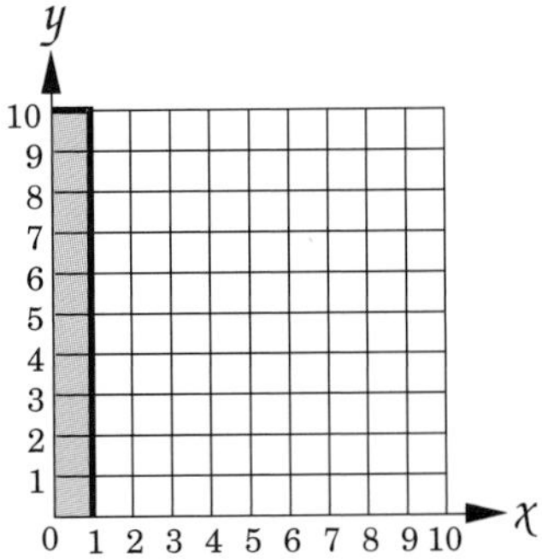

c. 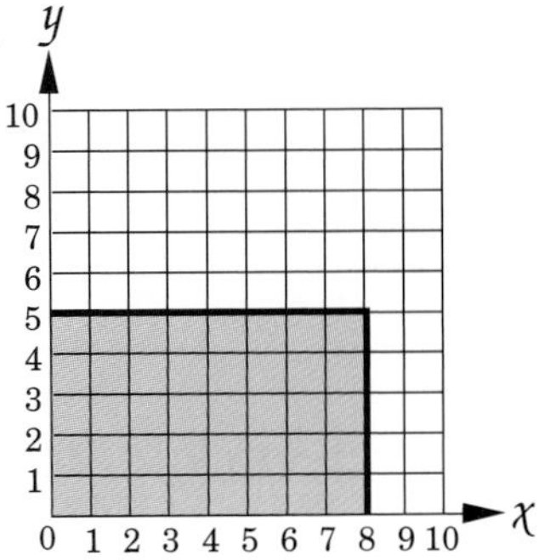

Independent Work

Part 5 Copy and work each problem.

a. $4 \times \frac{5}{6} = \blacksquare$

b. $6 - \frac{1}{10} = \blacksquare$

c. $\frac{15}{2} - 3 = \blacksquare$

d. $6 \times \frac{4}{5} = \blacksquare$

e. $\frac{5}{8} \times \frac{1}{8} = \blacksquare$

f. $\frac{5}{8} - \frac{1}{8} = \blacksquare$

Part 6 Copy and work each problem.

a. $8\overline{)3254}$

b. $8\overline{)9276}$

c. $2\overline{)9276}$

Part 7 Copy and complete each equation. If the fractions are not equivalent, circle the larger fraction. If the fractions are equivalent, circle the equal sign.

a. $\frac{4}{7}\left(\blacksquare\right) = \frac{20}{35}$

b. $\frac{2}{9}\left(\blacksquare\right) = \frac{40}{180}$

c. $\frac{9}{5}\left(\blacksquare\right) = \frac{180}{60}$

d. $\frac{7}{8}\left(\blacksquare\right) = \frac{112}{120}$

Part 8

For each item, make a ratio equation and answer the question. Write the answer as a whole number or a mixed number.

a. A work team makes 4 feet of highway every 3 hours. How long would it take the team to make 35 feet of highway?

b. The park has 7 bushes for every 2 trees. The park has 50 trees. How many bushes are there?

c. The ratio of fleas to spiders is 9 to 7. There are 126 fleas. How many spiders are there?

d. If it takes 3 years for a tree to grow 5 feet, how many feet will the tree grow in 11 years?

Part 9

Write the complete equation for each item.

a. $4 = \frac{■}{20}$ b. $6 = \frac{■}{3}$ c. $18 = \frac{■}{4}$ d. $5 = \frac{■}{120}$

Part J

a. $62\overline{)228}$ 4, −248; $62\overline{)228}$ 3, −186, 42, $3\frac{42}{62}$

b. $28\overline{)170}$ 5, −140, 30, $5\frac{30}{28}$; $28\overline{)170}$ 6, −168, 2, $6\frac{2}{28}$

c. $94\overline{)677}$ 6, −564, 113, $6\frac{113}{94}$; $94\overline{)677}$ 7, −658, 19, $7\frac{19}{94}$

Lesson 66

Part 1

- You're going to round 2-digit numbers to the nearest **ten.**

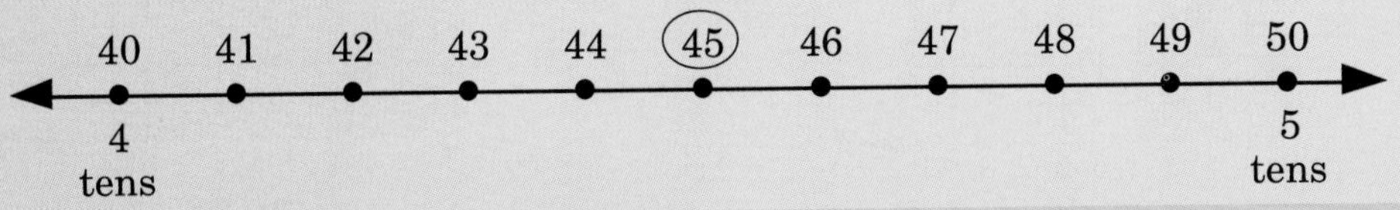

- Some numbers are closer to 4 tens.

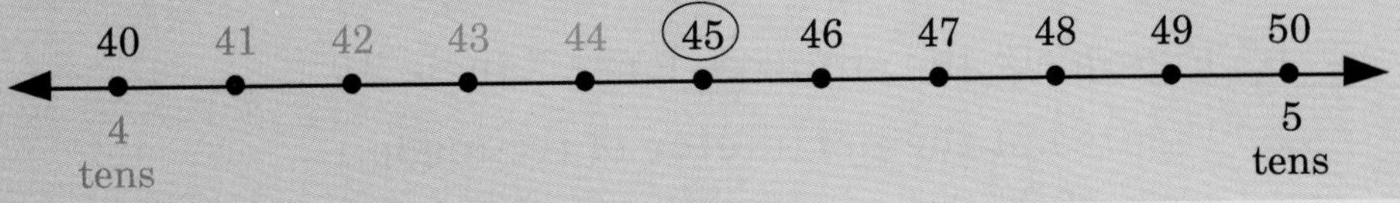

- Some numbers are closer to 5 tens.

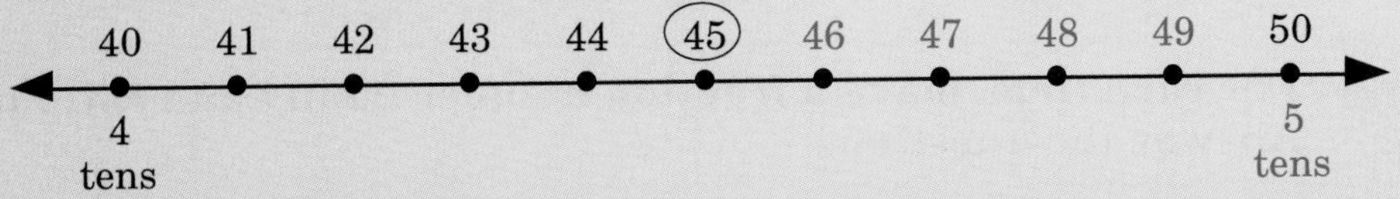

- 45 is in the middle. But we'll always round up if the second digit is 5. So 45 rounds to 5 tens.

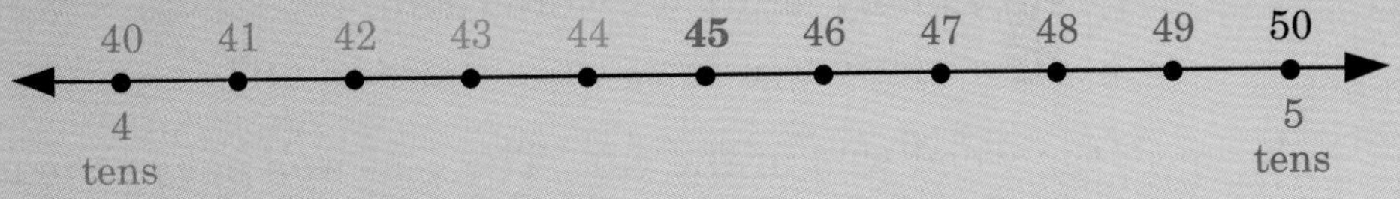

Part 2

For each item, write the number of tens each value rounds to.

a. 47 b. 82 c. 15 d. 36 e. 53

Part 3 **Work each item. Remember the unit name.**

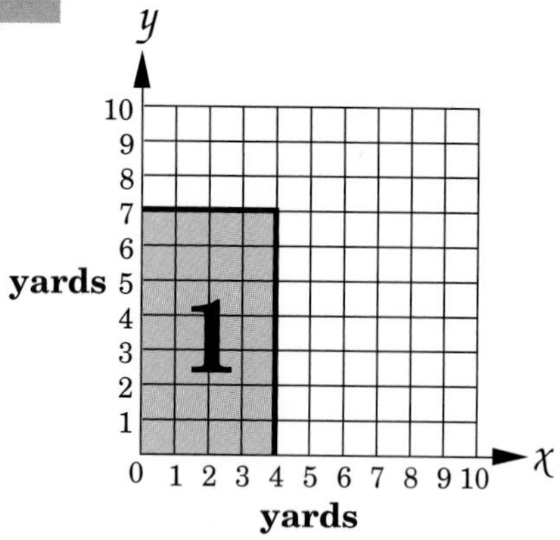

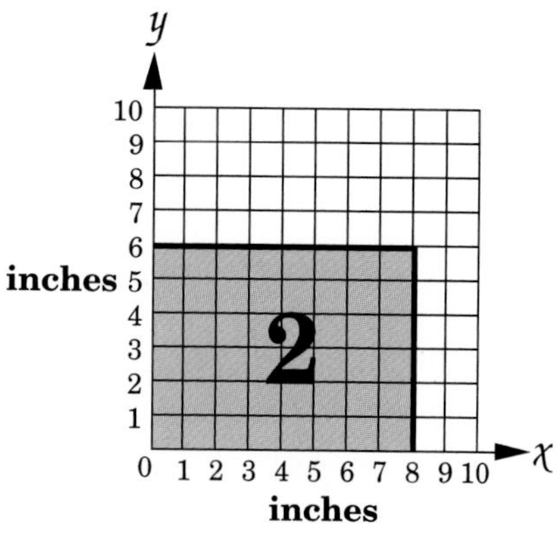

a. Figure out the **squares** for rectangle 1.

b. Figure out the **squares** for rectangle 2.

c. Figure out the **perimeter** of rectangle 1.

d. Figure out the **perimeter** of rectangle 2.

Part 4 **For each item, make a fraction number family and ratio table. Answer the questions.**

a. In a building, $\frac{5}{8}$ of the windows were dirty. There were 555 dirty windows.
   1. How many windows were clean?
   2. How many windows were there in all?

b. $\frac{3}{5}$ of the wood was in the car. The rest was not in the car. There were 327 pounds of wood in the car.
   1. How many pounds were not in the car?
   2. How many pounds were there in all?

Independent Work

Part 5 **Copy each problem. Rewrite the whole number. Copy the fraction and the sign. Then work the problem.**

a. $6 + \frac{7}{3}$

b. $4 - \frac{5}{6}$

c. $\frac{25}{8} - 2$

d. $\frac{4}{7} + 5$

Part 6 **Make a table. Answer the questions.**

Squirrels and foxes lived in Blue Ridge Park and Mountain Park. The total number of squirrels in both parks was 240. 51 foxes lived in Mountain Park. The total number of squirrels and foxes in Blue Ridge Park was 188. 57 squirrels lived in Blue Ridge Park.

a. How many squirrels lived in Mountain Park?

b. What is the total number of foxes and squirrels in both places?

c. Which park had more squirrels?

Part 7 **Copy each problem and multiply. Rewrite each problem with the correct answer and work it.**

a. $36\overline{)285}$ with 8 above

b. $55\overline{)275}$ with 4 above

c. $23\overline{)133}$ with 6 above

d. $47\overline{)220}$ with 5 above

Part 8 **Answer the question each problem asks.**

a. Ray is 32 inches shorter than Mike. If Mike is 68 inches tall, how many inches tall is Ray?

b. There were 247 monkeys in a zoo. There were 129 fewer tigers than monkeys. How many tigers were there?

c. There are 94 birds in John's pet shop. If John's shop has 88 more birds than Dave's shop, how many birds are in Dave's shop?

Part 9 **Copy and complete this equation.**

$$7 = \frac{\blacksquare}{5} = \frac{\blacksquare}{11} = \frac{\blacksquare}{66} = \frac{\blacksquare}{25}$$

Lesson 67

Part 1 **For each problem, make a ratio table and answer the questions.**

a. $\frac{4}{9}$ of the workers in a factory wore glasses. 76 workers wore glasses.
   1. How many workers did not wear glasses?
   2. How many workers were there in all?

b. There was a mixture of sand and cement. The ratio of sand to cement was 7 to 2. The whole mixture weighed 342 pounds.
   1. How many pounds of sand were in the mixture?
   2. How many pounds of cement were in the mixture?

c. $\frac{3}{8}$ of the students in the school had chicken pox. 125 students did not have chicken pox.
   1. How many students had chicken pox?
   2. How many students were there in all?

Part 2 **For each item, write the number of tens each value rounds to.**

a. 86 b. 44 c. 35 d. 73 e. 27

Part 3 **Copy and complete each item. Show the first common number as the answer for both problems.**

a. 4 x ■ = ■
   6 x ■ = ■

b. 10 x ■ = ■
   5 x ■ = ■

c. 6 x ■ = ■
   9 x ■ = ■

Part 4

- You've worked addition and subtraction problems that have a whole number and a fraction.

$$\begin{array}{r} 3 \\ +\frac{2}{5} \\ \hline \end{array}$$

- You change the whole number into a fraction with the right denominator.

$$\begin{array}{rcr} 3 & = & \frac{15}{5} \\ +\frac{2}{5} & = & +\frac{2}{5} \\ \hline \end{array}$$

- When the denominators are the same, you can work the problem.

$$\begin{array}{rcr} 3 & = & \frac{15}{5} \\ +\frac{2}{5} & = & +\frac{2}{5} \\ \hline & & \frac{17}{5} \end{array}$$

- You do something similar when two fractions do not have the same denominator. You find the **lowest common denominator.**

$$\begin{array}{r} \frac{1}{4} \\ +\frac{2}{3} \\ \hline \end{array}$$

- To find the **lowest common denominator,** you ask this question: **What's the first common number you reach when counting by 4 and counting by 3?**

$$\begin{array}{rcr} \frac{1}{4} & = & \frac{}{12} \\ +\frac{2}{3} & = & +\frac{}{12} \\ \hline \end{array}$$

- That number is 12. So 12 is the lowest common denominator.
- You write 12 as the denominator of each fraction.
- Now you figure out the missing numerator of the fraction that equals $\frac{1}{4}$. That's 3.
- And you figure out the numerator of the fraction that equals $\frac{2}{3}$. That's 8.

$$\begin{array}{rcr} \frac{1}{4}\left(\frac{3}{3}\right) & = & \frac{3}{12} \\ +\frac{2}{3}\left(\frac{4}{4}\right) & = & +\frac{8}{12} \\ \hline \end{array}$$

- Now you can add the fractions. The answer is $\frac{11}{12}$.

$$\begin{array}{rcr} \frac{1}{4}\left(\frac{3}{3}\right) & = & \frac{3}{12} \\ +\frac{2}{3}\left(\frac{4}{4}\right) & = & +\frac{8}{12} \\ \hline & & \frac{11}{12} \end{array}$$

Part 5

- Remember the steps:
  - ✔ Find the first common number you reach when you count by the number in each denominator.
  - ✔ Write the first common number as the denominator for **both fractions.**
  - ✔ Work equivalent-fraction problems to figure out the numerators.
  - ✔ Then add or subtract.

$$\begin{array}{r} \frac{7}{8}\left(\blacksquare\right) = \ \blacksquare \\ +\frac{5}{6}\left(\blacksquare\right) = +\blacksquare \\ \hline \end{array}$$

Independent Work

Part 6

Write the number of tens each value rounds to.

a. 74 b. 46 c. 88 d. 83 e. 85

Part 7

Copy each problem and multiply. Rewrite each problem with the correct answer and work it.

a. $\begin{array}{r} 6 \\ 52\overline{)310} \end{array}$ b. $\begin{array}{r} 4 \\ 94\overline{)536} \end{array}$ c. $\begin{array}{r} 3 \\ 19\overline{)85} \end{array}$ d. $\begin{array}{r} 3 \\ 49\overline{)136} \end{array}$

Part 8

Work each ratio problem. Then write the answer as a whole number or mixed number and a unit name.

a. There are 3 groups for every 9 people. How many groups can be formed with 27 people?

b. There are 3 eggs for every 2 birds. How many eggs are there if there are 18 birds?

c. The ratio of shovels to workers is 6 to 4. If there are 44 workers, how many shovels are there?

d. Sandra earns $12 for every 5 hours of yard work. How many hours must Sandra work to earn $25?

Part 9 Copy and complete each pair of equations.

a. 7J = 3
1J = ■

b. 3M = 4
1M = ■

c. 12P = 17
1P = ■

d. 5R = 3
1R = ■

Part 10 Figure out the squares for each rectangle. Use the equation: squares = $x \times y$. Write each answer with a number and a unit name.

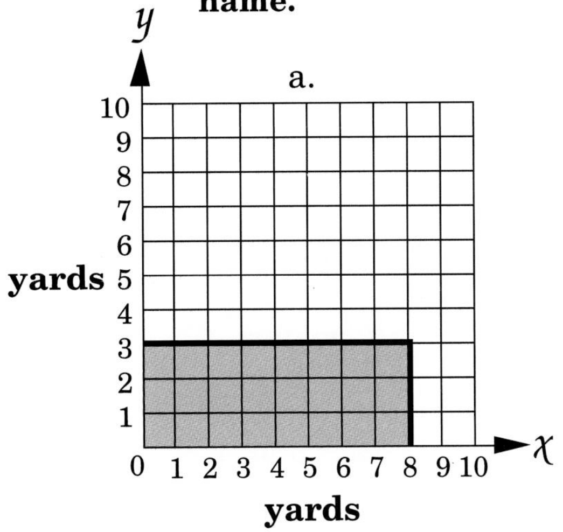

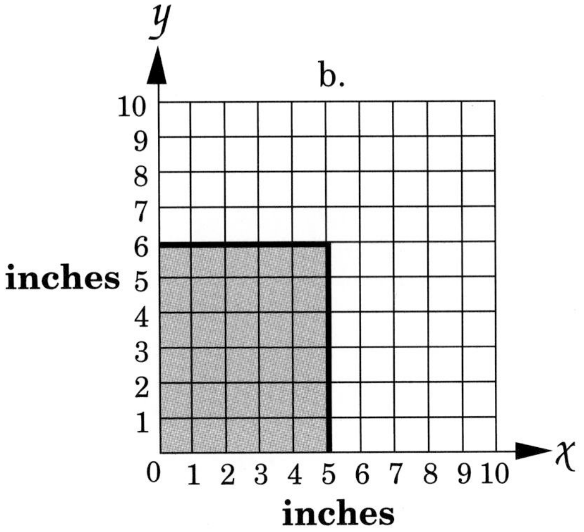

Part 11 Copy and complete the table. Write the names and the ratio numbers in the first box. Then complete each fraction. Answer each question. Remember the unit name.

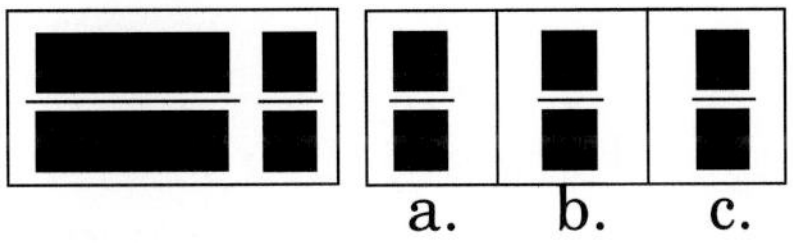

In the mountains, the ratio of blue butterflies to yellow butterflies is 7 to 3.

a. When 49 blue butterflies were counted, how many yellow butterflies were counted?

b. When 300 yellow butterflies were counted, how many blue butterflies were counted?

c. When 420 yellow butterflies were counted, how many blue butterflies were counted?

Lesson 68

Part 1 **Work each item.**

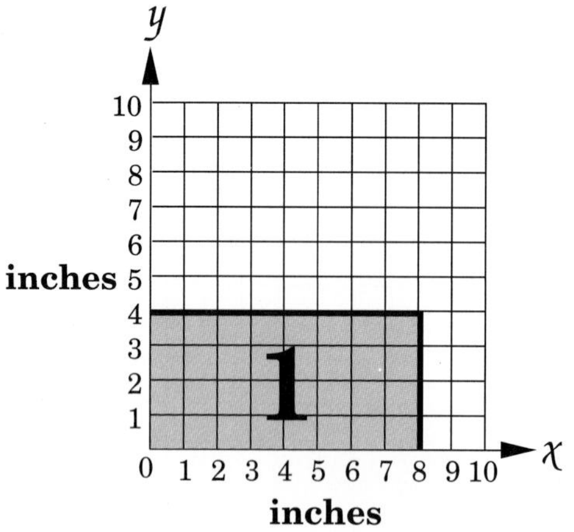

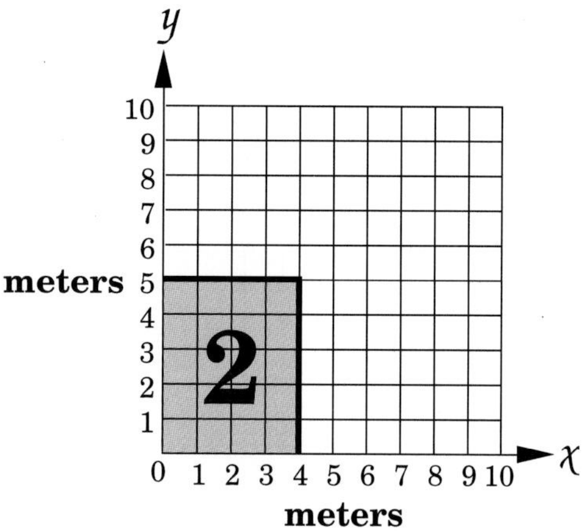

a. Find the perimeter of rectangle 1.

b. Find the number of squares for rectangle 1.

c. Find the number of squares for rectangle 2.

d. Find the perimeter of rectangle 2.

Part 2 **For each problem, make a ratio table and answer the questions.**

a. In a cake recipe, there are 2 cups of water for every 5 cups of milk. The total amount of liquid used was 84 cups.
   1. How many cups of water were used?
   2. How many cups of milk were used?

b. $\frac{5}{7}$ of the people on vacation in Bonner's Resort went skiing. 95 people went skiing.
   1. How many people were on vacation?
   2. How many people did not go skiing?

c. On $\frac{4}{5}$ of the days the bus was on time. The rest of the days the bus was late. The bus was late on 52 days.
   1. On how many days was the bus on time?
   2. How many days were there in all?

Part 3

- The best way to work division problems that divide by 2-digit numbers is to **round the number you divide by.**

- Here's a division problem: $49\overline{)308}$

- You're dividing by 49.
  The estimated answer is 6. $\begin{array}{r}6\\5\overline{)30}\end{array}$ $\begin{array}{r}6\\49\overline{)308}\end{array}$

- Here's a different problem: $41\overline{)308}$

- You're dividing by 41.
  The estimated answer is 7. $\begin{array}{r}7\\4\overline{)30}\end{array}$ $\begin{array}{r}7\\41\overline{)308}\end{array}$

Independent Work

Part 4 **For each item, make a number family. Answer the question.**

a. Mrs. Jones had a glass collection. She sold 36 glasses. 17 glasses were broken when she moved her collection. She gave away 13 glasses. She ended up with 457 glasses. How many glasses did she start out with?

b. Al's Toy Store had 247 toys in stock. On Monday, 166 toys were delivered to Al's store. On Monday, the store sold 49 toys. On Tuesday, another 500 toys were delivered. On Tuesday, the store sold 119 toys. On Wednesday, the store sold 392 toys. How many toys did the store end up with?

Part 5 **Copy and complete each pair of equations.**

a. $6T = 2$	b. $6T = 7$	c. $94J = 3$
$1T = ■$	$1T = ■$	$1J = ■$

Part 6 For each item, figure out the first common number. Write the complete equations.

a. 5 x ■ = ■
6 x ■ = ■

b. 3 x ■ = ■
5 x ■ = ■

c. 9 x ■ = ■
4 x ■ = ■

d. 6 x ■ = ■
4 x ■ = ■

Part 7 Make a ratio table. Answer the questions.

a. At Hidden Beach, there were seagulls and terns. The ratio of seagulls to terns was 4 to 3. There were 560 birds.
   1. How many were terns?
   2. How many were seagulls?

b. At Ace Factory, there were 5 married workers for every 2 unmarried workers. There were 355 married workers.
   1. How many total workers were there?
   2. How many unmarried workers were there?

Part 8 Copy and work each problem.

a. $5 \times \frac{4}{7} =$ ■

b. $\frac{4}{8} \times \frac{3}{8} =$ ■

c. $\frac{6}{8} - \frac{1}{8}$

d. $3 + \frac{11}{5}$

Part 9 Copy and complete the table.

	Fraction	Mixed number
a.	$\frac{52}{3}$	
b.		$11\frac{5}{9}$
c.	$\frac{18}{7}$	
d.		$6\frac{2}{5}$

Lesson 69

Part 1

- When you work some common denominator problems, you change only one of the fractions.

Here's:

$$\begin{array}{r} \frac{1}{4} \\ +\frac{1}{8} \\ \hline \end{array}$$

- The first common number for 4 and 8 is 8. So you don't change $\frac{1}{8}$ into another fraction.

$$\begin{array}{rl} \frac{1}{4} & \\ +\frac{1}{8} & = \frac{1}{8} \\ \hline \end{array}$$

- You change $\frac{1}{4}$ into $\frac{2}{8}$.

$$\begin{array}{rl} \frac{1}{4}\left(\frac{2}{2}\right) & = \frac{2}{8} \\ +\frac{1}{8} & = \frac{1}{8} \\ \hline \end{array}$$

- Then you add.
- Remember, if one of the denominators is the lowest common denominator, just copy the fraction with that denominator.

$$\begin{array}{rl} \frac{1}{4}\left(\frac{2}{2}\right) & = \frac{2}{8} \\ +\frac{1}{8} & = +\frac{1}{8} \\ \hline & \quad \frac{3}{8} \end{array}$$

Part 2

Copy each problem. Rewrite the fractions with a common denominator. Work the problem.

a. $\begin{array}{r} \frac{5}{12} \\ +\frac{7}{3} \\ \hline \end{array}$

b. $\begin{array}{r} \frac{3}{2} \\ -\frac{7}{8} \\ \hline \end{array}$

c. $\begin{array}{r} \frac{5}{6} \\ -\frac{1}{4} \\ \hline \end{array}$

Part 3

For each problem, make a ratio table and answer the questions.

a. $\frac{2}{15}$ of the leaves had beetles on them. There were 64 leaves with beetles.
   1. How many leaves were there in all?
   2. How many leaves did not have beetles?

b. The ratio of red buttons to black buttons was 4 to 11. There were 120 buttons in all.
   1. How many buttons were red?
   2. How many buttons were black?

Part 4

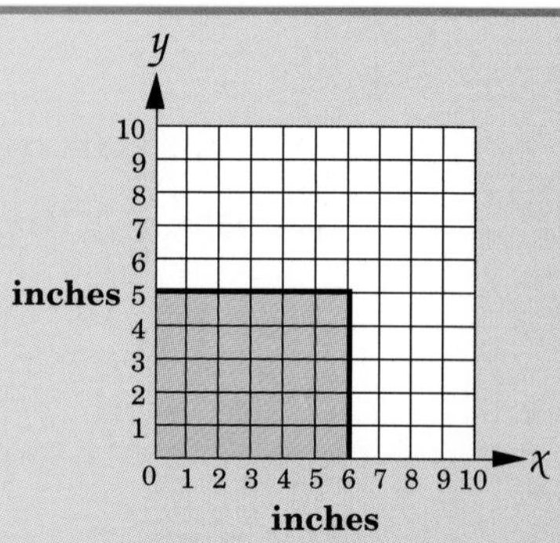

- When you find the number of square units in a figure, you find the **area** of the figure.

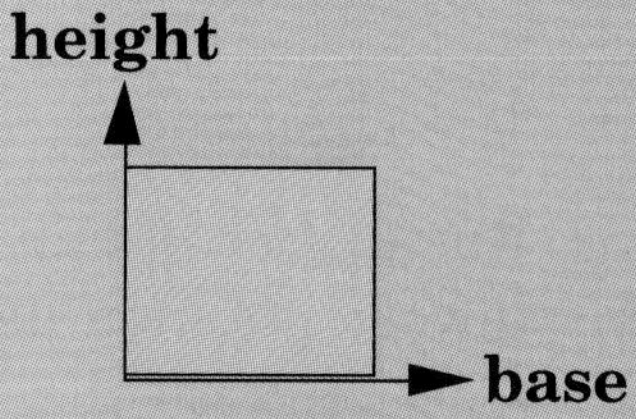

- The area is always the number of squares, even when the figure is not shown on the coordinate system.
- Here's the equation for finding the area of a rectangle: **Area □ = base x height**
  - The base is the x value.
  - The height is the y value.

- Here's a rectangle:

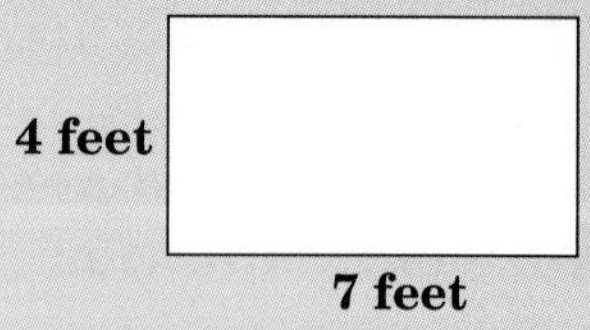

- The base is 7 feet. The height is 4 feet.

Area □ = base x height

Area = 7 x 4

28 square feet

Part 5 Work each item.

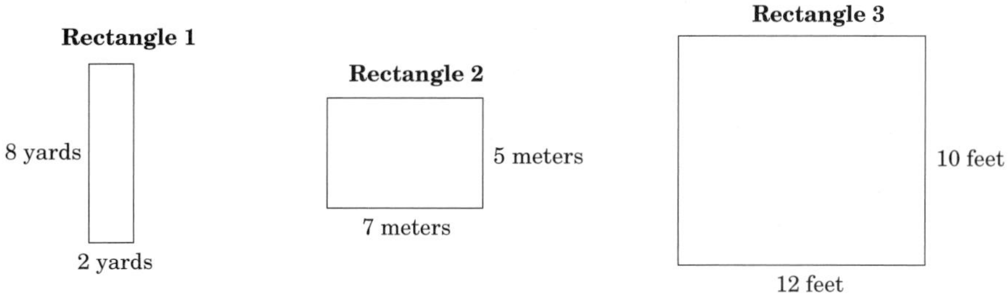

a. Find the area of rectangle 1.

b. Find the area of rectangle 2.

c. Find the perimeter of rectangle 3.

d. Find the area of rectangle 3.

e. Find the perimeter of rectangle 2.

Independent Work

Part 6 Write the number of tens each value rounds to.

a. 98 b. 25 c. 37 d. 54 e. 63

Part 7 Copy and complete each equation. If the fractions are not equivalent, circle the larger fraction. If the fractions are equivalent, circle the equal sign.

a. $\frac{4}{7}\left(\blacksquare\right) = \frac{28}{28}$ b. $\frac{6}{7}\left(\blacksquare\right) = \frac{480}{560}$

c. $\frac{5}{3}\left(\blacksquare\right) = \frac{100}{75}$ d. $\frac{4}{9}\left(\blacksquare\right) = \frac{200}{459}$

Part 8 Copy each problem and multiply. Rewrite each problem with the correct answer and work it.

a. $\begin{array}{r} 5 \\ 29\overline{)182} \end{array}$ b. $\begin{array}{r} 7 \\ 37\overline{)297} \end{array}$ c. $\begin{array}{r} 7 \\ 65\overline{)428} \end{array}$ d. $\begin{array}{r} 3 \\ 51\overline{)128} \end{array}$

Part 9 Make a table. Answer the questions.

During November and December, some snow fell and some rain fell in Bell City. 14 inches of snow fell during November. The total amount of snow and rain during December was 21 inches. The total amount of rain for both months was 17 inches. Only 1 inch of rain fell during December.

a. How many inches of rain fell during November?

b. Was there more total snowfall or total rainfall?

c. During December, was there less rainfall or less snowfall?

Part 10 Copy and complete each pair of equations.

a. 4R = 11
1R = ■

b. 2J = 1
1J = ■

c. 53D = 1
1D = ■

Part 11 For each item, make a number family. Then answer the question.

a. Shirley is 13 pounds heavier than her brother. If her brother weighs 97 pounds, how many pounds does Shirley weigh?

b. There are 45 fewer bicycles parked at Filmore School than at Emerald School. There are 193 bicycles parked at Emerald School. How many bicycles are parked at Filmore?

c. The blue jar contains 235 more beans than the red jar. There are 581 beans in the blue jar. How many beans are in the red jar?

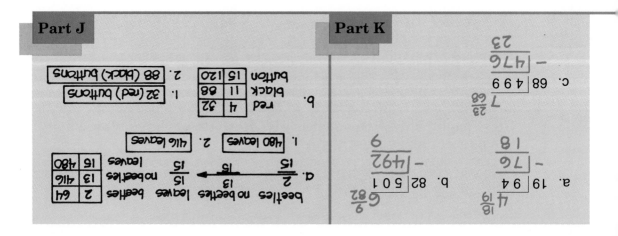

Part J

a. beetles $\frac{2}{15}$ no beetles $\frac{13}{15}$ → leaves $\frac{15}{15}$

beetles	2	64
no beetles	13	416
leaves	15	480

1. 480 leaves 2. 416 leaves

b.

red	4	32
black	11	88
button	15	120

1. 32 (red) buttons 2. 88 (black) buttons

Part K

a. 19 | 94 → $4\frac{18}{19}$; −76; 18

b. 82 | 501 → $6\frac{9}{82}$; −492; 9

c. 68 | 499 → $7\frac{23}{68}$; −476; 23

Lesson 70

Part 1

Work each item.

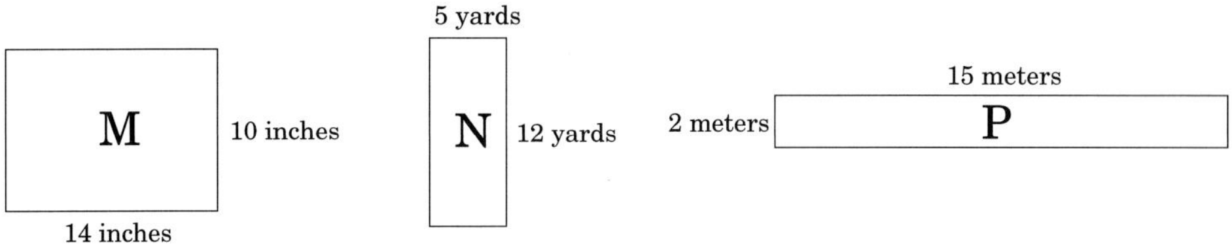

a. Figure out the area of rectangle M.

b. Figure out the area of rectangle N.

c. Figure out the perimeter of rectangle N.

d. Figure out the perimeter of rectangle P.

e. Figure out the area of rectangle P.

Part 2

- Sometimes, you find the lowest common denominator by multiplying the denominators together.

- Here the denominators are 6 and 7: The lowest common denominator is 6 x 7.

$$\frac{\blacksquare}{6}\left(\frac{7}{7}\right) = \frac{\blacksquare}{42}$$
$$+\frac{\blacksquare}{7}\left(\frac{6}{6}\right) = \frac{\blacksquare}{42}$$

- Here the denominators are 2 and 3: The lowest common denominator is 2 x 3.

$$\frac{\blacksquare}{2}\left(\frac{3}{3}\right) = \frac{\blacksquare}{6}$$
$$-\frac{\blacksquare}{3}\left(\frac{2}{2}\right) = \frac{\blacksquare}{6}$$

- Remember, for any two denominators, you can find a common denominator by multiplying the denominators together. For some problems, that denominator is the **lowest** common denominator.

Part 3 **Copy each problem. Find the lowest common denominator. Work the problem.**

a. $\begin{array}{r} \frac{5}{9} \\ -\frac{3}{10} \\ \hline \end{array}$

b. $\begin{array}{r} \frac{3}{4} \\ +\frac{10}{9} \\ \hline \end{array}$

c. $\begin{array}{r} \frac{7}{4} \\ -\frac{5}{8} \\ \hline \end{array}$

Part J

c. 12
12
5
+ 5
34 yards

d. 2
2
15
+ 15
34 meters

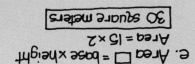

e. Area □ = base × height
Area = 15 × 2
30 square meters

Test 7

Part 1 **For each problem, make a ratio table and answer the questions.**

a. $\frac{2}{5}$ of the children wore shorts. 60 children did not wear shorts.
   1. How many children wore shorts?
   2. How many children were there in all?

b. $\frac{1}{8}$ of the cars were pink. There were 976 cars in all.
   1. How many cars were not pink?
   2. How many cars were pink?

c. $\frac{4}{5}$ of the rabbits were gray. There were 100 rabbits that were gray.
   1. How many rabbits were not gray?
   2. How many total rabbits were there?

Part 2 **Copy and complete each pair of equations.**

a. $7P = 1$
$1P = ■$

b. $2M = 12$
$1M = ■$

c. $65T = 27$
$1T = ■$

Part 3 **Copy each problem and multiply. Rewrite each problem with the correct answer. Work the problems. Write each answer as a mixed number.**

a. $\begin{array}{r} 8 \\ 53\overline{)420} \end{array}$ b. $\begin{array}{r} 7 \\ 36\overline{)292} \end{array}$ c. $\begin{array}{r} 8 \\ 94\overline{)851} \end{array}$

Part 4 **Work each ratio problem. Write the answer as a whole number or mixed number and a unit name.**

a. It takes 45 students to make 3 teams. How many students are needed for 2 teams?

b. A store sells 15 cans of lemonade for every 4 cans of ginger ale. The store sells 36 cans of ginger ale. How many cans of lemonade does the store sell?

c. A recipe requires 4 pounds of flour for every 3 pounds of sugar. The cook uses 11 pounds of flour. How many pounds of sugar will the cook need?

Part 5 **Copy each problem. Rewrite the whole number as a fraction. Work the problem. Write the answer as a fraction.**

a. $\begin{array}{r} 3 \\ -\frac{2}{7} \\ \hline \end{array}$ b. $\begin{array}{r} \frac{4}{9} \\ +6 \\ \hline \end{array}$

Part 6 **Write the number of tens each value rounds to.**

a. 32 b. 75

c. 84 d. 66

Part 7 **For each item, figure out the first common number (least common multiple). Write the complete equation with the first common number after the equal sign.**

a. 4 x ■ = ■
3 x ■ = ■

b. 4 x ■ = ■
6 x ■ = ■

Part 8 **Copy and complete the table. Then answer the questions.**

There are 5 sunnys days for every 3 rainy days.

		a.	b.	c.
sunny	■	15	■	■
rainy	■	■	12	6

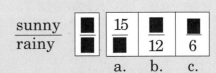

a. How many rainy days are there for 15 sunny days?
b. How many sunny days are there for 12 rainy days?
c. How many sunny days are there for 6 rainy days?

Lesson 71

Part 1

millions	hundred thousands	ten thousands	thousands	hundreds	tens	ones
7,	6,	5,	4,	3,	2,	1

- These digits show the rules for place value. The digits are 1 through 7. 1 is in the ones column and 7 is in the millions column.
- If a number has **7 digits,** it's a **millions** number.
- If a number has **6 digits,** it's a number for **hundred thousands.**
- A number with **5 digits** tells about **ten thousands.**
- The digits show the comma rule:
  - ✔ You start at the ones column. After the first three digits, you put a comma. That gives you a comma for thousands. After the next three digits, you put another comma. That comma is for millions.

Part 2 **Say the column name for each arrowed digit.**

a. 5,743,214 b. 6,394,172 c. 8,569,421 d. 9,123,617

Part 3 **Write the column name for each arrowed digit.**

a. 5,716,204 b. 4,125,823 c. 1,219,174 d. 8,210,427 e. 9,200,628

Part 4

Copy each problem. Find the lowest common denominator. Work the problem.

a. $\frac{3}{7} - \frac{1}{10}$

b. $\frac{1}{5} - \frac{1}{10}$

c. $\frac{4}{8} + \frac{7}{10}$

Part 5

For each item, write the multiplication problem and the answer.

a. What is $\frac{5}{3}$ of 21?

b. What is $\frac{3}{8}$ of 24?

c. What is $\frac{2}{5}$ of $\frac{1}{3}$?

d. What is $\frac{5}{9}$ of 45?

Part 6

- An angle is formed when two lines come together.
- The angle is shown as a part of a circle between the lines.

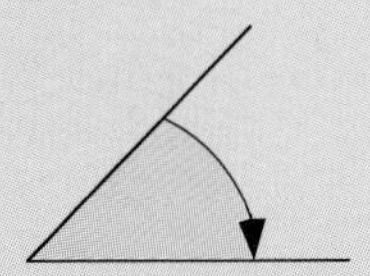

- We can measure angles in units called **degrees.**
- Here's an angle of 5 degrees: 
- Here's how to write 5 degrees: **5**°
- An angle with more than 5 degrees shows a bigger part of the circle. Here's an angle of 30 degrees:

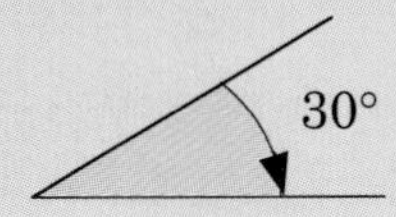

- Each of these angles is 80 degrees:

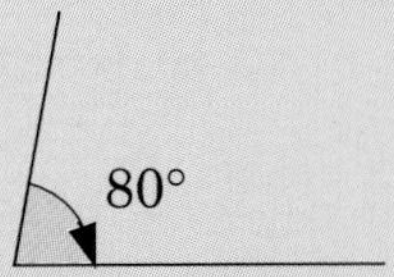

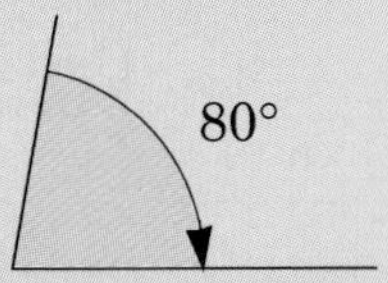

- The same angle can be shown in different positions. All these angles are 30 degrees:

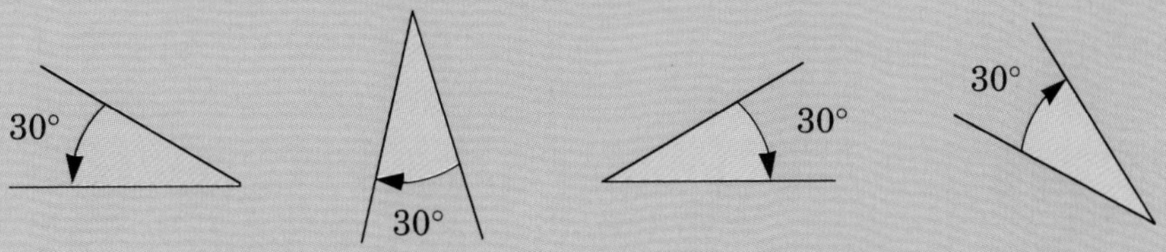

Part 7

Here are important facts about degrees:

- The angle for the corner of a room or the corner of a rectangle is 90 degrees.

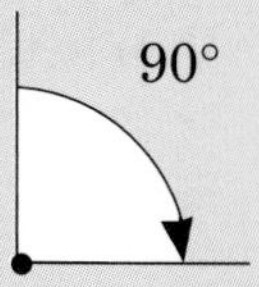

- The angle for half a circle is 180 degrees.

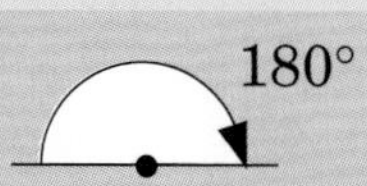

- The angle for a complete circle is 360 degrees.

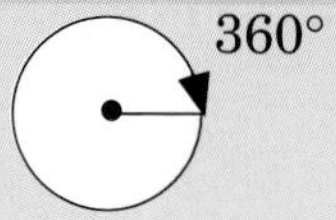

Part 8 **Answer each question.**

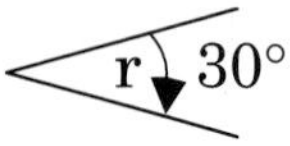

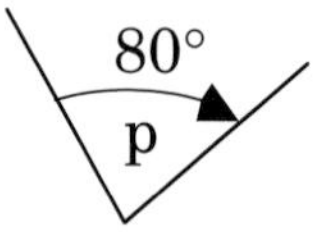

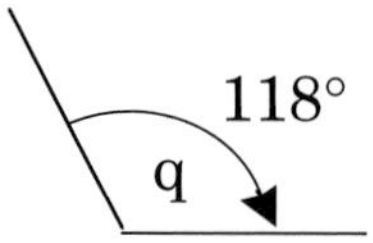

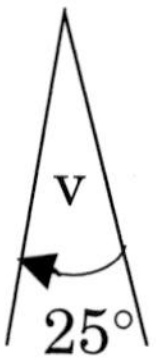

a. Write the degrees for the largest angle.
b. How many more degrees is angle p than angle r?
c. How many degrees are in a whole circle?
d. How many degrees are in half a circle?
e. What's the letter of the smallest angle?

Part 9 **Use an estimate to work each problem.**

Sample problem:
$28\overline{)192}$

a. $36\overline{)95}$ b. $62\overline{)268}$ c. $43\overline{)88}$

Part 10

- You've worked problems that deal with sets of equivalent fractions.

$\frac{3}{2}$

$\frac{9}{6} = \frac{15}{10} = \frac{6}{4} = \frac{12}{8}$

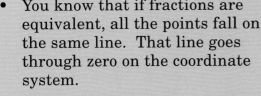

- You can work those problems quickly by using what you know about the coordinate system.

- You know that if fractions are equivalent, all the points fall on the same line. That line goes through zero on the coordinate system.
- Here's a fact:
  There were 3 ripe berries for every 2 unripe berries.
- You make a line that goes through the point: $y = 3$, $x = 2$.

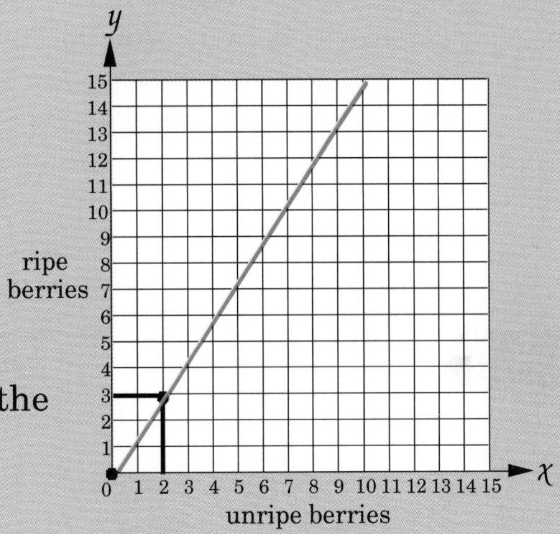

- The line goes through the corner of some squares on the coordinate system. You can make a point at each of those corners. And the points show different numbers for **ripe berries** and **unripe berries.**

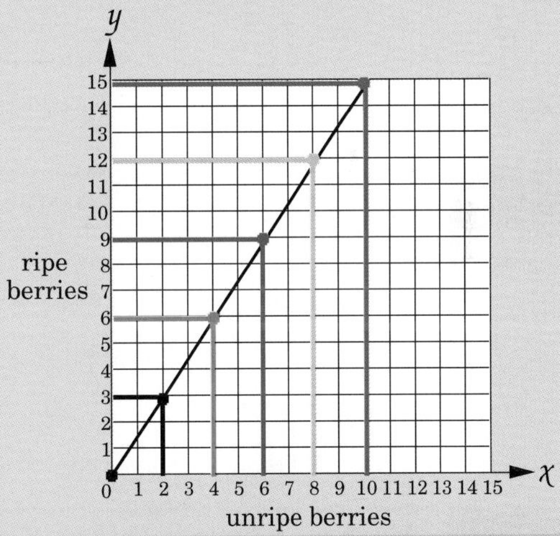

- You can look at the coordinate system and answer questions about ripe berries and unripe berries.
  a. If there are 6 ripe berries, how many unripe berries are there?
  b. If there are 10 unripe berries, how many ripe berries are there?
  c. If there are 6 unripe berries, how many ripe berries are there?

Independent Work

Part 11 **For each problem, make a fraction number family and a ratio table. Answer the questions.**

a. At a factory, $\frac{6}{11}$ of the employees were men. There were 300 women at the factory.
   1. How many men were there?
   2. How many employees were there?

b. $\frac{3}{4}$ of the mixture was water. The total mixture weighed 660 pounds.
   1. How much of the mixture was water?
   2. How much of the mixture was not water?

c. In $\frac{5}{8}$ of the towns, the temperature was below freezing. The temperature was not below freezing in 240 towns.
   1. How many towns were there in all?
   2. In how many towns was the temperature below freezing?

Part 12 **Copy each problem. Find the lowest common denominator. Work the problem.**

a. $\frac{3}{5} - \frac{1}{15}$

b. $\frac{2}{6} + \frac{5}{8}$

c. $\frac{6}{13} + 2$

Part 13 **Write the number of tens each number rounds to.**

a. 56
b. 13
c. 85
d. 54

Part 14 **Copy and complete each equation. If the fractions are not equivalent, circle the larger fraction. If the fractions are equivalent, circle the equal sign.**

a. $\frac{4}{5}\left(\blacksquare\right) = \frac{40}{45}$

b. $\frac{7}{10}\left(\blacksquare\right) = \frac{77}{110}$

c. $\frac{3}{2}\left(\blacksquare\right) = \frac{57}{40}$

d. $\frac{7}{3}\left(\blacksquare\right) = \frac{49}{21}$

Part 15 **Work each ratio problem. Write the answer as a whole number and a unit name.**

a. The ratio of children to balloons is 4 to 9. If there are 468 balloons, how many children are there?

b. 4 boxes hold 72 pencils. How many pencils do 7 boxes hold?

c. 42 plates fit on 3 shelves. How many plates fit on 5 shelves?

d. There are 8 bowls of soup for every 24 crackers. If there are 11 bowls of soup, how many crackers are there?

Part 16 Copy and complete each pair of equations.

a. 3J = 7
1J = ■

b. 17B = 15
1B = ■

c. 2C = 11
1C = ■

d. 5T = 4
1T = ■

Part J

a. $\frac{3}{7}\left(\frac{10}{10}\right) = \frac{30}{70}$
$-\ \frac{1}{10}\left(\frac{7}{7}\right) = -\ \frac{7}{70}$
$\frac{23}{70}$

b. $\frac{1}{5}\left(\frac{2}{2}\right) = \frac{2}{10}$
$-\ \frac{1}{10} = -\ \frac{1}{10}$
$\frac{1}{10}$

c. $\frac{4}{8}\left(\frac{5}{5}\right) = \frac{20}{40}$
$+\ \frac{7}{10}\left(\frac{4}{4}\right) = +\ \frac{28}{40}$
$\frac{48}{40}$

Part K

a. $36\overline{)95}$ -72 23 $2\frac{23}{36}$

b. $62\overline{)268}$ -248 20 $4\frac{20}{62}$

c. $43\overline{)88}$ -86 2 $2\frac{2}{43}$

Lesson 72

Part 1

Write the column name for each arrowed digit.

a. 7,210,623
b. 1,922,006
c. 4,306,015
d. 8,025,218
e. 5,128,439
f. 2,085,400

Part 2

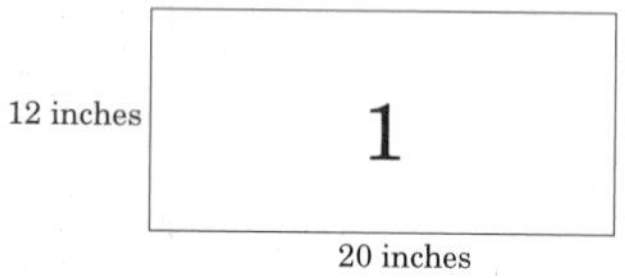

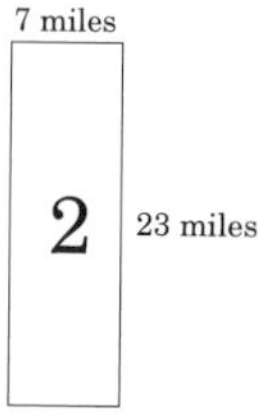

a. What's the area of rectangle 1?
b. What's the perimeter of rectangle 2?
c. What's the perimeter of rectangle 1?

Part 3

For each problem, make a number family with three letters. Then work the problem.

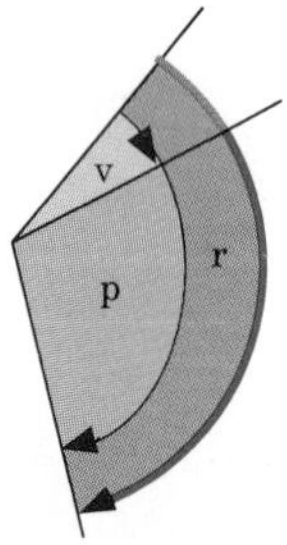

a. Angle v is 22°.
Angle r is 125°.
Figure out angle p.

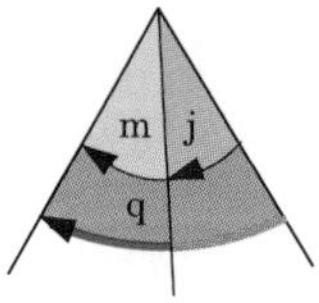

b. Angle m is 32°.
Angle j is 29°.
Figure out angle q.

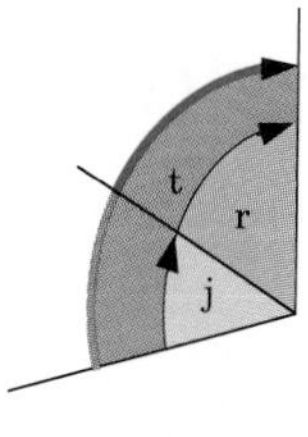

c. Angle t is 105°.
Angle j is 47°.
Figure out angle r.

Part 4

Copy each problem. Estimate the answer by rounding the number you divide by. Then work the problem.

a. $38\overline{)169}$
b. $71\overline{)580}$
c. $86\overline{)641}$

Part 5

Answer each question. Write answers that are more than 1 as whole numbers or mixed numbers.

a. What's $\frac{3}{7}$ of 49?

b. What's $\frac{5}{8}$ of 40?

c. What's $\frac{7}{4}$ of 50?

Part 6

For each item, figure out the cost of one object.

a. 10 pens = 2 dollars
   1 pen = ■

b. 5 rabbits = 42 dollars
   1 rabbit = ■

c. 2 radios = 125 dollars
   1 radio = ■

d. 25 magazines = 19 dollars
   1 magazine = ■

Independent Work

Part 7

Make a table. Answer the questions.

Poppies and roses are grown in Rock Park and Einstein Park. There are 603 poppies in Rock Park. There are 283 poppies in Einstein Park. There are 640 roses in Einstein Park. There are 124 fewer roses in Rock Park than in Einstein Park.

a. How many total poppies and roses grow in Rock Park?

b. Do more roses or more poppies grow in Rock Park?

c. Is the total of roses and poppies more in Rock Park or in Einstein Park?

Part 8

Copy each problem. Rewrite the whole number as a fraction. Then work the problem.

a. $6 + \frac{2}{5}$

b. $3 - \frac{14}{8}$

c. $\frac{8}{9} + 2$

d. $\frac{11}{7} - 1$

Part 9

Copy each mixed number. Write the fraction it equals.

a. $3\frac{4}{7}$ = ■ b. $4\frac{5}{8}$ = ■ c. $6\frac{3}{10}$ = ■ d. $5\frac{1}{2}$ = ■ e. $7\frac{5}{12}$ = ■

Part 10 For each problem, make a number family and answer the question.

a. Before Monday, a store had 349 pairs of shoes. On Monday, the store sold 39 pairs of shoes. On Tuesday, the store sold 187 pairs of shoes. The store also received a delivery of 400 pairs of shoes. On Wednesday, the store sold 48 pairs of shoes. On Thursday, the store sold 51 pairs of shoes. How many pairs of shoes did the store have at the end of Thursday?

b. The rocket traveled 420 miles per hour faster than the jet. The rocket traveled at the rate of 987 miles per hour. How fast did the jet travel?

c. At Willis Camp, there were 112 more campers than counselors. There were 38 counselors. How many campers were there?

d. The train started out with some passengers in it. At the first stop, 12 passengers got off. At the next stop, 20 passengers got off. There were now 33 passengers on the train. How many passengers were there on the train to begin with?

Part 11 For each item, make a ratio equation. Answer the question.

a. John worked 3 hours to earn $9. How many dollars did he earn in 75 hours?

b. If 14 boxes hold 8 pounds of flour, how many boxes hold 4 pounds of flour?

c. There were 2 groups for every 6 people. How many groups were there if there were 96 people?

Part 12 Make a table to show the x and y values for each point.

	x	y
A	■	■
B	■	■
C	■	■

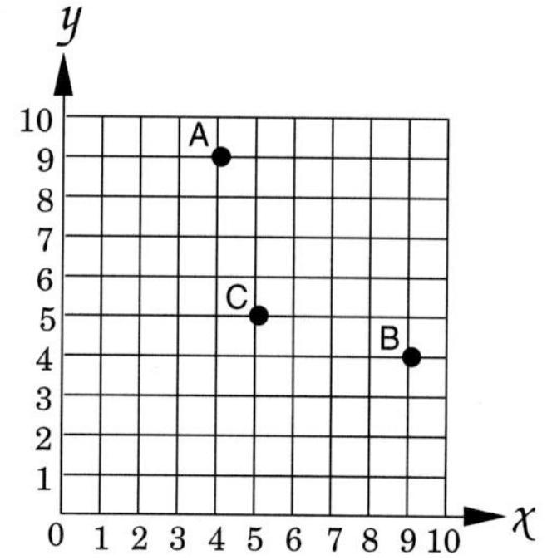

Part J

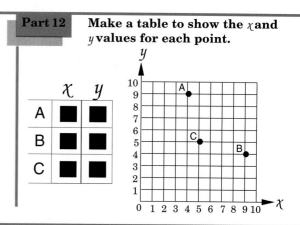

a. Area□ = base × height
Area = 20 × 12
240 square inches

b. 23
23
7
+ 7
60 miles

c. 12
12
20
+ 20
64 inches

Part K

a. $38\overline{)169}$ $4\frac{17}{38}$
−152
17

b. $71\overline{)580}$ $8\frac{12}{71}$
−568
12

c. $86\overline{)641}$ $7\frac{39}{86}$
−602
39

Lesson 73

Part 1 **Write the column name of the digit described in each item.**

a. This digit is third from the end.

b. This digit is the end digit.

c. This digit is seventh from the end.

d. This digit is fourth from the end.

Part 2

- The arrow is pointing to the digit that is fourth from the end. The digit is 9.

  3,469,453

  9,000

- If you had only the value shown by that digit, you would have 9 **thousand.** That's a four-place number. The first digit is 9 and all the other digits are zeros.

- Here's another example:

  3,469,453

  50

- The arrow is pointing to the digit that is second from the end. That digit is 5.
- If you had only the value shown by that digit, you would have 5 **tens.** That's a two-place number. The first digit is 5. The other digit is zero.
- Remember, to show what the arrowed digit is worth, copy the digit and show the correct number of zeros after the digit.

Part 3 **Write the value for each arrowed digit.**

a. 5,803,649 b. 24,539 c. 56,791 d. 157,264 e. 91,325

Part 4

Sample problem:

11 cars weigh 34 tons. What does 1 car weigh?

1 car = $\frac{34}{11}$ tons

a. 3 toys weigh 16 ounces. What does 1 toy weigh?

b. 20 buttons cost 4 dollars. What does 1 button cost?

c. They built 4 houses in 15 months. How long did it take to build 1 house?

Part 5

Make a number family with three letters. Answer each question.

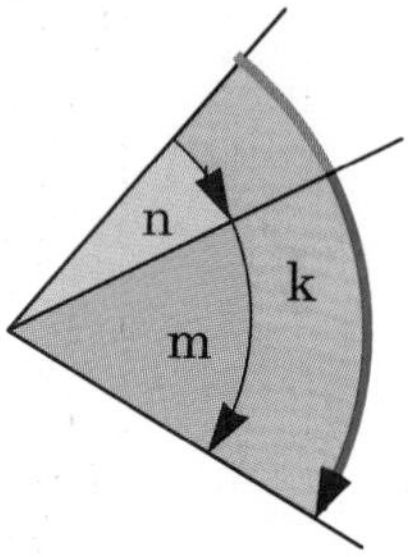

a.
Angle m is 56°.
Angle k is 80°.
How large is angle n?

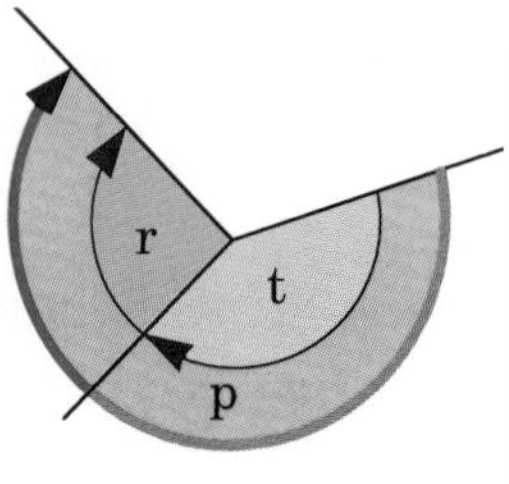

b.
Angle p is 254°.
Angle r is 90°.
How large is angle t?

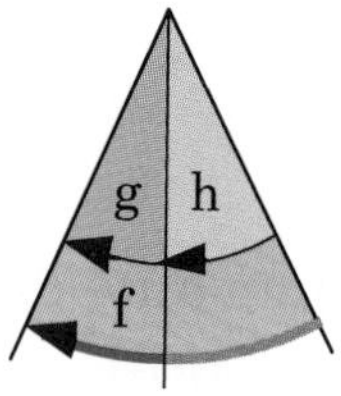

c.
Angle g is 24°.
Angle h is 28°.
How large is angle f ?

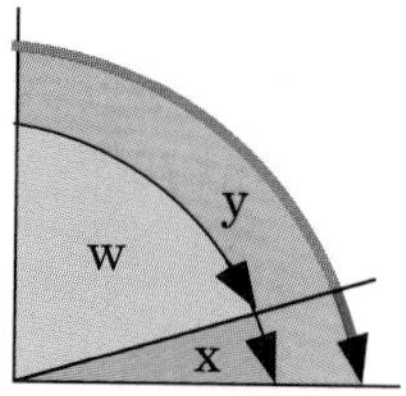

d.
Angle w is 76°.
Angle y is 90°.
How large is angle x?

Part 6

Work each item. Write answers that are more than 1 as whole numbers or mixed numbers.

a. What is $\frac{7}{3}$ of $\frac{2}{3}$?

b. What is $\frac{5}{8}$ of 10?

c. What is $\frac{2}{3}$ of 30?

Part 7

Copy each problem and work it. Rewrite the problem if you need to.

a. $\frac{2}{3} \times \frac{4}{5}$

b. $\frac{2}{3} + \frac{4}{5}$

c. $5 - \frac{8}{3}$

d. $\frac{5}{1} \times \frac{8}{3}$

Part 8 Write each item as a column problem and work it.

a. \$16.25 + \$2.07 + \$110.72 b. \$100.80 – \$28.17 c. \$527.62 + \$95.19

Independent Work

Part 9 Copy each problem. Estimate the answer by rounding the number you divide by. Then work the problem.

a. $64\overline{)527}$ b. $18\overline{)84}$

c. $49\overline{)352}$ d. $72\overline{)597}$

Part 10 Copy and complete the table.

	Fraction	Decimal	Mixed number
a.			$2\frac{17}{100}$
b.		2.3	
c.		5.038	
d.			$24\frac{3}{10}$

Part 11 Make a ratio table for each problem. If the problem tells about a fraction, also make a fraction number family. Answer the questions.

a. Cars and buses went on the turnpike. There were 16 cars for every 3 buses. A total of 4560 vehicles were on the turnpike.
   1. How many were cars?
   2. How many were buses?

b. A large building was getting its windows cleaned. $\frac{3}{10}$ of the windows were already cleaned. 259 windows were not yet cleaned.
   1. How many windows were in the building?
   2. How many were clean?

c. In a field, there were yellow flowers and white flowers. The ratio of yellow flowers to white flowers was 9 to 7. The field had 288 yellow flowers.
   1. How many white flowers were there?
   2. How many flowers were there in all?

Part 12 Copy and complete each pair of equations. If possible, write each answer as a whole number or mixed number.

a. 17P = 3
   1P = ■

b. 2M = 56
   1M = ■

c. 5J = 11
   1J = ■

d. 2R = 124
   1R = ■

Part 13 **Make a table. Answer the questions.**

Two schools bought history books and science books. The schools were Adams Elementary and Polk Elementary. Together, the schools bought 298 history books. Together, the schools bought 266 science books. Adams Elementary bought 145 history books. Polk Elementary bought a total of 210 books.

a. What was the total number of books bought by both schools?

b. Were more science books bought by Polk Elementary or by Adams Elementary?

c. Which school bought fewer history books?

d. How many history books did Polk Elementary buy?

Part 14 **Write the answer to each question.**

a. $\frac{3}{14}$ of the students were tired. What fraction of the students were not tired?

b. $\frac{1}{8}$ of the cars were speeding. What fraction of the cars were not speeding?

Part J

a. $16.25 + 2.07 + 110.72 = $129.04

b. $100.80 − 28.17 = $72.63

c. $527.62 + 95.19 = $622.81

Lesson 74

Part 1

Make a number family for each statement.

Sample problem:
M is $\frac{7}{4}$ of 1.

a. M is $\frac{7}{8}$ of 1.

b. M is $\frac{11}{9}$ of 1.

c. M is $\frac{2}{8}$ of 1.

d. M is $\frac{8}{5}$ of 1.

Part 2

Write the value for each arrowed digit.

a. 72,019 (arrow under 2)

b. 615 (arrow under 1)

c. 5,017,210 (arrow under 5)

d. 23,908 (arrow under 9)

e. 265 (arrow under 6)

Part 3

Copy each problem and work it. Rewrite the problem if you need to.

a. $\frac{3}{7} \times \frac{4}{1}$

b. $\frac{5}{10} + \frac{3}{5}$

c. $\frac{8}{9} - \frac{1}{6}$

d. $\frac{2}{3} \times \frac{1}{2}$

Part 4

- If problems add mixed numbers with the same denominator, you can work the problems by first adding the fractions, then adding the whole numbers.

$$\begin{array}{r} 3\frac{2}{5} \\ +\ 8\frac{1}{5} \\ \hline \end{array}$$

- The fractions have the same denominator, so you add them.

$$\begin{array}{r} 3\frac{2}{5} \\ +\ 8\frac{1}{5} \\ \hline \frac{3}{5} \end{array}$$

- Then you add the whole numbers—3 and 8. That's 11. The answer to the problem is $11\frac{3}{5}$.
- Remember, first add the fractions. Then add the whole numbers.

$$\begin{array}{r} 3\frac{2}{5} \\ +\ 8\frac{1}{5} \\ \hline 11\frac{3}{5} \end{array}$$

Part 5 **Copy and work each problem. First add the fractions. Then add the whole numbers.**

a. $\begin{array}{r} 11\frac{3}{8} \\ +10\frac{4}{8} \\ \hline \end{array}$

b. $\begin{array}{r} 12\frac{5}{9} \\ +\ 1\frac{2}{9} \\ \hline \end{array}$

c. $\begin{array}{r} \frac{2}{15} \\ +\ 6\frac{9}{15} \\ \hline \end{array}$

d. $\begin{array}{r} 28\frac{1}{4} \\ +\ 2\frac{1}{4} \\ \hline \end{array}$

Part 6

Sample problem:

How many degrees are in $\frac{1}{4}$ of a circle?

a. How many degrees are in $\frac{2}{5}$ of a circle?

b. How many degrees are in $\frac{7}{10}$ of a circle?

c. How many degrees are in $\frac{2}{9}$ of angle p?

d. How many degrees are in $\frac{3}{5}$ of angle y?

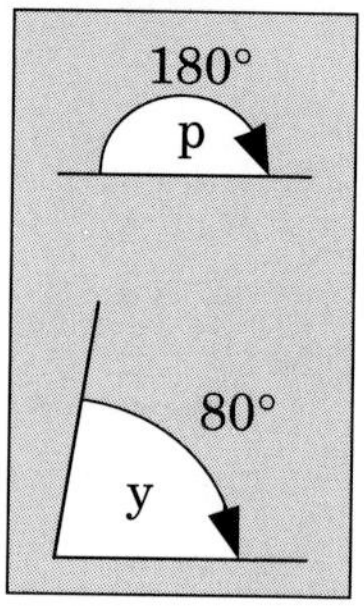

Part 7 You can find the area of triangles shown on the coordinate system.

- You just start with a rectangle and draw a DIAGONAL line. That line goes from one corner to the opposite corner.

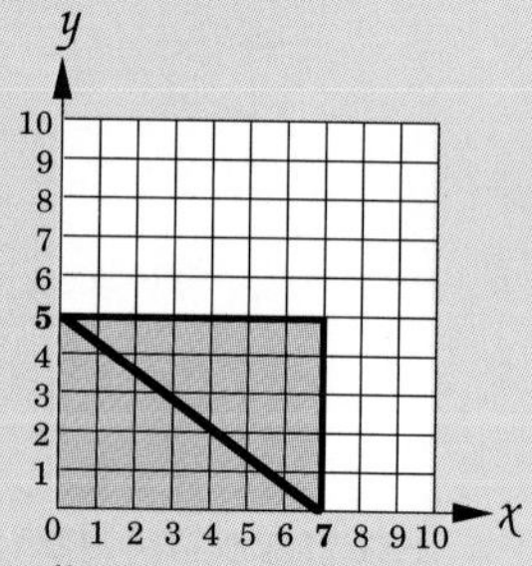

- The line divides the rectangle into two triangles. Each triangle has exactly $\frac{1}{2}$ the area of the rectangle you started with.

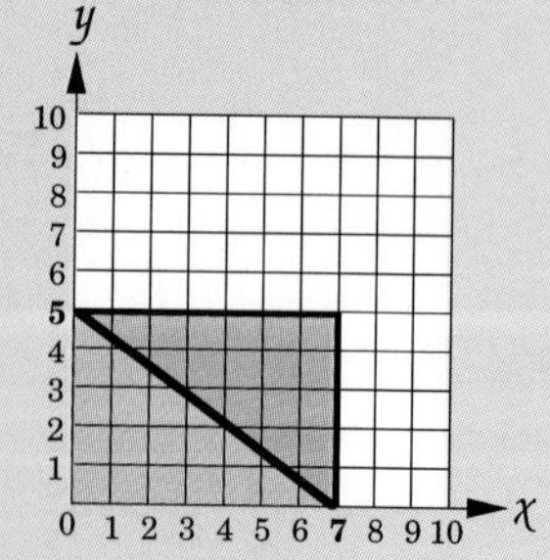

- Here's a triangle shown on the coordinate system:
- You know that the area of the triangle is $\frac{1}{2}$ the area of a rectangle with the same base and the same height.

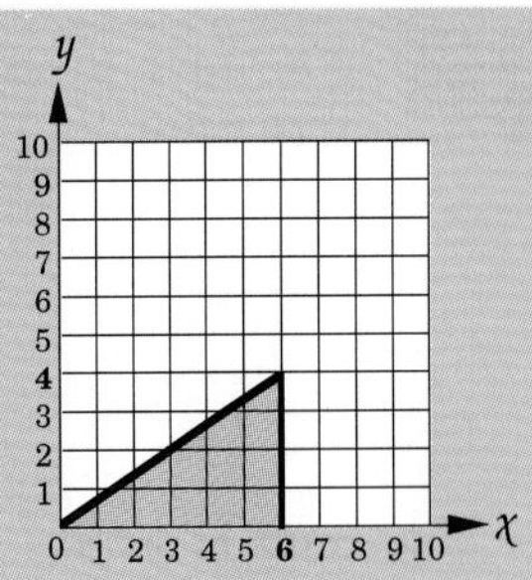

- So you complete the rectangle.

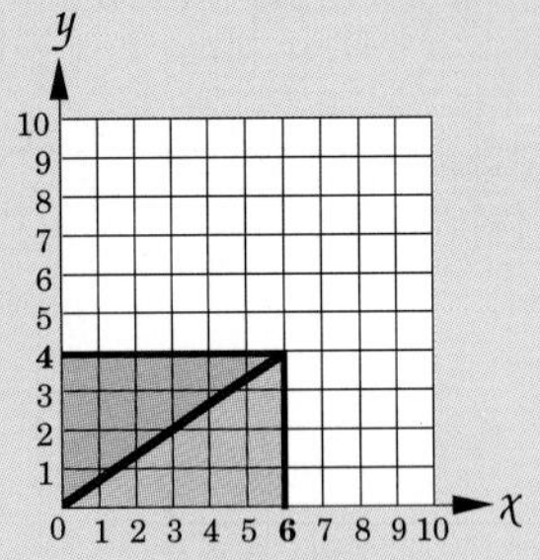

- To figure out the area of the triangle, you figure out the area of the entire rectangle: Area □ = 6 x 4 = **24**
- Then you just divide that area in half: Area △ = $\frac{24}{2}$ = **12 squares**
- Here's the equation for the area of a triangle: Area △ = $\frac{\text{base x height}}{2}$

Independent Work

Part 8 **Copy each problem. Estimate the answer by rounding the number you divide by. Then work the problem.**

a. $57\overline{)384}$ b. $93\overline{)346}$

c. $24\overline{)53}$ d. $78\overline{)615}$

Part 9 **For each item, show the equation. Simplify the answer.**

a. What is $\frac{3}{5}$ of 40?

b. What is $\frac{2}{3}$ of 24?

c. What is $\frac{1}{8}$ of 96?

d. What is $\frac{4}{7}$ of 56?

Part 10 For each problem, make a number family with three letters. Answer each question.

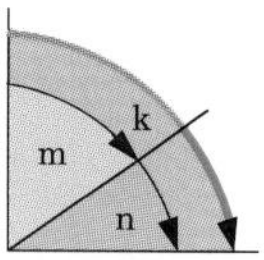

a.
Angle m is 56°.
Angle k is 90°.
How large is angle n?

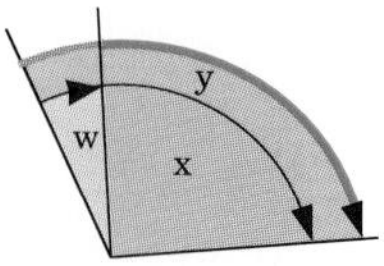

b.
Angle w is 12°.
Angle x is 98°.
How large is angle y?

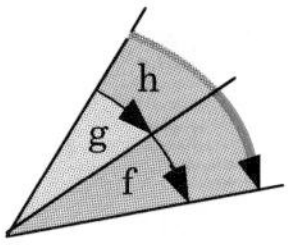

c.
Angle g is 24°.
Angle h is 48°.
How large is angle f?

Part 11 Copy and complete the table.

	Fraction	Mixed number
a.	$\frac{45}{4}$	
b.		$2\frac{7}{8}$
c.		$3\frac{5}{16}$
d.	$\frac{189}{5}$	

Part 12 Copy and complete each pair of equations.

a. 5P = 3
1P = ■

b. 12T = 20
1T = ■

c. 4J = 3
1J = ■

d. 5M = 1
1M = ■

Part 13 Make a ratio table for each problem. If the problem tells about a fraction, also make a fraction number family. Answer the questions.

a. In a pond, there are bass and catfish. $\frac{3}{8}$ of the fish are bass. There are 360 catfish.
1. How many bass are in the pond?
2. How many fish are in the pond?

b. A mixture is made up of lime and water. The ratio of lime to water is 3 to 4. There are 98 pounds in the whole mixture.
1. How many pounds of lime are there?
2. How many pounds of water are there?

c. A kennel had cats and dogs. $\frac{5}{9}$ of the animals were cats. There were 440 dogs in the kennel.
1. How many cats were there?
2. How many total animals were there?

Part 14 Copy and complete each equation.

a. $9 = \frac{■}{3} = \frac{■}{8} = \frac{■}{2} = \frac{■}{4}$

b. $6 = \frac{■}{10} = \frac{■}{5} = \frac{■}{3} = \frac{■}{7}$

Part J

a. $\frac{3}{7} \times \frac{4}{1}$ = $\frac{12}{7}$

b. $\frac{5}{10}$ = $\frac{5}{10}$
$+ \frac{3}{5}\left(\frac{2}{2}\right) = +\frac{6}{10}$
$\frac{11}{10}$

c. $\frac{8}{9}\left(\frac{2}{2}\right) = \frac{16}{18}$
$- \frac{1}{6}\left(\frac{3}{3}\right) = -\frac{3}{18}$
$\frac{13}{18}$

d. $\frac{2}{3} \times \frac{1}{2}$ = $\frac{2}{6}$

Lesson 75

Part 1

- When you multiply dollar amounts by a whole number, the answer will always have two places after the decimal point.
- After you multiply, you start with the ones digit of the answer and count off two places for the decimal point. Also, make sure the answer has a dollar sign.

$33.28

$$\begin{array}{r} \$\ 8.32 \\ \times \quad 4 \\ \hline \$33.28 \end{array}$$

Part 2

Copy each problem and work it. Remember the decimal point in your answer.

a. $\begin{array}{r} \$7.20 \\ \times \quad 3 \\ \hline \end{array}$ b. $\begin{array}{r} \$15.35 \\ \times \quad 2 \\ \hline \end{array}$ c. $\begin{array}{r} \$7.08 \\ \times \quad 9 \\ \hline \end{array}$

Part 3

Make a number family for each statement.

a. J is $\frac{1}{7}$ of 1. b. J is $\frac{8}{7}$ of 1. c. P is $\frac{5}{2}$ of 1. d. M is $\frac{15}{9}$ of 1.

Part 4

Copy and work each problem. First add the fractions. Then add the whole numbers.

a. $\begin{array}{r} 14\frac{5}{9} \\ +21\frac{3}{9} \\ \hline \end{array}$ b. $\begin{array}{r} 6\frac{1}{10} \\ +11\frac{6}{10} \\ \hline \end{array}$ c. $\begin{array}{r} 35\frac{8}{17} \\ +\ 1\frac{2}{17} \\ \hline \end{array}$

Part 5 Answer each question.

a. How many degrees are in $\frac{3}{8}$ of a circle?

b. How many degrees are in $\frac{4}{9}$ of a circle?

c. How many degrees are in $\frac{1}{2}$ of angle v?

d. How many degrees are in $\frac{2}{5}$ of angle w?

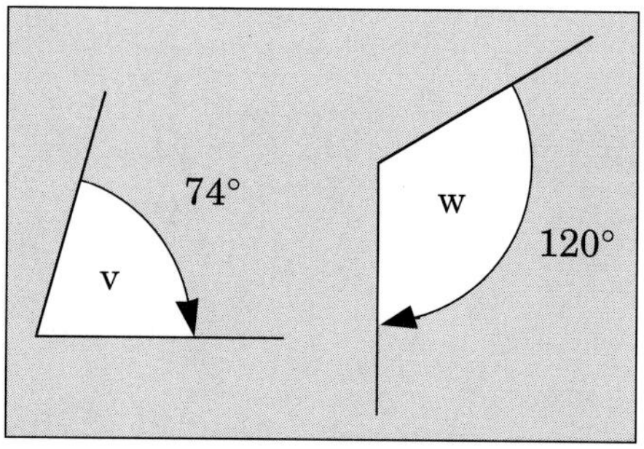

Part 6

- You can show what an arrowed digit is worth by replacing the digit with zero and subtracting the number with zero from the original number.
- Here's a number with the digit for 7 thousand arrowed: 57,328 (↑ under 7)
- We replace that digit with zero. That makes the number 50,328. 50,328
- Now we subtract 50,328 from the original number.

$$\begin{array}{r} 57{,}328 \\ -\ 50{,}328 \\ \hline 7{,}000 \end{array}$$

- We showed that the arrowed digit is worth 7,000.

Part 7 Replace the arrowed digit with zero. Subtract the number with zero from the original number.

a. 54,617   b. 794   c. 34,196   d. 21,491

Part 8 Write each problem as a column problem. Figure out the answer.

a. $3 - \frac{7}{4} = ■$

b. $\frac{3}{8} \times \frac{11}{8} = ■$

c. $\frac{1}{5} + \frac{3}{10} = ■$

d. $\frac{13}{5} \times \frac{1}{2} = ■$

Independent Work

Part 9 — Make a table. Answer the questions.

There were two factories—a cake factory and a fishstick factory. Men and women worked at each factory. The cake factory employed a total of 156 workers. That factory employed 45 men. The fishstick factory employed 600 people. 268 of those workers were women.

a. Do more men or more women work at the fishstick factory?

b. Do more people work at the fishstick factory or at the cake factory?

c. How many men work at the fishstick factory?

d. What's the total number of people that work at both factories?

Part 10 — For each item, make a number family with three letters. Answer each question.

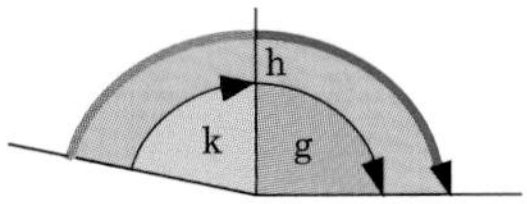

a. Angle h is 168°.
Angle g is 90°.
How large is angle k?

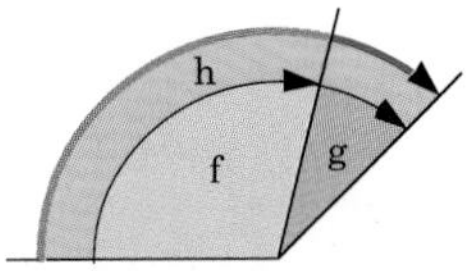

b. Angle f is 105°.
Angle g is 31°.
How large is angle h?

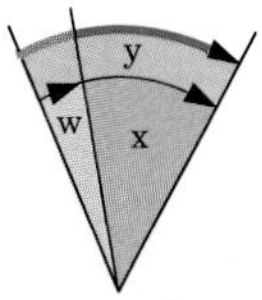

c. Angle x is 39°.
Angle w is 13°.
How large is angle y?

Part 11 — For each item, write the equation. Simplify the answer.

a. What is $\frac{3}{8}$ of 48?

b. What is $\frac{9}{5}$ of 20?

c. What is $\frac{15}{4}$ of 100?

d. What is $\frac{4}{15}$ of 120?

Part 12 — Copy each problem. Find the lowest common denominator. Work the problem.

a. $\frac{2}{8} + \frac{9}{4}$

b. $\frac{11}{4} + \frac{4}{3}$

c. $5 - \frac{3}{10}$

Part 13 — Copy and work each problem.

a. $9\overline{)7884}$ b. $4\overline{)184}$ c. $6\overline{)436}$

d. $7\overline{)2315}$ e. $8\overline{)672}$

Part 14 **Make a ratio table for each problem. If the problem tells about a fraction, also make a fraction number family. Answer the questions.**

a. $\frac{2}{7}$ of the bugs in Martha's garden were ladybugs. There were 903 bugs in her garden.
   1. How many were ladybugs?
   2. How many were not ladybugs?

b. In a sports store, the ratio of skis to snowshoes was 4 to 6. There were 420 skis in the store.
   1. How many snowshoes were there?
   2. What was the total number of skis and snowshoes?

c. $\frac{1}{17}$ of the children in Franklin School had gone to Alaska. 24 children had gone to Alaska.
   1. How many children were in Franklin School?
   2. How many had not gone to Alaska?

Part 15 **For each problem, make a number family and answer the question.**

a. Tom had 456 stamps in his collection. He bought 13 more stamps. He found 21 new stamps on letters. Then he sold some stamps. He ended up with 304 stamps in his collection. How many did he sell?

b. A farm had 21 tons of corn in the silo. In the fall, the farmer put another 78 tons in the silo. During the winter, the farm used 93 tons of corn. How much corn was in the silo after the winter?

Part J

b. $\text{Area}\,\triangle = \frac{\text{base} \times \text{height}}{2}$

$\text{Area} = \frac{4 \times 5}{2} = \frac{20}{2}$

10 square feet

c. $\text{Area}\,\triangle = \frac{\text{base} \times \text{height}}{2}$

$\text{Area} = \frac{12 \times 10}{2} = \frac{120}{2}$

60 square inches

Lesson 76

Part 1

- You've worked with sentences that compare something to 1. Sentences that compare something **to a letter** work the same way.
- The letter at the end of this sentence equals 1: J is $\frac{3}{4}$ of B.
- That sentence works just like the sentence: J is $\frac{3}{4}$ of 1.
- Here's the number family:

$$\begin{array}{ccc} \text{Dif} & \text{J} & \text{B} \\ \frac{1}{4} & \frac{3}{4} & \rightarrow \frac{4}{4} \end{array}$$

- Here's a different sentence: M is $\frac{8}{3}$ of T.
- That's just like the sentence: M is $\frac{8}{3}$ of 1.

$$\begin{array}{ccc} \text{Dif} & \text{T} & \text{M} \\ \frac{5}{3} & \frac{3}{3} & \rightarrow \frac{8}{3} \end{array}$$

Part 2

Write a fraction number family for each sentence.

***Sample sentence:* J is $\frac{1}{4}$ of T.**

a. M is $\frac{7}{3}$ of B.

b. R is $\frac{5}{8}$ of B.

c. K is $\frac{9}{4}$ of B.

d. J is $\frac{5}{6}$ of T.

e. V is $\frac{7}{2}$ of P.

Your big number is smaller than your small numbers. Why is your family like that?
Dif V P
e. 5/2 7/5 → 2/5
Because my big sister is younger than I am?

Part 3

- You can round whole numbers to tens, hundreds, or thousands.
- If you round to hundreds, all the digits **after hundreds** are zeros:

  600 1,500 200 8,700 2,100

- If you round to thousands, all the digits **after thousands** are zeros:

  5,000 12,000 17,000 1,000 128,000

- The arrowed digit shows the place you'll round to. You'll round this numeral to thousands. — 17,569 (arrow under 7)
- When you round to thousands, you look at the digit after thousands. If the digit is 5 or more, you round up. — 17,569 (arrow under 7) → 8,000
- The numeral 17,569 rounds to 18,000. — 17,569 → 18,000
- The numeral 17,369 rounds to 17,000. — 17,369 → 17,000

Part 4

Round each number. The arrow shows the place you round to.

a. 94,833 (arrow under 4)   b. 78,399 (arrow under 8)   c. 43,645 (arrow under 6)   d. 43,681 (arrow under 6)   e. 43,384 (arrow under 8)

Part 5

ABBREVIATIONS

LENGTH

inches : in
feet : ft
yards : yd
miles : mi
centimeters : cm
meters : m
kilometers : km

AREA

square inches : sq in
square feet : sq ft
square yards : sq yd

WEIGHT

ounces : oz
pounds : lb
grams : g
kilograms : kg

Part 6 Find the area of each figure.

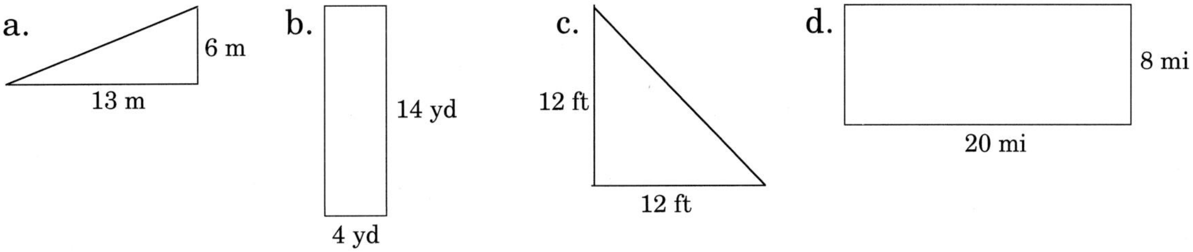

Part 7

- Some problems that add or subtract have a whole number **and** a mixed number.
- When you work **addition** problems, you just copy the fraction in the answer. Then you add the whole numbers.
- You're adding nothing to $\frac{5}{7}$:

$$\begin{array}{r} 34 \\ +\ 13\frac{5}{7} \\ \hline \frac{5}{7} \end{array} \qquad \begin{array}{r} 34 \\ +\ 13\frac{5}{7} \\ \hline 47\frac{5}{7} \end{array}$$

You copy the fraction in the answer. → $\frac{5}{7}$

Then you add 34 and 13. → 47

- Here's a different problem:

The fraction is $\frac{12}{57}$.

$$\begin{array}{r} 75\frac{12}{57} \\ +\ 18 \\ \hline \frac{12}{57} \end{array} \qquad \begin{array}{r} 75\frac{12}{57} \\ +\ 18 \\ \hline 93\frac{12}{57} \end{array}$$

You copy that fraction in the answer. → $\frac{12}{57}$

Then you add the whole numbers 75 and 18. → 93

- Some **subtraction** problems work the same way. If the **top number** in the problem is the mixed number, you just copy the fraction in the answer.
- For this problem, the mixed number is on top.

$$\begin{array}{r} 25\frac{17}{19} \\ -\ \ 9 \\ \hline \frac{17}{19} \end{array} \qquad \begin{array}{r} 25\frac{17}{19} \\ -\ \ 9 \\ \hline 16\frac{17}{19} \end{array}$$

You're subtracting nothing from $\frac{17}{19}$, so the fraction part of the answer is $\frac{17}{19}$. → $\frac{17}{19}$

- Then you subtract 9 from 25. → 16

Part 8 Copy and work each problem.

a. $10\frac{25}{38} + 47$

b. $45\frac{7}{11} - 13$

c. $29 + 7\frac{10}{19}$

Part 9 For each problem, write the answer as a simple equation that shows the unit name.

a. 5 pills weigh 11 grams. What does 1 pill weigh?

b. 4 identical bottles hold a total of 45 ounces. How many ounces does 1 bottle hold?

c. 10 identical cards cost 8 dollars. How much does 1 card cost?

d. 3 identical machines made 78 buttons. How many buttons did 1 machine make?

Independent Work

Part 10 Write each problem as a column problem and work it.

a. $4.27 + $15.08 + $2.60

b. $194.28 – $56.03

Part 11 Work each problem. If the answer is too big, work the problem again with the correct answer.

a. $87\overline{)560}$ with 7 written above

b. $83\overline{)592}$ with 7 written above

c. $55\overline{)367}$ with 7 written above

d. $95\overline{)665}$ with 7 written above

Part 12 For each problem, make a number family. Answer the questions.

a. In August, the horse weighed 68 pounds more than it weighed in May. If the horse weighed 1111 pounds in August, how much did it weigh in May?

b. The horse weighed 1040 pounds in January. In February, it gained 41 pounds. In March, it lost 8 pounds. In April, it gained 38 pounds. How much did the horse weigh at the end of April?

c. $\frac{3}{4}$ of the workers wore hard hats.
   1. What's the fraction for all the workers?
   2. What fraction of the workers did not wear hard hats?

d. A deck of cards has 52 cards. 4 of those cards are kings.
   1. What fraction of the cards are kings?
   2. What fraction of the cards are not kings?

Part 13 **Find the area and perimeter of each rectangle. Use abbreviations.**

a.

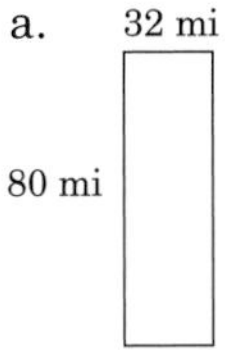

b.

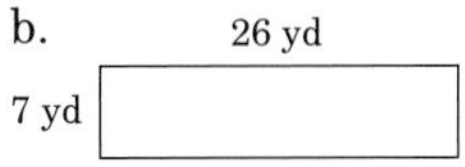

Part 14 **Answer the questions.**

The line shows that the ratio of girls to boys is 3 to 2.

a. If there are 12 boys, how many girls are there?

b. If there are 12 girls, how many boys are there?

c. If there are 18 girls, how many boys are there?

d. How many girls are there for 10 boys?

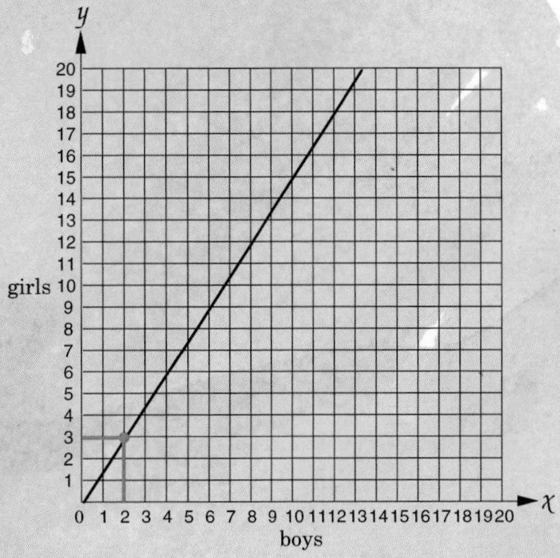

What I want to know is how 3 boys and 2 girls will fit on that line.

Lesson 77

Part 1 Round each numeral to the place indicated by the arrow.

a. 4,082   b. 7,098   c. 4,326   d. 8,888   e. 5,793

Part 2 For each item, make a number family with three letters. Then work the problem.

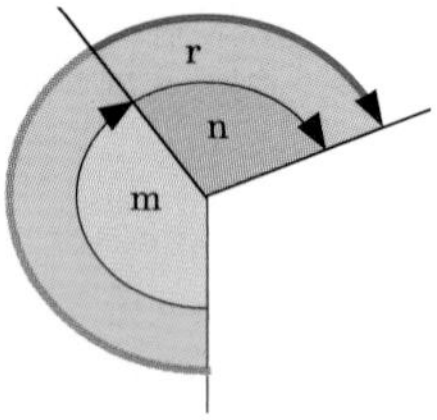

a.

Angle m is $\frac{2}{5}$ of a circle.
Angle r is 250°.
Figure out angle n.

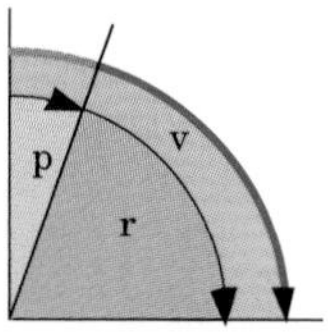

b.

Angle p is 20°.
Angle v is $\frac{1}{4}$ of a circle.
Figure out angle r.

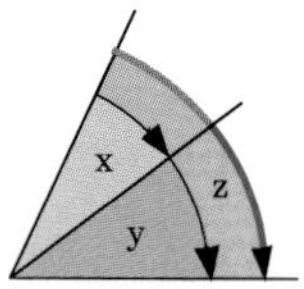

c.

Angle y is $\frac{1}{10}$ of a circle.
Angle x is 28°.
Figure out angle z.

Part 3

- You've worked with sentences that compare letters. The sentences you've worked with have the word **of.**
- Sentences that do not have the word **of** work the same way.
- Here's a sentence that compares: F is $\frac{7}{5}$ **as much as** R.
- You're comparing something to R. So R is 1. F is more than R, so F is the big number.
- Here's the family with F as the big number and R as 1:

Dif	R	F
	$\frac{5}{5}$ →	$\frac{7}{5}$

- Here's another sentence: T is $\frac{5}{6}$ **as long as** Y.
- Here's the family with T as a small number and Y as 1:

Dif	T	Y
	$\frac{5}{6}$ →	$\frac{6}{6}$

Part 4 **For each item, make a fraction number family.**

a. P is $\frac{5}{6}$ as tall as H.

b. R is $\frac{9}{7}$ of T.

c. J is $\frac{4}{3}$ as much as D.

d. V is $\frac{1}{2}$ of P.

Part 5 **Copy and work each problem.**

a. $18 + 2\frac{7}{15}$

b. $38\frac{9}{21} - 7$

c. $55\frac{12}{19} - 41$

d. $34\frac{1}{3} + 68$

Part 6 **Find the area of each figure.**

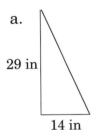

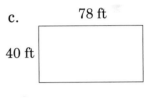

a.

29 in

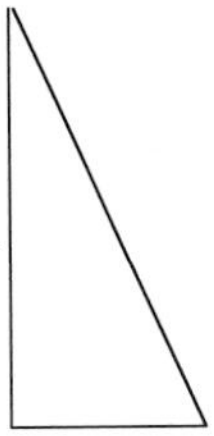

14 in

b.

36 mi

85 mi

c.

78 ft

40 ft

Independent Work

Part 7 **For each item, make a ratio table. Answer the questions.**

a. $\frac{7}{8}$ of the students passed the test. There were 400 students in all.
   1. How many students passed the test?
   2. How many students did not pass the test?

b. The ratio of aces to other cards in a deck is 1 to 12. There are 48 cards that are not aces.
   1. How many cards are aces?
   2. How many cards are there in all?

Part 8 **Complete each equation.**

a. $4 = \frac{\blacksquare}{8} = \frac{\blacksquare}{50} = \frac{\blacksquare}{125}$

b. $3 = \frac{\blacksquare}{12} = \frac{\blacksquare}{36} = \frac{\blacksquare}{180}$

Part 9 **Make a table and answer the questions.**

There are black-tail deer and white-tail deer in two locations. The locations are Elk Ridge and Horn Mountain. The total number of white-tail deer for both locations is 400. At Horn Mountain, there are 48 black-tail deer. At Elk Ridge, there is a total of 210 deer. At Elk Ridge, there are 145 black-tail deer.

a. How many white-tail deer are at Horn Mountain?

b. Are there more white-tail deer or black-tail deer at Elk Ridge?

c. At which place are there fewer white-tail deer?

d. What's the total number of deer for both locations?

Part 10 **Copy each problem. Estimate the answer by rounding the number you divide by. Then work the problem.**

a. $91\overline{)779}$ b. $49\overline{)329}$

Part 11 **Copy and complete the table.**

	Decimal	Fraction	Mixed number
a.		$\frac{38}{10}$	
b.			$4\frac{3}{100}$
c.	16.915		
d.		$\frac{265}{100}$	

Part J

a. Area △ = $\frac{\text{base} \times \text{height}}{2}$

Area = $\frac{14 \times 29}{2} = \frac{406}{2}$

203 sq in

b. Area △ = $\frac{\text{base} \times \text{height}}{2}$

Area = $\frac{36 \times 85}{2} = \frac{3060}{2}$

1530 sq mi

c. Area □ = base × height

Area = 78 × 40

3120 sq ft

Lesson 78

Part 1

- You've worked with sentences that compare letters. Sentences that compare things work the same way.
- Here's a sentence: **The radio costs $\frac{3}{7}$ as much as the toaster.**
- The sentence compares a radio to a toaster. So the toaster is 1. The radio costs less, so the radio is a small number. The toaster is the big number.
- Here's the number family:

Dif	Radio	Toaster
$\frac{4}{7}$	$\frac{3}{7}$ →	$\frac{7}{7}$

- Here's a different sentence:

The cost of dinner was $\frac{8}{5}$ the cost of lunch.

- The cost of dinner was more than the cost of lunch. So the cost of dinner is the big number.
- Here's the family:

Dif	Lunch	Dinner
$\frac{3}{5}$	$\frac{5}{5}$ →	$\frac{8}{5}$

Part 2

Make a number family for each sentence.

a. The train was $\frac{3}{4}$ as long as the station.

b. The cost of the book was $\frac{5}{3}$ the cost of the radio.

c. Dinner cost $\frac{4}{5}$ as much as the show.

d. John's weight is $\frac{7}{5}$ of his father's weight.

e. The rainfall in August was $\frac{9}{7}$ as much as the rainfall in July.

Part 3

Copy and work each problem.

a. $\begin{array}{r} \$6.14 \\ \underline{\times \quad 13} \end{array}$

b. $\begin{array}{r} \$\ 7.03 \\ 51.00 \\ \underline{+ \quad 9.16} \end{array}$

c. $\begin{array}{r} \$53.06 \\ \underline{\times \qquad 4} \end{array}$

d. $\begin{array}{r} \$56.03 \\ \underline{- \quad 3.99} \end{array}$

Part 4 Work each item.

a. 8,743 Round the numeral to the nearest hundred.

b. 18,409 Round the numeral to the nearest ten.

c. 8,720,201 Round the numeral to the nearest million.

d. 218,599 Round the numeral to the nearest thousand.

e. 2,063,514 Round the numeral to the nearest ten thousand.

Part 5 Write each problem as a column problem and work it. Write the answer as a fraction and box it.

a. $\frac{5}{3} \times \frac{1}{2} =$ [redacted]

b. $\frac{5}{3} + \frac{1}{2} =$ [redacted]

c. $\frac{5}{3} + 2 =$ [redacted]

d. $\frac{6}{1} \times \frac{5}{8} =$ [redacted]

e. $3 - \frac{2}{15} =$ [redacted]

Part 6 For each item, make a number family with three letters. Then work the problem.

a.

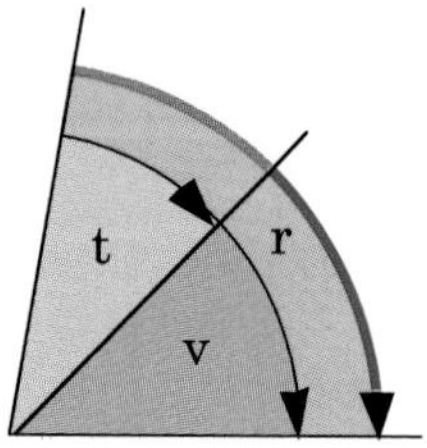

Angle r is $\frac{2}{9}$ of a circle.
Angle t is 35°.
Figure out angle v.

b.

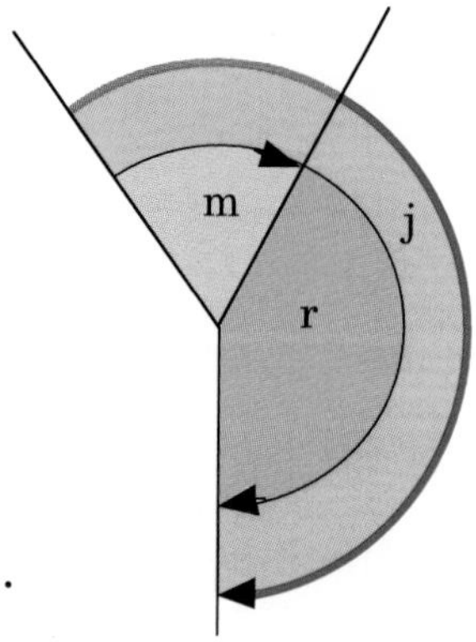

Angle m is 65°.
Angle j is $\frac{3}{5}$ of a circle.
Figure out angle r.

c.

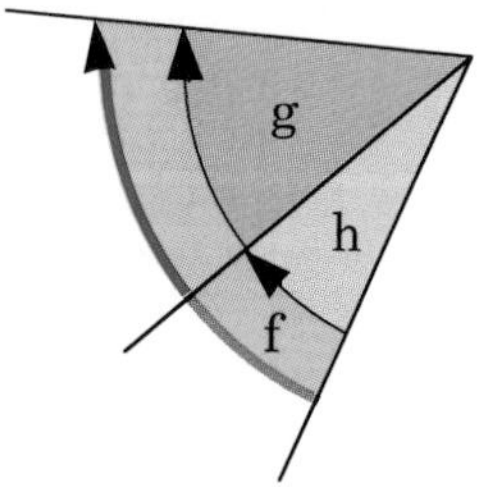

Angle h is 25°.
Angle g is $\frac{1}{8}$ of a circle.
Figure out angle f.

Part 7

Answer each question. For some problems, you do not need to make a ratio equation.

a. 4 pills weigh 15 grams. What does 1 pill weigh?

b. 4 pills weigh 15 grams. What do 6 pills weigh?

c. If 3 identical bottles hold 120 ounces, how many bottles are needed to hold 280 ounces?

d. If 7 identical vases weigh 84 pounds, how many pounds does 1 vase weigh?

Independent Work

Part 8

Some answers are too big. Some are too small. Copy each problem and multiply. Work the problems again with the correct answer.

a. $\begin{array}{r} 5 \\ 96\overline{)576} \end{array}$ b. $\begin{array}{r} 5 \\ 53\overline{)228} \end{array}$

c. $\begin{array}{r} 5 \\ 41\overline{)262} \end{array}$ d. $\begin{array}{r} 5 \\ 88\overline{)530} \end{array}$

Part 9

Copy and complete the equation.

$$\frac{5}{3} = \boxed{\frac{\blacksquare}{21} = \frac{25}{\blacksquare} = \frac{200}{\blacksquare}}$$

Part 10

For each item, make a ratio equation. Answer the question.

a. The ratio of perch to sunfish is 2 to 7. If there are 245 sunfish, how many perch are there?

b. A cook uses 6 onions for every 4 cloves of garlic. If she uses 21 cloves of garlic, how many onions does she need?

c. A bus travels at the rate of 160 miles every 3 hours. If the bus travels for 2 hours, how many miles does it go?

d. In a mixture, there are 5 pounds of lime for every 1 pound of sand. If there are 56 pounds of sand, how many pounds of lime are there?

Part 11

Copy and work each problem.

a. $\begin{array}{r} 15 \\ +\ 2\frac{7}{8} \\ \hline \end{array}$ b. $\begin{array}{r} 11\frac{3}{8} \\ -\ 4 \\ \hline \end{array}$ c. $\begin{array}{r} 10\frac{13}{15} \\ -\ 9 \\ \hline \end{array}$

Part 12 **Make a number family for each problem. Figure out the answer to each question.**

a. Donna's bank account had $300 at the beginning of January. In January, she took out some money. In February, she put $120 in her account. In March, she put $86 in her account. At the end of March, she had $299 in her account. How much money did she take out of her account in January?

b. $\frac{3}{8}$ of the eggs were rotten. There was a total of 2200 eggs.
   1. How many were rotten?
   2. How many were not rotten?

Part 13 **For each item, write the multiplication problem and the answer. Simplify the answer if you can.**

a. What is $\frac{3}{5}$ of 80?

b. What is $\frac{9}{4}$ of 28?

c. What is $\frac{1}{3}$ of $\frac{5}{9}$?

d. What is $\frac{1}{2}$ of 300?

Part 14 **Copy each problem and work it. Rewrite the problem if you need to. Write the answer as a fraction and box it.**

a. $4 + \frac{5}{4}$

b. $\frac{1}{6} + \frac{3}{4}$

c. $\frac{11}{6} + \frac{1}{9}$

Part J

a. $6.14 × 13 = 18 42 + 61 40 = $79.82

b. $ 7.03 + 51.00 + 9.16 = $67.19

c. $53.06 × 4 = $212.24

d. $56.03 − 3.99 = $52.04

Part K

a. $\frac{5}{3} \times \frac{1}{2} = \boxed{\frac{5}{6}}$

b. $\frac{5}{3}\left(\frac{2}{2}\right) = \frac{10}{6}$; $+\frac{1}{2}\left(\frac{3}{3}\right) = +\frac{3}{6}$; $\boxed{\frac{13}{6}}$

c. $\frac{5}{3} = \frac{5}{3}$; $+2 = +\frac{6}{3}$; $\boxed{\frac{11}{3}}$

d. $\frac{6}{1} \times \frac{5}{8} = \boxed{\frac{30}{8}}$

e. $3 = \frac{45}{15}$; $-\frac{2}{15} = -\frac{2}{15}$; $\boxed{\frac{43}{15}}$

Lesson 79

Part 1

- If the fraction part of a mixed number equals 1, you can write the mixed number as a whole number. You just add 1.
- Here's: $3\frac{14}{14}$

  The fraction equals 1. So the mixed number equals 3 + 1. $3\frac{14}{14} = 4$
- Here's another mixed number: $19\frac{7}{7}$

  $19\frac{7}{7} = 20$

Part 2

Rewrite each mixed number if the fraction equals 1.

a. $8\frac{5}{5}$ b. $9\frac{6}{7}$ c. $12\frac{3}{3}$ d. $53\frac{2}{2}$ e. $4\frac{30}{30}$ f. $4\frac{27}{30}$

Part 3

Work each item.

a. 17,298,608 Round the numeral to the nearest million.

b. 25,523 Round the numeral to the nearest thousand.

c. 4,284 Round the numeral to the nearest ten.

d. 188,610 Round the numeral to the nearest ten thousand.

e. 1,204,543 Round the numeral to the nearest hundred.

Part 4

- You've used this equation: **Area □ = base x height.**
- You can use this same equation to find the area of any **parallelogram.**

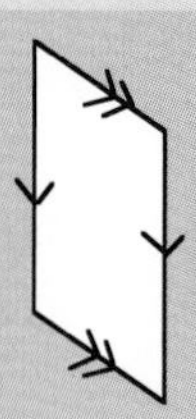

- A parallelogram is a 4-sided figure that has two pairs of parallel sides.
- All these figures are parallelograms:

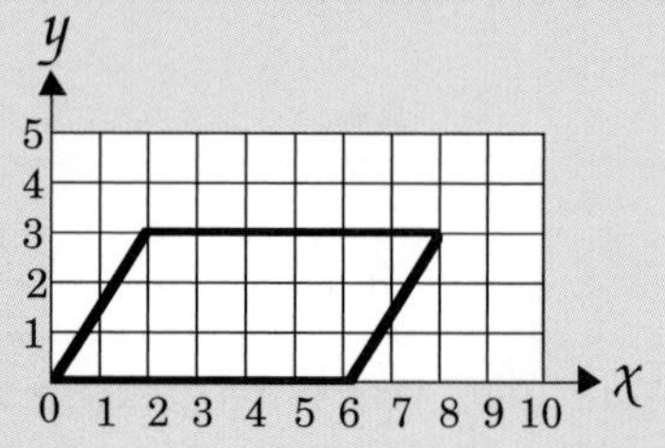

- **Area □ = base x height.**
- The equation works with parallelograms because a parallelogram has the same area as a rectangle with the same base and the same height.

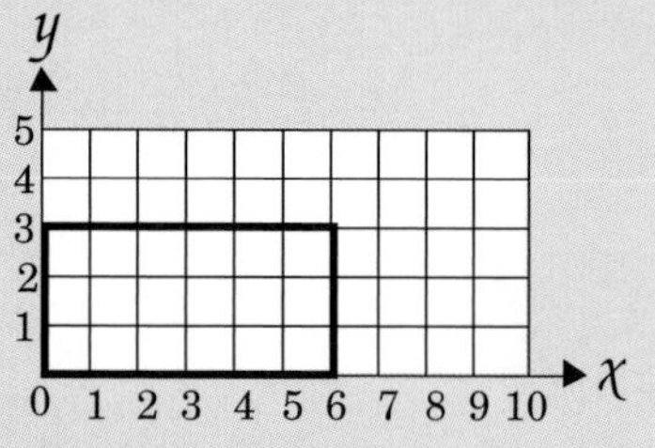

- Remember, the height of a parallelogram on the coordinate system is always a line that is parallel to the *y* axis.

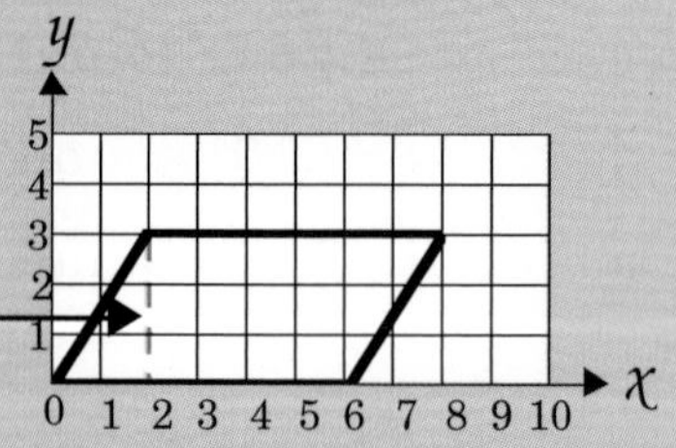

- This is the height:
- This is **not** the height:

- Remember, use this equation: **Area □ = base x height.**

Part 5 Figure out the area of each parallelogram.

a.

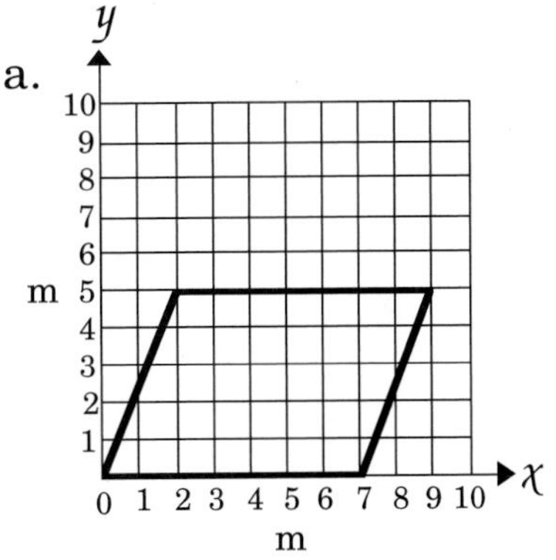

b.

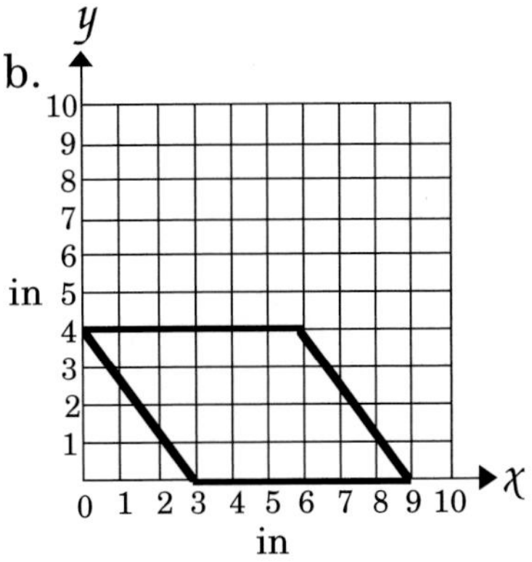

c.

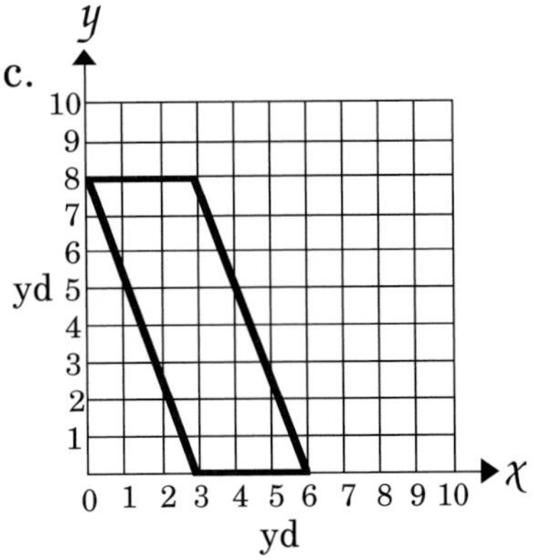

d.

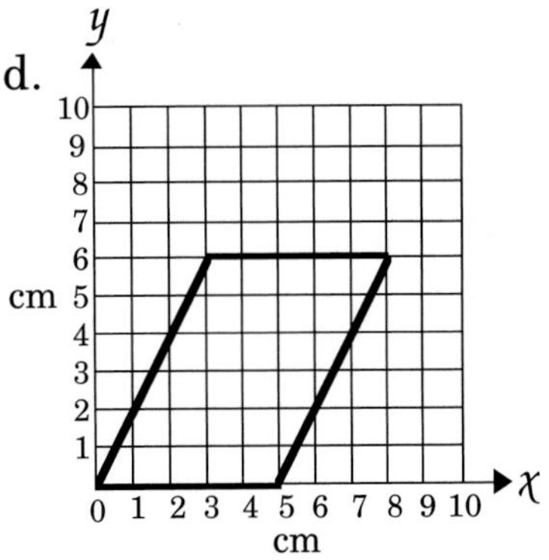

Part 6 For each item, make a number family with three letters. Then work the problem.

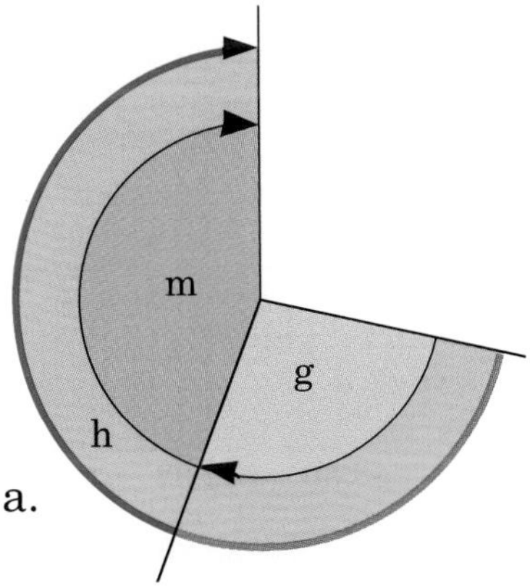

a.

Angle h is $\frac{7}{10}$ of a circle.
Angle g is 93°.
Figure out angle m.

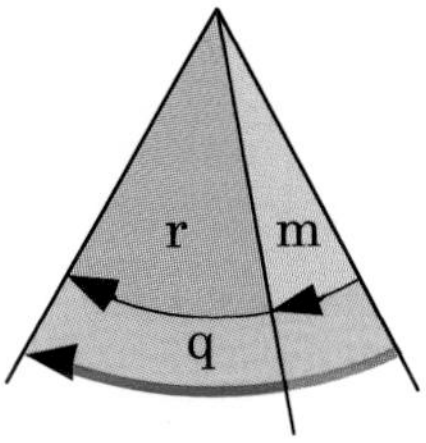

b.

Angle r is 40°.
Angle m is $\frac{1}{20}$ of a circle.
Figure out angle q.

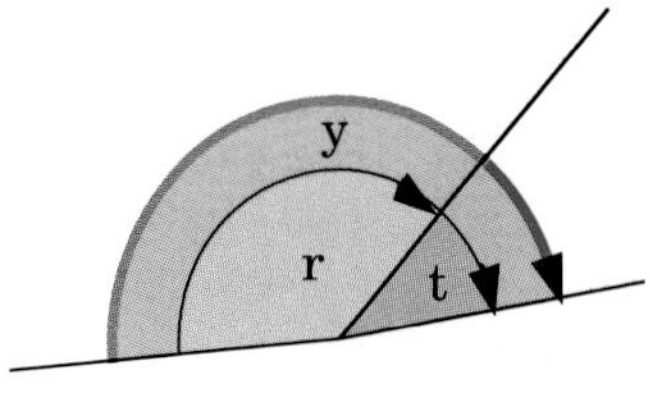

c.

Angle r is $\frac{3}{8}$ of a circle.
Angle y is 175°.
Figure out angle t.

Part 7

Answer each question. For some problems, you do not need to make a ratio equation.

a. 9 boots weigh 12 ounces. What do 6 boots weigh?

b. 12 marbles weigh 42 grams. What does 1 marble weigh?

c. 8 textbooks cost 120 dollars. What does 1 textbook cost?

d. 14 machines grind 56 tons of wood. How much wood do 5 machines grind?

Part 8

Make a fraction number family for each sentence.

a. Ronald runs $\frac{7}{8}$ as far as Ginger.

b. Today's temperature is $\frac{8}{5}$ of yesterday's temperature.

c. The tower is $\frac{13}{10}$ as high as the apartment building.

d. Factory B produced $\frac{3}{8}$ of the amount that factory C produced.

Independent Work

Part 9

For each item, answer the questions. Box the answers.

a. A rectangle has a base of 16 meters and a height of 19 meters. What is the perimeter of the rectangle? What is the area of the rectangle?

b. A field is the shape of a rectangle that has a base of 380 feet and a height of 88 feet. What's the area of the field?

Part 10

Figure out the area of each triangle. Remember to start with the equation for the area of a triangle.

a.

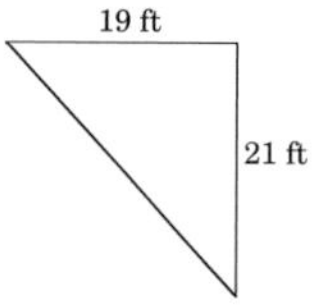

b.

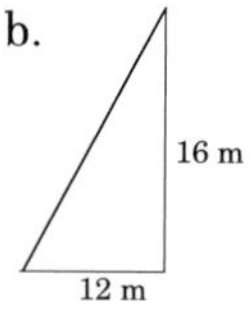

Part 11

For each item, make a number family and answer the question the problem asks.

a. A tire had 28 pounds of air in it. 5 pounds of air leaked out. Somebody pumped 15 pounds of air into the tire. 6 pounds of air leaked out. How many pounds of air were left in the tire?

b. Fran had some money in her savings account. She took out $30. Then she took out $14. She still had $16 in her account. How much was in her account to begin with?

Part 12

Write each item as a column problem and work it.

a. \$3.56 + \$12.08

b. \$14.71 – \$2.30

c. \$1.03 + \$17.24 + \$9.68

Part 13 **Write each problem as a column problem and work it. Box the answer.**

a. $\frac{4}{7} + \frac{1}{2} =$ ■   b. $\frac{6}{1} \times \frac{15}{4} =$ ■   c. $\frac{3}{20} + \frac{2}{10} =$ ■

Golly, Edna, I don't think that's what the teacher had in mind when he said to write the problems as **column** problems!
a. 4/7 + 1/2
b. 6/1 × 15/4

Part 14 **Copy and complete each pair of equations. Show the first common number.**

a. 4 x ■ = ■
   8 x ■ = ■

b. 9 x ■ = ■
   6 x ■ = ■

c. 7 x ■ = ■
   3 x ■ = ■

Part 15 **Copy and complete each pair of equations.**

a. 4R = 11
   1R = ■

b. 7D = 17
   1D = ■

c. 15R = 2
   1R = ■

Lesson 80

Part 1

- **Area □ = base x height.**
- Here's a rectangle on the coordinate system:

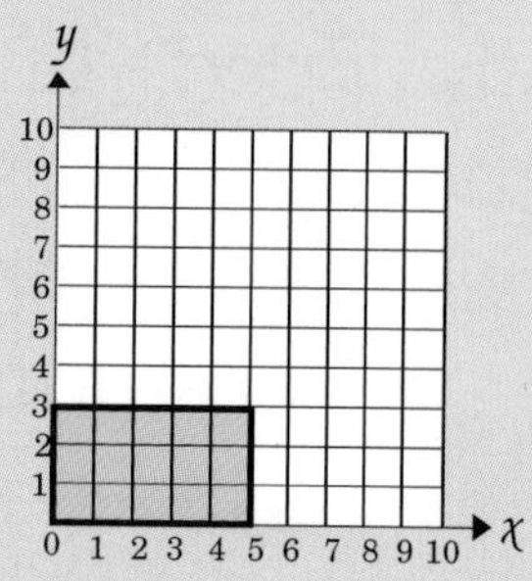

- To find the area of the rectangle you multiply: 5 x 3. The area is 15 square units.
- We'll move part of the rectangle. The figure will still have 15 square units because we are not adding any units or taking any units away.

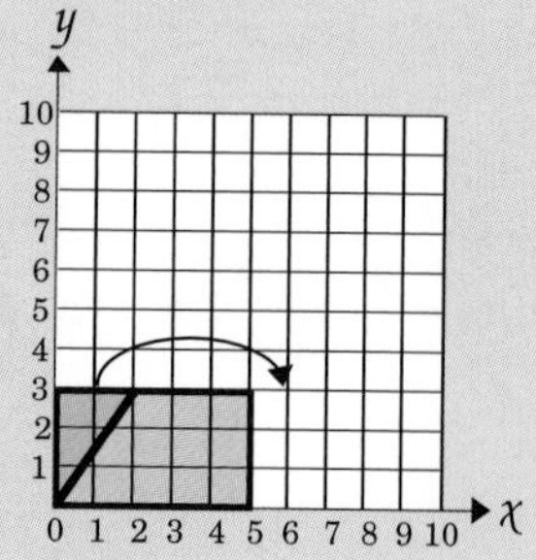

- The figure still has the same number of squares it started out with.

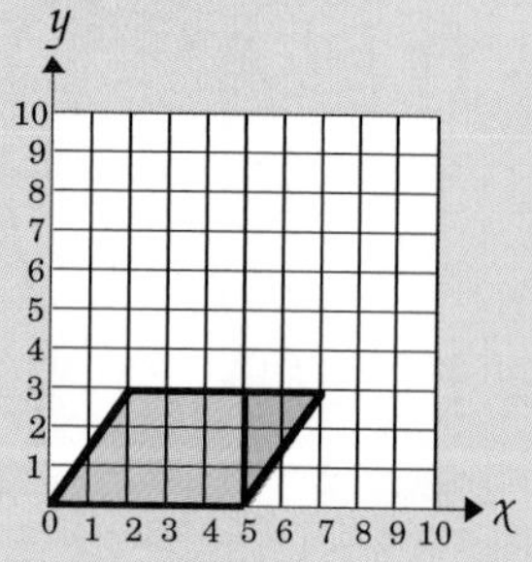

- We can create different parallelograms that have the same base and the same height as the rectangle we started with. Each of these parallelograms has a base that is 5 and a height that is 3. So each parallelogram has the same area.

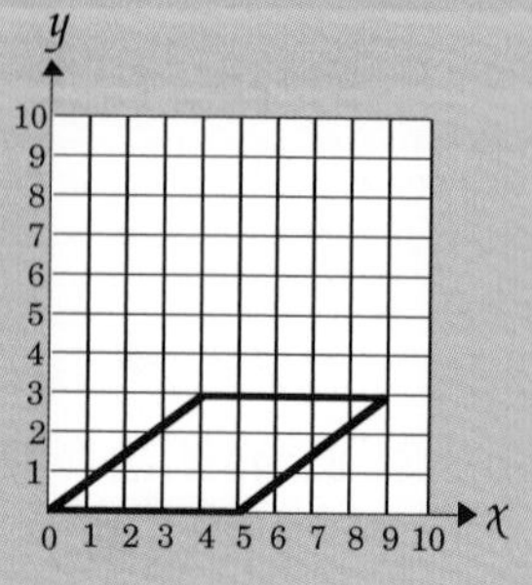

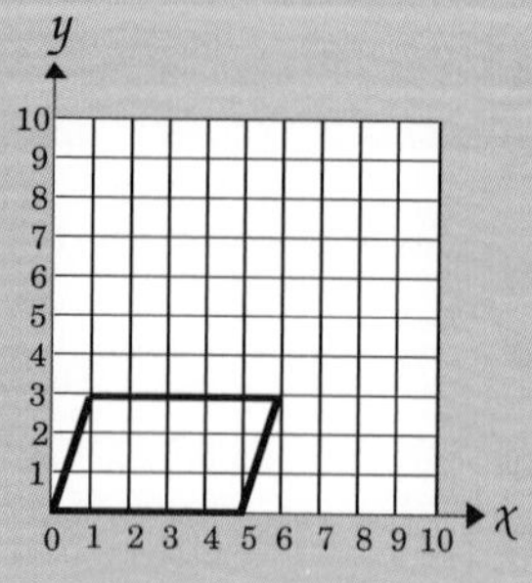

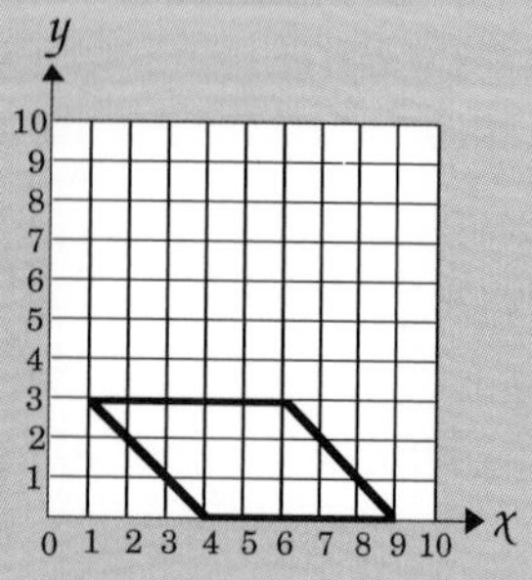

Part 2 Find the area of each figure.

a.

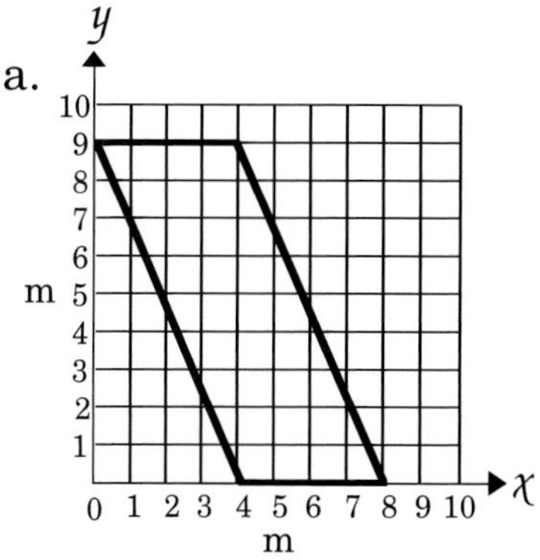

b.

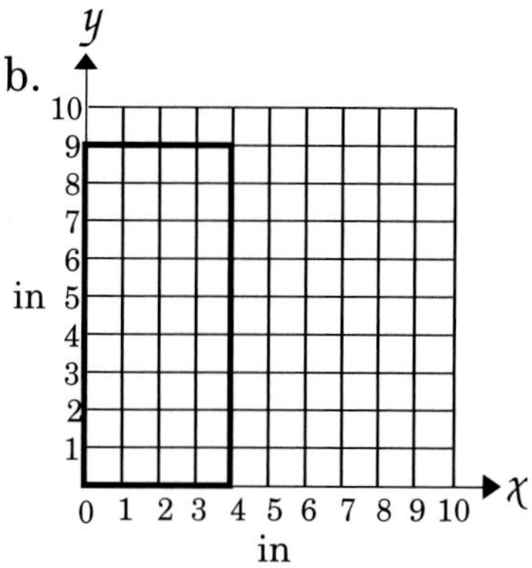

c.

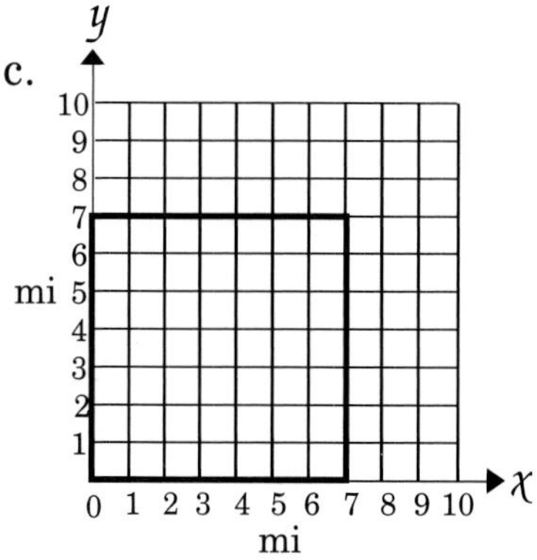

d.

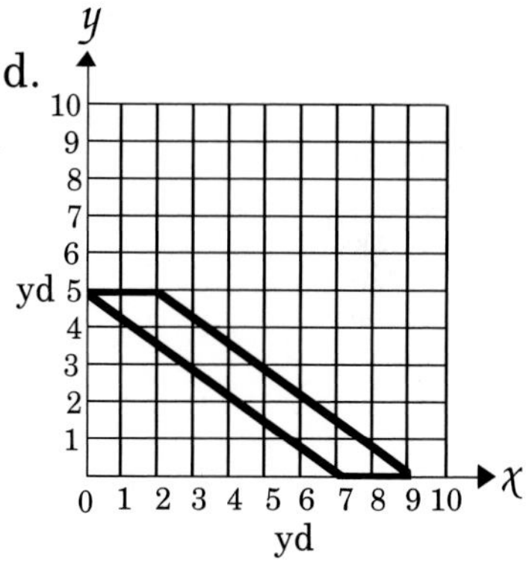

Part 3 Copy and work each problem. If the answer has a fraction that equals 1, rewrite it.

Sample problem:

$$\begin{array}{r} 3\frac{1}{5} \\ +\ 7\frac{4}{5} \\ \hline 10\frac{5}{5} = 11 \end{array}$$

a. $\begin{array}{r} 9\frac{7}{10} \\ +\ 5\frac{3}{10} \\ \hline \end{array}$

b. $\begin{array}{r} 48\frac{1}{23} \\ +\ 8\frac{20}{23} \\ \hline \end{array}$

c. $\begin{array}{r} 3\frac{7}{15} \\ +\ 1\frac{8}{15} \\ \hline \end{array}$

d. $\begin{array}{r} 3\frac{4}{7} \\ +\ 50\frac{3}{7} \\ \hline \end{array}$

Part 4 Write the decimal value for each mixed number.

a. $5\frac{3}{12}$ b. $17\frac{4}{20}$ c. $1\frac{24}{25}$ d. $10\frac{7}{8}$

Test 8

Part 2 **Answer the questions for items a through c. For items d and e, make a number family with three letters. Answer the question.**

a. How many degrees are in $\frac{1}{4}$ of a circle?

b. How many degrees are in a whole circle?

c. How many degrees are in $\frac{1}{2}$ of a circle?

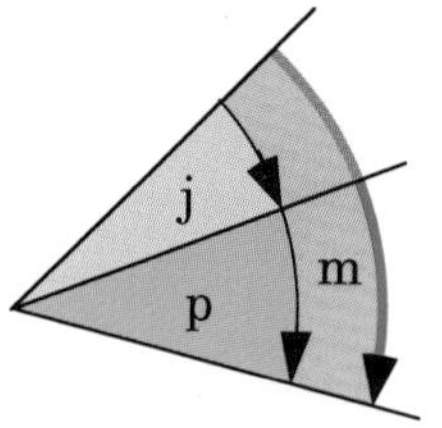

d.
Angle m is 82°.
Angle j is 24°.
What is angle p?

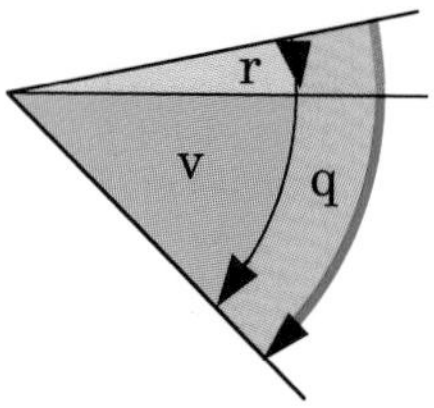

e.
Angle r is 11°.
Angle v is $\frac{1}{8}$ of a circle.
What is angle q?

Part 3 **For each item, show the equation. Simplify the answer.**

a. What is $\frac{5}{4}$ of 192?

b. What is $\frac{1}{8}$ of $\frac{3}{5}$?

c. How many degrees are in $\frac{3}{8}$ of a circle?

Part 4 **Write each problem in a column and work it.**

a. \$13.80 x 4

b. \$7.60 + \$48.01 + \$1.36

Part 5 **Copy each problem. Find the lowest common denominator. Work each problem. Write the answer as a fraction.**

a. $3 - \frac{2}{9}$

b. $\frac{5}{8} - \frac{3}{6}$

c. $\frac{3}{10} + \frac{8}{5}$

Part 6 **For each item, make a fraction number family.**

a. B is $\frac{9}{4}$ of D.

b. J is $\frac{1}{15}$ as much as R.

Part 7

Work each item.

a. Round 14,671 to the nearest hundred.

b. Round 14,671 to the nearest thousand.

c. Round 14,671 to the nearest ten.

Part 8

Write the answer as an equation. Simplify the answer.

a. 3 identical machines produce 450 shoes. How many shoes does 1 machine produce?

Part 9

Copy each problem. Estimate the answer by rounding the number you divide by. Then work the problem.

a. $69\overline{)508}$

b. $92\overline{)770}$

Part 10

Find the area and perimeter of each figure.

a.

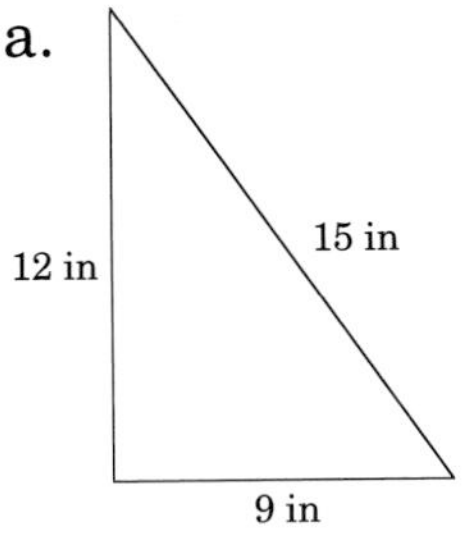

b.

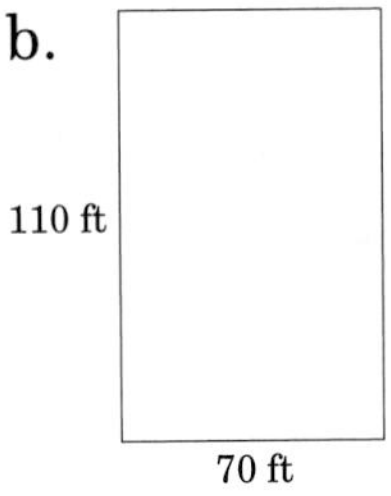

Lesson 81

Part 1

- You've worked number-family problems that have names for **in, out** and **end up.**
- You can use these families to work money problems.
- The amount for **in** is the amount you **give the person.** That's the amount that goes **in** the cash register.

- The amount for **out** is the cost of what you buy.

- The amount for **end up** is the change you receive.

Part 2

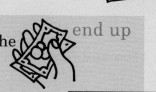

For each item, make a number family. Answer the question.

Sample problem: Linda purchased the mask and the dive watch. She gave the clerk $50. How much change did she receive?

a. Tim purchased the swim fins and two dive watches. He received $11 change. How much money did he give the clerk?

b. Ginger bought the fins, a mask, a belt and a shirt. She gave the clerk a check for $100. How much change did she get?

c. Anne bought a mask and two shirts. She paid for the items and received $5 in change. How much money did she give the clerk?

Part 3 For each item, work a problem with rounded values.

Sample problem:

$$\begin{array}{r} 5626 \\ -\ 1761 \\ \hline \end{array}$$

a. $\begin{array}{r} 157 \\ -\ 103 \\ \hline \end{array}$

b. $\begin{array}{r} 2940 \\ \times\quad 4 \\ \hline \end{array}$

c. $\begin{array}{r} 281 \\ +\ 1326 \\ \hline \end{array}$

Part 4 Copy and work each problem.

a. $\begin{array}{r} 1\frac{1}{2} \\ +\ 3\frac{1}{2} \\ \hline \end{array}$

b. $\begin{array}{r} 7\frac{3}{8} \\ +\ 2\frac{4}{8} \\ \hline \end{array}$

c. $\begin{array}{r} 26\frac{4}{10} \\ +\ 1\frac{1}{10} \\ \hline \end{array}$

d. $\begin{array}{r} 8\frac{3}{16} \\ +\ 8\frac{13}{16} \\ \hline \end{array}$

Part 5

- You know how many degrees are in half a circle.

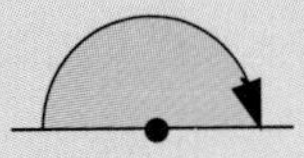

- You know how many degrees are in a corner of a rectangle.

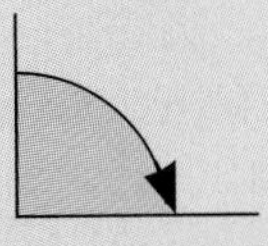

- There's a special angle marker for 90° angles. The degree marker looks like the corner of a rectangle.

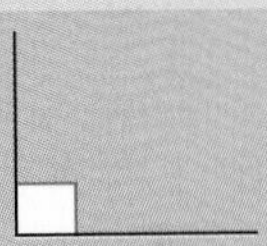

- If you know that the whole angle is 90 degrees or 180 degrees, you can work problems that show the whole angle divided into two smaller angles.

Sample problem:

Angle **m** is 95°.

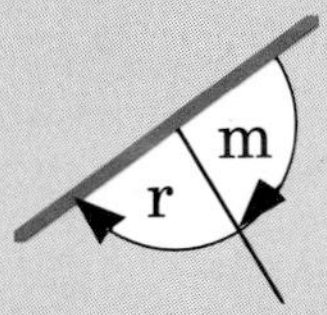

How many degrees are in angle **r**?

Part 6 For each item, answer the question.

Angle **j** is 110°.

a.

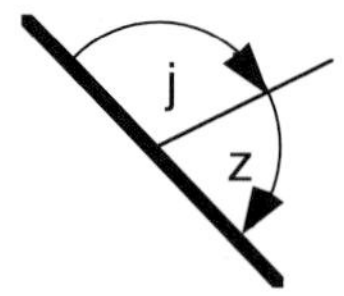

How many degrees are in angle **z**?

Angle **k** is 48°.

b.

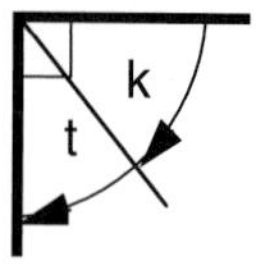

How many degrees are in angle **t**?

Angle **r** is 74°.

c.

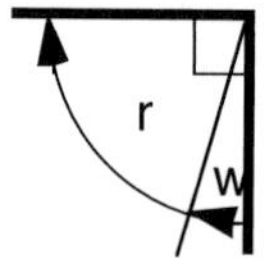

How many degrees are in angle **w**?

Angle **p** is 49°.

d.

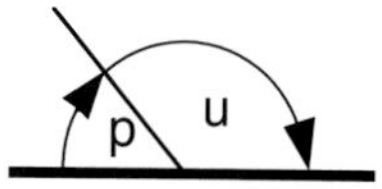

How many degrees are in angle **u**?

Part 7 For each item, answer the question.

a. 1 block weighs 13 ounces. 11 blocks weigh how many ounces?

b. 1 basket costs $24. How much do 6 baskets cost?

c. 1 egg makes 3 waffles. 40 eggs make how many waffles?

Part 8 Find the area and perimeter of each figure.

a.

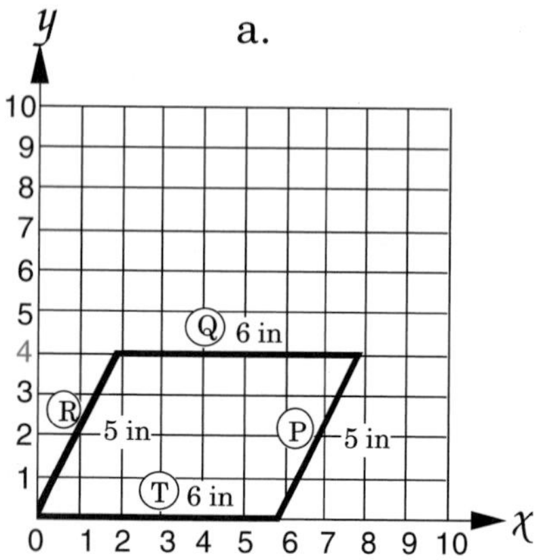

b.

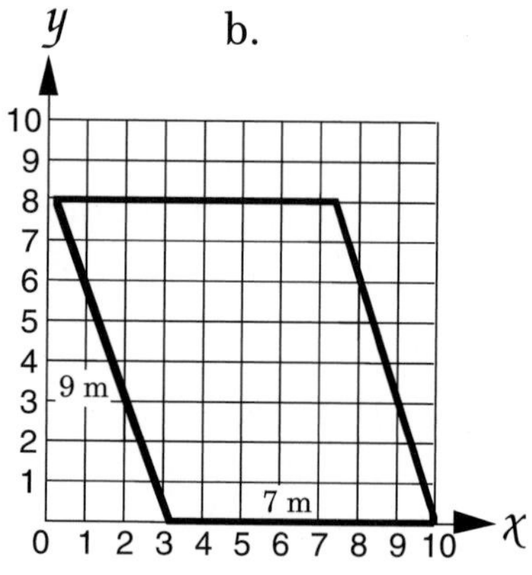

c.

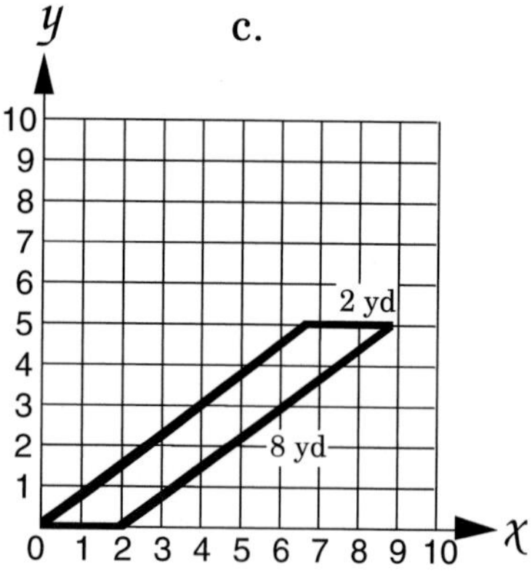

Independent Work

Remember to work the problems in part 3. Compare the answers to the estimated answers.

Part 9 **Copy each problem and work it.**

a. $\frac{5}{7} + \frac{1}{4}$

b. $\frac{2}{9} + \frac{5}{9}$

c. $\frac{7}{3} - \frac{7}{6}$

d. $\frac{13}{4} - \frac{5}{6}$

Part 10 **For each problem, make a ratio table. Answer the questions.**

a. $\frac{1}{3}$ of the elephants were ill. 300 elephants were not ill.
   1. How many elephants were ill?
   2. How many elephants were there in all?

b. The ratio of green bottles to brown bottles is 5 to 6. There are 198 bottles.
   1. How many brown bottles are there?
   2. How many green bottles are there?

Part 11 **Round each number to the nearest hundred.**

a. 5,698 b. 19,231 c. 586 d. 12,091 e. 13,111

Part 12 **For each item, write the equation with a fraction and a unit name.**

a. 8 identical machines weigh 37 tons. What does 1 machine weigh? 1M = ■ ▬

b. 4 boats hold 576 fish. How many fish does 1 boat hold? 1B = ■ ▬

c. If 7 boxes hold 364 matches, how many matches are in 1 box? 1B = ■ ▬

Part 13 **Copy and work each problem.**

a. 374×50

b. $6\overline{)582}$

c. $29\overline{)139}$

d. $\frac{36}{5} \times \frac{11}{8} =$ ■

Lesson 82

Part 1 **For each item, make a number family. Answer the question.**

a. Big Jed ordered two hamburgers, a large salad and a glass of milk. He gave the clerk $10. How much change did he get?

b. Jan and Edna bought a milk, a large soft drink, a hamburger and a fish sandwich. They paid $5. How much change did they receive?

c. Henry ordered a small salad, a hot dog and a large soft drink. He received 90 cents in change. How much money did he give the clerk?

Part 2 **For each item, work a problem with values rounded to the place named in the box.**

a. 561 [hundreds]
440
+ 706

b. 316 [hundreds]
− 112

c. 5610 [hundreds]
+ 2848

d. 58 [tens]
37
+ 91

Part 3

- Some ratio-table problems have sentences that compare two things.
- Here's a comparison problem:

> The sand weighed $\frac{2}{5}$ as much as the cement. The cement weighed 720 pounds.
> 1. How much did the sand weigh?
> 2. How much heavier was the cement than the sand?

- You work that problem just like other ratio-table problems.
  - ✔ You make the fraction number family.
  - ✔ Then you use the numerators as ratio numbers.
- Here's the first sentence of the problem:

The sand weighed $\frac{2}{5}$ as much as the cement.

- That sentence compares sand to cement. It gives information for making a fraction number family.

Dif **Sand** **Cement**

$\frac{3}{5} \quad \frac{2}{5} \longrightarrow \frac{5}{5}$

- You use the numerators as ratio numbers for the ratio table. The table shows those ratio numbers.
- The problem tells that the cement weighed 720 pounds. The table shows that number.

	Ratio	
Dif	3	
Sand	2	
Cement	5	**720**

Part 4

Make a fraction number family and a ratio table. Then answer the questions.

a. The amount the Craner family spent on dinner was $\frac{7}{4}$ of the amount spent on breakfast. Breakfast cost $56.
   1. How much did dinner cost?
   2. How much more did dinner cost than breakfast?

b. Abbey Hill is $\frac{3}{8}$ as high as Howard Hill. Abbey Hill is 240 feet high.
   1. How high is Howard Hill?
   2. How much higher is Howard Hill than Abbey Hill?

Part 5 **For each item, answer the question.**

Angle **h** is 166°.

a. 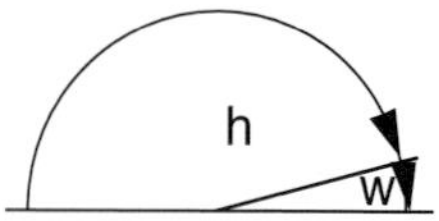

How many degrees are in angle **w**?

Angle **p** is 71°.

b. 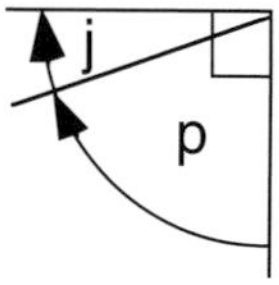

How many degrees are in angle **j**?

Angle **t** is 119°.

c. 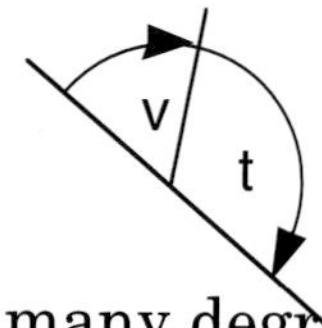

How many degrees are in angle **v**?

Part 6

- You know how to work problems that tell about more than 1 and ask about 1. You just write the answer as a fraction.
- You can work those problems as division problems because the fraction you write can also be written as a division problem.
- If the fraction is $\frac{45}{9}$, you can write the fraction as the division problem: $9\overline{)45}$
- **You can work any problem that tells about more than 1 and asks about 1 as a division problem.**
- Here are the rules:
  - ✔ Find the **name** for 1.
  - ✔ Find the other **number** with **that name.**
  - ✔ Divide by that number.
- Here's a problem:

  If 34 identical dresses cost $476, how much does 1 dress cost?

- The problem asks about 1 dress. You find the other number for dresses and divide by that number.

  $\boxed{\$14}$
  $34\overline{)476}$

- Here's another problem:

  If 15 identical pens cost $3, how many pens can you buy for $1?

  $\boxed{5 \text{ pens}}$
  $3\overline{)15}$

Part 7 Work each problem. Answer the question.

a. The cook uses 17 ounces of oil to make 100 donuts. How many ounces of oil does she use for 1 donut?

b. A cook uses 9 ounces of oil for 72 donuts. How many donuts could the cook fix with 1 ounce of oil?

c. 1 cake uses 9 ounces of milk. How many ounces of milk are needed for 15 cakes?

d. 7 dresses use 84 buttons. How many buttons are on 1 dress?

Part 8 Find the area and perimeter of each figure.

a.

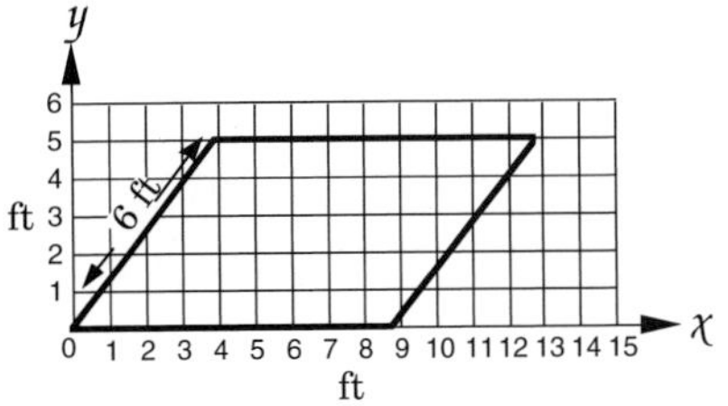

b.

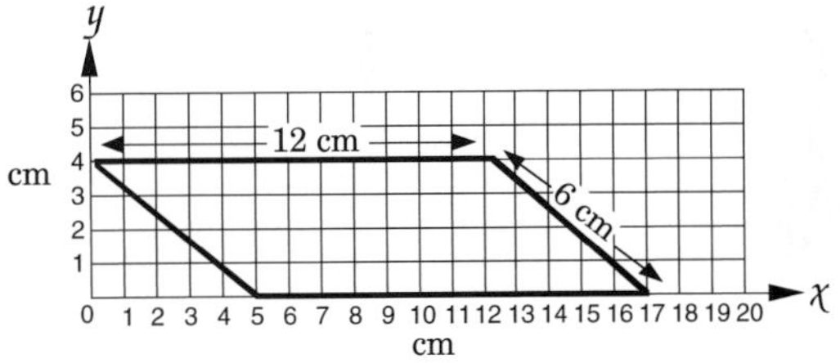

Independent Work

Remember to work the problems in part 2. Compare the answers to the estimated answers.

Part 9 For each problem, make a number family. Answer the questions.

a. Martha is 15 years younger than Becky. If Becky is 44 years old, how old is Martha?

b. $\frac{4}{9}$ of the employees were women.
   1. What fraction of the employees were men?
   2. What's the fraction for all the employees?

c. There are 17 carrots in a bag. 5 of the carrots are green.
   1. What fraction of the carrots are not green?
   2. What fraction of the carrots are green?

Part 10 **Copy and complete the table.**

	Mixed number	Fraction
a.	$2\frac{3}{7}$	
b.		$\frac{12}{11}$
c.		$\frac{5}{2}$
d.	$7\frac{2}{5}$	

Part 11 **Find the area and perimeter of each figure.**

a.

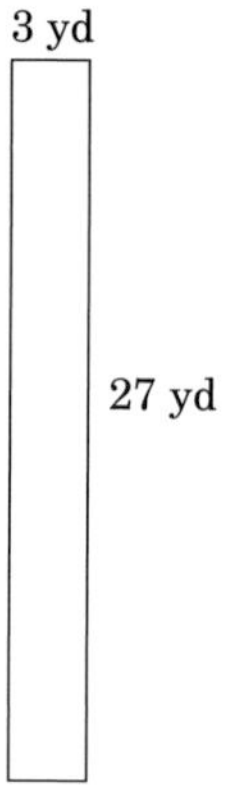

b.

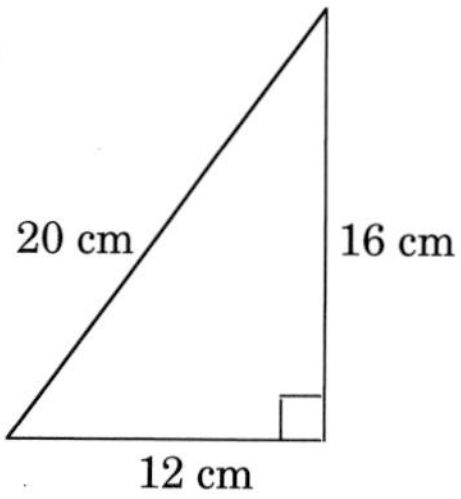

Part 12 **Copy and work each problem. If the answer has a fraction that equals 1, rewrite the answer.**

a. $\begin{array}{r} 14\frac{4}{5} \\ -\ 6\frac{1}{5} \\ \hline \end{array}$

b. $\begin{array}{r} 3\frac{7}{9} \\ +\ 11\frac{2}{9} \\ \hline \end{array}$

c. $\begin{array}{r} 27\frac{4}{13} \\ -\ 6 \\ \hline \end{array}$

d. $\begin{array}{r} 64\frac{3}{8} \\ +\ 6\frac{2}{8} \\ \hline \end{array}$

Part 13 **The answers shown are incorrect. Copy each problem and multiply. Rewrite the problem with the correct answer and work it.**

a. $57\overline{)464}$ with answer 7

b. $20\overline{)118}$ with answer 6

c. $24\overline{)120}$ with answer 4

d. $82\overline{)654}$ with answer 8

Part 14 **Answer each question. If the fraction is more than 1, write it as a whole number or mixed number.**

a. What's $\frac{4}{5}$ of 90?

b. How many degrees are in $\frac{1}{2}$ of a circle?

c. How many degrees are in the corner of a rectangle?

d. How many degrees are in $\frac{3}{5}$ of a circle?

e. What's $\frac{2}{3}$ of $\frac{7}{8}$?

Lesson 83

Part 1 Work each problem. Answer the question.

a. A plane travels at the steady rate of 415 miles in 1 hour. How far will the plane travel in 6 hours?

b. A train travels 250 miles in 4 hours. How far does it travel in 1 hour?

c. If a factory burns 12 tons of coal in 3 days, how many days does it take the factory to burn 1 ton?

d. 10 T.V. dinners cost $45. What does 1 T.V. dinner cost?

e. In 1 minute, a machine makes 180 yards of paper. How much paper does the machine make in 3 minutes?

Part 2 For each item, make a number family. Answer the question.

a. Edna and Amy bought a shovel and a hoe. The shovel cost $5.60. The hoe cost $11.80. They gave the clerk $20. How much change did they get?

b. Mrs. Anderson bought a dozen eggs, a loaf of bread and a half gallon of milk. The eggs cost 90 cents, the bread cost 80 cents and the milk cost $1.05. She gave the clerk $20. How much change did she receive?

c. Jan bought two pairs of socks and a pair of running shoes. Each pair of socks cost $1.20. The running shoes cost $38.50. She received change of $9.10. How much money did she give the clerk?

Part 3 Find the area and the perimeter of each parallelogram.

a.

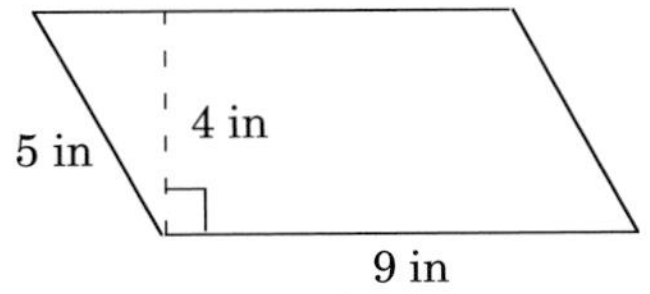

b.

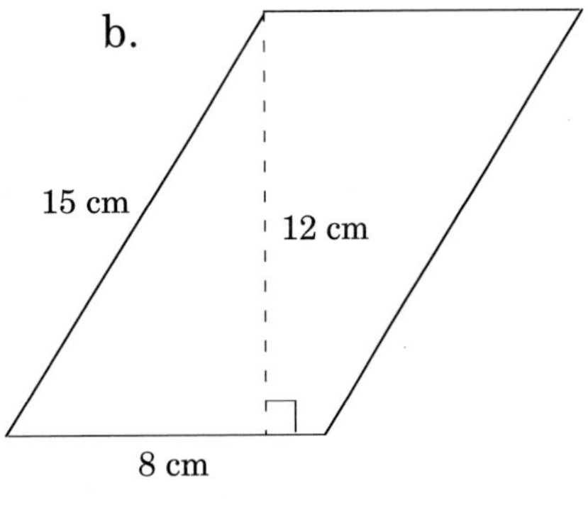

Part 4

Make a fraction number family and a ratio table. Then answer the questions.

a. There were $\frac{3}{5}$ as many students in the chess club as in the Spanish club. There were 51 students in the chess club.

   1. How many students were in the Spanish club?
   2. How many fewer students were in the chess club than in the Spanish club?

b. The lunchroom holds $\frac{7}{4}$ the number of students the gymnasium holds. The gymnasium holds 128 students.

   1. How many students does the lunchroom hold?
   2. The lunchroom holds how many more students than the gymnasium holds?

c. In March, Amy earned $\frac{9}{10}$ of the amount she earned in April. She earned $85 less in March than she earned in April.

   1. How much did she earn in March?
   2. How much did she earn in April?

Part 5

- A line that intersects parallel lines **creates the same angle at each parallel line.**
- The intersecting line creates the same angle at the top line:

  and at the bottom line:

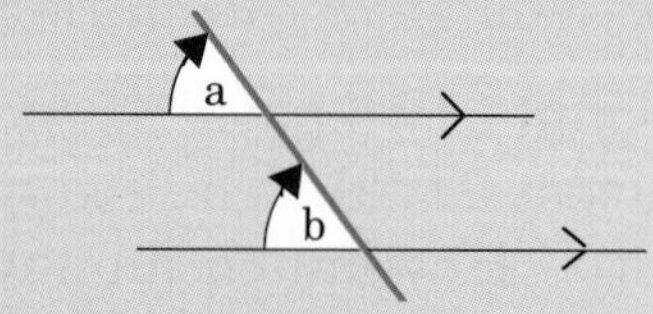

- Angle **a** equals angle **b.**
- Those angles are called **corresponding angles** because they are in the same position.

- Here's angle **m** at the top line and corresponding angle **n** at the bottom line:
- They're equal to each other.

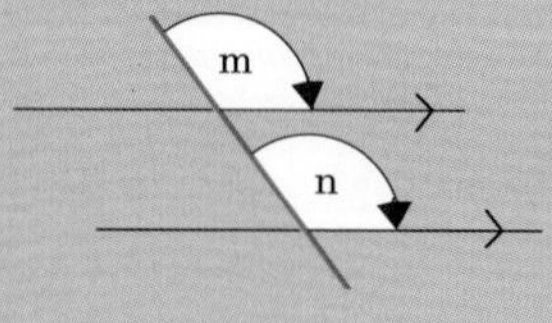

Part 6 Write the letters of the angles your teacher describes.

a.

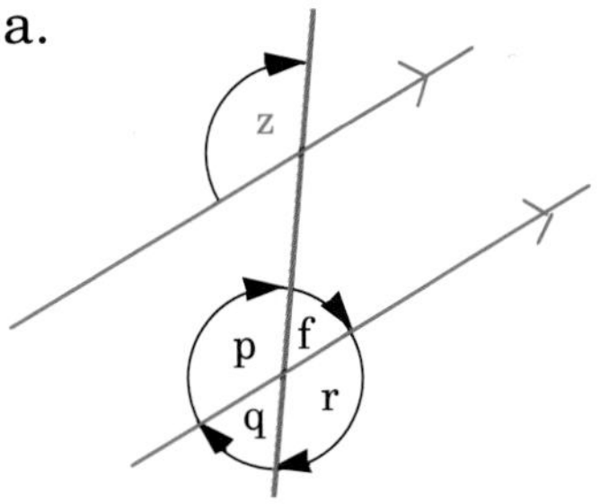

b.

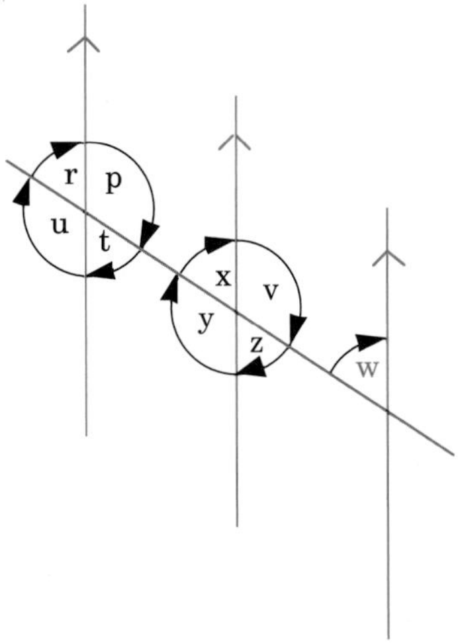

c.

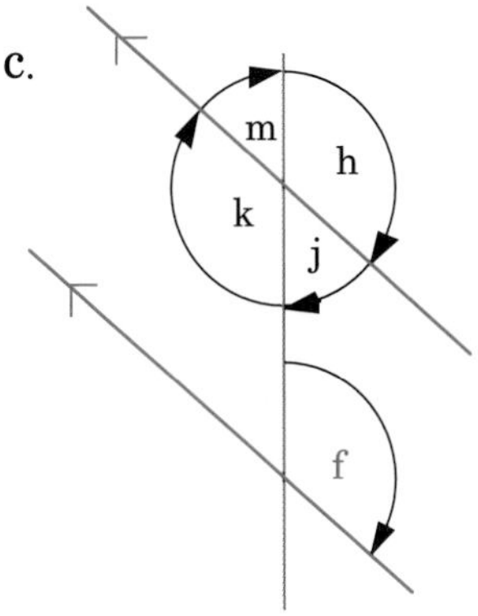

Part 7 Write the equation for the corresponding angles.

a. ∠v = 97°.

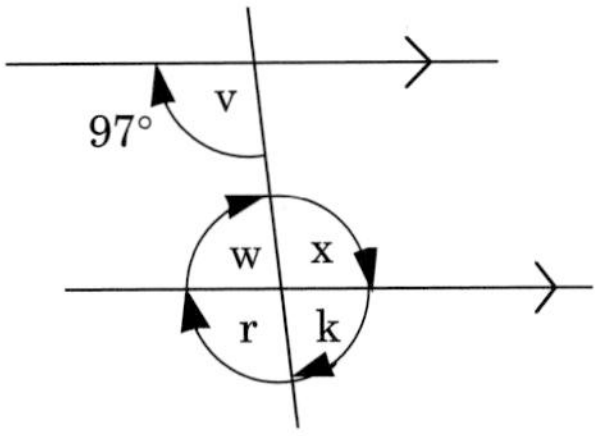

b. ∠j = 61°.

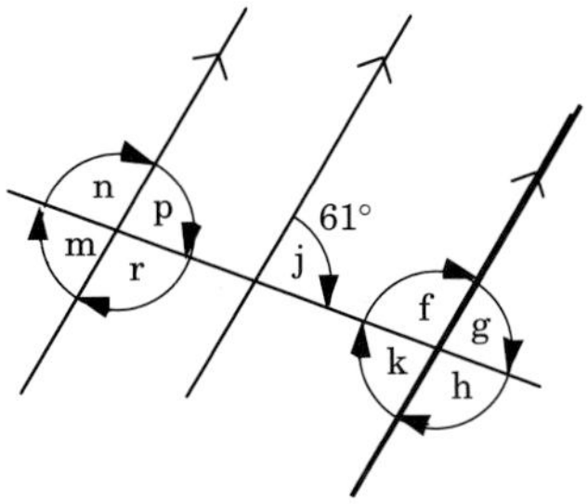

c. ∠k = 45°.

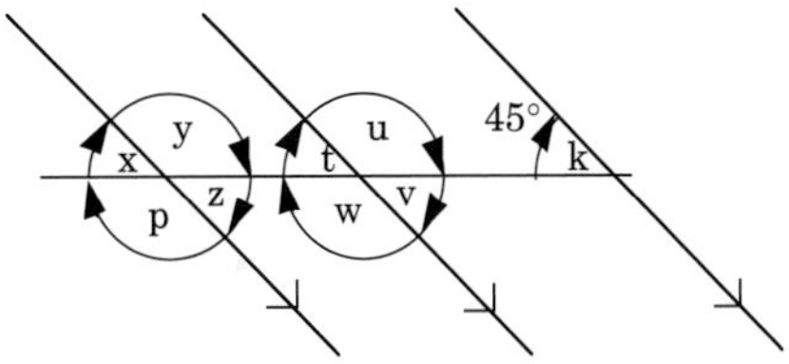

Independent Work

Remember to work problem c in part 4.

Part 8 Round each value to the nearest thousand. Work the rounded problems.

a.
```
  5,432
– 1,689
```

b.
```
  17,208
+ 12,911
```

c.
```
  12,340
   7,200
+ 60,802
```

Part 9 Make a number family for each problem. Answer the question.

a. A train started out with 111 people. At the first stop, 312 people got in the train. 34 people got off the train. At the next stop, 181 people got in the train. 301 people got off the train. How many people were still in the train?

b. A truck started out with 34 gallons in the tank. At the first stop, 50 gallons were added to the tank. At the next stop, 14 gallons were added. At the end of the trip, there were still 11 gallons in the tank. How many gallons were used on the entire trip?

Part 10 Make a table. Answer the questions.

Pete and Milly collected United States and foreign stamps. Together, they had 875 foreign stamps. Pete had a total of 510 stamps. Milly had 158 United States stamps. Milly's collection had 280 more foreign stamps than United States stamps.

a. Who had more foreign stamps?

b. What was the total number of stamps in both collections?

c. Did Pete have fewer United States stamps or foreign stamps?

Part 11 For each statement, make a fraction number family.

a. R is $\frac{9}{5}$ of V.

b. T is $\frac{7}{8}$ of J.

c. Z is $\frac{26}{11}$ of M.

Part 12 Make a number family. Answer the questions. Use the equation $\angle ■ = ■°$.

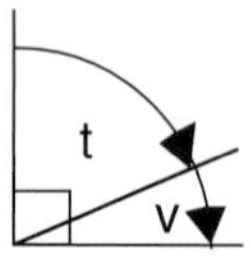

a. $\angle v = 28°$

What is $\angle t$?

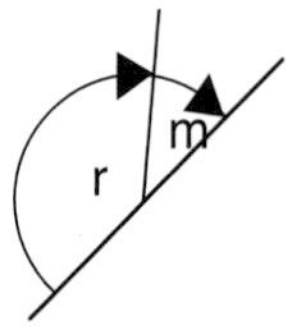

b. $\angle m = 39°$

What is $\angle r$?

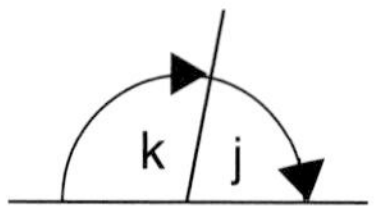

c. $\angle k = 100°$

What is $\angle j$?

Lesson 84

Part 1

- For some mixed-number subtraction problems, you can't just copy the fraction in the answer. Those problems **start** with a whole number and **subtract a mixed number.**
- Here's $47 - 13\frac{7}{8}$:

  You can't just copy $\frac{7}{8}$ in the answer because you're subtracting $\frac{7}{8}$ from 47.

$$\begin{array}{r} 47 \\ -\ 13\frac{7}{8} \\ \hline \end{array}$$

- To work the problem, you borrow 1 from **47.**

$$\begin{array}{r} 4\overset{6}{\cancel{7}} \\ -\ 13\frac{7}{8} \\ \hline \end{array}$$

- You write the **1** you borrowed as a fraction with the same denominator as $\frac{7}{8}$.

$$\begin{array}{r} 4\overset{6\frac{8}{8}}{\cancel{7}} \\ -\ 13\frac{7}{8} \\ \hline \end{array}$$

- Now you subtract in each column, starting with the fractions.
- The answer is $33\frac{1}{8}$.

$$\begin{array}{r} 4\overset{6\frac{8}{8}}{\cancel{7}} \\ -\ 13\frac{7}{8} \\ \hline 33\frac{1}{8} \end{array}$$

Part 2

Copy and work each problem.

a. $\begin{array}{r} 5 \\ -\ 2\frac{1}{4} \\ \hline \end{array}$

b. $\begin{array}{r} 9 \\ -\ 4\frac{6}{7} \\ \hline \end{array}$

c. $\begin{array}{r} 27 \\ -\ 3\frac{5}{10} \\ \hline \end{array}$

Part 3

- You've worked with ratio-table sentences that **compare two things.**
- You've also worked with sentences that tell about a fraction of a **whole group.**
- If the sentence compares two things, the number family has the name **difference.**
- If the sentence tells about the fraction of a whole group, the number family does **not** have the name **difference.** It names the whole group and the two parts that make up the whole group.
- Here are sentences that compare two things:

The boys ate $\frac{3}{4}$ as much as the girls ate.

Dif	Boys	Girls
$\frac{1}{4}$	$\frac{3}{4}$ →	$\frac{4}{4}$

The price of dinner was $\frac{7}{5}$ the price of lunch.

Dif	Lunch	Dinner
$\frac{2}{5}$	$\frac{5}{5}$ →	$\frac{7}{5}$

- The families for these sentences have the name **difference.**
- Here are sentences that tell about the fraction of a whole group:

$\frac{9}{10}$ of the children were sleeping.

Sleeping	Not sleeping	Children
$\frac{9}{10}$	$\frac{1}{10}$ →	$\frac{10}{10}$

Ginger had eaten $\frac{2}{9}$ of the food.

Eaten	Not eaten	Food
$\frac{2}{9}$	$\frac{7}{9}$ →	$\frac{9}{9}$

$\frac{3}{5}$ of the mixture was sand, and the rest was cement.

Sand	Cement	Mixture
$\frac{3}{5}$	$\frac{2}{5}$ →	$\frac{5}{5}$

$\frac{2}{15}$ of the cars were yellow.

Yellow	Not yellow	Cars
$\frac{2}{15}$	$\frac{13}{15}$ →	$\frac{15}{15}$

- Remember, if the sentence compares two things, your family has the name **difference.** Otherwise, it has the names of the two parts that make up the whole group.

Part 4 For each sentence, make the number family.

a. The car was $\frac{4}{9}$ as long as the trailer.

b. $\frac{7}{8}$ of the trucks were dirty.

c. Donna ran $\frac{7}{5}$ as far as Rodney ran.

d. $\frac{9}{10}$ of the trees were old.

Part 5 For each problem, make a number family. Answer the question.

a. Jan had $45 in her bank account. Then she put in another $28. She took out some money. She still had $16 in her bank account. How much money did she take out?

b. Ginger purchased a salad for $3.60, an ice cream cone for $1.20, and a soft drink for 75 cents. She gave the clerk some money and received $14.45 in change. How much money did she give the clerk?

c. Al had $12.25 in a jar. On Wednesday, he took out $1.60. On Thursday, he put 90 cents in the jar. On Friday, he took out $3.20 and put in $6.20. On Saturday, he took out $11.70. How much money was still in the jar?

Part 6 Make a fraction number family and a ratio table. Answer the questions.

a. A store sold items for $\frac{3}{2}$ the amount the store paid for the items. The store paid a total of $1700 for the items.
   1. When the store sold the items, how much did the store receive?
   2. What was the difference between the amount the store paid and the amount the store received?

b. The rope was $\frac{3}{5}$ as strong as the cable. The rope can hold 72 pounds.
   1. How much weight can the cable hold?
   2. How much more weight can the cable hold than the rope?

Part 7 Work each problem. Answer the question.

a. If 6 identical bottles hold 4 pints, how many pints are in 1 bottle?

b. If a snail moves at a steady rate of 140 centimeters in 3 minutes, how far does it move in 1 minute?

c. 3 fishsticks weigh 102 grams. What does 1 fishstick weigh?

d. 36 pounds of seed fill 18 bags. What does 1 bag of seed weigh?

Part 8

- You've learned about corresponding angles.
- A line that intersects parallel lines creates equal angles at each parallel line. Those angles are called **corresponding angles.**
- You can use the rule about corresponding angles to work difficult problems.

How many degrees are in angle t?

- Here's a pair of parallel lines and an intersecting line:

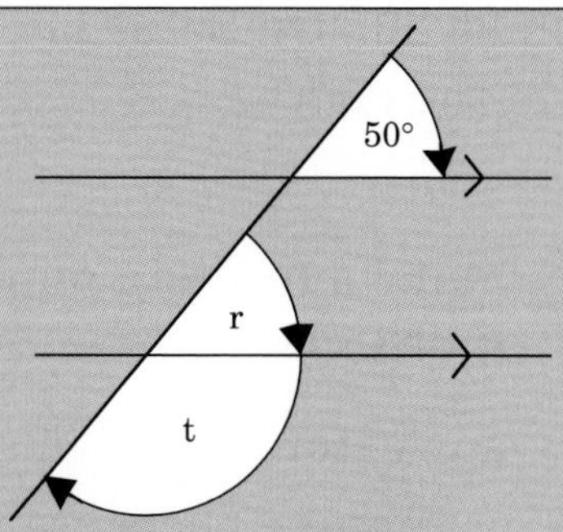

- The angle at the top parallel line is 50°. So the corresponding angle at the bottom line is 50°. That's angle **r.**
- Together, angles **r** and **t** are 180°. You know that angle **r** is 50°.
- So angle **t** must be 180° – 50°. That's 130°.

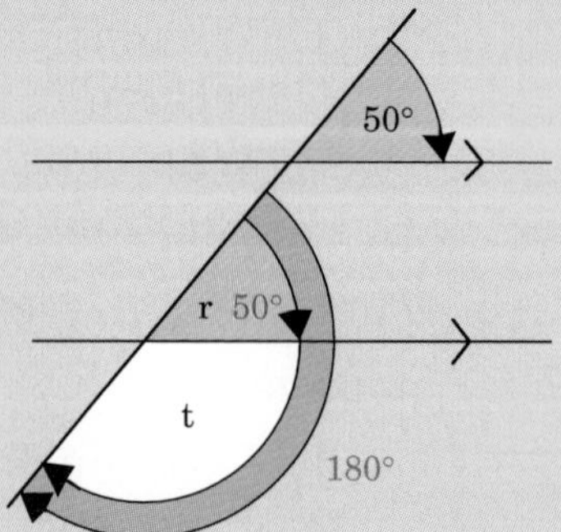

Independent Work

Remember to work problem b in part 6 and problems c and d in part 7.

Part 9 **Simplify each fraction. If the fraction is more than 1, write it as a mixed number.**

a. $\frac{4}{24}$ b. $\frac{21}{7}$ c. $\frac{18}{12}$ d. $\frac{5}{25}$ e. $\frac{30}{6}$ f. $\frac{6}{12}$

Part 10 **Find the area and perimeter of each parallelogram.**

a.

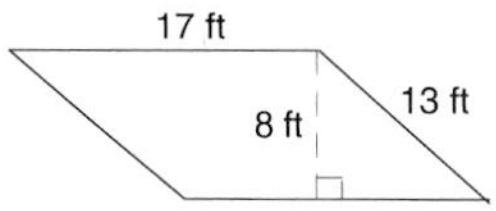

b.

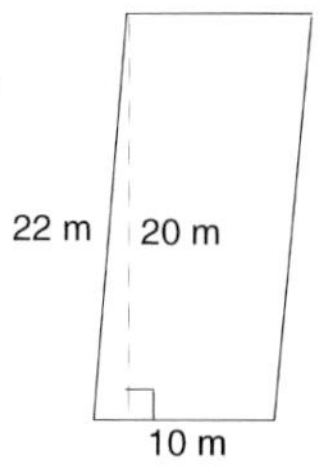

Part 11 **Copy and complete the table.**

	Decimal	$\frac{■}{100}$
a.		$\frac{101}{100}$
b.	.30	
c.	.48	
d.		$\frac{9}{100}$

Part 12 **Copy and complete each equation. If the fractions are not equivalent, circle the larger fraction. If the fractions are equivalent, circle the equal sign.**

a. $\frac{2}{3}(■) = \frac{18}{24}$ b. $\frac{1}{5}(■) = \frac{3}{15}$

c. $\frac{7}{3}(■) = \frac{35}{12}$ d. $\frac{5}{2}(■) = \frac{30}{16}$

Part 13 **Work each problem. Answer the question.**

a. There are 2 teachers for every 10 pieces of chalk. If there are 9 teachers, how many pieces of chalk are there?

b. A piggy bank contained 120 nickels. Somebody put another 45 nickels in the bank. Somebody took 81 nickels out of the piggy bank. Somebody else took 14 nickels out of the bank. How many nickels were left in the piggy bank?

c. Fran recycles 8 newspapers every 3 minutes. How many newspapers does she recycle in 20 minutes?

Part 14 **Copy and work each problem.**

a. $4\frac{3}{11} + 2\frac{5}{11}$ b. $4\frac{5}{8} + 7\frac{3}{8}$ c. $6\frac{13}{15} - 5$

Lesson 85

Part 1

- You're going to add decimal values. The decimal points must be lined up.
- Here are three values to be added: **4.3 + 7.089 + 413.42**
- Here they are written with the decimal points lined up:

$$\begin{array}{r} 4.3 \\ 7.089 \\ +\ 413.42 \\ \hline \end{array}$$

- Before you add, you make zeros so that all the values have digits to the thousandths.
- Then you add and carry the way you normally would.

$$\begin{array}{r} \overset{1}{4}.300 \\ 7.089 \\ +\ 413.420 \\ \hline 424.809 \end{array}$$

- Remember, make zeros so that all the numbers end at the same decimal place. Then add.

Part 2

Rewrite each problem in columns, then work it.

a. 14.82 + 1.705 + .6

b. 10.697 + 158.3 + 5.04

c. 15.06 + .3 + 110.7

Part 3

Find the area and the perimeter of each parallelogram.

a.

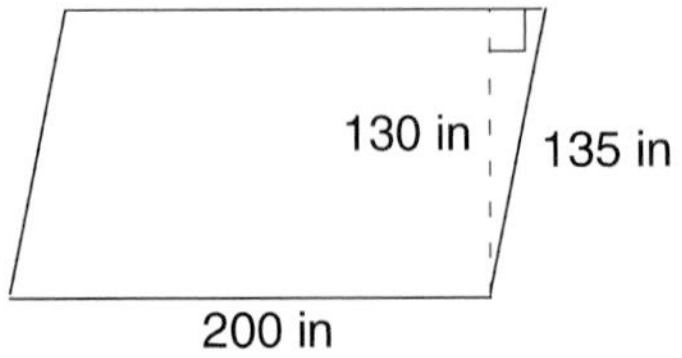

b.

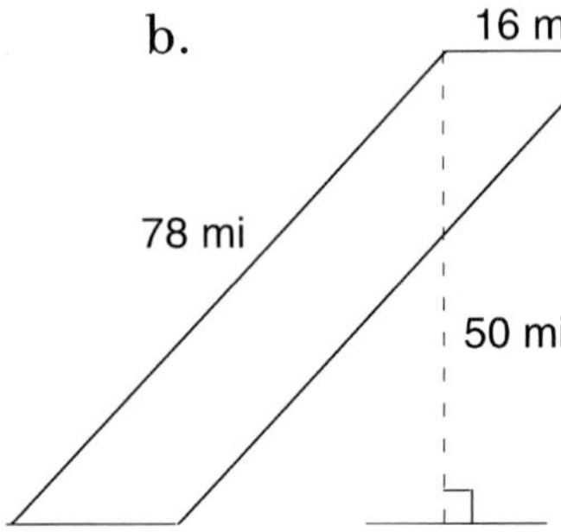

Part 4 Copy and work each problem.

a. $12 - 10\frac{3}{7}$

b. $16 - 5\frac{3}{20}$

c. $17 - 14\frac{2}{5}$

d. $208 - 200\frac{7}{15}$

Part 5 Tell whether each sentence compares.

a. The height of the tower was $\frac{4}{9}$ the height of the redwood.

b. Mary ran $\frac{8}{5}$ the distance that Julie ran.

c. $\frac{7}{8}$ of the women were married.

d. $\frac{3}{5}$ of the mixture was water.

Part 6 For each sentence, make the number family.

a. The cat weighed $\frac{2}{7}$ as much as the dog weighed.

b. $\frac{4}{5}$ of the hot dogs were cold.

c. The car travelled at $\frac{9}{5}$ the speed of the train.

d. The mixture weighed $\frac{5}{6}$ as much as the box.

e. $\frac{7}{9}$ of the boxes were filled.

Part 7 Work each problem. Answer the question.

a. It takes 15 hours for a machine to make 24 garments. How many hours does it take the machine to make 1 garment?

b. It takes 1 hour for a machine to produce 18 hats. How many hats does the machine produce in 3 hours?

c. 4 worker bees produce 1 ounce of honey. How many worker bees produce 280 ounces of honey?

d. 86 bars of soap weigh 9 pounds. How many bars of soap weigh 1 pound?

Independent Work

Part 8 **Copy each problem. Figure out the missing numerator.**

a. $2 = \frac{■}{8}$ b. $4 = \frac{■}{9}$ c. $7 = \frac{■}{3}$ d. $8 = \frac{■}{4}$ e. $3 = \frac{■}{6}$

Part 9 **Make a table. Answer the questions.**

On Monday and Tuesday, a machine filled blue bottles and green bottles. On Monday, the machine filled 628 green bottles and 150 blue bottles. The total number of blue bottles filled on both days was 349. The total number of green bottles was 1605 more than the total number of blue bottles.

a. How many green bottles were filled on Tuesday?
b. Were fewer blue bottles filled on Monday or Tuesday?
c. On Tuesday, did the machine fill more blue bottles or green bottles?

Part 10 **Copy each problem. Estimate the answer by rounding. Then work the problem.**

a. $32\overline{)97}$ b. $48\overline{)405}$

c. $54\overline{)247}$ d. $91\overline{)640}$

Part 11 **Simplify each fraction. If the fraction is more than 1, write it as a mixed number.**

a. $\frac{42}{6}$ b. $\frac{25}{25}$ c. $\frac{9}{45}$

d. $\frac{27}{3}$ e. $\frac{7}{28}$ f. $\frac{20}{30}$

Part 12 **For each problem, make a ratio table. Answer the questions.**

a. The ratio of children to staff at Clark School was 70 to 3. There was a total of 365 people at Clark School.
   1. How many staff people were there?
   2. How many children were there?

b. $\frac{4}{7}$ of the cherries were ripe. There were 540 unripe cherries.
   1. How many ripe cherries were there?
   2. How many cherries were there in all?

Part 13 **Find the area and perimeter of the rectangle.**

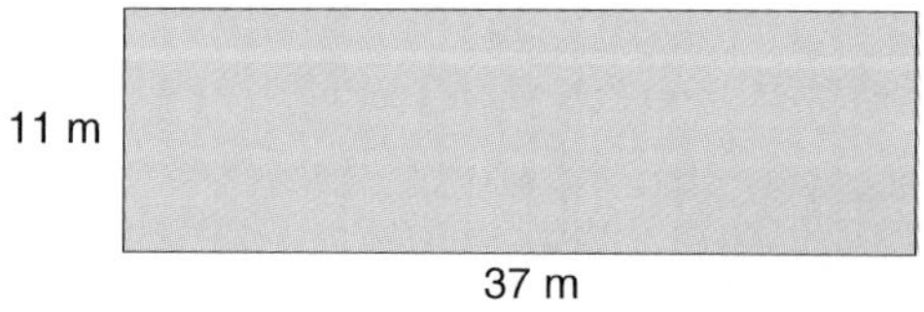

Part J

a. Area□ = b×h
Area = 200 × 130
26.000 sq in

135
135
200
+ 200
670 in

b. Area□ = b×h
Area = 16 × 50
800 sq mi

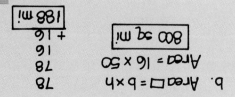

78
78
16
+ 16
188 mi

Lesson 86

Part 1 Copy and work each problem.

a. $82\overline{)240}$ b. $68\overline{)152}$ c. $25\overline{)185}$ d. $90\overline{)673}$

Part 2 Find the area of each figure.

a.

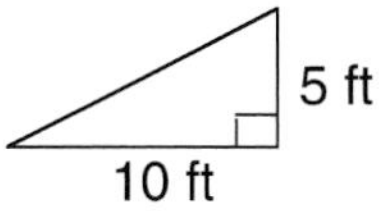

b.

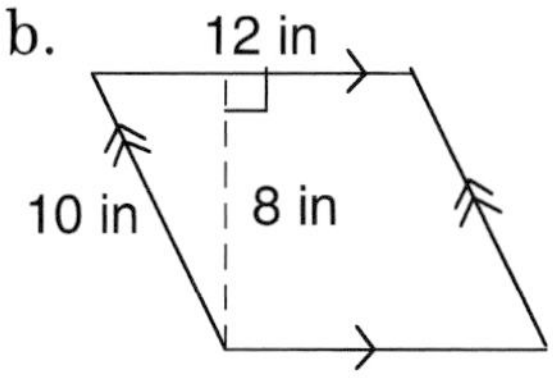

c.

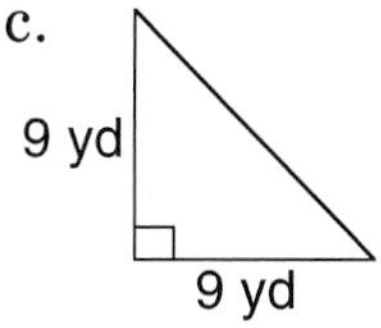

d.

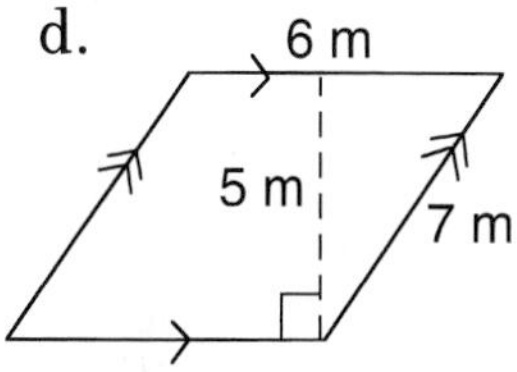

Part 3 Make a fraction number family for each sentence.

a. $\frac{3}{4}$ of the books were sold.

b. Tim read at $\frac{5}{3}$ the rate that Jay read.

c. In a factory, $\frac{2}{15}$ of the workers wore suspenders.

d. Factory A employs $\frac{8}{7}$ as many workers as Factory B.

e. In a kennel, $\frac{1}{5}$ of the dogs are white.

Part 4 Copy and work each problem.

a. $\begin{array}{r} 24 \\ -\ 12\frac{2}{7} \\ \hline \end{array}$ b. $\begin{array}{r} 44\frac{7}{8} \\ -\ 5 \\ \hline \end{array}$ c. $\begin{array}{r} 11\frac{3}{5} \\ +\ 25 \\ \hline \end{array}$ d. $\begin{array}{r} 40 \\ +\ 28\frac{5}{9} \\ \hline \end{array}$ e. $\begin{array}{r} 40 \\ -\ 28\frac{5}{9} \\ \hline \end{array}$

Part 5 Rewrite each problem in columns, then work it.

a. 15.4 – 2.76 b. 3.16 – 1.2 c. 9.28 – 1.076

d. 14.59 – 3.08 e. 5.08 – .835 f. 10.286 – 7.59

Part 6 Write the complete equation for each lettered angle.

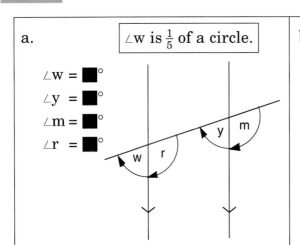

a.

$\angle w$ is $\frac{1}{5}$ of a circle.

$\angle w = \blacksquare^\circ$
$\angle y = \blacksquare^\circ$
$\angle m = \blacksquare^\circ$
$\angle r = \blacksquare^\circ$

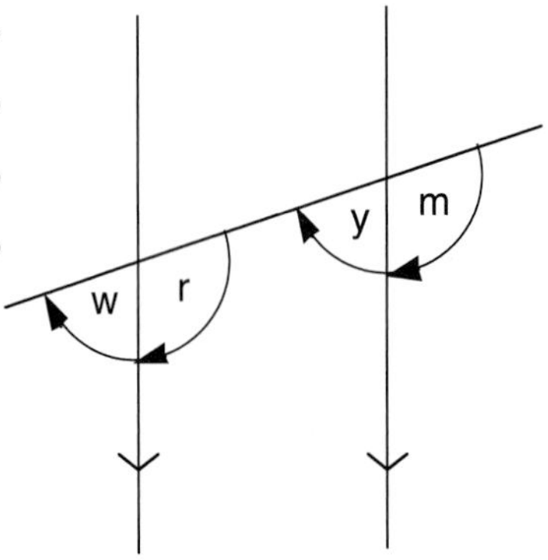

b.

$\angle g$ is $\frac{1}{3}$ of a circle.

$\angle g = \blacksquare^\circ$
$\angle p = \blacksquare^\circ$
$\angle r = \blacksquare^\circ$
$\angle v = \blacksquare^\circ$

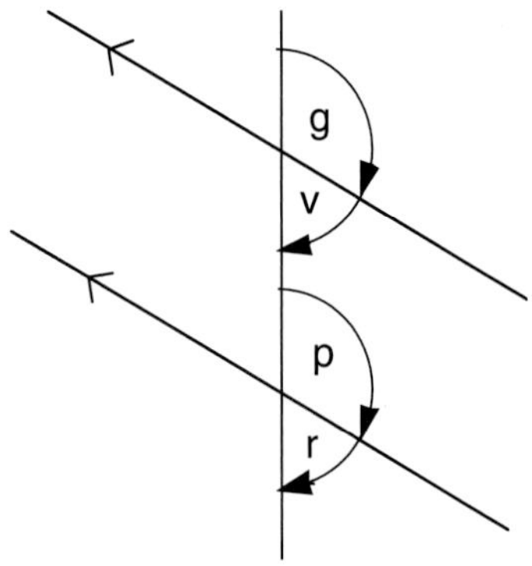

Independent Work

Remember to work problems d, e and f in part 5.

Part 7 Work each problem.

a. 14 identical bugs weigh 13 grams. How many grams does 1 bug weigh?

b. If 8 pounds of grass seed cost $5, how many pounds can you buy for $1?

c. If 8 cases hold 480 bottles, how many bottles are in 1 case?

d. If a train travels 68 feet in 4 seconds, how many seconds does it take the train to travel 1 foot?

Part 8 Work each problem.

a. $68\overline{)428}$ b. $78\overline{)572}$ c. $88\overline{)567}$

Part 9

Copy the table and complete it by rounding each number to the nearest ten, hundred and thousand.

		Nearest ten	Nearest hundred	Nearest thousand
	4128	4130	4100	4000
a.	4628			
b.	8019			
c.	6543			

Part 10

For each item, make a number family. Answer the question.

a. On Monday, a piggy bank had some money in it. On Tuesday, 15 cents was removed from the bank. On Wednesday, $2.13 was taken out of the bank. At the end of Wednesday, the bank had $11.77 in it. How much was in the bank to begin with?

b. John traded baseball cards. He started out with 72 cards. On Monday, he gave away 17 cards and got 5 cards in return. On Tuesday, he bought 53 cards. On Wednesday, he gave away 6 cards and got 15 cards in return. How many cards did he end up with?

c. A person purchased a hamburger for $2.45, milk for $ .49 and a salad for $2.78. He gave the clerk $10.00. How much change did he receive?

d. Another person ordered a salad for $2.78 and a fish sandwich for $1.95. The person received $5.27 in change. How much money did the person give the clerk?

Part J

a. $24 - 12\frac{2}{7}$ = $11\frac{5}{7}$

b. $44\frac{7}{8} - 5$ = $39\frac{7}{8}$

c. $11\frac{3}{5} + 25$ = $36\frac{3}{5}$

d. $40 + 28\frac{5}{6}$ = $68\frac{5}{6}$

e. $40 - 28\frac{5}{6}$ = $11\frac{4}{6}$

Lesson 87

Part 1

- To work **goal** problems, you'll **compare** the amount the person has **now** with the **goal.**
- If the goal is more than the person has, the goal is the big number.

- If the goal is less than the person has, the goal is a small number.

- The other small number is always the **difference number.**

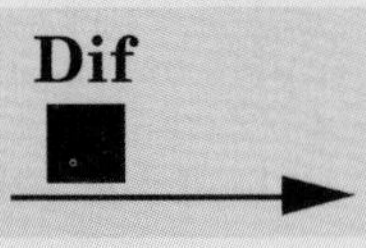

a. Betty must lose 15 pounds to reach her goal.

b. Don needs $18 more to reach his goal.

Part 2

For each problem, make a number family. Answer the question.

a. Sally needs to lose 28 pounds to reach her goal. Her goal is to weigh 120 pounds. How much does she weigh now?

b. John's goal is to have $45. He already has $29. How much more money does he need to reach his goal?

c. John's goal is to spend $17 week less than he spends now. He spends $75 a week. How much will he spend each week if he reaches his goal?

Part 3

Copy and work each problem.

a. $48 + 12\frac{5}{9}$

b. $55 - 7\frac{4}{10}$

c. $30\frac{8}{11} + 49\frac{1}{11}$

d. $17 - 12\frac{2}{3}$

Part 4

Make a fraction number family and a table. Answer the questions.

a. The number of red boats on a lake was $\frac{4}{3}$ the number of white boats. There were 90 white boats.
   1. How many red boats were there?
   2. How many more red boats than white boats were there?

b. $\frac{5}{8}$ of the boats on a lake were white. There were 400 boats on the lake.
   1. How many boats were white?
   2. How many boats were not white?

c. The salt weighs $\frac{1}{3}$ as much as the flour. The flour weighs 273 pounds.
   1. How much does the salt weigh?
   2. How much less does the salt weigh than the flour weighs?

Part 5

The words **each** and **per** mean **1.**

- If **each sheet** costs 4¢,
  1 sheet costs 4¢.

- If a car travels 20 miles **per hour,**
  the car travels 20 miles in **1 hour.**

Part 6

Find the name that tells about 1 thing.

a. A wagon travels at the rate of 96 feet per minute.

b. There were 16 pounds in each package.

c. Each box holds 45 grams.

Part 7 Work each problem. Answer the question.

a. If 5 paper clips weigh 8 grams, how much does each paper clip weigh?

b. The train traveled at a steady rate of 85 miles per hour. How far did the train travel in 5 hours?

c. How much do 7 baskets cost if each basket costs $9.50?

d. There are 7 students on each team. How many students are on 8 teams?

e. In 2 minutes, a snail moves 5 centimeters. How many centimeters per minute does it move?

Part 8 Rewrite each problem in columns, then work it.

a. 128.32 + 5.953   b. 389.2 – 96.74   c. 14.72 – 8.675

Independent Work

Part 9 For each item, make a number family. Answer the question.

The price tags show the cost of different items.

a. John bought the shirt, the clock and two pens. He received $7.55 in change. How much did he give the clerk?

b. Jan had $67.80. She spent $13.45 on Wednesday and $21 on Tuesday. On Thursday, she earned $34. On Friday, she earned $11.90. How much money did she end up with?

c. Jan bought the sweater, the clock and a watch. She gave the clerk $60. How much change did she get?

d. Dan bought the hat, the sunglasses and the shirt. He received $17.41 in change. How much did he give the clerk?

Part 10 Copy and complete each equation.

a. $6 = \frac{■}{17}$ b. $12 = \frac{■}{3}$ c. $2 = \frac{■}{3}$ d. $5 = \frac{■}{5}$

Part 11 Write complete equations to show the number of degrees in each angle that is lettered.

∠h is 41°.

∠j = ■°

∠k = ■°

∠m = ■°

∠n = ■°

∠p = ■°

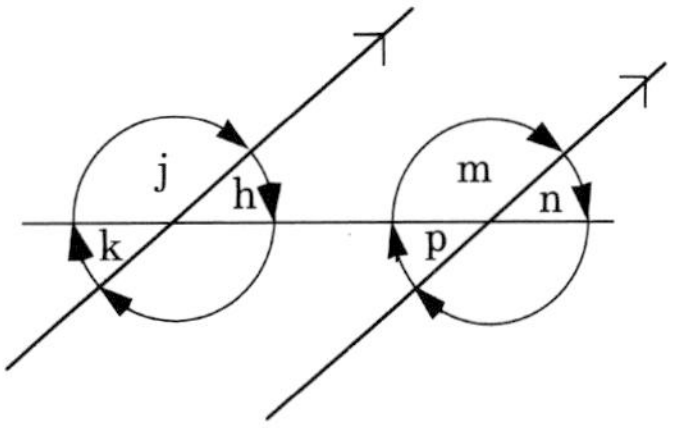

Part 12 Copy and complete the table by rounding each value.

		Nearest ten	Nearest hundred	Nearest thousand
a.	2003			
b.	1999			
c.	8273			

Part 13 Copy and complete the second equation. Show the answer as a fraction.

a. 5J = 31

1J = ■

b. 24R = 11

1R = ■

c. 2P = 1

1P = ■

d. 5M = 3

1M = ■

Part 14 For each item, make a ratio equation. Answer the question.

a. The ratio of fish to worms was 3 to 15. If there were 30 worms, how many fish were there?

b. A machine made 5 shirts every 4 minutes. How many shirts would the machine make in 60 minutes?

c. Farmer Brown transported goats in wagons. There were 5 wagons for every 13 goats. There were 260 wagons. How many goats were there?

Lesson 88

Part 1 Work each item. Answer the question.

a. If there are 7 parts in each unit, how many parts are there in 13 units?

b. If 15 marbles weigh 6 ounces, how many ounces does each marble weigh?

c. With $13 you can buy 4 pounds of nuts. What is the cost of each pound?

d. A car travels at the rate of 45 miles per hour. How many miles does the car travel in 12 hours?

Part 2 For each problem, make a number family. Answer the question.

a. Tammy's goal is to reduce the time it takes her to run a course. It currently takes her 81 seconds to the run the course. Her goal is to run the course in 17 fewer seconds. When she reaches her goal, how long will it take her to run the course?

b. Mr. Robinson's goal is to jump high enough to touch a mark 130 inches high. To reach that goal, Mr. Robinson would have to jump 13 inches higher than he currently jumps. How high can he reach now when he jumps?

c. Nancy's goal is to pick pears from 100 trees. She has already picked pears from 42 trees. How many more trees does she have to pick to reach her goal?

d. For next year, Fran's goal is to spend $940 less than she spent this year. This year, she spent $3600. What's her spending goal for next year?

Part 3

- For some ratio-table problems, you have to work with mixed numbers.
- Here's a ratio table:

	■	■
	■	$11\frac{1}{3}$
Total	■	36

- You can figure out the missing value in the second column by subtracting. The subtraction problem is: $36 - 11\frac{1}{3}$.
- You work the problem by rewriting 36 as a mixed number:
- Then you subtract and get $24\frac{2}{3}$.

$$\begin{array}{r} \overset{5\frac{3}{3}}{3\cancel{6}} \\ -\ 11\frac{1}{3} \\ \hline 24\frac{2}{3} \end{array}$$

- Remember, if the number you **subtract** is a **mixed number,** you have to **start** with a mixed number.

4
C. Total
Jerry still hasn't caught on to the idea of mixed numbers.

Part 4 For each table, work the mixed number problem to figure out the missing value in the second column.

a.

	■	$12\frac{3}{7}$
	■	■
Total	■	25

b.

	■	$11\frac{3}{8}$
	■	$14\frac{5}{8}$
Total	■	■

c.

	■	4
	■	$29\frac{3}{5}$
Total	■	■

Part 5 For each item, make a fraction number family and a table. Answer the questions.

a. $\frac{1}{3}$ of the motorcycles in the store are used. There are 58 new motorcycles in the store.
   1. How many used motorcycles are there?
   2. How many motorcycles are there in all?

b. The chef earned $\frac{9}{7}$ as much as the waitress earned. The chef earned $84 more than the waitress.
   1. How much did the chef earn?
   2. How much did the waitress earn?

c. The weight of the book is $\frac{3}{5}$ the weight of the parcel. The book weighs 36 ounces.
   1. How much does the parcel weigh?
   2. How much more does the parcel weigh than the book?

Part 6 For each item, figure out all the angles in the circle.

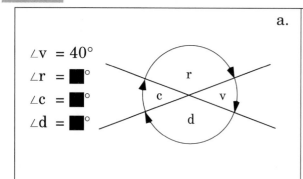

a.

$\angle v = 40°$

$\angle r =$ ■°

$\angle c =$ ■°

$\angle d =$ ■°

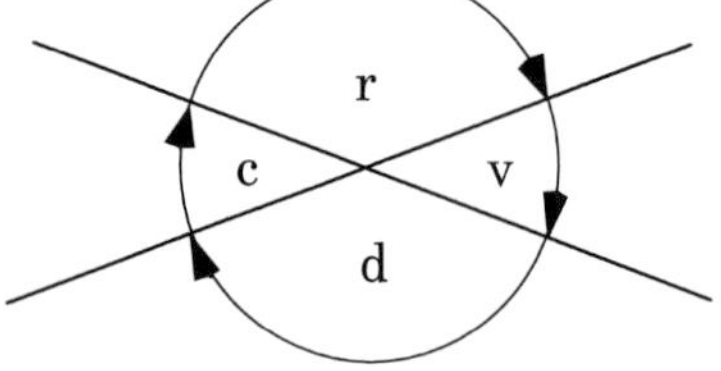

b.

$\angle m = 110°$

$\angle f =$ ■°

$\angle t =$ ■°

$\angle p =$ ■°

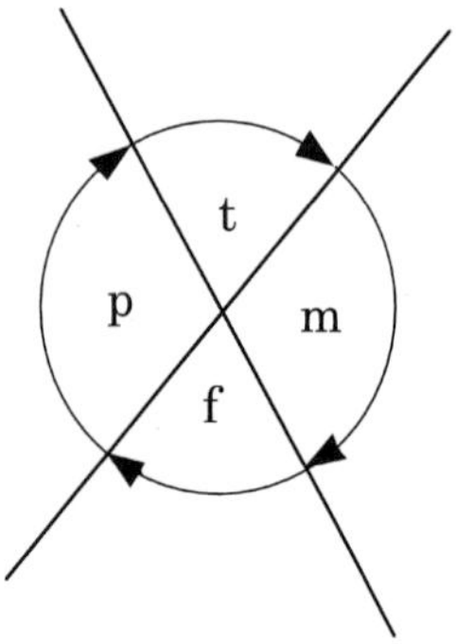

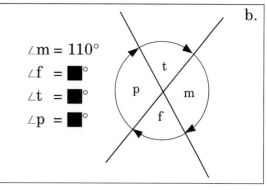

Independent Work

Part 7 **Work each item.**

a. 5 shirts costs \$78. How much does 1 shirt cost?

b. 1 straw hat costs \$6.50. How much do 3 straw hats cost?

c. If it takes a train 1 second to go 19 feet, how far does the train go in 600 seconds?

d. If 11 identical buildings have 44 windows, how many windows are in 1 building?

Part 8 **Work each problem.**

a. $\frac{5}{3} + \frac{2}{7}$

b. $\frac{9}{4} - \frac{5}{6}$

c. $\frac{7}{8} + \frac{5}{2}$

Part 9 **Copy and work each problem.**

a. $146 - 12\frac{3}{8}$

b. $20\frac{3}{10} + 14\frac{5}{10}$

c. $63\frac{1}{4} + 19\frac{3}{4}$

d. $29\frac{4}{5} - 22\frac{4}{5}$

Part 10 **Copy and work each problem. Then round each answer to the nearest hundred.**

a. $2462 - 1231$

b. $5679 + 4444$

c. $576 + 328 + 195 + 612$

d. $294 - 103$

Part 11 **Make a table. Then answer the questions.**

Two students collected baseball cards and football cards. The students were Milly and George. Milly had 27 baseball cards in her collection. George had 52 football cards. Milly had 25 more football cards than George. George had a total of 75 cards.

a. How many baseball cards did George have?
b. How many football cards did both students have?
c. Which student had fewer total cards?

Part 12 **Find the area and perimeter of each figure.**

a.
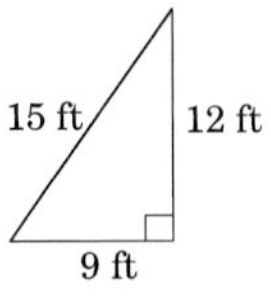

b.
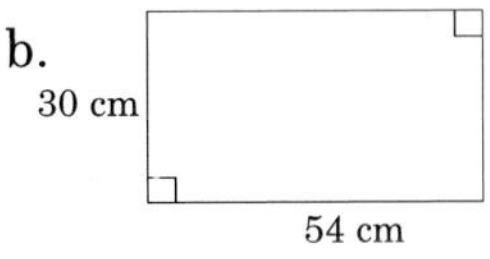

c.
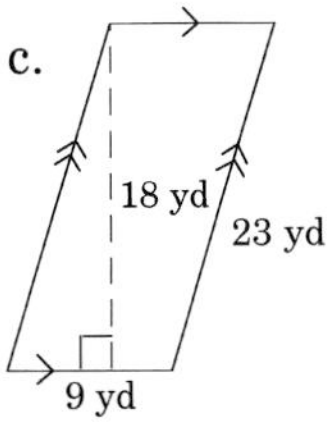

Part J

d. 45 × 12 = 540 mi

c. 4 1/3 — $34

b. 15 1/6 — 6)0 15 oz

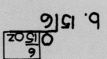

Lesson 89

Part 1 Work each item as a ratio problem. Answer the question.

a. Each lot costs $3000. How much do 16 lots cost?

b. If 7 clips weigh 5 grams, how much does each clip weigh?

Part 2 Work each item the fastest way you can. Answer the question.

a. If 12 baskets hold 42 pounds, how many pounds does 1 basket hold?

b. If 9 baskets hold 100 pounds, how many pounds would 8 baskets hold?

c. If each basket holds 56 pounds, how many pounds do 8 baskets hold?

d. If 2 baskets hold 32 pounds, how many baskets are needed to hold 160 pounds?

Part 3 Rewrite each problem and work it.

a. 130.71 + 42 + 3.5 b. 156 – 95.371 c. 98.3 – 40.58

Part 4 For each table, work the mixed number problem to figure out the missing value in the second column.

a.

	■	$14\frac{3}{10}$
	■	$25\frac{7}{10}$
Total	■	■

b.

	■	■
	■	$16\frac{5}{9}$
Total	■	38

c.

	■	$14\frac{5}{12}$
	■	$3\frac{7}{12}$
Total	■	■

Part 5 Copy and work each problem.

a. $68\overline{)479}$ b. $84\overline{)322}$

Part 6 For each item, make a number family. Answer the question.

a. Fran's goal is to buy a bike. The bike she wants costs $249. Fran has only $186. How much more money does she need?

b. Billy's goal is to lose weight. When he reaches his goal, he'll weigh 27 pounds less than he weighs now. He wants to weigh 158 pounds. How much does he weigh now?

c. Ms. Brown's goal is to reduce the amount of ice in the cold storage room. When she reaches her goal, the storage room will have 500 pounds of ice in it. To reach her goal, she must remove 865 pounds of ice. What's the amount of ice in the cold storage room?

d. Mr. Hanson has collected 194 baseball cards. He needs 106 more cards to reach his goal. How many cards will he have when he reaches his goal?

Part 7 Figure out all the angles in each circle.

a. $\angle x$ is $\frac{1}{6}$ of a circle.

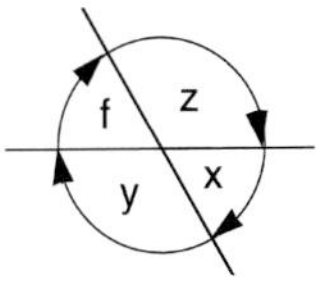

$\angle x$ = ■°

$\angle y$ = ■°

$\angle z$ = ■°

$\angle f$ = ■°

b. $\angle r$ is $\frac{3}{8}$ of a circle.

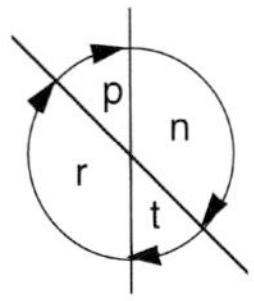

$\angle r$ = ■°

$\angle p$ = ■°

$\angle t$ = ■°

$\angle n$ = ■°

c. $\angle v$ is $\frac{2}{9}$ of a circle.

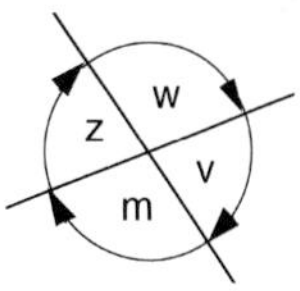

$\angle v$ = ■°

$\angle w$ = ■°

$\angle m$ = ■°

$\angle z$ = ■°

Independent Work

Part 8 Work each item. Answer the question.

a. If you can buy 1 pencil for 16 cents, 30 pencils cost how much?

b. If 56 bricks weigh 23 pounds, 1 brick weighs how many pounds?

c. 3 identical cars weigh 5640 pounds. 1 car weighs how many pounds?

d. 1 bicycle weighs 17 pounds. How much do 50 bicycles weigh?

Part 9 Write the complete equation for each angle marked with a letter.

∠p is 155°.

∠m = ■° ∠q = ■°

∠r = ■° ∠n = ■°

∠t = ■°

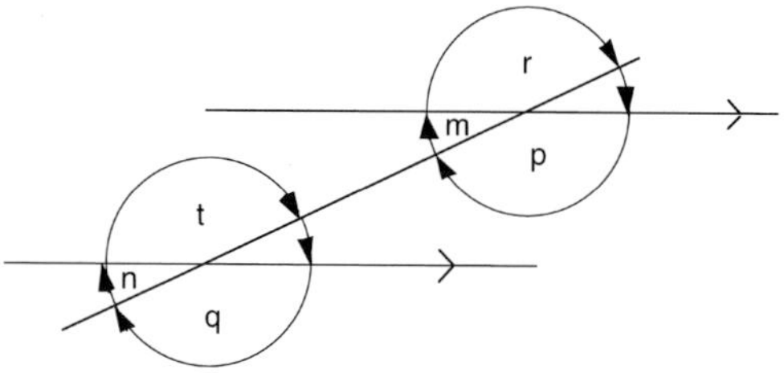

Part 10 Copy each problem. Figure out the missing numerator.

a. $5 = \frac{\blacksquare}{7}$ b. $8 = \frac{\blacksquare}{5}$ c. $4 = \frac{\blacksquare}{6}$ d. $7 = \frac{\blacksquare}{8}$ e. $3 = \frac{\blacksquare}{4}$

Part 11 Rewrite and work each problem.

a. 13 + 5.38 + 12.2

b. 26 + 3.19 + 12.002 + 1.8

c. 87 – 4.26

Part 12 Copy and complete the table.

	Fraction	Decimal	Mixed number
a.	$\frac{404}{100}$		
b.		3.5	
c.		7.16	
d.			$4\frac{11}{100}$
e.			$2\frac{3}{100}$

Part 13 For each item, make a fraction number family and a table. Answer the questions.

a. $\frac{3}{4}$ of the shoes in a store had rubber soles. There were 340 shoes that did not have rubber soles.
   1. How many shoes had rubber soles?
   2. How many shoes were in the store?

b. In the store, there were $\frac{7}{5}$ as many ties as shirts. There were 40 more ties than shirts.
   1. How many shirts were there?
   2. How many ties were there?

Part J

a. $12\overline{)42}$, -36, remainder 6 → $3\frac{6}{12}$ lb

b. $\frac{\text{baskets}}{\text{lb}} \; \frac{9}{100}\left(\frac{\frac{8}{9}}{\frac{8}{9}}\right) = \frac{8}{\frac{800}{9}}$ → $88\frac{8}{9}$ lb

c. 56×8 → 448 lb

d. $\frac{\text{baskets}}{\text{lb}} \; \frac{2}{32}\left(\frac{5}{5}\right) = \frac{10}{160}$ → 10 baskets

Part K

a. Dif, N 186, G 249

$249 - 186$ → \$ 63

b. Dif 27, G 158, N

$27 + 158$ → 185 lb

c. Dif 865, G 500, N

$865 + 500$ → 1365 lb

d. Dif 106, N 194, G

$106 + 194$ → 300 cards

Lesson 90

Part 1 **Copy and complete each equation.**

a. $\frac{210}{7}\left(\blacksquare\right)=\frac{\blacksquare}{1}$

b. $\frac{1}{16}\left(\blacksquare\right)=\frac{9}{\blacksquare}$

c. $\frac{3}{276}\left(\blacksquare\right)=\frac{1}{\blacksquare}$

d. $\frac{15}{8}\left(\blacksquare\right)=\frac{\blacksquare}{1}$

Part 2 **Copy each equation. Circle the big number. Figure out the missing value.**

a. $86 + \blacksquare = 400$ b. $127 - \blacksquare = 104$ c. $\blacksquare - 88 = 21$

d. $\blacksquare + 151 = 609$ e. $\blacksquare - 103 = 7$

Part 3

- You've rounded whole numbers. You round decimal numbers the same way.
- If the digit after the arrowed digit is 5 or more, you round the **arrowed digit up.**
- The arrowed digit points to the tenths. The digit after the tenths is more than 5, so you round the tenths to $\frac{3}{10}$.

  7.281
  ↑

- Here's the tenths rounded to 3 and two zeros after the 3:

  7.300
  ↑

- You don't have to show zeros when you round decimal numbers because zeros after the last decimal digit don't change the value.

  7.3
  ↑

- Remember, round the arrowed digit up if you have to. Don't show any zeros after the rounded digit.

Part 4 **Round each value. Each arrow shows the decimal place you'll round to.**

a. 19.249 b. 23.471 c. 2.5380 d. 12.0394 e. 1.836

Part 5

This is an inequality sign: >

- It has a large side and a point. Whatever is next to the large side is more than the value next to the point.
- Here's 56 on the large side and 55 on the point side: $56 > 55$
- Here's 14 on the point side and 20 on the large side: $14 < 20$
- Here's 3 x 5 on the large side and 7 x 2 on the point side: $3 \times 5 > 7 \times 2$
- 15 is more than 14. $15 > 14$

Part J

a. $400 - 86 = 314$ b. $127 - 104 = 23$ c. $88 + 21 = 109$ d. $609 - 151 = 458$ e. $103 + 7 = 110$

Part K

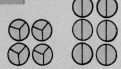

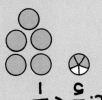

b. $2 > \frac{7}{7}$ c. $\frac{3}{5} < \frac{5}{1}$ d. $27 - 27 < 1$ e. $\frac{14}{2} > \frac{12}{3}$

Test 9

Part 1 **For each item, make a number family. Answer the question.**

a. A train started out with 569 gallons of fuel. At the first stop, another 112 gallons were added. At the next stop, another 99 gallons were added. The train used up 702 gallons on the trip. How much fuel did the train have at the end of the trip?

b. Tim bought film for $2.50. He bought paper for $.85. He bought a T-shirt for $7.95. He received $3.70 in change. How much did he give the clerk?

c. A bus started out with 37 people in it. At the first stop, 4 people got off and 12 people got in the bus. At the next stop, 15 people got in and 25 people got off the bus. How many people were still on the bus?

d. Jan bought a T-shirt for $7.95. She also bought a camera for $13.45. She gave the clerk $30. How much change did she receive?

Part 2 **Copy and work each problem.**

a. $73\overline{)215}$ b. $62\overline{)593}$ c. $58\overline{)356}$

Part 3 **Find the area and perimeter of the parallelogram and the triangle.**

a.

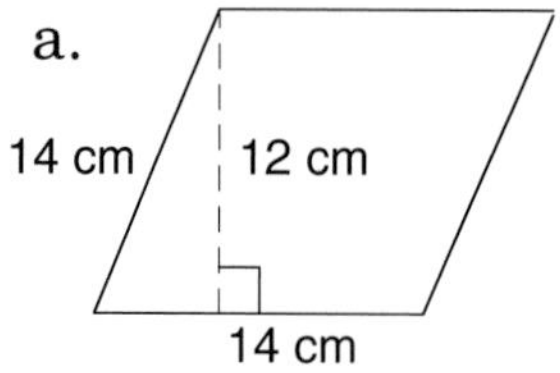

b.

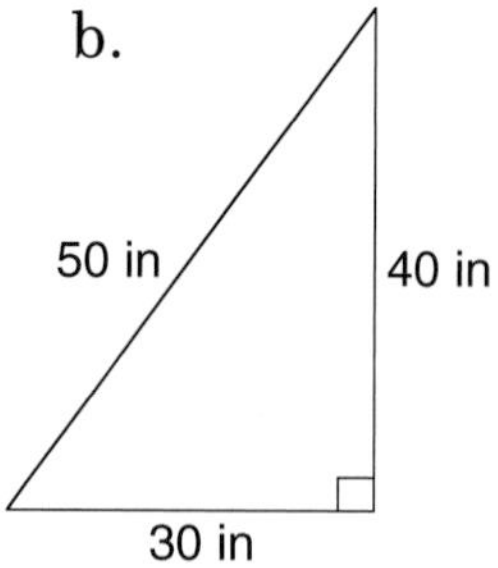

Part 4 Copy and work each problem.

a. $52 - 15\frac{5}{9}$

b. $14\frac{7}{20} + 10\frac{13}{20}$

c. $2\frac{7}{15} + 14 + 8\frac{6}{15}$

Part 5 For each item, make a fraction number family and a ratio table. Answer the questions.

a. Bill was $\frac{4}{3}$ the height of his sister. His sister was 57 inches tall.
   1. How much taller is Bill than his sister?
   2. How tall is Bill?

b. $\frac{3}{8}$ of the trucks had new tires. There were 88 trucks.
   1. How many trucks had new tires?
   2. How many trucks had tires that were not new?

Part 6 Write the complete equation for each angle marked with a letter.

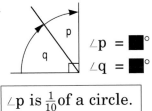

a.

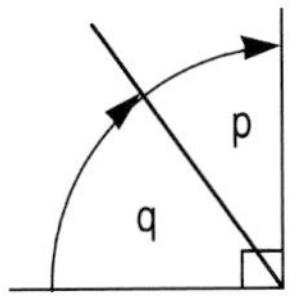

$\angle p =$ ■°

$\angle q =$ ■°

$\angle p$ is $\frac{1}{10}$ of a circle.

b.

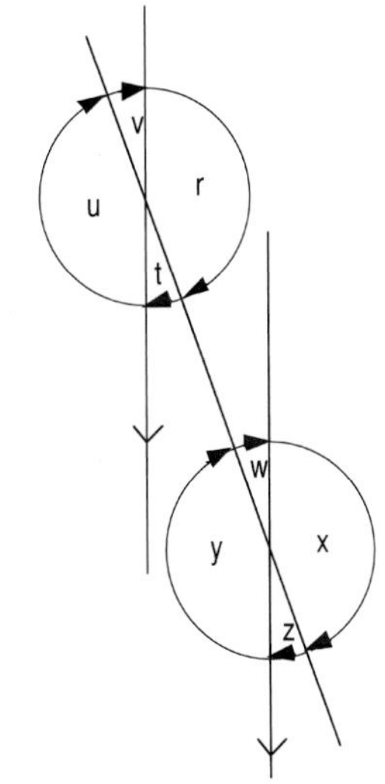

$\angle y = 160°$

$\angle w =$ ■°

$\angle x =$ ■°

$\angle z =$ ■°

$\angle u =$ ■°

$\angle v =$ ■°

$\angle r =$ ■°

$\angle t =$ ■°

Part 7 Work each item. Answer the question.

a. If 1 box holds 150 paper clips, how many paper clips do 12 boxes hold?

b. 7 boxes weigh 9 ounces. How many ounces does 1 box weigh?

c. 3 pounds of coffee make 160 cups. How much coffee is needed for each cup?

d. If each ant can carry 2 grams, how many grams can 15 ants carry?

Part 8 Rewrite each problem and work it.

a. 15.85 + 300 + 1.391

b. 300.4 – 108.75

c. 4 – 2.38

Part 9 For each item, work a problem with values rounded to the place named in the box.

a. $\begin{array}{r} 5671 \\ -\ 2008 \\ \hline \end{array}$ tens

b. $\begin{array}{r} 2586 \\ 3498 \\ +\ 1360 \\ \hline \end{array}$ hundreds

c. $\begin{array}{r} 5602 \\ 1294 \\ +\ 1861 \\ \hline \end{array}$ thousands

Yes, Jerry, you made **round** numbers, but you were supposed to make **rounded** numbers.

Lesson 91

Part 1

- You've learned that the distance around any figure with straight sides is called the **perimeter.**

- A circle doesn't have any straight sides. So it doesn't have a perimeter. The distance around a circle is called the **circumference.**
- The first part of that name has the same letters as the word **circle: C-I-R-C.**
- To figure out the distance around a circle, you can't add up the length of each side because there are no sides. But you can **measure** the circumference of a circle.
- One way is to roll the circle and see how long the path is when the circle rotates one time.

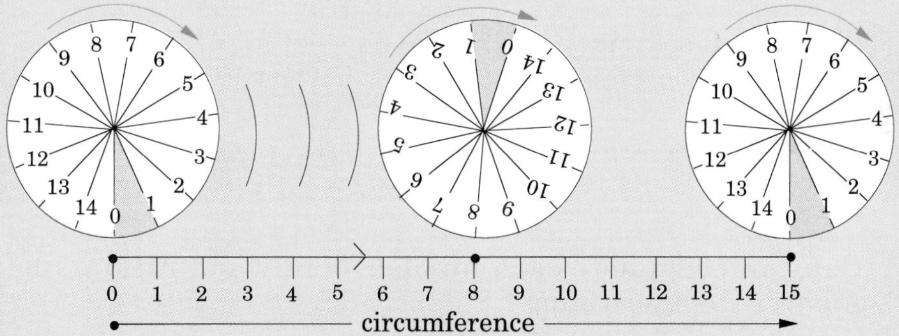

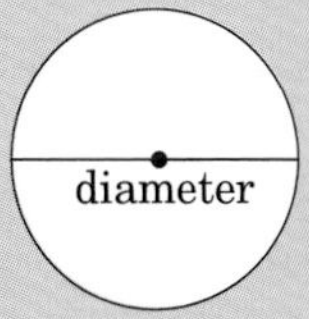

- The circumference of any circle is related to a line that goes through the center of that circle. That line is called the **diameter.**

Part 2 For each circle, write the complete equation with numbers. Figure out the decimal value for each fraction.

		Equation
a.	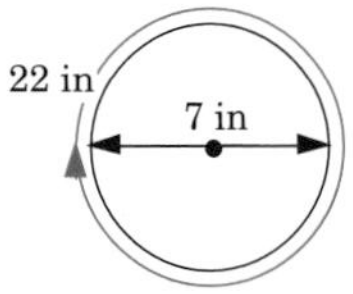	D $\left(\frac{■}{■}\right)$ = C
b.	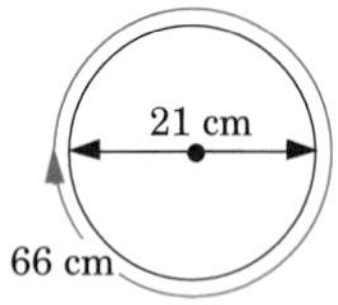	■ $\left(\frac{■}{■}\right)$ = ■
c.	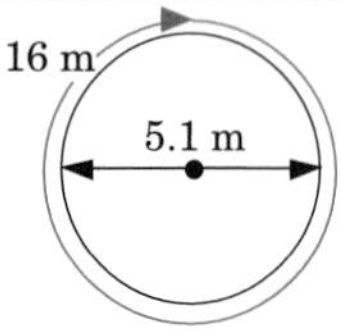	■ $\left(\frac{■}{■}\right)$ = ■

Part 3 Figure out all the angles that are shown.

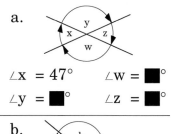

a. 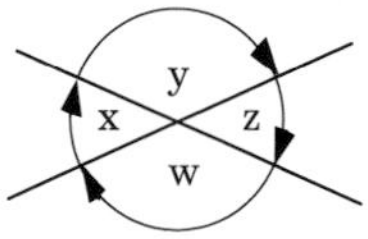

∠x = 47° ∠w = ■°
∠y = ■° ∠z = ■°

b. 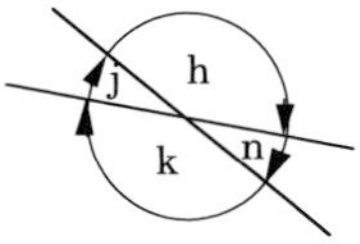

∠j = 28° ∠h = ■°
∠k = 152° ∠n = ■°

c. 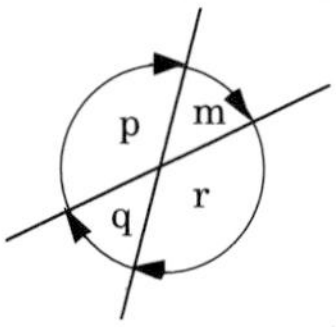

∠m = 50° ∠p = ■°
∠q = ■° ∠r = ■°

Part 4 Write each statement with the correct sign.

a. $\frac{1}{2}$ ■ $\frac{1}{3}$ b. $\frac{1}{10}$ ■ $\frac{1}{4}$ c. $\frac{2}{5}$ ■ $\frac{1}{5}$ d. $\frac{1}{8}$ ■ $\frac{1}{7}$ e. $\frac{9}{10}$ ■ $\frac{10}{5}$

Part 5 Copy and complete each number family and ratio table. Answer the questions.

a. Sand $\frac{2}{5}$ — Gravel $\frac{3}{5}$ → Mixture

S	■	11
G	■	■
M	■	■

1. How many pounds does the gravel weigh?
2. How many pounds does the whole mixture weigh?

b. Dif — Tree $\frac{7}{7}$ → Pole $\frac{9}{7}$

Dif	■	■
T	■	■
P	■	50

1. How many feet tall is the tree?
2. How much shorter is the tree than the pole?

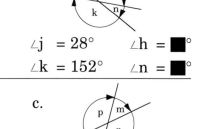

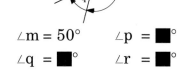

Part 6 **Copy each equation. Circle the big number. Figure out the missing value.**

a. 607 + ■ = 999 b. ■ – 348 = 19

c. ■ + 203 = 591 d. 607 – ■ = 444

Part 7

- Some numbers are **odd** and some are **even.**
- You can figure out whether numbers are **even** by dividing the number by 2.
- If the answer is a whole number, the number you started with is **even.**
- If you don't get a whole-number answer when you divide by 2, the number is not even. It's **odd.**

Part 8 **Copy each item. Write E after each even number. Write O after each odd number.**

a. 6 b. 7 c. 119 d. 198 e. 412 f. 666 g. 255 h. 125

Part 9 **Round each decimal value.**

a. Round numeral A to the nearest tenth.
b. Round numeral B to the nearest hundredth.
c. Round numeral C to the nearest hundredth.
d. Round numeral D to the nearest hundredth.
e. Round numeral E to the nearest tenth.

	tens	ones	tenths	hundredths	thousandths
A		8.	1	6	0
B		7.	1	7	9
C	1	2.	0	4	3
D	1	5.	4	0	8
E	1	2.	7	5	2

Independent Work

Part 10 **For each item, make a number family. Answer the questions.**

a. Sara Johnson's goal is to buy a car that costs $11,200. She needs $5,412 more than she has now. How much does she have now?

b. The store wants to reduce the number of items it has. It currently has 5100 items. The store wants to have only 4750 items. How many items must the store sell to reach its goal?

c. The goal of River City is to use 45,000 fewer gallons of water each day. The city uses 99,400 gallons of water each day. If the city reaches its goal, how many gallons of water will it use each day?

Part 11 **Rewrite each problem and work it.**

a. 21 – 13.12

b. 9 + 2.03 + 15.8

c. 93.7 – 25.045

Part 12 **Copy and work each problem.**

a. $58\overline{)406}$

b. $94\overline{)820}$

c. $71\overline{)365}$

Part 13 **For each item, make a fraction number family and a table. Answer the questions.**

a. In a factory, $\frac{8}{9}$ of the workers wear gloves. There are 459 workers in the factory.
   1. How many wear gloves?
   2. How many do not wear gloves?

b. The snail moved at $\frac{2}{7}$ the rate of the beetle. The beetle went 56 feet.
   1. How far did the snail move in the same time?
   2. How much farther did the beetle move than the snail moved?

c. In a hospital, $\frac{2}{3}$ of the babies were sleeping. 55 babies were not sleeping.
   1. How many babies were in the hospital?
   2. How many were sleeping?

d. The cost of a typewriter was $\frac{12}{5}$ the cost of a camera. The typewriter cost $300.
   1. How much did the camera cost?
   2. How much less was the cost of the camera compared to the cost of the typewriter?

Part 14 **Find the area and perimeter of each figure.**

a.

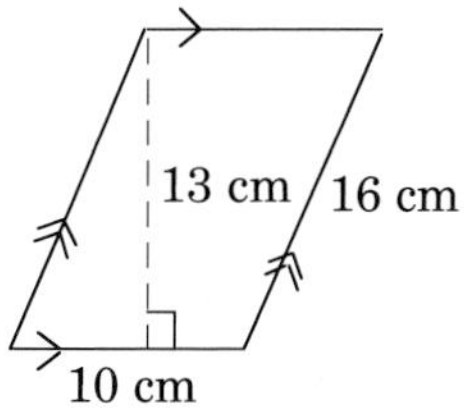
13 cm
16 cm
10 cm

b.

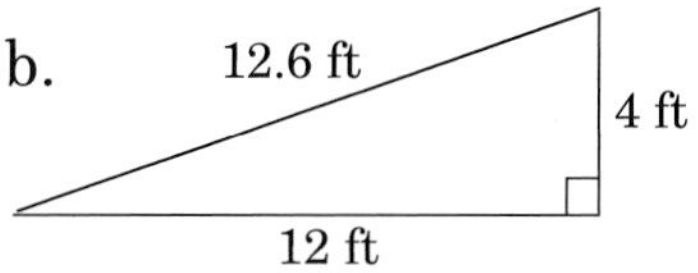
12.6 ft
4 ft
12 ft

Part 15 **Copy and complete the table.**

	Fraction	Mixed number
a.	$\frac{93}{9}$	
b.		$4\frac{3}{7}$
c.		$9\frac{2}{23}$
d.	$\frac{100}{3}$	

Can you find the area of that large triangular lot ?
Sure, it's easy to find. It's right over there.

Part J

a. $\frac{1}{2} > \frac{1}{3}$ b. $\frac{1}{10} < \frac{1}{4}$ c. $\frac{2}{5} > \frac{1}{5}$ d. $\frac{1}{8} < \frac{1}{7}$ e. $\frac{9}{10} < \frac{10}{5}$

Part K

a. $999 - 607 = \boxed{392}$ b. $348 + 19 = \boxed{367}$ c. $591 - 203 = \boxed{388}$ d. $607 - 444 = \boxed{163}$

Lesson 92

Part 1 **Copy each equation. Circle the big number. Figure out the missing value.**

a. 207 – ■ = 67

b. ■ + 13 = 800

c. ■ – 13 = 800

d. 211 + ■ = 800

Part 2

- The diameter of any circle is related to the circumference of the circle. The circumference is always **3.14 times the diameter.**

- That's true of small circles and large circles.

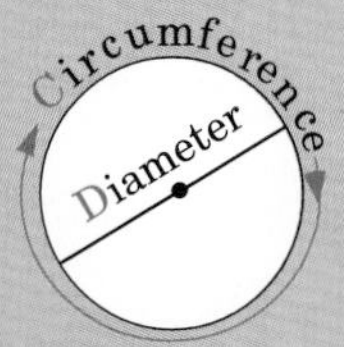

D(3.14) = C

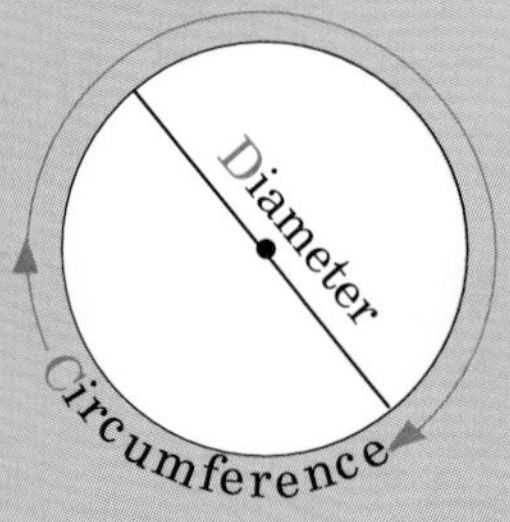

D(3.14) = C

- The number 3.14 has a special symbol: π
  It's called **pi.**

- You write the equation for working with circles as: **D x π = C**

  Or you can use the equation: **π x D = C**

- Either equation says the same thing.
  It tells you that the circumference is
  3.14 times the diameter: **3.14 x D = C**

Part 3 Figure out the circumference of each circle.

$\pi \times D = C$

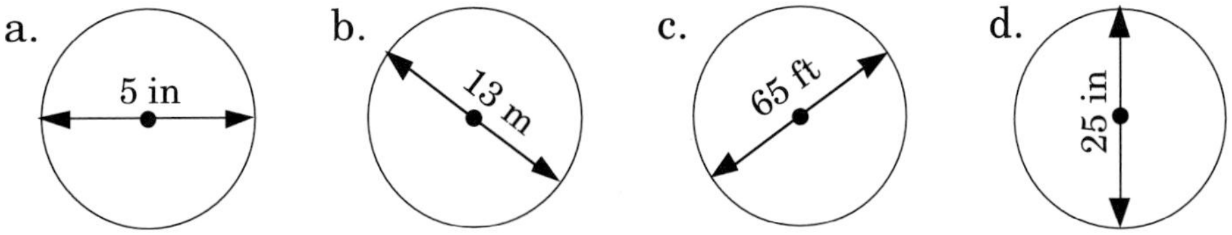

Part 4 Round each decimal value.

a. Round 3.05882 to the nearest thousandth.

b. Round 20.3102 to the nearest tenth.

c. Round 6.77777 to the nearest thousandth.

d. Round 14.85431 to the nearest hundredth.

e. Round 4.20309 to the nearest hundredth.

Part 5 Copy each item. Write E after each even number. Write O after each odd number.

a. 27 b. 193 c. 58 d. 102 e. 80 f. 577

Part 6 Figure out all the angles marked with a letter.

a. ∠n = 30° ∠w = ■°
∠r = ■° ∠t = ■°
∠p = ■° ∠v = ■°
∠q = ■° ∠x = ■°

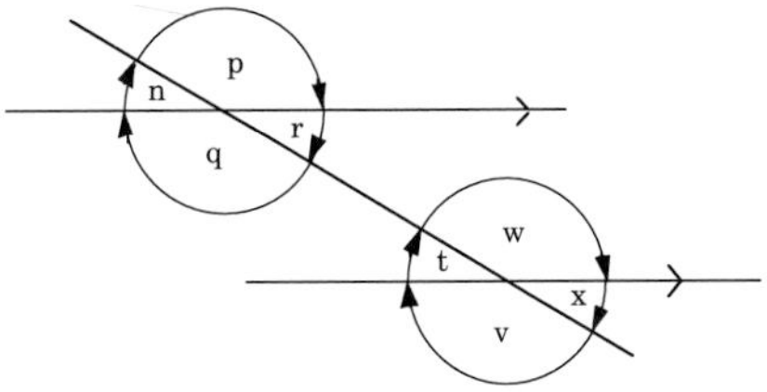

---

b. ∠g = 86° ∠x = ■°
∠j = ■° ∠y = ■°
∠k = ■° ∠p = ■°
∠h = ■° ∠v = ■°

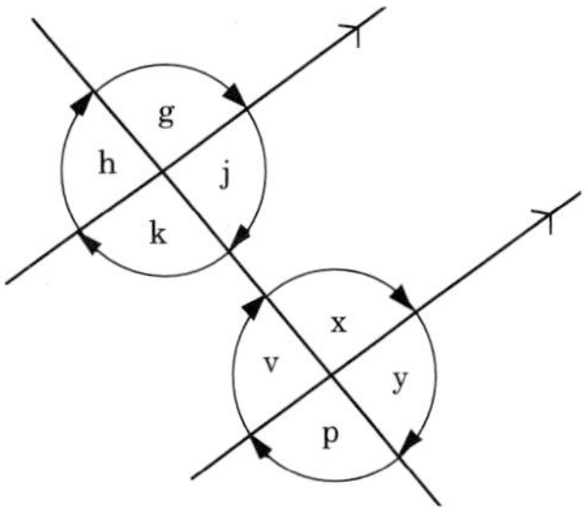

Part 7

- Some problems tell about percents. A percent number is a hundredths number.
- 16% is $\frac{16}{100}$.
- 235% is $\frac{235}{100}$.
- You can rewrite any hundredths fraction as a percent value.
- The percent number has the same digits as the numerator of the fraction. $\frac{45}{100} = 45\%$
- You write the percent sign instead of the denominator. $\frac{6}{100} = 6\%$

Independent Work

Part 8

Copy and complete each statement with the appropriate sign: >, < or =.

a. $\frac{3}{2}$ ■ $\frac{10}{10}$ b. $\frac{6}{10}$ ■ $\frac{8}{10}$ c. 5 ■ $\frac{20}{5}$ d. $\frac{11}{1}$ ■ $\frac{66}{6}$

Part 9

Work each item. Answer the question.

a. If each classroom has 28 desks, how many classrooms would be needed for 308 desks?

b. If 62 identical classrooms have 310 chalkboards, how many chalkboards are in each classroom?

c. If each classroom has 12 windows, how many windows are there in 37 classrooms?

d. If 4 classrooms have 112 books, how many classrooms would have 84 books?

Part 10 **Rewrite each problem and work it.**

a. 35.01 + 3.3

b. 56.09 – 3.17

c. 15 + 3.45

Part 11 **For each item, make a number family. Answer the question.**

a. Big Zig's goal is to lose 35 pounds. He currently weighs 235 pounds. How much will Zig weigh when he reaches his goal?

b. The goal is to load a truck with gravel. When the truck is fully loaded, it will weigh 1800 pounds more than it weighs now. The truck weighs 4927 pounds now. How much will it weigh when it is fully loaded?

c. Tina's goal is to have $340 in her savings account. She currently has $14.65 in her account. How much more money must go into the account before Tina reaches her goal?

Part 12 **Copy each equation and show the missing value as a fraction.**

a. 7 x ■ = 46 b. 90 x ■ = 12

c. 20 x ■ = 1004 d. 17 x ■ = 1

Part 13 **For each item, make a fraction number family and a table. Answer the questions.**

a. The regular price of jeans is $\frac{5}{4}$ the sale price. You would save $4 by buying the jeans on sale.
   1. How much is the regular price?
   2. How much is the sale price?

b. The sale price of dinnerware is $\frac{3}{5}$ the regular price. A full set of dinnerware on sale costs $69.
   1. What is the regular price of the dinnerware?
   2. How much would a person save by purchasing the dinnerware on sale?

Part J

a. 207 − 67 = 140

b. 800 − 13 = 787

c. 800 + 13 = 813

d. 800 − 211 = 589

Lesson 93

Part 1

- You've worked with vertical number families in tables.
- The two top numbers are small numbers. The value at the end of the arrow is the big number.

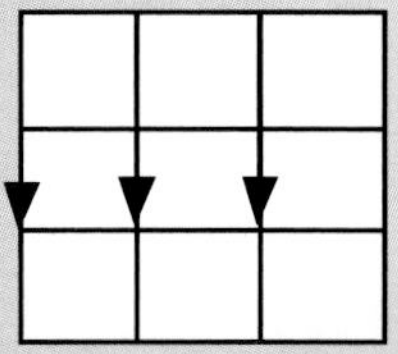

- If the big number is missing, you add.

16
25
■

- If a small number is missing, you subtract.

16 ■
■ 25
41 41

- You can use vertical number families for word problems that tell about **in** or **out.** You make a box for the missing value.

in

- Here's a problem: **Tom had some money.**

■

Then he received $16 more.

16

He ended up with $48.

48

16 25
I guess you could call that a vertical number family, but there's an easier way to do it.

Part 2 For each item, make a number family. Answer the question.

Sample problem:	John lost some weight in March. Then he lost another 14 pounds in April. The total amount of weight he lost during both months was 23 pounds. How much weight did he lose in March?

a. John had some money. Then he earned $45 more. He ended up with $98. How much money did he have to begin with?

b. Jerry picked 167 pears in the morning. In the afternoon, he picked more pears. In all, he picked 411 pears. How many pears did he pick in the afternoon?

c. Bernie collected 34 seashells last year. This year, she collected 134 more. How many shells did she collect during the two-year period?

d. Ginger sold some garments on two occasions. On the second occasion, she sold 26 garments. She sold a total of 88 garments. How many garments did she sell on the first occasion?

e. Rodney ate 156 grams of cheese. Later, he ate some more cheese. In all, he ate 201 grams. How much cheese did he eat on the second occasion?

Part 3 Complete each equation.

∠p = 32°	∠q = ■°
∠■ = ■°	∠■ = ■°
∠k = ■°	∠v = ■°
∠■ = ■°	∠■ = ■°

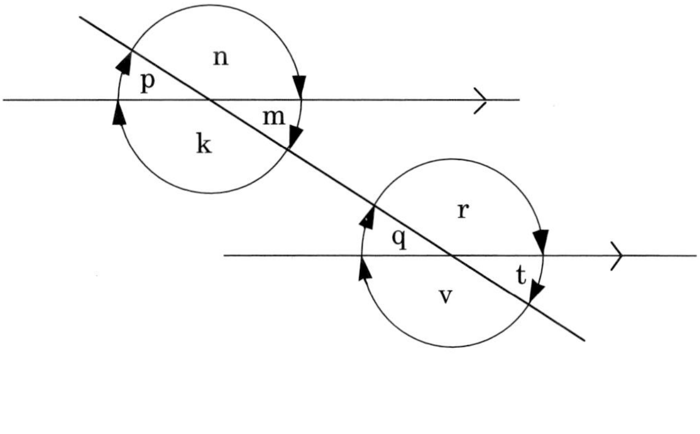

Part 4

- You've divided numbers by 2 to figure out if they are **odd** or **even.**
- The first even numbers are: **0, 2, 4, 6, 8, 10.**
- If you divide any of these numbers by 2, the answer is a whole number.
- Here's a fact: If the **last digit** of any number is 0, 2, 4, 6, or 8, the entire number is **even.**
- If the last digit is **not** 0, 2, 4, 6 or 8, the number is **odd.**
- Here's a number: **547.**
  The last digit is 7. That's **not** an even number.
  So **547 is not even.** It's odd.
- Here's a different number: **548.**
  The last digit is 8. That's an even number. So **548 is even.**
- Remember, look at the last digit. It it's even, the entire number is even.

Part 5

Copy each item. Write E after each even number. Write O after each odd number.

a. 314 b. 413 c. 30 d. 51 e. 17 f. 90 g. 136

Part 6

Work each item.

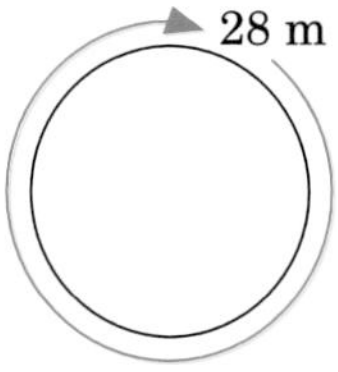

a. Find the diameter.

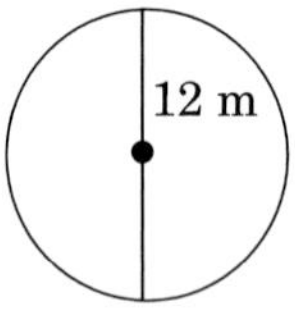

b. Find the circumference.

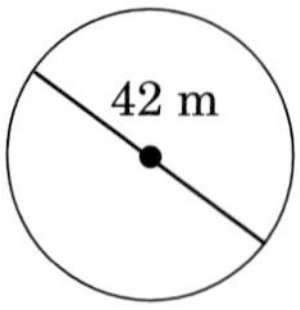

c. Find the circumference.

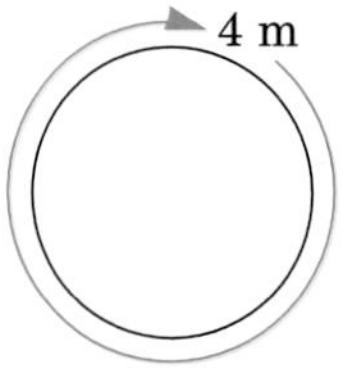

d. Find the diameter.

Part 7

- You've made ratio tables for some problems without first making a fraction number family.
- Those problems don't tell about fractions. They have sentences like these:

> **The ratio of boys to girls is 4 to 3.**
>
> **The ratio of cows to all the farm animals is 2 to 9.**
>
> **There were 3 cracked plates for every 5 plates that were not cracked.**
>
> **4 out of every 7 plates are blue.**

- You **can** make a fraction number family for all these sentences. Each family will have a big number that equals 1.
- To make the family, you ask whether the sentence gives the name for the big number.
- Here's the family for: **The ratio of boys to girls is 4 to 3.**

boys	girls	children
$\frac{4}{7}$	$\frac{3}{7}$ →	$\frac{7}{7}$

Part 8 Make a fraction number family for each sentence.

a. There are 5 children for every 9 people.

b. In a mixture, the ratio of sand to gravel is 5 to 3.

c. 3 out of every 100 parts are broken.

d. There are 6 clean plates for every 11 dirty plates.

e. The ratio of frogs to all the animals in the pond is 2 to 15.

Independent Work

Part 9 **Work each item. Answer the question.**

a. If the cost of 1 vacation day at Breen Mountain is $185, how much is the cost of 7 vacation days?

b. If the cost of each vacation day at Preen Lake is $126, how many days could you stay for $756?

c. If the cost of 5 vacation days at Vern's Hollow is $400, how long could you stay at Vern's Hollow for $960?

d. If the cost of 7 vacation days at Nina's Hide Away is $196, how much does each day cost?

e. Which of the vacation resorts in items a through d costs the least amount each day?

Part 10 **Copy each equation. Circle the big number. Figure out the missing value.**

a. 156 – ■ = 29

b. ■ + 84 = 709

c. ■ – 183 = 9

d. 560 + ■ = 641

Part 11 **Write each rounded value.**

a. Round 56.062 to the nearest tenth.

b. Round 4.198 to the nearest tenth.

c. Round 4.075 to the nearest hundredth.

d. Round 3.1238 to the nearest hundredth.

e. Round 0.7874 to the nearest thousandth.

Part 12 **Make a number family for each item. Answer the question.**

a. Al gave a clerk $50 to pay for his purchase. The clerk gave Al $13.70 in change. What was the price of the item Al purchased?

b. A hotel had guests that came and left. On Monday morning, the hotel had 212 guests. During that day, 104 guests arrived and 71 guests left the hotel. On Tuesday, 65 guests left the hotel and 52 guests arrived. On Wednesday, 150 left the hotel and 38 arrived. How many guests stayed in the hotel Wednesday night?

c. Cindy purchased a camera that cost $48.30. She gave the clerk $60. How much change did she receive?

d. Tim started out with some money in his account. Then he took out $450. Later he took out another $120. Finally, he took out $56. He still had $92 in his account. How much did he have in his account to start with?

e. Betty went to the store and bought some items. She gave the clerk a check for $25. She received $16.45 in change. What was the cost of the items she bought?

Part 13 Copy and work each problem.

a. $23\overline{)177}$

b. $45\overline{)270}$

c. $51\overline{)305}$

Part 14 Copy and complete each statement. Use the sign <, > or =.

a. 1 ■ $\frac{100}{100}$ b. $\frac{10}{5}$ ■ $\frac{24}{4}$ c. 5×8 ■ 39

d. $\frac{6}{10}$ ■ $\frac{5}{10}$ e. $\frac{20}{100}$ ■ $\frac{100}{4}$

I don't think that's the way you're supposed to use those signs.
Use the sign<, >or =.
a. 1 100/100 b. 10/5 24/4

Part J

	Decimal	Fraction	Percent
a.	.09	$\frac{9}{100}$	9%
b.	1.42	$\frac{142}{100}$	142%
c.	.26	$\frac{26}{100}$	26%
d.	5.18	$\frac{518}{100}$	518%
e.	.03	$\frac{3}{100}$	3%

Lesson 94

Part 1 **For each item, make a number family. Answer the question.**

a. Sally had some trading cards. Then she bought 64 more cards. She ended up with 206 cards. How many cards did she start out with?

b. Sam had 460 plants in his nursery. He bought some more plants and ended up with 546 plants. How many plants did he buy?

c. Walter, the whale, went on a diet. On Monday, he lost 25 pounds. On Tuesday, he lost another 18 pounds. On Wednesday, he lost 42 pounds. How much weight did Walter lose altogether?

d. Hilda sold some stamps to Barbara. Then she gave 13 stamps to Alex. She got rid of 85 stamps in all. How many stamps did Hilda sell to Barbara?

Part 2

- You can figure out the surface area of containers by adding the area of each face.
- A box has 6 faces. Each face is a flat surface that is the shape of a rectangle.

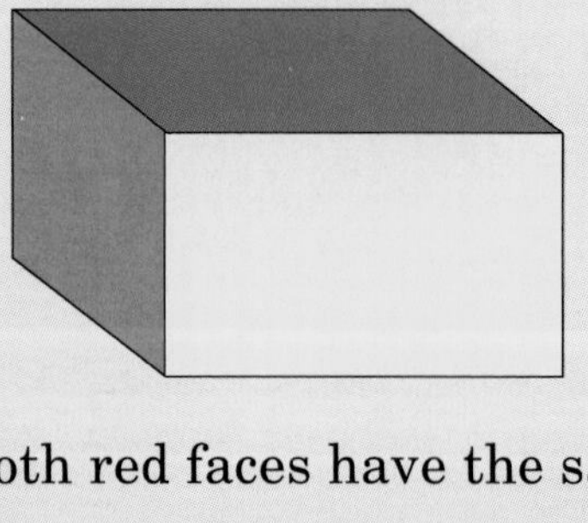

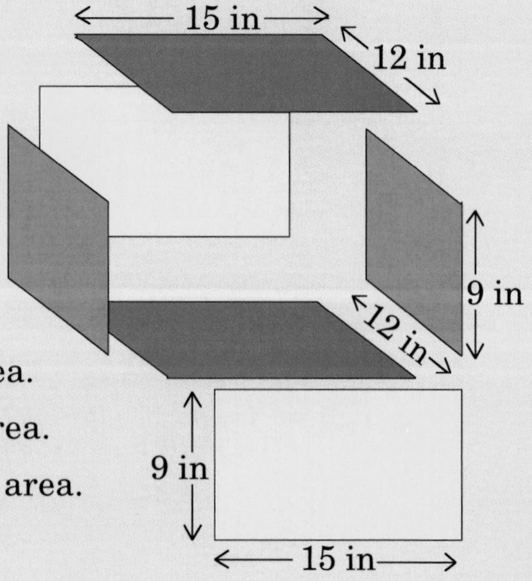

- Both red faces have the same area.
- Both blue faces have the same area.
- Both yellow faces have the same area.

Part 3 Find the surface area of the box.

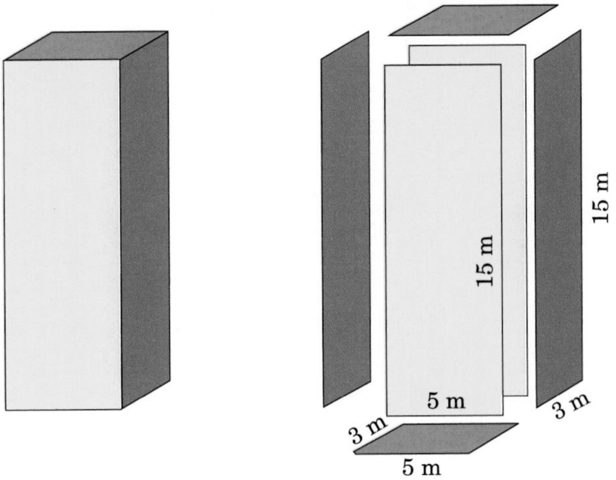

Part 4 Use your calculator to work each item.

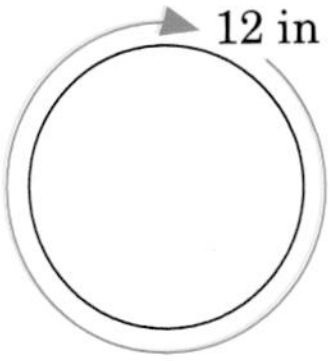

a. Find the diameter.

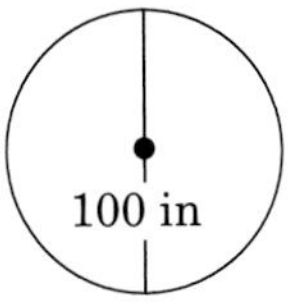

b. Find the circumference.

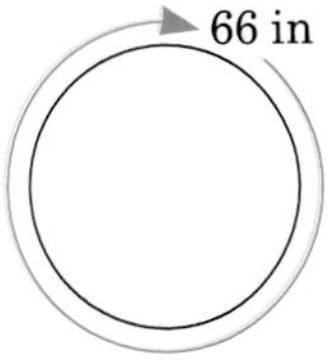

c. Find the diameter.

If this box has six faces, how come I can't find one single nose or eye?

Part 5

- Here's an important rule about any whole number that ends in one zero. The number equals the rest of the digits times 10.

340

340 = 34 x 10

Here's 50: **50**
It ends in one zero.
It equals 5 x 10. **50 = 5 x 10**

7890

7890 = 789 x 10

- Numbers that end in two zeros equal the rest of the digits times 100.

Here's 300: **300**
It equals 3 x 100. **300 = 3 x 100**

5400
5400 = 54 x 100

- Numbers that end in three zeros equal the rest of the digits times 1000.

Here's 3000: **3000**
It equals 3 x 1000. **3000 = 3 x 1000**

56,000 = ■ x ■

Here's 420: **420 = ■ x ■**

600 = ■ x ■

Here's 6000: **6000 = ■ x ■**

Part 6

Write the multiplication for each item.

Sample problem: **4500 = 45 x 100**

a. 76,000 b. 48,700 c. 270 d. 300

Part 7 Make a fraction number family for each sentence.

a. The ratio of perch to all the fish was 3 to 13.

b. There were 5 men for every 3 women.

c. The ratio of flat tires to good tires is 1 to 9.

Part 8 For each item, make a fraction number family and a ratio table with four numbers.

a. The ratio of green bottles to clear bottles is 4 to 5. There are 63 bottles in all.
   1. How many clear bottles are there?
   2. How many green bottles are there?

b. 2 out of every 7 bottles were empty. There were 84 empty bottles.
   1. How many bottles were not empty?
   2. How many bottles were there in all?

Independent Work

Remember to complete the ratio tables and answer the questions for part 8 of your textbook.

Part 9 Work each item.

a. A store wants to sell \$4500 worth of merchandise by the end of Saturday. By noon on Saturday, the store had sold \$2120 worth of merchandise. How much more money must the store take in to reach its goal?

b. The truck must deliver 68,200 pounds of gravel by the end of the day. The truck has delivered some gravel but must still deliver 13,780 pounds before reaching its goal. How much has the truck already delivered?

c. The rangers want to reduce the water level in a lake by 478 inches. The water level is currently 1560 inches. When the water level is reduced, how many inches of water will be in the lake?

d. Farmer Vern wants to sell all his corn. He has already sold 6800 pounds of corn. He still needs to sell 14,200 pounds. When he reaches his goal, how much corn will he have sold?

Part 10 Work each item.

a. Round 11.0715 to the nearest thousandth.

b. Round 6.8537 to the nearest hundredth.

c. Round 0.1723 to the nearest tenth.

d. Round 120.904 to the nearest tenth.

Part 11 Copy each equation. Circle the big number. Figure out the missing value.

a. $\blacksquare - 146 = 312$

b. $\blacksquare + 146 = 312$

c. $45 + \blacksquare = 206$

d. $792 - \blacksquare = 206$

Part 12 **Copy each equation. Show the missing value as a fraction.**

a. 11 x ■ = 56

b. 80 x ■ = 1

c. 63 x ■ = 84

d. 420 x ■ = 18

e. 15 x ■ = 3

f. 7 x ■ = 10

Part 13 **Find the area and perimeter of each figure.**

a.

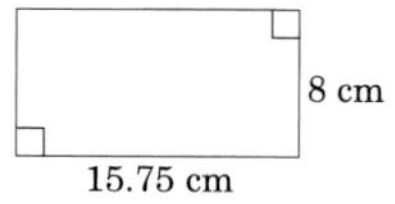

b.

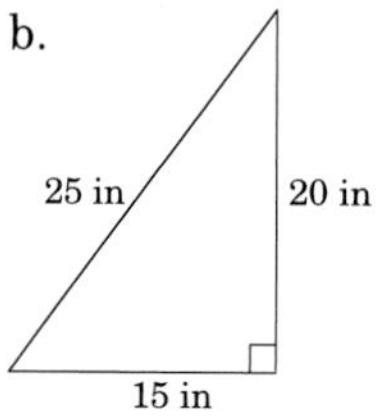

Part 14 **Write the letter O or E for each number.**

a. 700 b. 257 c. 256 d. 1772 e. 209

Part 15 **For each item, make a fraction number family and a table. Answer the questions.**

a. In a factory, the time required to cut out a shirt is $\frac{7}{3}$ the time required to cut out a tie. The time for cutting out a tie is 19 seconds.
   1. How much time is required for a shirt?
   2. How much more time is required for a shirt than for a tie?

b. A recipe calls for 4 cups of flour for every 9 cups of water. A person follows the recipe and uses 14 cups of water.
   1. How many cups of flour are needed?
   2. How much more water than flour does the person use?

c. A job requires a painter to use blue paint and white paint. The ratio of blue paint to white paint is 3 to 1. The painter uses a total of 25 gallons of paint.
   1. How much blue paint does the painter use?
   2. How much white paint does the painter use?

Part 16 **Rewrite each problem and work it.**

a. 170 – 3.81 = ■ b. 15.2 – 13.86 = ■ c. 20.8 + 1.003 = ■ d. 28 + 3.03 + 100.7 = ■

Part J

b. 48,700 = 487 × 100
c. 270 = 27 × 10
d. 300 = 3 × 100

Part K

	Decimal	Fraction	Percent
a.	1.00	$\frac{100}{100}$	100%
b.	8.02	$\frac{802}{100}$	802%
c.	4.03	$\frac{403}{100}$	403%
d.	.08	$\frac{8}{100}$	8%
e.	.90	$\frac{90}{100}$	90%

Lesson 95

Part 1

- You've written the multiplication for numbers that end in zeros. Remember, the number of zeros tells whether you multiply digits by 10, 100 or 1000.
- The number **560** has one zero. It equals 56 x 10. **560 = 56 x 10**
- Some **fractions** have numerators and denominators that end in zero. You can simplify those fractions by showing the multiplication.
- The numerator and denominator have values multiplied by 10. So when you cross out $\frac{10}{10}$, you have the simplified fraction.

$$\frac{40}{370} = \frac{4 \times 10}{37 \times 10}$$

$$\frac{40}{370} = \frac{4 \times \cancel{10}}{37 \times \cancel{10}} = \frac{4}{37}$$

- Both numerator and denominator have values multiplied by 100.
- So when you cross out $\frac{100}{100}$, you have the simplified fraction $\frac{4}{37}$.

$$\frac{400}{3700} = \frac{4 \times \cancel{100}}{37 \times \cancel{100}} = \frac{4}{37}$$

Part 2

For each fraction, write the multiplication for the numerator and the denominator. Then write the simplified fraction.

a. $\frac{300}{1700}$ b. $\frac{50}{1410}$ c. $\frac{680}{30}$ d. $\frac{11,000}{19,000}$

Part 3 For each item, make a number family. Answer the question.

a. On Monday, Sally gave away 28 stamps. On Thursday, she gave away 16 more stamps. How many stamps did she give away in all?

b. Billy had some money in the bank. On Friday, he put another $55 in the bank. In all, he had $317 in his account. How much money did he have in the bank to start with?

c. 14 people got off the bus at the first stop. At the next stop, some more people got off. In all, 29 people got off the bus. How many got off at the second stop?

d. On Monday, it rained 31 millimeters. On Tuesday, it rained another 14 millimeters. On Wednesday, it rained 11 millimeters. What was the total rainfall for all three days?

Part 4 Find the surface area of each box.

a.

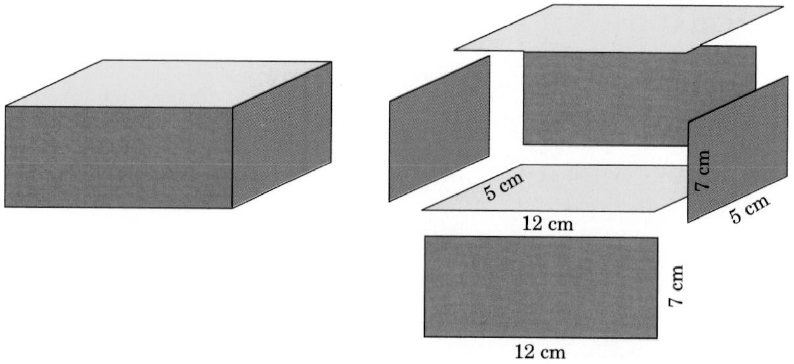

b.

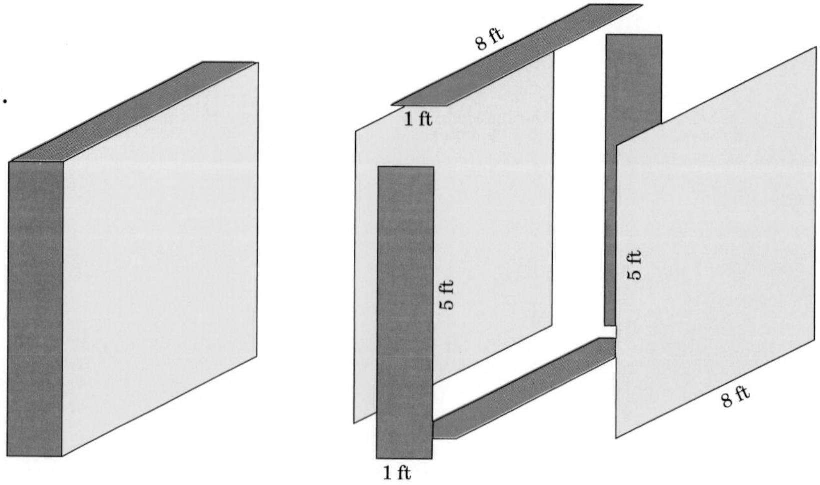

Part 5

Write the equation to show the decimal that equals each percent value.

a. 137% = [redacted]

b. 4% = [redacted]

c. 56% = [redacted]

d. 209% = [redacted]

e. 99% = [redacted]

Part 6

For each item, make a fraction number family and a ratio table with four numbers.

a. On Uncle Jack's farm, the ratio of farm animals to goats is 7 to 2. 155 of the animals are not goats.
   1. How many farm animals are there?
   2. How many goats are there?

b. In the classrooms at Brown's school, there are children and teachers. There are 32 children for every 4 teachers. There are 180 people in the classrooms at Brown's school.
   1. How many children are there?
   2. How many teachers are there?

c. In a forest, there were oak trees and fir trees. There were $\frac{5}{3}$ as many oak trees as fir trees. There were 42 more oak trees than fir trees.
   1. How many oak trees were there?
   2. How many fir trees were there?

Part 7

Work each item. If necessary, round your answer to hundredths.

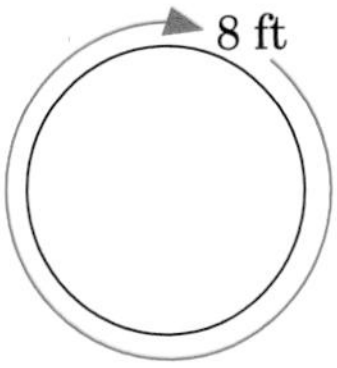

a. Find the diameter.

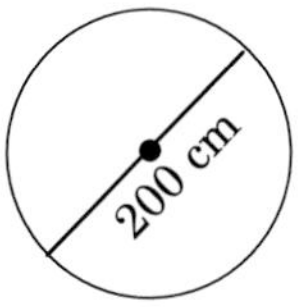

b. Find the circumference.

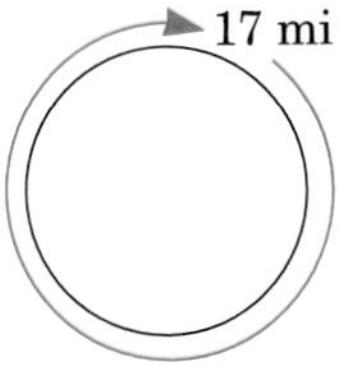

c. Find the diameter.

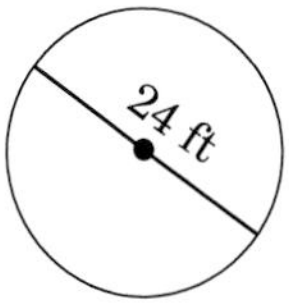

d. Find the circumference.

Independent Work

Remember to complete the ratio tables and answer the questions for part 6 of your textbook.

Part 8 **For each item, make a number family and a table. Answer the questions.**

a. In a pet store, $\frac{8}{9}$ of the pets are kittens. There are 450 pets in the store.
   1. How many are kittens?
   2. How many are not kittens?

b. Mrs. Mathews earns $\frac{10}{9}$ the amount her husband earns. Mrs. Mathews earns $2500 each month.
   1. How much does her husband earn each month?
   2. How much more does Mrs. Mathews earn each month than her husband earns?

c. $\frac{3}{7}$ of a mixture is sulphur. The mixture has 56 pounds of sulphur.
   1. How much does the total mixture weigh?
   2. How many pounds of the mixture are not sulphur?

Part 9 **Write a complete equation for each lettered angle.**

$\angle k$ is $\frac{2}{5}$ of a circle.

$\angle k$ = ■°	∠■ = ■°
∠■ = ■°	∠■ = ■°
$\angle p$ = ■°	∠■ = ■°
∠■ = ■°	∠■ = ■°

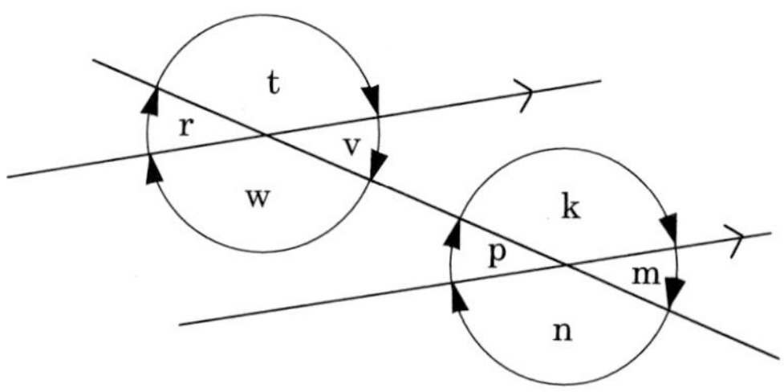

Part 10 **Copy and work each problem.**

a. $\begin{array}{r} 560\frac{1}{30} \\ -\ 68 \\ \hline \end{array}$

b. $\begin{array}{r} 11\frac{15}{22} \\ +\ 82\frac{7}{22} \\ \hline \end{array}$

c. $\begin{array}{r} 123 \\ -\ 14\frac{5}{9} \\ \hline \end{array}$

d. $\begin{array}{r} 14\frac{1}{8} \\ 29 \\ +\ 32\frac{5}{8} \\ \hline \end{array}$

Part 11 **Write the letter O or E for each number.**

a. 151

b. 252

c. 350

d. 149

e. 5683

Part 12 **Work each item.**

a. Round 50.110 to the nearest tenth.

b. Round 4.9873 to the nearest hundredth.

c. Round 100.0249 to the nearest hundredth.

d. Round 1.20551 to the nearest thousandth.

Part 13 For each item, make a number family. Answer the question.

a. Ginger's goal is to run a mile in 35 fewer seconds than the time it takes her to run a mile now. When she reaches her goal, she will run a mile in 295 seconds. How long does it take her to run a mile now?

b. At the beginning of June, Memorial Hospital had 451 patients. In June, 562 more patients entered the hospital. In June, 345 patients left the hospital. How many patients were still in the hospital at the end of June?

c. Tom purchased a clock. He gave the clerk \$50. He received \$11.11 in change. How much did the clock cost?

d. Mary bought a bicycle for \$130.95. She received \$9.05 in change. How much did she give the clerk?

e. Sandra wants to buy a TV. The set she wants costs \$123 more than she has. She has \$253. How much does the TV cost?

Part 14 Copy and complete each statement. Use the sign <, > or =.

a. $\frac{10}{10}$ ■ $\frac{6}{6}$ b. $\frac{8}{2}$ ■ $\frac{60}{20}$ c. $\frac{5}{8}$ ■ $\frac{6}{8}$

Part J

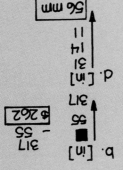

a. [out] 28 16 → 44 stamps

b. [in] ■ 55 → 317
317 − 55 = \$262

c. [out] 14 ■ → 29
29 − 14 = 15 people

d. [in] 31 14 11 → 56 mm

Part K

b. $\pi \times D = C$
$3.14 \times 200 = C$
C = 628 cm

c. $\pi \times D = C$
$3.14\left(\frac{17}{3.14}\right) = 17$
D = 5.41 mi

d. $\pi \times D = C$
$3.14 \times 24 = C$
C = 75.36 ft

Lesson 96

Part 1

- You've simplified fractions that have zeros in both the numerator and denominator. $\frac{160}{50} = \frac{16 \times \cancel{10}}{5 \times \cancel{10}} = \frac{16}{5}$
- You can simplify these fractions the fast way by just crossing out zeros. $\frac{16\cancel{0}}{5\cancel{0}} = \frac{16}{5}$
- You must cross out the **same number of zeros** in the numerator and denominator.
- If you cross out two zeros in the numerator, you must cross out two zeros in the denominator.
- **That's crossing out $\frac{100}{100}$.** $\frac{2\cancel{00}}{13\cancel{00}} = \frac{2}{13}$

$\frac{67\cancel{0}}{30\cancel{0}} = \frac{67}{30}$

Part 2

Copy each fraction. Cross out zeros and write the simplified fraction.

a. $\frac{860}{4000} = $ ■   b. $\frac{10,700}{36,000} = $ ■   c. $\frac{3010}{700} = $ ■

But I crossed out the same number of zeros on the top and the bottom.
$\frac{3\cancel{0}1\cancel{0}}{7\cancel{0}\cancel{0}} = \frac{31}{7}$

Part 3 For each item, make a number family. Answer the question.

a. There were 91 people in a train. At the first stop, more people got in the train. The train ended up with 133 people in it. How many people got in the train at the first stop?

b. There were some people in a train. 91 people got off the train. The train ended up with 133 people in it. How many people were in the train to begin with?

c. In the morning, the temperature was fairly high. Then the temperature went down 21°. The temperature ended up at 66°. What was the temperature in the morning?

d. In the morning, the temperature dropped 12°. Then the temperature dropped another 41°. How much did the temperature drop in all?

Part 4

- Some problems that tell about people's goals require **vertical** number families for **goal** or **now.**

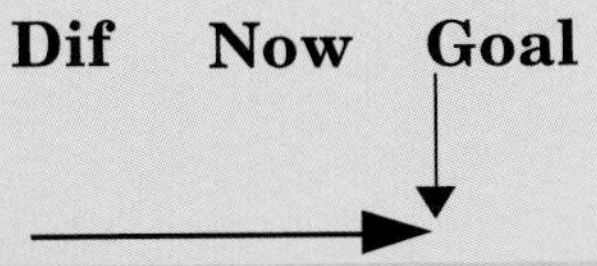

- Here's a problem that uses that kind of family:

A man wants enough money for a vacation. The airfare will cost $650. Staying at the hotel will cost $430. The man needs another $120 for spending money. The man currently has $910 in his savings account. How much more money will he need for the trip?

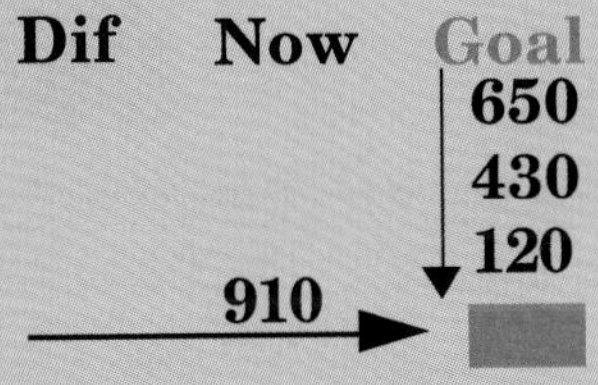

- The big number is the **goal.** It's more than the man has now. The goal is all the money the man will need.
- The amount the man has **now** is $910.
- The **difference** is the money the man needs to reach his goal.

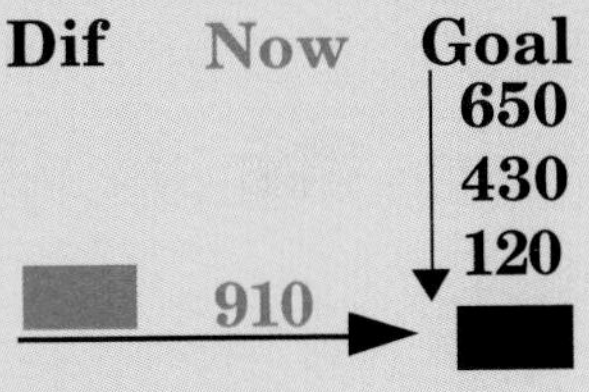

Part 5 **For each item, make a number family. Answer the question.**

a. Hilda's goal is to mow the large lot on the corner. In the morning, Hilda mowed 1850 square yards. In the afternoon, she mowed 3110 square yards. Before she reaches her goal, she has to mow 40 more square yards. How many square yards is her goal?

b. Ginger's goal is to buy soap, eggs, and chips at the store. Soap costs \$1.20; eggs cost \$.90; chips cost \$.90. Ginger has \$2.70. How much more money does she need to reach her goal?

c. Andy wants to buy a bike, a new mirror, and a tire pump. The bike costs \$210; the mirror costs \$21; the tire pump costs \$16. Andy has \$135 in his savings account. He has another \$11 in his wallet. Andy's mother will give Andy \$41 for work that he has done. How much more money will Andy need before he can buy all the items he wants?

Part 6 **Find the surface area of the box.**

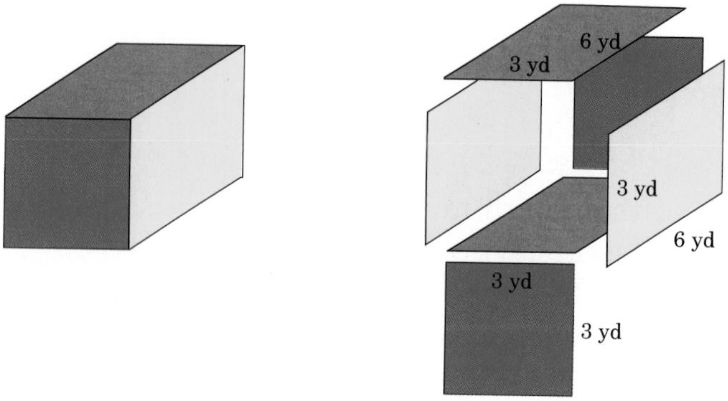

Part 7 **Write the equation to show the percent that equals each decimal value.**

a. 2.56 = [redacted] b. .75 = [redacted] c. .01 = [redacted] d. .40 = [redacted] e. 3.00 = [redacted]

Part 8

- You've worked with triangles that have one side parallel to the y axis.
- You can show that the area of that triangle is half the area of a rectangle with the same base and same height. You just complete the rectangle.

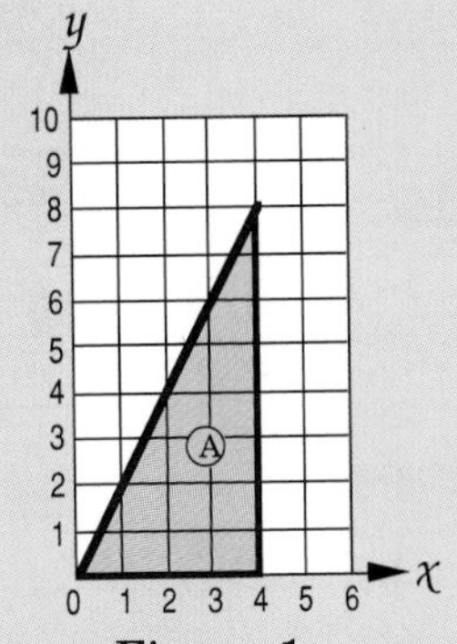

Figure 1

- When you complete the rectangle, you actually make another triangle that is exactly the same size as triangle A.
- Triangle A and triangle B are identical. The only difference is that B is upside down.

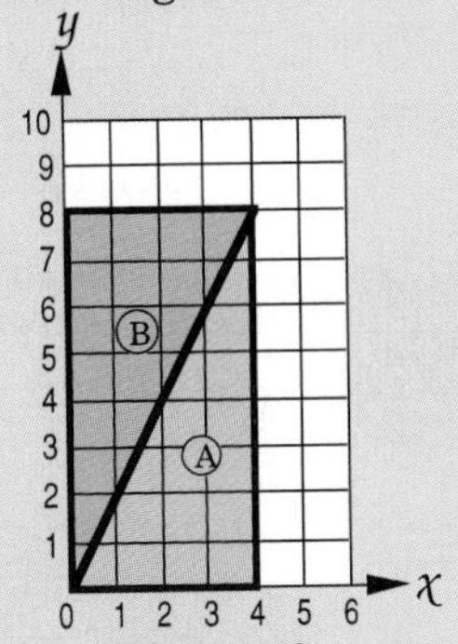

Figure 2

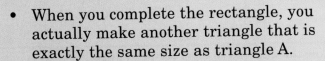

- You can use upside-down triangles to show that the area of **any triangle** is half the area of a **parallelogram** with the same base and same height.

- Here's triangle C:
  It has no side parallel to the y axis.
- We can make a parallelogram by combining triangle C with another triangle that is exactly the same size and shape. That's triangle D.

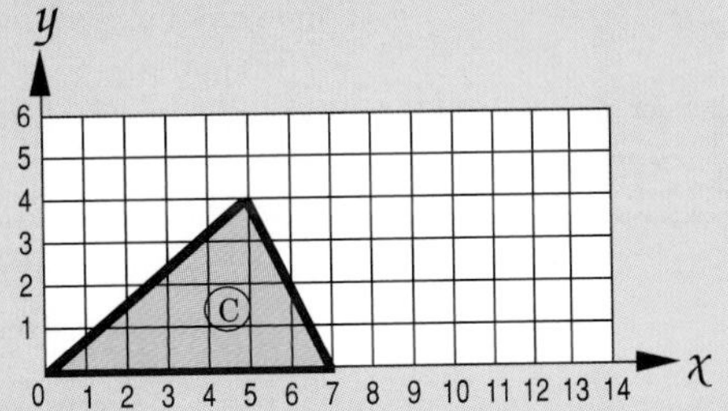

Figure 3

- In figure 4, triangle C is combined with triangle D to form a parallelogram.
- The base is 7 and the height is 4. So the whole parallelogram has an area of 28 square units.
- The area of triangle C is half that amount–14 square units.

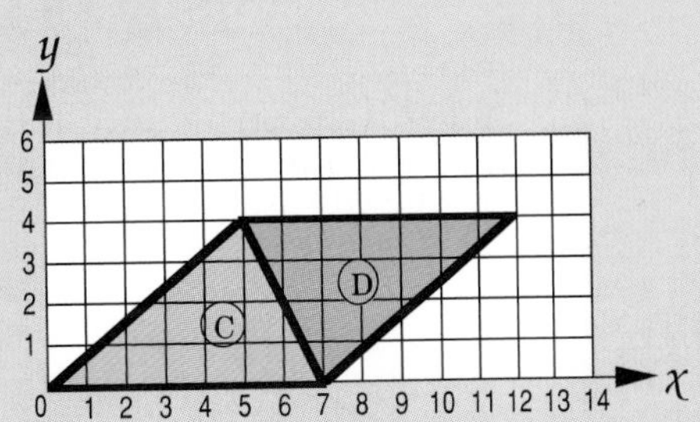

Figure 4

Independent Work

Part 9 **Copy and complete the table.**

	Decimal	$\frac{\blacksquare}{100}$	Percent
a.			302%
b.	.90		
c.		$\frac{50}{100}$	
d.	2.34		

Part 10 **Copy each fraction. Write the equation to show the crossed out zeros and the simplified fraction.**

a. $\frac{6010}{300}$

b. $\frac{1700}{500}$

c. $\frac{4030}{60}$

Part 11 **Write an equation to show the degrees in each lettered angle.**

∠v is $\frac{1}{8}$ of a circle.

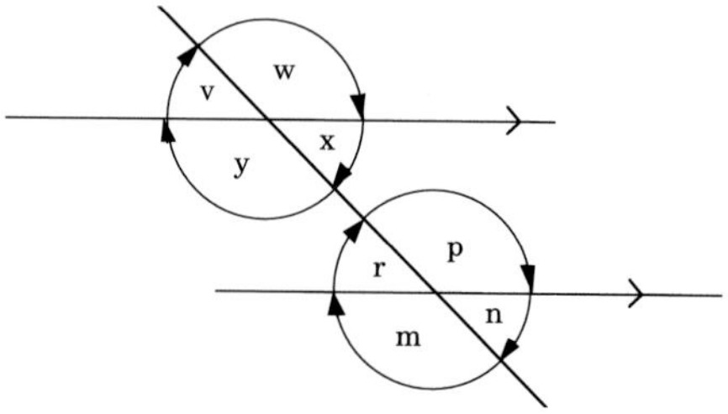

Part 12 **Make a ratio table. Answer the questions.**

a. $\frac{3}{4}$ of the paper is yellow. The rest is green. There were 860 sheets of paper.
   1. How much of the paper is yellow?
   2. How much of the paper is green?

b. The ratio of toads to frogs was 1 to 7. There were 567 frogs.
   1. How many of both animals were there?
   2. How many toads were there?

c. 2 out of every 15 students are in the band. 48 students are in the band.
   1. How many students are not in the band?
   2. How many students are there in all?

Part 13 **Start with the equation that has the symbol π. Work each item. If necessary, round your answer to hundredths.**

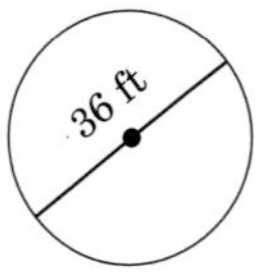

a. Find the circumference.

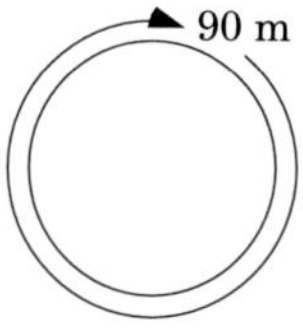

b. Find the diameter.

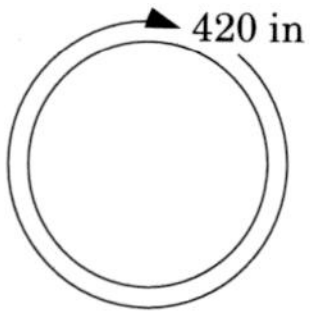

c. Find the diameter.

Lesson 97

Part 1 **Find the surface area of the box.**

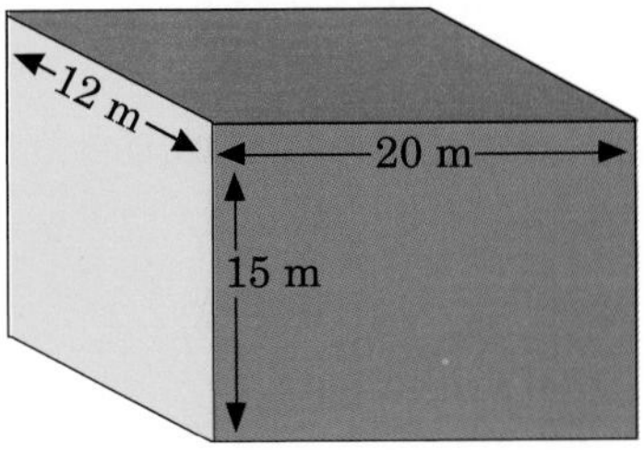

Part 2 **For each item, make a number family. Answer the question.**

a. On the first day, a group of mountain climbers went up 7100 feet. On the second day, they went up another 4200 feet. On the third day, they went up 3960 feet. The goal for the group of mountain climbers was to reach the top of the mountain. They still had to climb 4140 more feet to reach the top. How high is the top of the mountain?

b. The goal is to put 41 tons of gravel on the road. In the morning, the crew put 17 tons on the road. In the afternoon, the crew put another 13 tons on the road. To reach the goal, how much more gravel does the crew need to put on the road?

c. Tim's goal is to buy school supplies and a radio. The school supplies cost $16.50. The radio costs $23.95. Tim has coins that are worth $3.50. He also has a $20 bill. How much money does Tim still need to reach his goal?

Part 3 **Find the area and perimeter of each triangle.**

a.

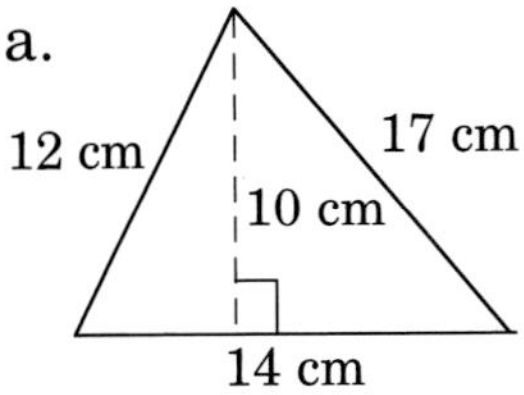

b.

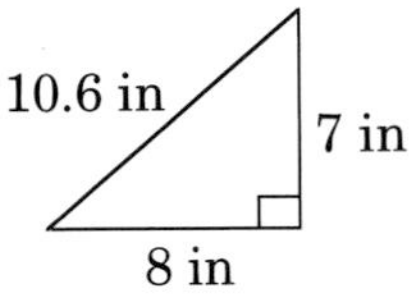

c.

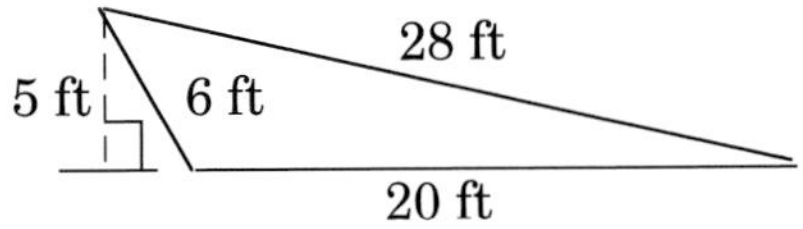

Part 4 For each item, make a number family. Answer the question.

a. The train slowed as it went up the mountain. Before crossing the bridge, the train slowed 18 miles per hour. After crossing the bridge, the train slowed more. In all, it slowed down 41 miles per hour. How much did it slow down after the bridge?

b. A man had some money. Then he earned $458 more. He ended up with $905. How much did he have at first?

c. Jenny put $873 in the bank. Later she took out $440. How much money was still in her bank account?

d. On Monday, the hot dog stand sold 89 cups of chili. On Tuesday, the stand sold even more chili. The total for both days was 315 cups of chili. How many cups were sold on Tuesday?

e. A bus started out with 64 people on it. At the first stop, some people got off the bus. The bus still had 48 people on it. How many people got off the bus?

Part 5 For each item, write an equation. Start each equation with the value that is shown.

a. Write the percent value that equals $\frac{17}{100}$.

b. Write the percent value that equals $\frac{502}{100}$.

c. Write the hundredths fraction that equals 800%.

d. Write the percent value that equals 3.14.

e. Write the decimal value that equals 5%.

f. Write the hundredths fraction that equals .09.

Part 6

- Some division problems that divide by a 2-digit number have an answer with two digits.
- Here's a problem: $21\overline{)905}$
- The first digit of the answer goes above the last digit of 90.

$$\begin{array}{r} 4 \\ 21\overline{)\underline{90}5} \end{array} \qquad \begin{array}{r} 4 \\ 2\overline{)9} \end{array}$$

- When you multiply 21 by 4, you get 84.
- You subtract 84 from 90.

$$\begin{array}{r} 4 \\ 21\overline{)\underline{90}5} \\ -\underline{84} \\ 6 \end{array}$$

- You **bring down the ones digit** of the number under the division sign.
- Now you have a division problem for the ones column. →

$$\begin{array}{r} 4 \\ 21\overline{)\underline{90}5} \\ -\underline{84}\downarrow \\ 65 \end{array}$$

- You multiply 21 by 3 and subtract from 65.
- The remainder is 2.

$$\begin{array}{r} 43 \\ 21\overline{)\underline{90}5} \\ -\underline{84} \\ \underline{6}5 \\ -\underline{63} \\ 2 \end{array} \qquad \begin{array}{r} 3 \\ 2\overline{)6} \end{array}$$

- Remember these steps:
  - ✔ Work a problem for the underlined digits.
  - ✔ The answer goes in the tens column.
  - ✔ Multiply and write the number **below the underlined digits.**
  - ✔ Subtract.
  - ✔ Bring down the last digit.
  - ✔ You work another division problem.
  - ✔ The answer goes in the ones column.
  - ✔ Subtract and show the remainder as a fraction.

$$\begin{array}{r} 43\tfrac{2}{21} \\ 21\overline{)\underline{90}5} \\ -\underline{84} \\ \underline{6}5 \\ -\underline{63} \\ 2 \end{array}$$

Independent Work

Part 7 **Start with the equation that has the symbol π. Work each item.**

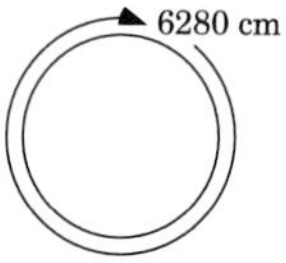

a. Find the diameter.

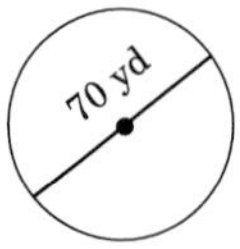

b. Find the circumference.

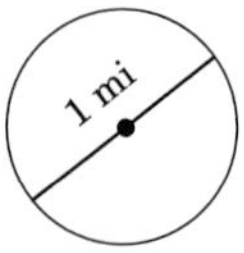

c. Find the circumference.

Part 8 **For each item, circle the big number. Figure out the missing value.**

a. 156 – ■ = 12

b. ■ + 118 = 300

c. ■ – 118 = 300

d. 481 + ■ = 500

Part 9 **Copy each fraction. Cross out zeros and write the simplified fraction.**

a. $\frac{6000}{300} =$ ■

b. $\frac{40{,}020}{400} =$ ■

c. $\frac{100}{8000} =$ ■

Part 10 **Work each item.**

a. Round 2.659 to the nearest tenth.

b. Round 1.30081 to the nearest thousandth.

c. Round 0.0559 to the nearest hundredth.

d. Round 18.411 to the nearest hundredth.

Part 11 **Make a ratio table. Answer the questions.**

a. On Tuesday, $\frac{3}{4}$ of the eggs at Herbie's Hatchery hatched. 240 eggs did not hatch.
   1. How many eggs were there in all?
   2. How many eggs hatched?

b. $\frac{2}{3}$ of a circle is yellow. The rest is red.
   1. How many degrees are in the part that is red?
   2. How many degrees are in the part that is yellow?

c. Tina is $\frac{7}{5}$ the height of her younger sister. Tina is 59 inches tall.
   1. How tall is her younger sister?
   2. How much taller is Tina than her sister?

Part 12 **Copy and complete each statement. Use the sign <, > or =.**

a. $27 - 27$ ■ $\frac{16}{16}$

b. $\frac{45}{9}$ ■ $\frac{500}{100}$

c. $16 \div 2$ ■ 7

d. $\frac{9}{3}$ ■ $\frac{7}{3}$

Part J

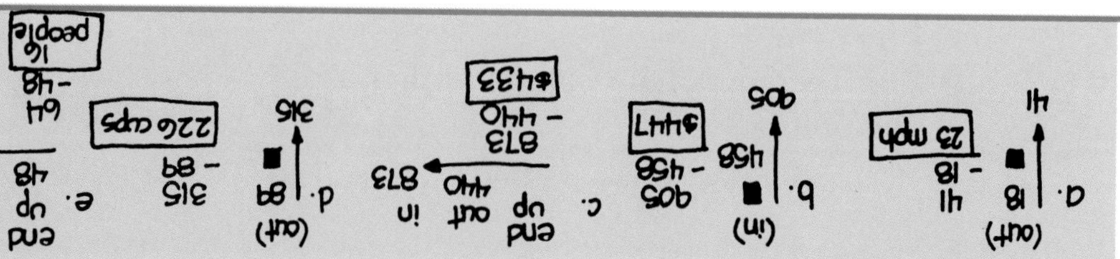

Lesson 98

Part 1

- Some word problems refer to dividing things into equal parts. You work those problems as division problems.
- Here's a problem:

> A pizza costs $12. We want to **divide** the pizza into 6 pieces that are the same size. How much will each piece cost?

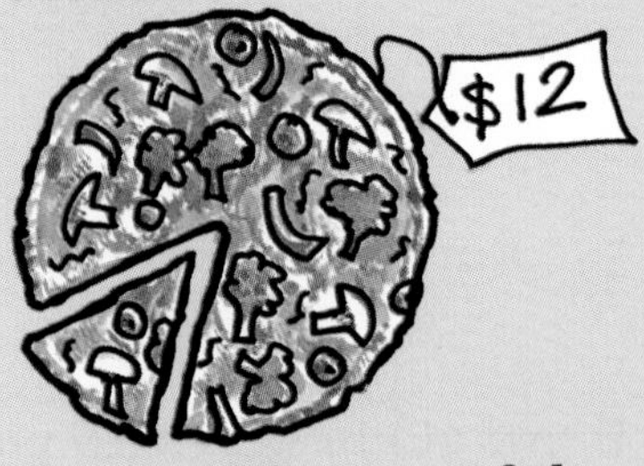

- The problem asks about the cost of each piece. The cost of the whole pizza is the cost of 6 pieces.
- So you just divide by 6 to get the cost of each piece.
- When you divide 12 by 6, you get the cost of 1 piece.

$$6\overline{)12}\quad \boxed{\$2}$$

Part 2 Work each problem. Answer the question.

a. A parcel of land contains 145 acres. A farmer wants to divide that parcel into 7 fields that are the same size. How many acres will be in each field?

b. A king has 360 pounds of gold that he wants to divide equally among his 9 children. How much gold will each child receive?

c. Tim has 5 hours to do 4 jobs. He must spend exactly the same amount of time on each job. How many hours will he spend on each job?

Part 3 Find the area and perimeter of each figure.

a.
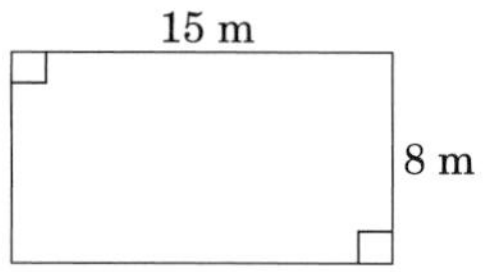

b.
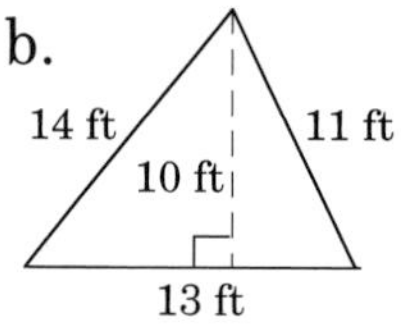

c.
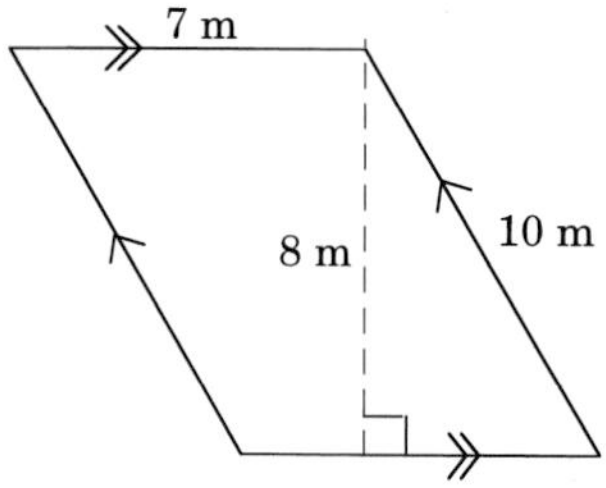

Part 4 For each item, make a number family. Answer the question.

a. Milly wants to weigh 15 pounds less than she weighs now. She weighs 132 pounds. What is her goal weight?

b. Mr. Smith's goal is to have a set of dinnerware. The plates cost \$58, the cups and saucers cost \$70 and the bowls cost \$35. So far he has saved \$98. How much more money does Mr. Smith need to reach his goal?

c. Jim needs to move 28 more tons of dirt to reach his goal. He moved 45 tons of dirt yesterday, and 18 tons of dirt this morning. When Jim reaches his goal, how much will he have moved?

d. Sandra's goal is to purchase the following items: a tent for \$85, a jacket for \$147, and snowshoes for \$88. To reach her goal, she needs \$45 more than she has now. How much does she have now?

Part 5 Copy each fraction. Cross out the same number of zeros on top and on the bottom. Write the simplified fraction.

a. $\frac{210}{3800} = \blacksquare$

b. $\frac{10{,}500}{100} = \blacksquare$

c. $\frac{280}{9000} = \blacksquare$

d. $\frac{509{,}000}{50{,}000} = \blacksquare$

Part 6

Find the surface area of the box.

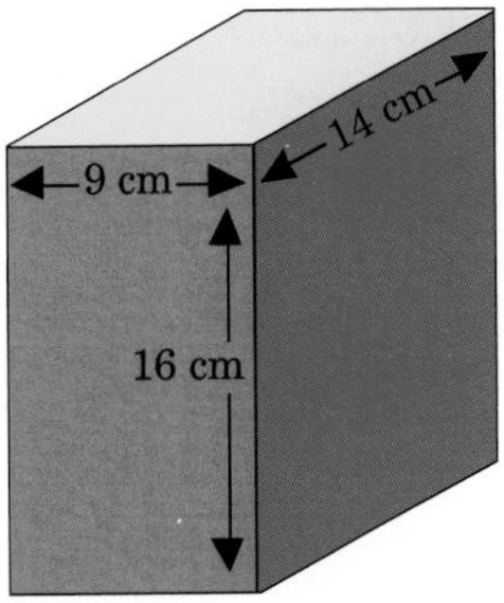

Part 7

For each item, write an equation. Start each equation with the value that is shown.

a. Write the hundredths fraction that equals 220%.

b. Write the hundredths fraction that equals 100%.

c. Write the percent value that equals .05.

d. Write the decimal value that equals $\frac{117}{100}$.

Independent Work

Part 8

For each item, make a number family and answer the question.

a. June walked 34 kilometers last week. This week, she walked some more. The total distance she walked in both weeks is 82 kilometers. How far did June walk this week?

b. There were lots of pears on the pear tree. After Peter picked 138 pears, there were 265 pears left on the tree. How many pears were on the tree to start with?

c. Mary grew 624 tomatoes last year. This year she grew 379 tomatoes. How many tomatoes did Mary grow during both years?

d. Walter grew 780 tomatoes last year. He grew 400 tomatoes this year. He sold a total of 1000 tomatoes. How many tomatoes did he keep?

Part 9

Copy and work each problem

a. $62\overline{)262}$ b. $36\overline{)95}$ c. $87\overline{)512}$

Part 10

Write an equation to show the degrees in each lettered angle.

$\angle$k is $\frac{1}{9}$ of a circle.

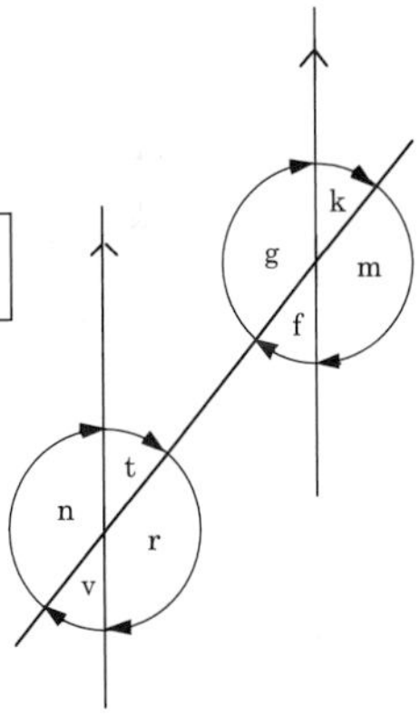

Part 11

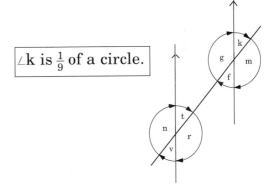

Start with the equation that has the symbol π. Work each item. If necessary, round to hundredths.

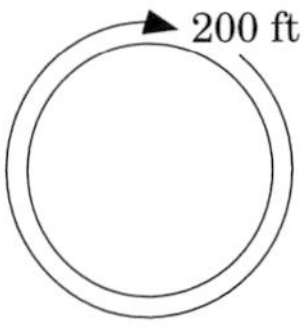

a. Find the diameter.

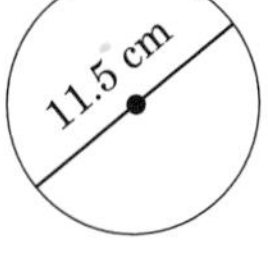

b. Find the circumference.

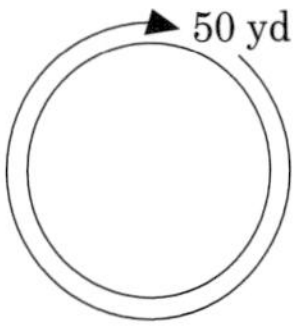

c. Find the diameter.

Part 12 Rewrite each problem as a column problem and work it.

a. 56 – 19.02 b. 11.7 + 110.65 + 0.392 c. 69 + 56.75 d. 11.7 – 8.68 e. 150 – 149.2

Part J

a. Area□ = b × h
Area = 15 × 8
120 sq m

15
15
8
+ 8
46 m

b. Area△ = $\frac{b \times h}{2}$
Area = $\frac{13 \times 10}{2} = \frac{130}{2}$
65 sq ft

14
11
+ 13
38 ft

c. Area□ = b × h
Area = 7 × 8
56 sq m

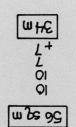

10
10
7
+ 7
34 m

Part K

a. $\frac{210}{3800} = \frac{21}{380}$ b. $\frac{10,500}{100} = \frac{105}{1}$ c. $\frac{280}{9000} = \frac{28}{900}$ d. $\frac{509,000}{50,000} = \frac{509}{50}$

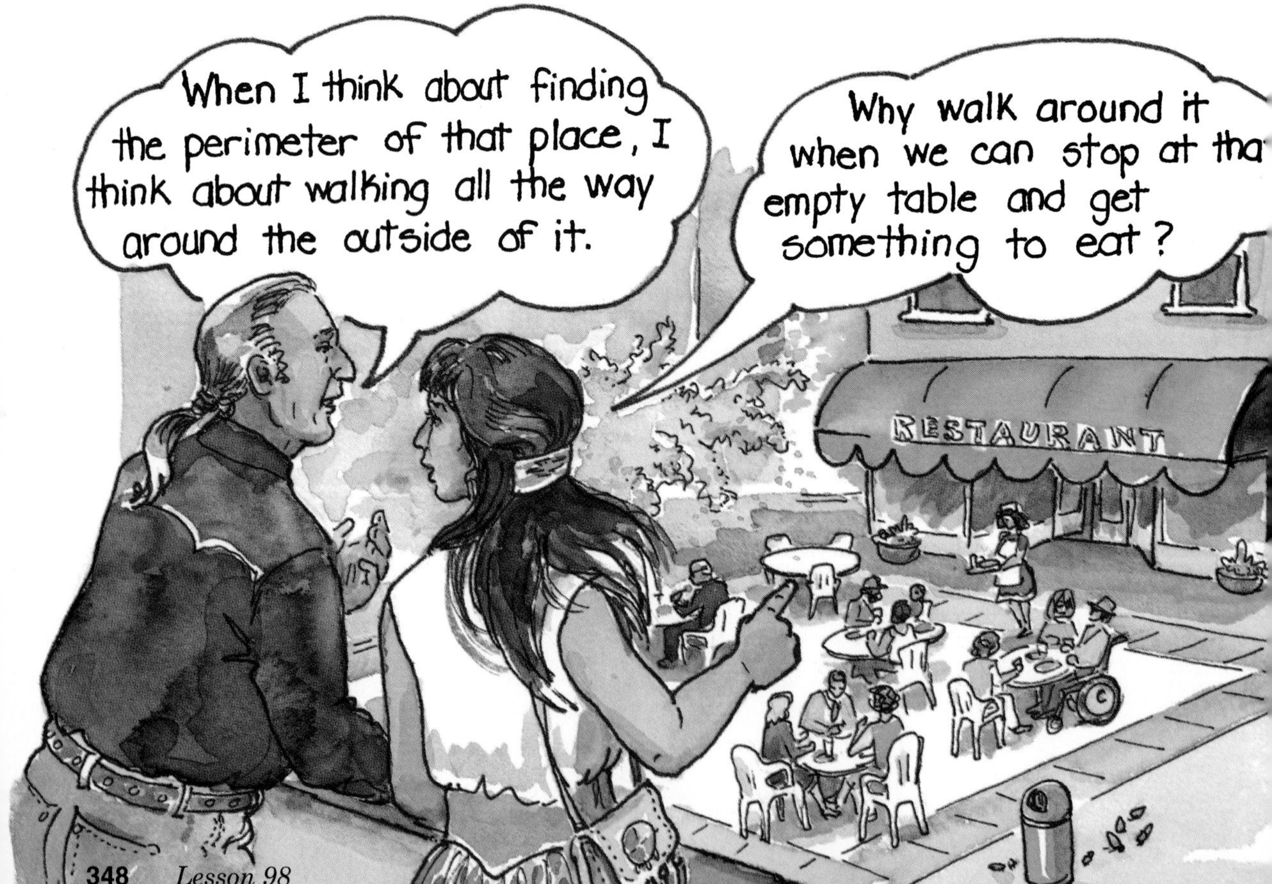

Lesson 99

Part 1 **Find the surface area of the pyramid.**

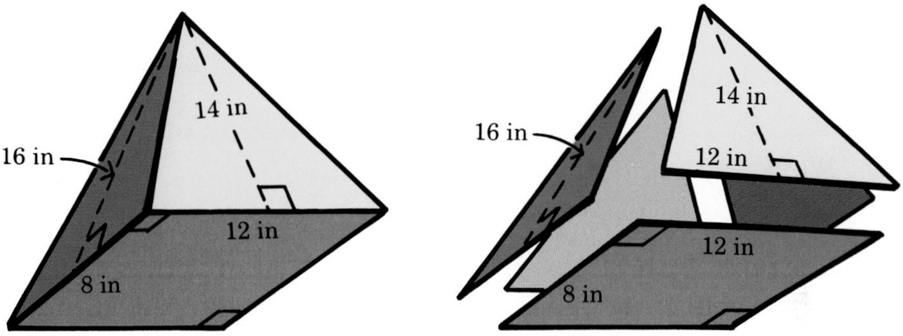

Part 2

- When you multiply by a decimal value, you end up with an answer that has a decimal point and digits after the decimal point.
- One way to work this problem is to change .4 into a fraction. Then multiply.
- You end up with the fraction $\frac{144}{10}$. That's 14.4

$36 \times .4 = ■.■$

$\frac{36}{1} \times \frac{4}{10} = \frac{144}{10} = 14.4$

Part 3 **Write each problem with the decimal shown as a fraction and work it .**

a. 23 x .3 = ■ b. 4 x .03 = ■ c. 14 x 1.5 = ■ d. 22 x .04 = ■

Part 4 Copy each problem and work it.

a. $\frac{120}{30}(\blacksquare) = \frac{100}{\blacksquare}$

b. $\frac{30}{200}(\blacksquare) = \frac{\blacksquare}{356}$

c. $\frac{500}{1000}(\blacksquare) = \frac{\blacksquare}{5}$

d. $\frac{60}{150}(\blacksquare) = \frac{120}{\blacksquare}$

Part 5 Work each problem.

a. Jan has a tank with 37 pints of water in it. Jan wants to put that water into 8 containers so that each container has the same amount. How many pints will be in each container?

b. Mr. Cleanit has 11 hours to clean 4 office buildings. Mr. Cleanit will spend the same amount of time in each building. How much time is that?

c. For 7 days, Jane gathered eggs. She gathered a total of 56 eggs. She collected the same number of eggs each day. How many eggs did she gather each day?

Part 6 Copy and work each problem.

a. $\frac{3}{5}(\blacksquare) = \frac{\blacksquare}{100}$

b. $\frac{7}{4}(\blacksquare) = \frac{\blacksquare}{100}$

c. $\frac{1}{10}(\blacksquare) = \frac{\blacksquare}{100}$

d. $\frac{20}{20}(\blacksquare) = \frac{\blacksquare}{100}$

e. $\frac{3}{2}(\blacksquare) = \frac{\blacksquare}{100}$

Independent Work

Part 7 **For each item, make a number family and answer the question.**

a. Tom's goal is to plant a total of 200 bulbs. Last week, he planted 78 bulbs. This week, he planted 47 bulbs. How many more bulbs must he plant to reach his goal?

b. Martin's goal is to weigh 165 pounds. To reach his goal, he must gain 13 pounds. How much does he weigh now?

c. The goal of Rita's pet shop is to have only 300 turtles in stock. The shop currently has 432 turtles. How many turtles must the shop sell to reach the goal?

d. For Roger's vacation, he'll need $450 for his plane trip, $220 for his hotel, and $320 for meals and other expenses. To reach his goal, he'll need $275 more than he has now. How much does he have?

Part 8 **Copy and work each problem.**

a. $32\overline{)185}$ b. $46\overline{)228}$

Part 9 **For each item, circle the big number. Figure out the missing value.**

a. $\blacksquare - 12 = 399$ b. $\blacksquare + 85 = 200$

c. $85 - \blacksquare = 13$ d. $\blacksquare - 401 = 68$

Part 10 **Write an equation for each item. Start with the value shown.**

a. Write the decimal value that equals 8%.

b. Write the fraction that equals 520%.

c. Write the percent value that equals $\frac{100}{100}$.

d. Write the decimal value that equals 63%.

Part 11 **For each item, write O for odd or E for even.**

a. 345 b. 300 c. 346 d. 261 e. 555 f. 444

Part 12 **Copy and work each problem.**

a. $\frac{2}{3} + \frac{5}{9}$

b. $1 - \frac{4}{7} = \blacksquare$

c. $\frac{7}{6} - \frac{3}{7}$

d. $\frac{6}{8} \times \frac{5}{8} = \blacksquare$

e. $\frac{21}{8} - \frac{15}{8} = \blacksquare$

Lesson 100

Part 1 Copy each problem and work it.

a. $\frac{40}{60}(\blacksquare) = \frac{75}{\blacksquare}$

b. $\frac{12{,}000}{3{,}600}(\blacksquare) = \frac{54}{\blacksquare}$

c. $\frac{50}{200}(\blacksquare) = \frac{\blacksquare}{2}$

Part 2 Find the surface area of the pyramid.

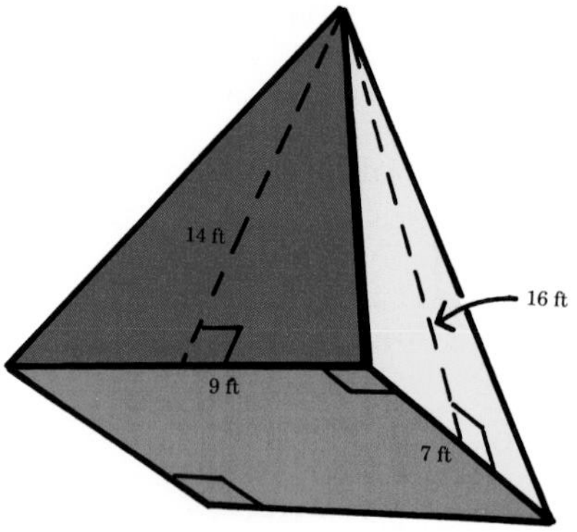

Part 3 Work each problem.

a. A parcel is 240 acres. A farmer wants to divide it into 3 fields that are the same size. How many acres will be in each field?

b. A store has 666 nails and wants to divide those nails so they are in 6 packets. Each packet must have the same number of nails. How many nails is that?

c. A stick is 36 centimeters long. A person wants to divide that stick into 5 pieces that are exactly the same length. How many centimeters long will each piece be?

Test 10

Part 1 **Make a fraction number family and ratio table. Answer the questions.**

The amount of paper Andy recycled this year is $\frac{6}{5}$ of the amount he recycled last year. This year, he recycled 155 tons.

1. How much paper did he recycle last year?
2. How much more paper did he recycle this year, compared to last year?

Part 2 **Find the area and the perimeter of the triangle.**

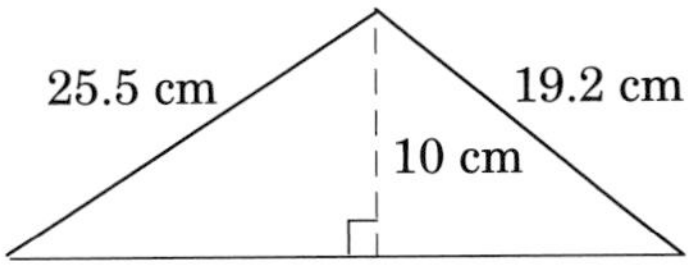

Part 3 **Copy each fraction. Cross out zeros and complete the equation with the simplified fraction.**

a. $\frac{4,030}{2,010} =$ ■ b. $\frac{70}{300} =$ ■ c. $\frac{11,000}{1,600} =$ ■

Part 4 **For each item, make a number family. Answer the question.**

a. A truck started out with 624 boxes. The truck made lots of deliveries. At the end of the day, there were 195 boxes on the truck. How many boxes were delivered?

b. Sarah had 590 buttons. She found some more buttons in a drawer. She now has a total of 626 buttons. How many buttons did she find?

c. In the morning, Mark went to the orchard and picked apples. Later, he picked 128 apples. In all he picked 300 apples. How many apples did Mark pick in the morning?

Part 5 Find the surface area of the box.

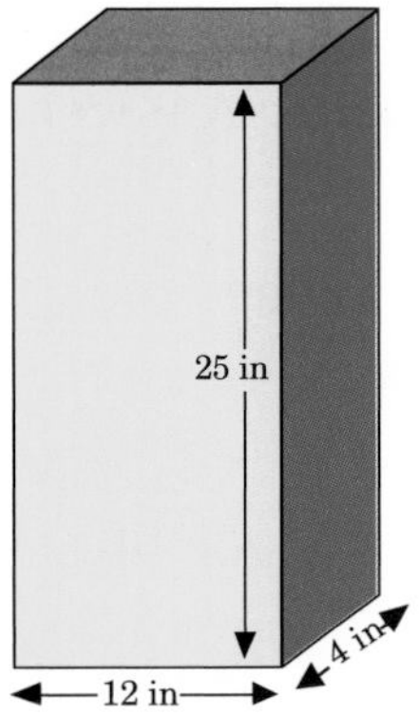

Part 6 Work each item.

a. Round 8.0749 to the nearest hundredth.

b. Round 0.6680 to the nearest tenth.

c. Round 9.6681 to the nearest thousandth.

Part 7 For each item, write O for odd or E for even.

a. 3029

b. 61

c. 96

d. 600

Part 8 Copy and complete the table.

	Decimal	$\frac{■}{100}$	Percent
a.	1.50		
b.			60%
c.		$\frac{5}{100}$	

Part 9 Write an equation to show the degrees in each lettered angle.

∠g is $\frac{3}{10}$ of a circle.

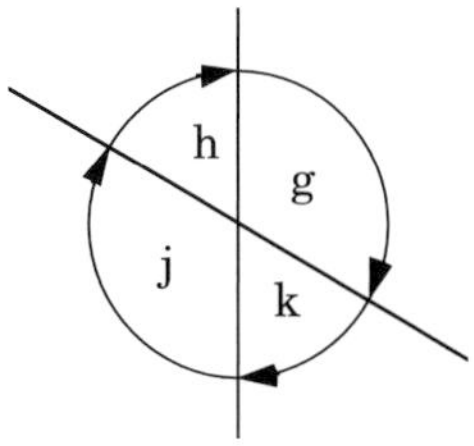

Part 10 For each item, make a number family. Answer the question.

a. A factory wants to reduce the amount of smoke it puts out each day by 50,000 cubic yards. When the factory reaches its goal, it will put out only 12,000 cubic yards of smoke per day. What is the amount of smoke the factory currently puts out each day?

b. For her camping trip, Rita needs a tent which costs $112, a camp stove which costs $29.50, and a sleeping bag which costs $65. She has $150. How much more money must she have to buy the equipment she needs?

Part 11 Start with the equation that has the symbol π. Work each item. If necessary, round your answer to hundredths.

a. Find the circumference.

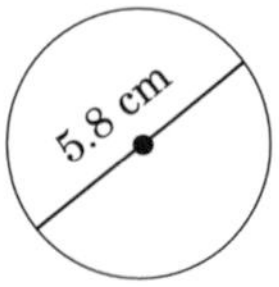

b. Find the diameter.

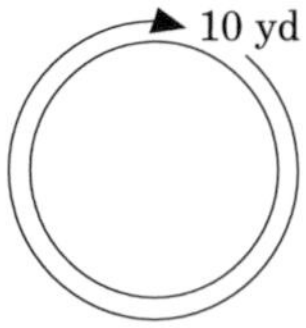

Lesson 101

Part 1

Rewrite each decimal value as a fraction and multiply.

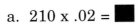

a. 210 x .02 = ■

b. 15 x 3.5 = ■

c. 55 x .4 = ■

d. 10 x .65 = ■

Part 2

Find the surface area of the pyramid.

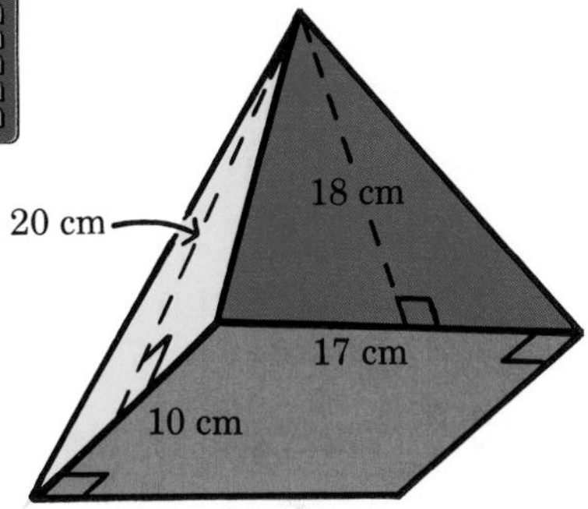

Part 3

Make a ratio equation. Answer each question. Remember the unit name.

a. It takes 120 staples to make 30 picture frames. How many frames can be made with 100 staples?

b. Tickets for 60 people cost $100. How much do tickets for 90 people cost?

c. In 10 seconds, a factory makes 200 fish sticks. How long does it take the factory to make 350 fish sticks?

d. There are 50 cups of milk used for 100 people. How many cups of milk are used for 5 people?

Part 4

Write the complete equation for each item.

a. $\frac{3}{4} = \frac{■}{100} = ■\%$

b. $\frac{7}{5} = \frac{■}{100} = ■\%$

c. $\frac{18}{10} = \frac{■}{100} = ■\%$

d. $\frac{1}{50} = \frac{■}{100} = ■\%$

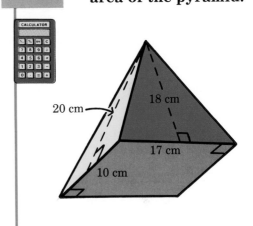

Part 5 Work each item.

a. 5 boys will carry a pile of sand that weighs 37 pounds. The pile will be divided so that each boy will carry the same amount. How much will each boy carry?

b. 3 identical machines make 72 garments. How many garments would 2 machines make in the same period of time?

c. Each cake weighs 25 ounces. What do 7 cakes weigh?

d. Each cake weighs 25 ounces. How many cakes weigh 250 ounces?

Part 6 For each item, write the complete statement with one value on each side.

a. $3 \times \frac{1}{3}$ ■ $\frac{1}{2}$

b. $4 \times \frac{7}{8}$ ■ 4

c. $\frac{1}{3} \times \frac{6}{5}$ ■ $\frac{1}{3}$

d. $\frac{10}{8}$ ■ $\frac{7}{8} + \frac{1}{8}$

Independent Work

Part 7 Figure out the area and the perimeter of each figure. Remember the unit names.

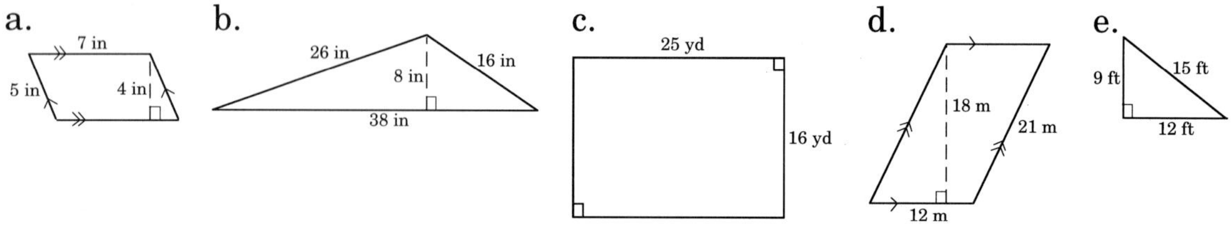

Part 8 For each item, make a fraction number family and ratio table. Answer the questions.

a. The temperature outside the icehouse is $\frac{3}{2}$ the temperature inside the house. The temperature outside is 44°.
   1. How much cooler is the temperature inside?
   2. How many degrees is the inside temperature?

b. $\frac{1}{8}$ of a circle is shaded. The rest is not shaded.
   1. How many degrees are shaded?
   2. How many degrees are not shaded?

c. $\frac{5}{9}$ of the adults were women. There were 200 men.
   1. How many women were there?
   2. How many adults were there in all?

Part 9 For each item, write E if the number is even and O if the number is odd.

a. 2805

b. 280

c. 28

d. 407

e. 13,001

Part 10 **For each problem, make the number family and answer the question.**

a. Mr. Jackson's goal is to reduce the amount he spends on car expenses each month. Currently, he pays a $250 car payment. He pays $28 for gas and $80 for insurance. He also pays $45 for parking. When Mr. Jackson reaches his goal, his expenses will be $255 each month. How much less will he spend each month if he reaches his goal?

b. The goal of the sixth grade is to raise money for the homeless. There are 3 classes. The goal for Ms. Franklin's class is to raise $150. The goal for Mr. James' class is to raise $200. The goal for Mrs. Isha's class is to raise $220. The sixth grade must raise another $284 to reach its goal. How much money has the sixth grade already raised?

Part 11 **Work each item. If necessary, round your answer to hundredths.**

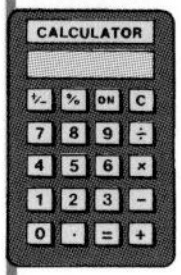

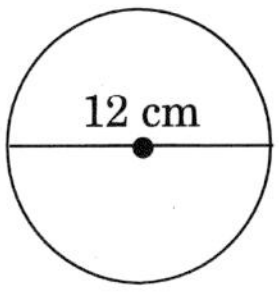

a. Find the circumference.

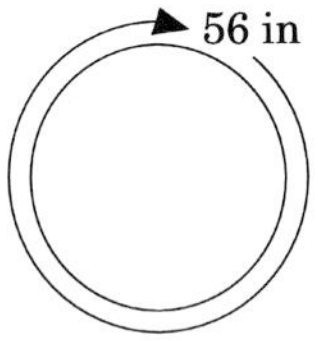

b. Find the diameter.

Part 12 **For each item, make a ratio table. Answer the questions.**

a. At the picnic, there were 12 children for every 7 adults. There were 152 people at the picnic.
   1. How many adults were there?
   2. How many children were there?

b. A recipe called for 2 cups of butter for every 7 cups of other ingredients. Someone used 45 cups of other ingredients.
   1. How many cups of butter were needed?
   2. How many cups of ingredients were used in the whole recipe?

Part 13 **Find the surface area of the box.**

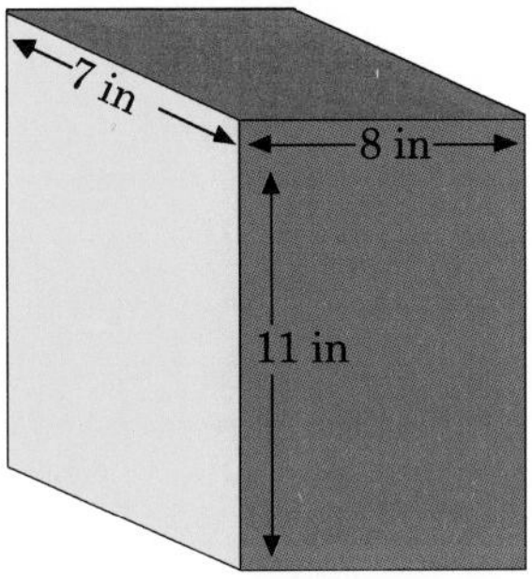

Part J

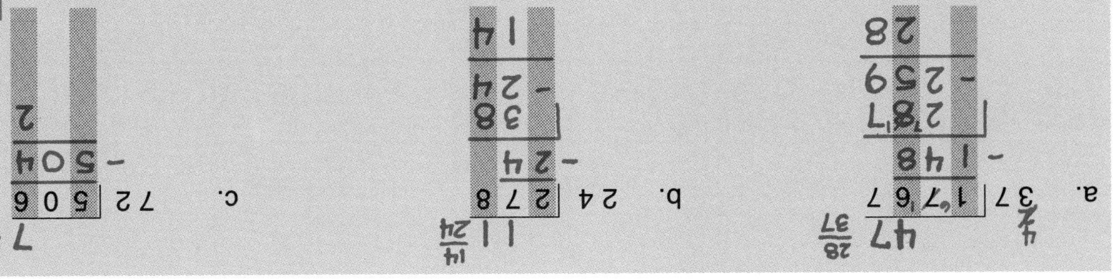

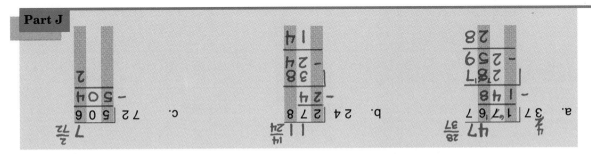

Lesson 102

Part 1 **For each item, write the complete statement with one value on each side.**

a. $6 \times \frac{9}{10} \blacksquare 6$ b. $\frac{1}{4} \blacksquare \frac{1}{3}$ c. $28 \div 7 \blacksquare \frac{36}{9}$ d. $\frac{4}{3} \times \frac{6}{5} \blacksquare \frac{3}{3}$

Part 2

- You've learned that if you multiply by more than 1, you end up with more than you start with. If you multiply by less than 1, you end up with less than you start with.
- You can use what you know about multiplying fractions to show that this rule works.
- For this problem, you end up with more than you start with, so 5 must be multiplied by **more than 1.** $5(\blacksquare) = 6$
- For this problem, you end up with the same value you start with, so 5 must be multiplied by **1.** $5(\blacksquare) = 5$
- For this problem, you end up with less than you start with, so 5 must be multiplied by **less than 1.** $5(\blacksquare) = 4$

Part 3 **Rewrite each decimal value as a fraction and multiply. Then write the answer as a decimal value.**

a. $.7 \times .3 = \blacksquare$ b. $.08 \times .9 = \blacksquare$ c. $.15 \times 4 = \blacksquare$ d. $.9 \times 2.5 = \blacksquare$

Part 4 Find the surface area of each pyramid.

a.

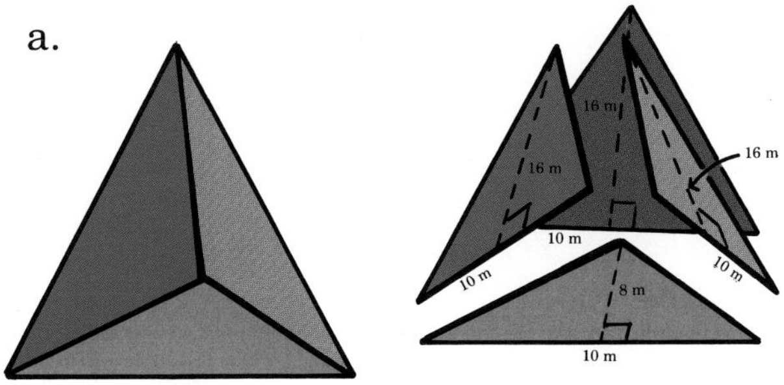

b.

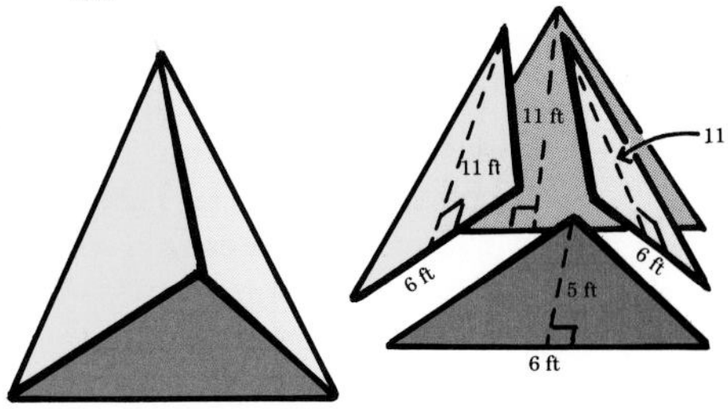

Part 5

- You can figure out which decimal values are larger by rewriting them so they have the same number of decimal places.
- Here's how to compare .4 and .30:
  You rewrite .4 so it has two places after the decimal point. Then you can see that .40 is more than .30.

.4	.40
.30	.30

- Here's how to compare .5, .50 and .500:
  You rewrite all the values so they have three decimal places.
- The values are identical. They are all .500.

.5	.500
.50	.500
.500	.500

- Here's how to compare 1 and .99:
  You rewrite 1 so it has two decimal places.
- 1 is 100-hundredths. It's larger than 99-hundredths.

1	1.00
.99	.99

Part 6 For each item, write the decimal numbers in order of size. Write the largest value on top and the smallest value on the bottom.

a.	b.	c.	d.
.4	.03	.30	1.00
.43	.30	.01	.99
.420	.3	.09	1.01

Independent Work

Part 7 **For each problem, make the number family and answer the question.**

a. The goal for our club is to collect 800 bottles for recycling. On Monday, we collected 134. On Tuesday, we collected 103. On Wednesday, we collected 119. How many more bottles do we have to collect to reach our goal?

b. The cook's goal was to use up all her potatoes over the weekend. On Saturday, she used up 32 pounds of potatoes. On Sunday, she used up 41 pounds of potatoes. She still had 111 pounds of potatoes left. If she had reached her goal, how many pounds of potatoes would the cook have used?

Part 8 **Figure out the area of each figure.**

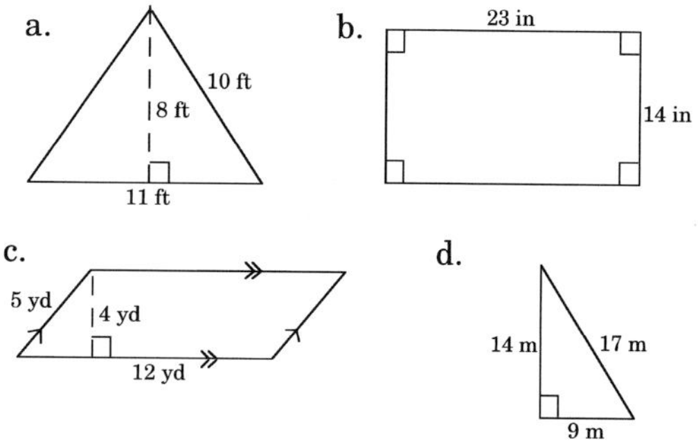

Part 9 **Make a ratio equation. Answer each question. Remember the unit name.**

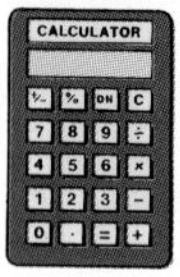

a. In a mixture, there were 420 pounds of sulphur for every 300 pounds of carbon. If the mixture had 26 pounds of carbon, how much sulphur was there?

b. In 360 days, Tinytown used 7050 tons of water. At that rate, how many tons of water would Tinytown use in 900 days?

Part 10 **Answer the question each problem asks. Remember the unit name.**

a. Rita spent $34 on school supplies. Then she spent some more money on presents. In all, she spent $94. How much did she spend on presents?

b. The submarine is 147 feet shorter than the battleship. The submarine is 95 feet long. How long is the battleship?

c. Peter had $103 in his savings account. He received $50 for his birthday which he put into his account. He took out $23 for tennis shoes and $55 for buying presents. How much did he have left in his account?

Part 11 **Copy and complete the table.**

	Percent	Decimal	$\frac{■}{100}$
a.	56%		
b.		.03	
c.			$\frac{9}{100}$
d.			$\frac{112}{100}$

Part 12 **Work each item.**

a. If each block weighs 13 ounces, how many ounces do 14 blocks weigh?

b. A pie is divided into 7 equal pieces. If the whole pie weighs 29 ounces, how much does each piece weigh?

c. It takes 14 minutes to clean 3 windows. How many minutes does it take to clean 11 windows?

Part J

a. $\frac{54}{10} < 6$ b. $\frac{1}{4} < \frac{1}{3}$ c. $4 = \frac{36}{9}$ d. $\frac{24}{15} > \frac{3}{3}$

Lesson 103

Part 1

Copy each problem. Underline the part you work first. Then work each problem.

a. $75\overline{)183}$ b. $89\overline{)6703}$ c. $51\overline{)239}$

Part 2

Write the complete equation for each item.

a. $\frac{8}{2} = \frac{\blacksquare}{100} = \blacksquare\%$

b. $\frac{7}{10} = \frac{\blacksquare}{100} = \blacksquare\%$

c. $\frac{9}{20} = \frac{\blacksquare}{100} = \blacksquare\%$

d. $\frac{5}{5} = \frac{\blacksquare}{100} = \blacksquare\%$

Part 3

- You've learned how to work multiplication problems that have decimal values. You've written values as fractions, then multiplied, then written the answer as a decimal value.

  $4 \times .8 = \blacksquare$

  $\frac{4}{1} \times \frac{8}{10} = \frac{32}{10} = 3.2$

- There's a faster way to work the problem. You can count the number of decimal places in the values you multiply together. That's the number of decimal places that are in the answer.
- Here's 4 times .8: $4 \times .8 = 3.2$
- There's one decimal place in the values that are multiplied, so there's one decimal place in the answer.
- Here's .4 times .8: $.4 \times .8 = .32$
- There are two decimal places in the values that are multiplied together. One place in .4 and one place in .8. So, there are two decimal places in the answer.

Part 3 continues on next page

- Here's .4 times .08: $.4 \times .08 = .032$
- There are three decimal places in the values that are multiplied together, so there are three decimal places in the answer.
- You do the same thing when problems are written in columns.
- First you multiply and you write digits in the answer.

$$\begin{array}{r} .4 \\ \underline{\times\ .08} \\ .032 \end{array}$$

- Then you count all the decimal places in the values that are multiplied. You show the same number of decimal places in the answer.

Part 4 Copy and work each item.

a. $\begin{array}{r} 3.2 \\ \underline{\times\ \ .5} \end{array}$ b. $\begin{array}{r} 1.89 \\ \underline{\times\ \ \ .3} \end{array}$ c. $\begin{array}{r} 12 \\ \underline{\times\ .8} \end{array}$ d. $\begin{array}{r} 11.2 \\ \underline{\times\ .38} \end{array}$

Part 5 For each item, write the complete statement with one value on each side.

a. $\frac{4}{3}$ ■ .65 b. 2.5 ■ 2.50 c. .7 ■ $\frac{9}{10}$

d. $\frac{12}{2}$ ■ 3.03 e. $\frac{1}{6}$ ■ $\frac{1}{5}$ f. 3 ■ $3 \times \frac{1}{2}$

Part 6 Find the surface area of the pyramid.

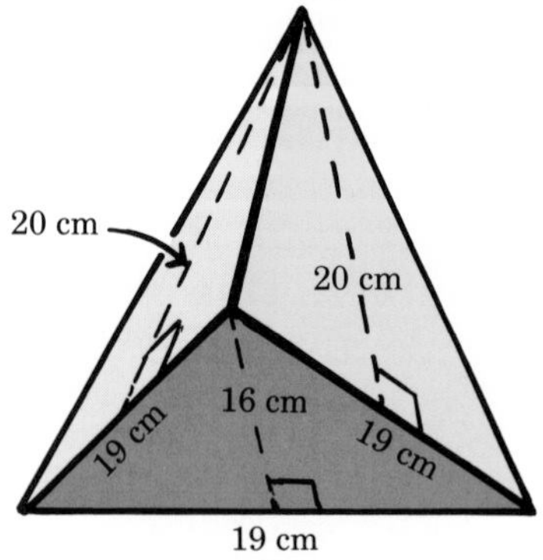

Part 7

For each item, write the decimal numbers in order of size. Write the largest value on top and the smallest value on the bottom.

a.	b.	c.	d.
.42	2.97	.57	.73
.4	2.95	5.50	.073
.41	3.00	.62	1.07

Part 8

Answer each question.

a. What do you get when you multiply the first odd number that comes after 5 by the even number that is 1 more than 5?

b. Start with the larger odd number between 24 and 28. Divide it by the odd number between 1 and 5. What's the answer?

c. Start with the second odd number after 27. Multiply by the first even number that follows 10. What's the answer?

d. Start with the even number that comes just before 311. Divide by the odd number that comes just before 7. What's the answer?

Independent Work

Part 9

For each item, make a ratio equation. Answer the question.

a. The ratio of crickets to frogs is 300 to 20. There were 10 frogs. How many crickets were there?

b. It took 270 tons of water to irrigate 140 acres. How many tons are needed for 11 acres?

Part 10

For each item, write O for odd or E for even.

a. 560

b. 3000

c. 51

d. 8409

e. 12

Part 11

Work each item. If necessary, round to hundredths.

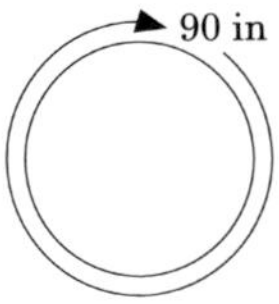

a. Find the diameter.

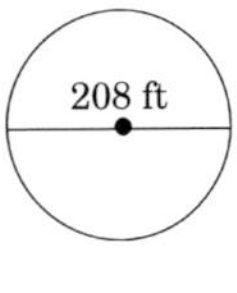

b. Find the circumference.

Part 12 **For each item, make a ratio table. Answer the questions.**

a. $\frac{2}{17}$ of the cars had dents. There were 102 cars with dents.
   1. How many cars were there in all?
   2. How many cars did not have dents?

b. Machine A works at $\frac{5}{3}$ the rate of machine B. Machine B produces 67 fewer garments than machine A.
   1. How many garments does machine A produce?
   2. How many garments does machine B produce?

Part 13 **Write the complete statement with one value on each side.**

a. 2.06 ■ $3 \times \frac{1}{3}$

b. $\frac{11}{15}$ ■ $.7 + .3$

c. $56 - 56$ ■ 7×0

Part 14 **Write the equations for the angles.**

∠r equals $\frac{3}{8}$ of a circle.

∠r = ■°　　∠w = ■°

∠p = ■°　　∠u = ■°

∠q = ■°　　∠y = ■°

∠t = ■°　　∠v = ■°

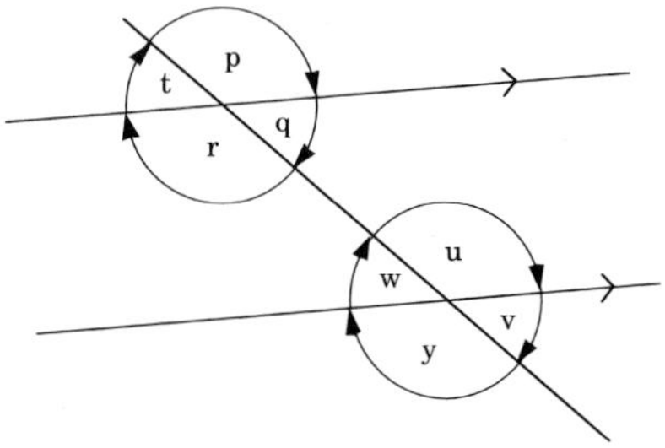

Part J

a. $\frac{8}{2}\left(\frac{50}{50}\right) = \frac{400}{100} = 400\%$

b. $\frac{7}{10}\left(\frac{10}{10}\right) = \frac{70}{100} = 70\%$

c. $\frac{9}{20}\left(\frac{5}{5}\right) = \frac{45}{100} = 45\%$

d. $\frac{5}{5}\left(\frac{20}{20}\right) = \frac{100}{100} = 100\%$

Part K

a. $\frac{4}{3} > .65$

b. $2.5 = 2.50$

c. $.7 < \frac{9}{10}$

d. $\frac{12}{2} > 3.03$

e. $\frac{1}{6} < \frac{1}{5}$

f. $3 > 3 \times \frac{1}{2}$

Lesson 104

Part 1

- You've figured out the surface area of boxes and pyramids. You can also find the **volume** of these figures.

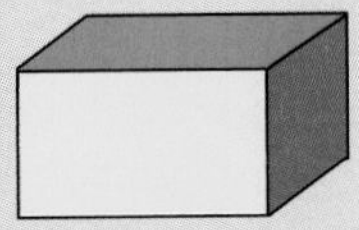

- The volume of a box is the amount of material the box can hold. The material is measured in **cubic units.**
- All cubic units are cubes. Cubes are the shape of dice.
- A cubic centimeter is 1 centimeter wide, 1 centimeter long, and 1 centimeter high.

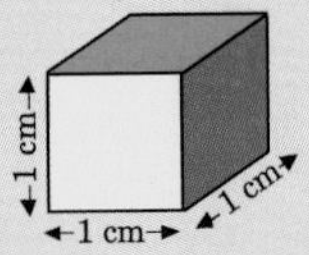

- A cubic inch is 1 inch wide, 1 inch long, and 1 inch high.

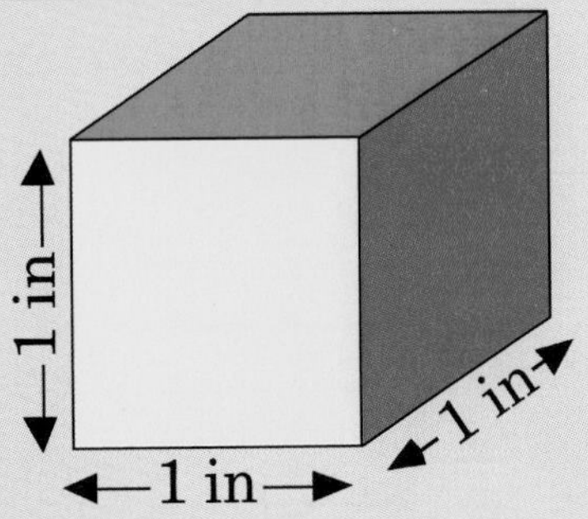

- To find the volume of a box, you use this equation:

Volume = Area of base x height

- You first find the area of the base. Then you multiply by the height.
- Here is a box:
- The base is red. The base is 7 inches long and 3 inches wide. So the **area** of the base is 21 square inches.

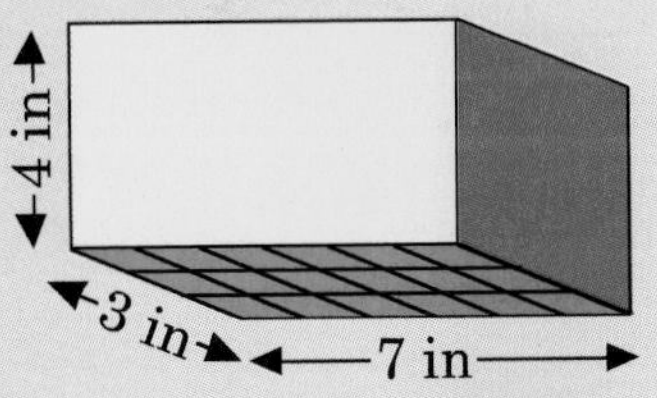

- The height is 4 inches. When you multiply 21 by the height, you get 84. That's the number of **cubic inches** the box holds.

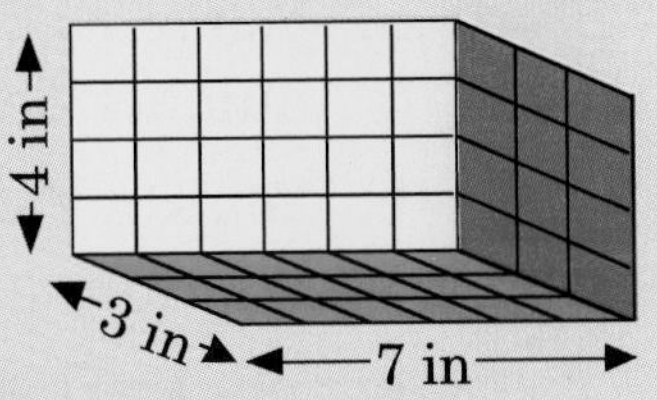

- Remember, figure out the **area of the base,** then **multiply by the height.** The unit name tells about cubes.

Part 2 Find the volume of each box.

Sample problem

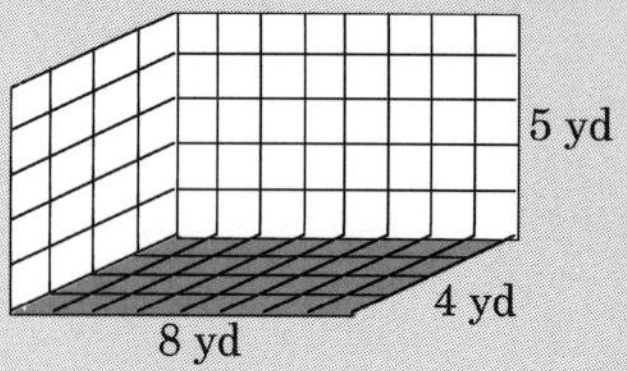

a.

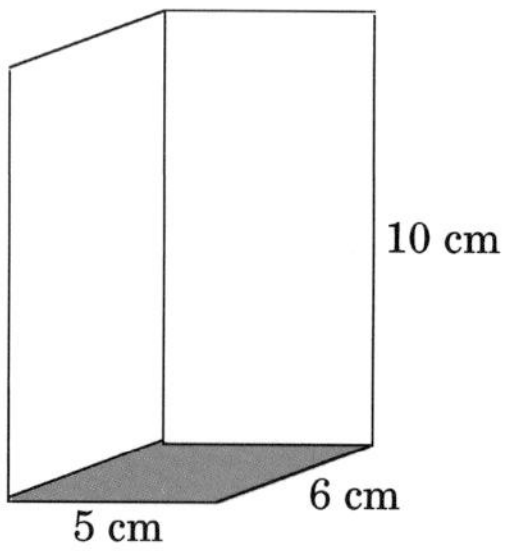

b.

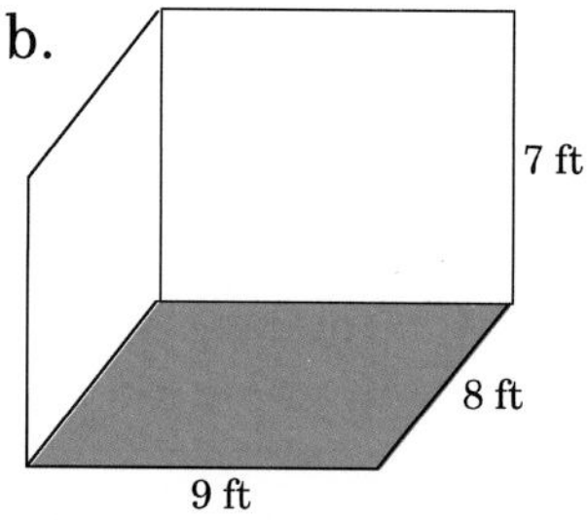

c.

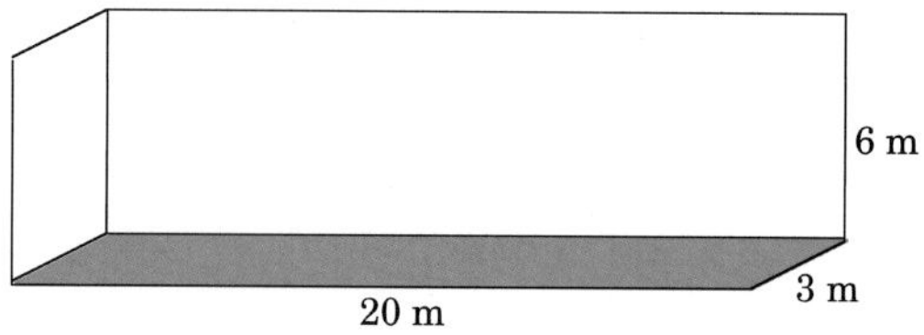

Part 3 Copy and work each problem.

a. $3\overline{)1420}$ b. $51\overline{)2448}$ c. $4\overline{)876}$ d. $27\overline{)156}$

Part 4 For each item, make two equations. Answer the question.

Sample problem

You start with 4 and multiply by 3. Then you add 5. What number do you end up with?

4 x 3 = ■
■ + 5 = ■ ?

a. You start with 26 and add 19. Then you divide by 5. What number do you end up with?

b. You start with 76 and subtract 20. Then you multiply by 4. What number do you end up with?

c. You start with 344 and divide by 4. Then you multiply by 3. What number do you end up with?

Part 5 Write the decimals in order of size. Write the largest value on top.

a. .99	b. .25	c. 6.1	d. .300	e. 1.89
1.08	.2	6.01	.3	.98
1.15	.27	6.10	.35	1.08

Part 6 Figure out the mystery number for each item.

a. The mystery number is an odd number between 22 and 30. This number is divisible by 3. What's the mystery number?

b. The mystery number is an even number between 22 and 30. This number is divisible by 3, by 4, and by 2. What's the mystery number?

c. The mystery number is divisible by 5. The number is more than 30 and less than 50. When you divide the mystery number by 5, you get an even number. What's the mystery number?

Part 7 Copy and work each problem.

a. $\begin{array}{r} .04 \\ \underline{\times\ .3} \end{array}$ b. $\begin{array}{r} 5.6 \\ \underline{\times\ .5} \end{array}$ c. $\begin{array}{r} .10 \\ \underline{\times\ .03} \end{array}$ d. $\begin{array}{r} 5.4 \\ \underline{\times\ 3} \end{array}$

Independent Work

Part 8 Work each item.

a. A large parcel of land produced 980 tons of wheat. If the parcel is divided into 7 equal-sized fields, how many tons of wheat did each field produce?

b. A machine produces 235 staples each minute. How many staples does the machine produce in 8 minutes?

c. How many degrees are in $\frac{5}{3}$ of a circle?

d. 2500 bees produced 300 pounds of wax. How many pounds of wax did 12 bees produce?

Part 9 Work each item.

a. Round 347 to the nearest ten.

b. Round 3.474 to the nearest hundredth.

c. Round .0345 to the nearest thousandth.

d. Round .452 to the nearest tenth.

Part 10 **Find the surface area of each figure.**

a.

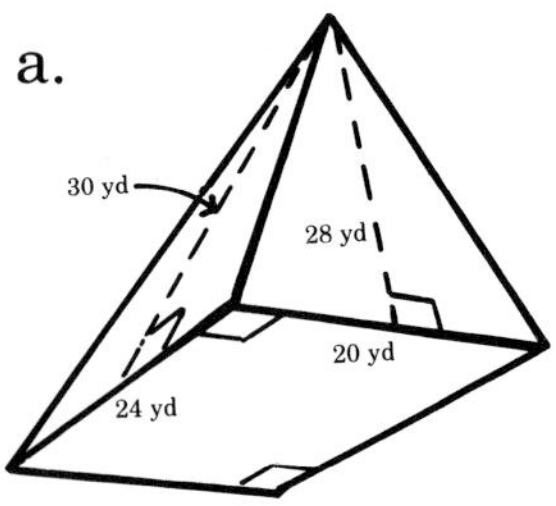

b.

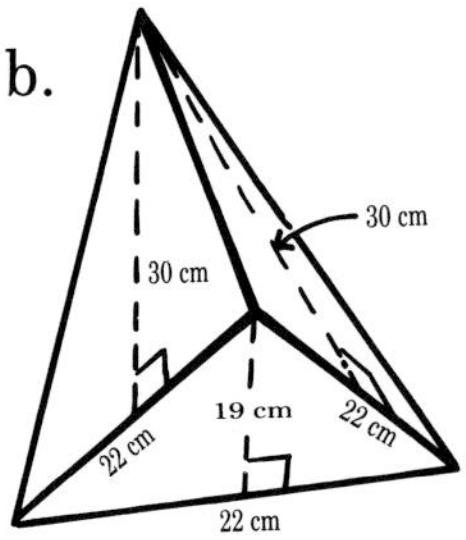

Part 11 **Write the complete equation for each item.**

a. $\frac{7}{4} = \frac{\blacksquare}{100} = \blacksquare\%$

b. $\frac{3}{5} = \frac{\blacksquare}{100} = \blacksquare\%$

c. $\frac{19}{20} = \frac{\blacksquare}{100} = \blacksquare\%$

Part 12 **Make a number family for each item. Answer the question.**

a. A train started out with 45 passengers. At the next stop, 38 people got in and 11 people got out. At the next stop, 44 people got in and 20 got out. At the next stop, 62 people got in and 84 got out. How many people were in the train after this stop?

b. Ted had a lot of trading cards. He sold 14 cards to Ernie. He sold 23 cards to Linda. He gave 7 cards to his younger brother. He still had 87 cards. How many did he start out with?

c. Jumbo, the elephant, went on a diet. In April, Jumbo lost 99 pounds. In May, Jumbo lost some more weight. During the two-month period, Jumbo lost 164 pounds. How much did Jumbo lose in May?

Lesson 105

Part 1

- Some ratio problems require a table. Those are problems that have **three names.** Problems that have only two names do not require a table.

- Here's a problem that requires a table:

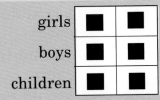

> The ratio of U. S. girls to children is 1 to 3. If there are 60 children, how many boys are there?

girls	■	■
boys	■	■
children	■	■

- The names are **girls, boys** and **children.** The problem requires a table.

- Here's a problem that does not require a table:

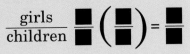

> The ratio of girls to children is 2 to 5. If there are 20 girls, how many children are there?

$$\frac{\text{girls}}{\text{children}} \quad \frac{\blacksquare}{\blacksquare}\left(\frac{\blacksquare}{\blacksquare}\right)=\frac{\blacksquare}{\blacksquare}$$

- The names are **girls** and **children.**

- Remember, if there are **three names,** you need a table. If there are only two names, you don't need a table. Also remember that one of the names may be in the question.

Part 2

Read each problem. Figure out whether or not you need to make a table. Work each problem.

a. There are 3 sunny days for every 4 days that are not sunny. If there are 60 total days, how many are sunny days?

b. The machine makes 16 garments every 3 hours. How many hours will it take for the machine to make 100 garments?

c. In a pond, 3 of every 4 fish are bass. If there are 90 fish that are not bass, how many fish are in the pond?

Part 3

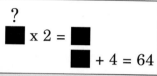

- This problem shows a mystery number as a question mark above the **first box.**

?
■ x 2 = ■
■ + 4 = 64

- To work problems of this type, you start at the **end** of the second equation and work **backward.** You **undo** each step that was done.
- Here are the rules for undoing:
  - ✔ If you **added,** you undo it by **subtracting** the same number.
  - ✔ If you **subtracted,** you undo it by **adding** the same number.
  - ✔ If you **multiplied,** you undo it by **dividing by** the same number.
- We work the problem a step at a time.
- First we undo adding 4:

?
■ x 2 = 60
60 + 4 = 64

$$\begin{array}{r} 64 \\ -\ 4 \\ \hline 60 \end{array}$$

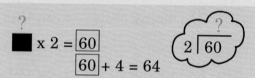

- Then we undo multiplying by 2:

?
■ x 2 = 60
60 + 4 = 64

$$\begin{array}{r} ? \\ 2\overline{)60} \end{array}$$

Part 4

Figure out the mystery number in each item.

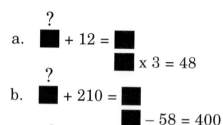

a. ?
■ + 12 = ■
■ x 3 = 48

b. ?
■ + 210 = ■
■ – 58 = 400

c. ?
■ x 5 = ■
■ + 16 = 76

Part 5

Copy and work each problem.

a. $28\overline{)245}$

b. $7\overline{)6203}$

c. $62\overline{)957}$

d. $9\overline{)9036}$

Part 6

Copy and work problems a through d. Then answer the questions in items e and f.

a. $\begin{array}{r} 10.2 \\ \times\ \ .5 \\ \hline \end{array}$

b. $\begin{array}{r} .45 \\ \times\ .02 \\ \hline \end{array}$

c. $\begin{array}{r} .007 \\ \times\ \ \ 7 \\ \hline \end{array}$

d. $\begin{array}{r} 3.89 \\ \times\ \ .6 \\ \hline \end{array}$

e. Which answer is the largest value?

f. Which answer is the smallest value?

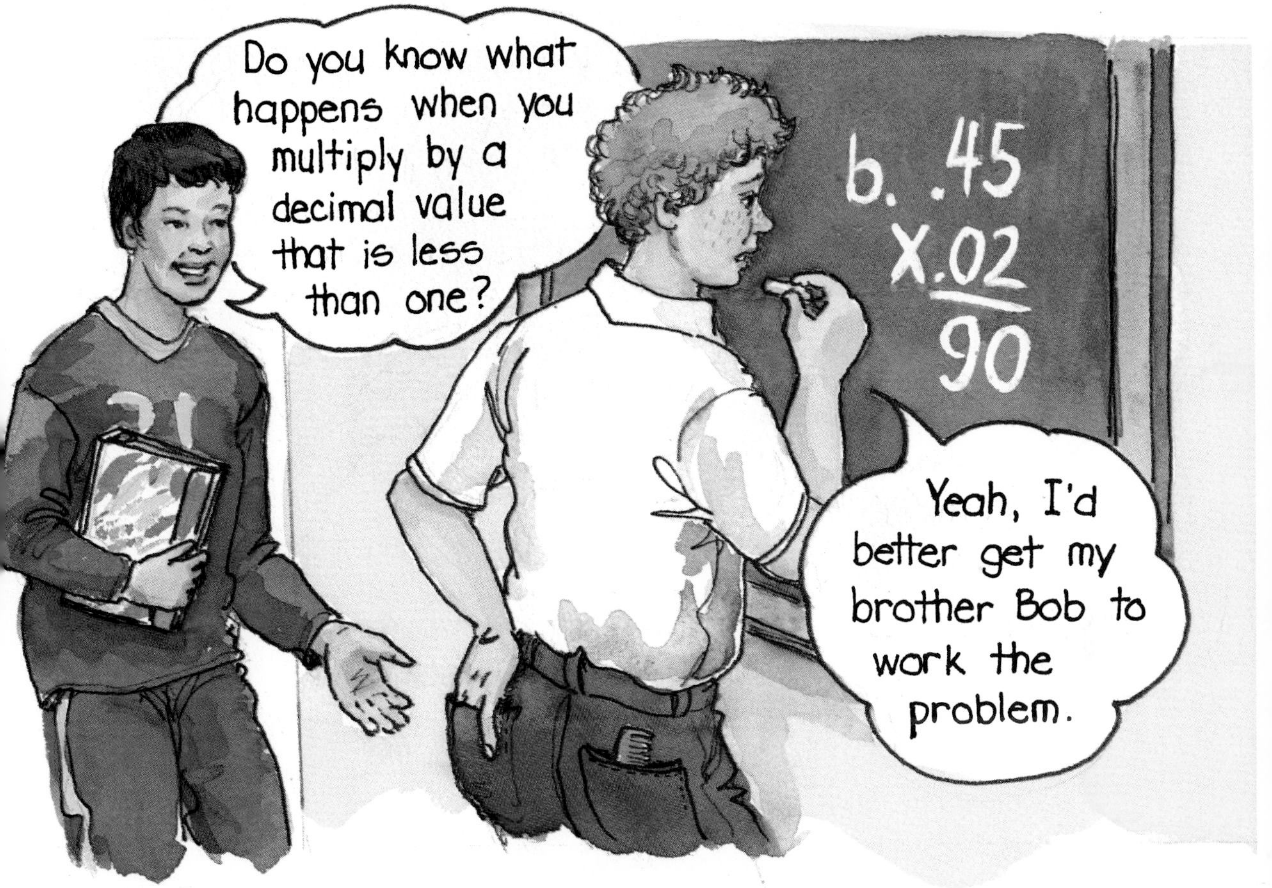

Part 7

Find the volume of each box.

a.

b.

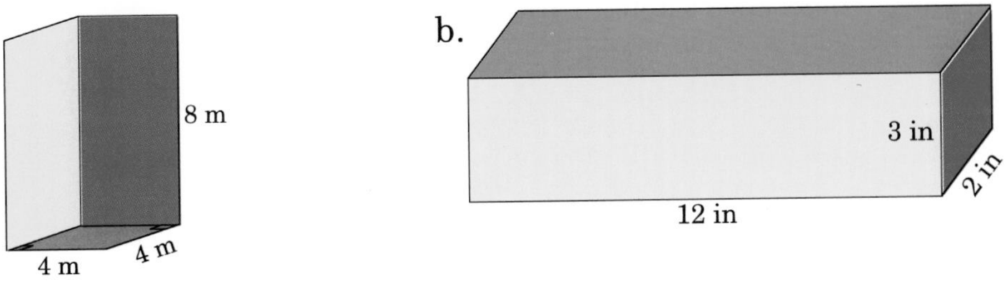

Part 8

- You've worked equivalent-fraction problems that show a series of fractions.

$$\boxed{\frac{2}{5}} = \frac{\blacksquare}{15} = \frac{16}{\blacksquare} = \frac{\blacksquare}{20}$$

a. b. c.

- You can work some measurement problems the same way. Those are problems that have related units for measuring the same thing–like **miles** and **feet,** or **pints** and **gallons.**
- Here are two problems:

  a. How many **inches** are in 3 **yards?**

  b. How many **yards** are 180 **inches?**

- To work the problems, you start with the fact about the two units:

1 yard is 36 inches.

- You put the larger unit on top. That's **yards.**

$$\frac{\text{yards}}{\text{inches}}\ \boxed{\frac{1}{36}} = \frac{3}{\blacksquare} = \frac{\blacksquare}{180}$$

a. b.

- The first problem gives the number **3** for **yards.** The other problem gives the number **180** for **inches.**
- Here's the complete equation:

$$\frac{\text{yards}}{\text{inches}}\ \boxed{\frac{1}{36}} = \frac{3}{108} = \frac{5}{180}$$

a. b.

- Remember:
  - ✔ Start with the fact.
  - ✔ Put the name for the larger unit on top.
  - ✔ Show the numbers for the fact.
  - ✔ Put in the numbers the problem gives.
  - ✔ Complete the fractions.

Independent Work

Remember to complete the problems for part 2 of your textbook.

Part 9

Copy and complete the table.

	Percent	Decimal	$\frac{\blacksquare}{100}$
a.	8%		
b.			$\frac{200}{100}$
c.	103%		
d.		4.15	

Part 10 **For each item, make a number family and answer the questions.**

a. A rancher's goal was to have 900 steers on his range. He started with 178 steers. He bought 320 steers at the market. He traded some farm equipment for 173 more steers. How many more steers does he need to reach his goal?

b. Terry's goal is to cut 19 seconds off the time it takes him to run a half a mile. Currently, it takes him 160 seconds to run the half mile. What will his time be after he reaches his goal?

c. Mike had a lot of stamps in his album. After 228 stamps were destroyed in a fire, he had only 33 stamps left. How many stamps did he have to start with?

d. 119 students joined the school choir in the fall. In the winter, some more students joined the choir, making 140 students in all. How many students joined the choir in the winter?

Part 11 **For each item, write the decimal numbers in order of size. Write the largest value on top and the smallest value on the bottom.**

a. .038	b. 9.00
3.08	8.68
8.03	8.72
c. .41	d. .37
.041	.3690
.40	.370

Part 12 **Make a ratio equation. Answer each question.**

a. At the bakery, loaves of rye bread and white bread are baked in the ratio of 7 to 4. If 28 loaves of white bread are baked, how many loaves of rye are baked?

b. There are 500 houses built every 40 days. How many houses are built in 29 days?

Part 13 **Figure out the number for each puzzle.**

a. Multiply the first odd number after 31 by the second number after zero.

b. Subtract the second even number after 24 from the second even number after 99.

c. Add the first and second odd numbers after 30 to the first odd number after 56.

Part J

a. 28)245 = $8\frac{21}{28}$; −224; 21

b. 7)6203 = $886\frac{1}{7}$

c. 62)957 = $15\frac{27}{62}$; −62; 337; −310; 27

d. 9)9036 = 1004

Lesson 106

Part 1

Find the volume of each figure.

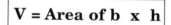

V = Area of b x h

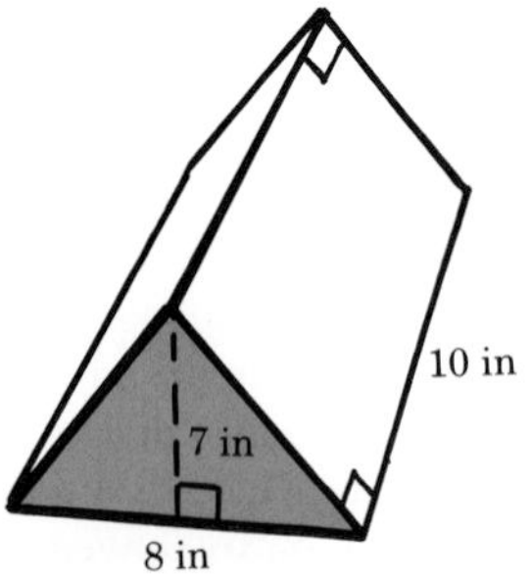

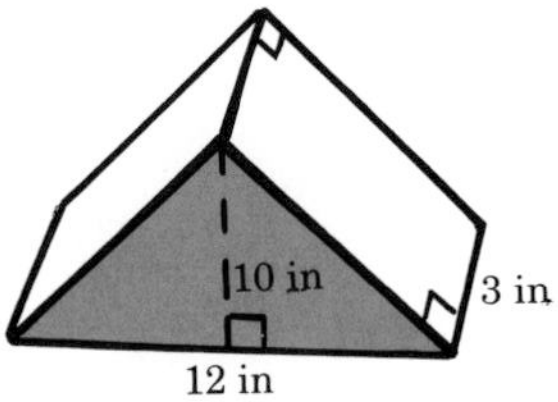

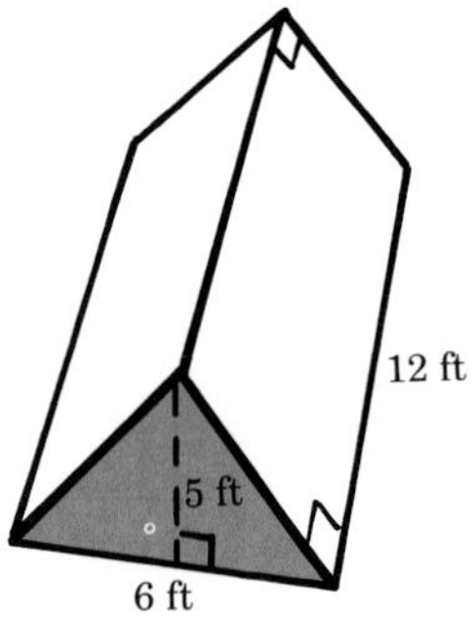

Part 2

- You've worked number family problems that have **fractions.** You can work the same kind of problems that involve **percents.**
- Remember, percents equal fractions with denominators of 100:

$$100\% = \frac{100}{100} \qquad 75\% = \frac{75}{100} \qquad 230\% = \frac{230}{100}$$

- If a problem gives percents, you can write fractions with denominators of 100.
- Here's a problem:

20% of the students rode their bikes to school. What fraction of the students rode their bikes? What fraction did not ride their bikes?

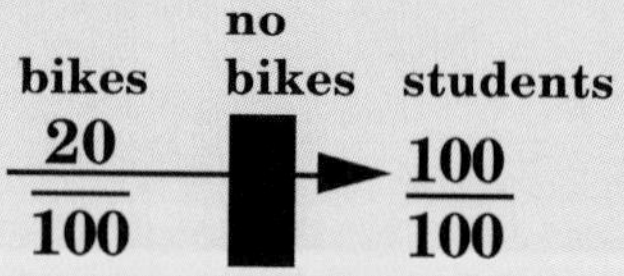

- The family shows a fraction for all the students.
- Remember, the fraction for all the students equals one whole. That's $\frac{100}{100}$.
- The fraction for students who did not ride their bikes is missing.

Part 3

For each item, make a fraction number family. Box the answer to the question.

a. 75% of the people wear glasses. What's the fraction for people who did not wear glasses?

b. The dog is 15% heavier than the cat. What's the fraction for the dog?

c. The pole is 20% higher than the tree. What's the fraction for the tree?

Part 4

For each item, answer the question. Remember the dollar signs.

a. Each day that Dan worked, he earned \$12.30. He worked for $\frac{4}{10}$ of a day. How much did he earn?

b. Rita earned \$44.80 for each full day she worked. She worked $\frac{3}{10}$ of a day. How much did she earn?

c. Reggie earns \$5.85 for each hour he works. He works $1\frac{5}{10}$ hours. How much does he earn?

d. Donna earned \$15.10 for each morning she worked. How much did she earn if she worked $3\frac{2}{10}$ mornings?

Part 5

Copy each problem. Figure out the mystery number.

a. ? ■ – 100 = ■
■ x 4 = 340

b. ? ■ – 97 = ■
■ – 11 = 31

Part 6

For each item, write table or no table. Work each problem.

a. There are 3 sunny days for every 5 days that are not sunny. If there are 66 sunny days, how many days are not sunny?

b. The ratio of girls to boys is 6 to 5. If there are 30 boys, how many girls are there?

c. At a school, there are students and employees. The ratio of employees to total people is 4 to 9. If there are 603 total people in the school, how many are employees? How many are students?

Part 7 Copy and complete the equation.

Each yard equals 3 feet.

$$\frac{\blacksquare}{\blacksquare}\boxed{\frac{\blacksquare}{\blacksquare}} = \frac{\blacksquare}{6} = \frac{10}{\blacksquare} = \frac{\blacksquare}{15} = \frac{\blacksquare}{2} = \frac{12}{\blacksquare}$$

Independent Work

Remember to complete the problems for part 6 of your textbook.

Part 8 Work each item.

a. Multiply the first odd number after 20 by the second odd number after 52.

b. Subtract the largest even number between 3 and 7 from 49.

c. Add the even number that comes just before 30 to the even number that comes just after 30.

Part 9 Work each item. Write the complete equations.

a. 7R = 13
1R = $\blacksquare$

b. 12J = 5
1J = $\blacksquare$

c. 9B = 1
1B = $\blacksquare$

Part 10 Work each item.

a. If each block weighs 14 ounces, how much do 9 blocks weigh?

b. A pizza costs $10. If it is divided into 8 equal-sized pieces, how much does each piece cost?

c. 3 cups hold 20 ounces of water. How much do 11 cups hold?

Part 11 Work each item.

a. What's $\frac{3}{4}$ of 196°?

b. What's $\frac{8}{7}$ of $\frac{2}{3}$?

c. How many degrees are in $\frac{4}{5}$ of a circle?

Part 12 Copy and work each item.

a. $\begin{array}{r} 3.05 \\ \times\ .70 \\ \hline \end{array}$

b. $\begin{array}{r} .03 \\ \times\ 2.5 \\ \hline \end{array}$

c. $\begin{array}{r} 11.5 \\ \times\ \ \ 6 \\ \hline \end{array}$

Part 13 Copy and complete each equation.

a. $\frac{7}{4} = \frac{\blacksquare}{100} = \blacksquare\%$

b. $\frac{21}{20} = \frac{\blacksquare}{100} = \blacksquare\%$

c. $\frac{15}{25} = \frac{\blacksquare}{100} = \blacksquare\%$

Lesson 107

Part 1 **For each item, make a fraction number family. Make a ratio table. Answer the questions the problem asks.**

a. 25% of the mushrooms were poisonous. There were 48 mushrooms.
   1. How many mushrooms were not poisonous?
   2. How many mushrooms were poisonous?

b. Martin weighed 50% less than his sister. His sister weighed 84 pounds.
   1. How much did Martin weigh?
   2. How much less did Martin weigh than his sister?

Part 2 **For each item, figure out the mystery number.**

a. ? ■ x 2 = ■
■ – 64 = 100

b. ? ■ – 501 = ■
■ x 3 = 12

c. ? ■ + 28 = ■
■ – 100 = 50

Part 3 **For each item, answer each question. Remember the dollar signs.**

a. Mark earns $5.60 for each full hour he works. If he works $1\frac{8}{10}$ hours, how much does he earn?

b. Each full day that Martha works, she earns $38.75. If she works for $\frac{8}{10}$ of a day, how much does she earn?

c. Bill earns $6.50 an hour. How much would he earn for 15 hours work?

d. Sandra worked for $\frac{6}{10}$ of a morning on Saturday. If she earns $14.15 for a full morning's work, how much money did she earn on Saturday?

Part 4 Find the volume of each figure.

a.
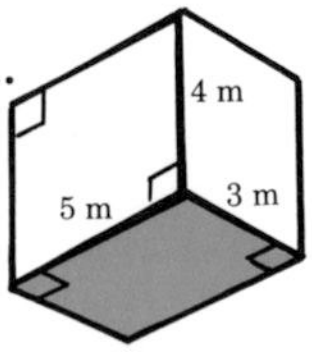

b.
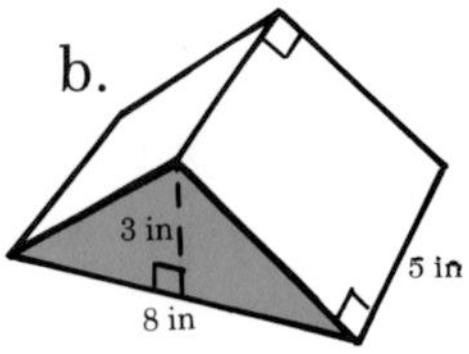

c.
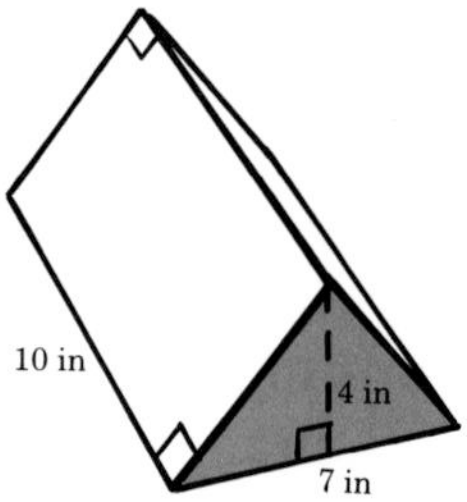

d.
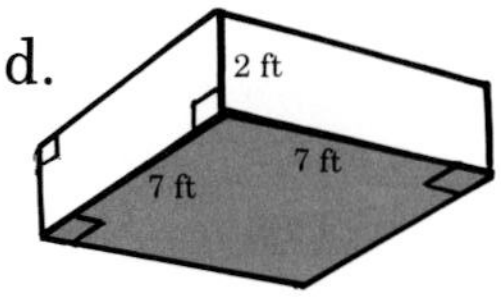

Part 5

- You can work some measurement problems by setting them up as equivalent fractions.
- Here's a problem:

Which is more, 4 gallons or 20 quarts?

- You start with a fact that tells the number of quarts in each gallon.

Each gallon is 4 quarts.

- Here's the names and the ratio numbers for the fact:

  $$\frac{\text{gallons}}{\text{quarts}}\ \boxed{\frac{1}{4}}$$

- To compare 4 gallons and 20 quarts, make two equivalent fractions. The first shows 4 gallons. The other shows 20 quarts.

  $$\frac{\text{gallons}}{\text{quarts}}\ \boxed{\frac{1}{4}} = \frac{4}{\blacksquare} = \frac{\blacksquare}{20}$$

- When you complete the fractions, one of the fractions will have a larger number for quarts and gallons. That fraction will tell which is more.

  $$\frac{\text{gallons}}{\text{quarts}}\ \boxed{\frac{1}{4}} = \frac{4}{16} = \frac{5}{20}$$

Part 6 **Answer each question.**

Each quart is 4 cups.

a. Which is more, 12 cups or 3 quarts?
b. Which is more, 36 cups or 8 quarts?
c. Which is more, 24 cups or 7 quarts?

Part 7 **For each item, make a ratio table. Answer the questions.**

a. The ratio of men to adults at a meeting was 3 to 7. If there were 560 adults, how many men were there?

b. Mountain D is $\frac{7}{5}$ the height of Mountain R. Mountain R is 4000 yards high. How much taller is Mountain D than Mountain R?

c. In a pond, $\frac{4}{9}$ of the fish were striped. If there were 125 fish that were not striped, how many total fish were in the pond?

d. Jan eats 80% as much as Donna eats. Donna eats 60 ounces of food.
   1. How much does Jan eat?
   2. How much more does Donna eat than Jan eats?

Independent Work

Remember to complete the problems for part 7 of your textbook.

Part 8 **Copy and work each item.**

a. $\begin{array}{r} 4 \\ \underline{\times\ 3.24} \end{array}$

b. $\begin{array}{r} 1.8 \\ \underline{\times\ 1.8} \end{array}$

c. $\begin{array}{r} .003 \\ \underline{\times\ 7.9} \end{array}$

Part 9 **Rewrite each item with the largest value on top.**

a.	b.	c.
.56	1.0	6.1
.555	.99	5.9
.5	.990	5.98

Part 10 **For each item, make a number family. Answer the question.**

a. By the end of December, Farmer Higgins wants to have 48 tons of corn in his silo. When he reaches his goal, the silo will have 136 tons less than it has now. How much corn is currently in his silo?

b. Rita's goal is to have enough money for her vacation. She will need \$620 for her airfare, \$315 for her hotel, \$175 for meals and \$150 for other expenses. She currently has \$615. How much more does she need to save to reach her goal?

c. The reservoir started out with 8110 tons of water in it. In the morning, 350 tons of water flowed out from the reservoir. In the afternoon and evening, 411 tons of water flowed out from the reservoir. During the day, 185 tons of water flowed into the reservoir. How much water was in the reservoir at the end of the day?

Part 11 **Copy and work each item.**

a. $\begin{array}{r} 17 \\ -\ 8\frac{3}{8} \\ \hline \end{array}$ b. $\begin{array}{r} 17\frac{2}{9} \\ +\ 8\frac{3}{9} \\ \hline \end{array}$ c. $\begin{array}{r} 503\frac{1}{7} \\ +\ 18\frac{6}{7} \\ \hline \end{array}$

Part 12 **Work each item.**

a. Subtract the largest even number between 102 and 107 from 200.

b. Multiply the odd number that comes just before 41 by the second even number after 10.

Part 13 **Work each item.**

a. $5\overline{)3708}$ b. $30\overline{)786}$ c. $75\overline{)450}$

Part 14 **Copy and complete each equation.**

a. $\frac{20}{20} = \frac{\blacksquare}{100} = \blacksquare\%$

b. $\frac{57}{10} = \frac{\blacksquare}{100} = \blacksquare\%$

c. $\frac{3}{50} = \frac{\blacksquare}{100} = \blacksquare\%$

Part J

a. ?
82 x 2 = 164
164 − 64 = 100

b. ?
505 − 501 = 4
4 x 3 = 12

c. ?
122 + 28 = 150
150 − 100 = 50

Lesson 108

Part 1

- You can use ratios to work problems that involve **averages.**
- Here's a problem:

> Donna drinks water each day. She drank 3 glasses on Monday, 2 glasses on Tuesday, 5 glasses on Wednesday and 2 glasses on Thursday. On the **average,** how many glasses of water did she drink **each day?**

- To find the **average,** you find out how much she would drink each day if the amount was the same for each day.
- Here's how you work the problem:
- You make a ratio equation for the number of glasses she drank on each day. The names are **glasses** and **days:** $\frac{\text{glasses}}{\text{days}}$
- You make a fraction that has the number of glasses for each day. Those numbers are added: $\frac{\text{glasses}}{\text{days}}\ \frac{3+2+5+2}{}$
- The problem tells that she drank water on **4 days.** So the number of days is 4: $\frac{\text{glasses}}{\text{days}}\ \frac{3+2+5+2}{4}$
- The problem asks about **each** day. That's 1 day: $\frac{\text{glasses}}{\text{days}}\ \frac{3+2+5+2}{4} = \frac{\blacksquare}{1}$
- Here's the ratio equation we work: $\frac{\text{glasses}}{\text{days}}\ \frac{12}{4}\left(\quad\right) = \frac{\blacksquare}{1}$
- The **total** number of glasses is 12. The **average** number of glasses she drank each day is 3. $\frac{\text{glasses}}{\text{days}}\ \frac{12}{4}\left(\frac{\frac{1}{4}}{\frac{1}{4}}\right) = \frac{\frac{12}{4}}{1}$
- If Donna drank the same amount each day for 4 days, she would drink 3 glasses a day. **3 glasses**

Part 2 Answer each question.

a. A pet shop has hamsters in cages. There are 4 hamsters in cage A. There are 7 hamsters in cage B. There are 3 hamsters in cage C. There are 5 hamsters in cage D. There is 1 hamster in cage E. On the average, how many hamsters are in each cage?

b. Miriam earned $234 one week, $152 the next week, and $319 the next week. On the average, how much money did she earn each week?

Part 3 For each item, figure out the mystery number.

a. ? (first box)
■ – 100 = ■
■ x 3 = 75

b. ? (first box)
■ x 2 = ■
■ – 420 = 10

Part 4 Rewrite each amount as dollars and cents.

a. 50¢ b. 234¢ c. 10,024¢

Part 5 For each item, make a fraction number family and a ratio table. Answer the questions the problem asks.

a. 25% of the mixture is sand. The rest of the mixture is gravel. The total mixture weighs 16 pounds.
   1. How many pounds of sand are in the mixture?
   2. How many pounds of gravel are in the mixture?

b. The height of the tree is 60% the height of the pole. The pole is 5 meters tall.
   1. How tall is the tree?
   2. How much taller is the pole than the tree?

c. There are 145% as many carnations as roses. There are 20 roses.
   1. How many carnations are there?
   2. How many fewer roses than carnations are there?

Part 6 **Answer each question.**

Each pint is 2 cups.

a. Which is more, 16 cups or 7 pints?

b. Which is more, 3 pints or 7 cups?

c. Which is more, 10 pints or 18 cups?

Part 7 **Find the surface area and volume of the figure.**

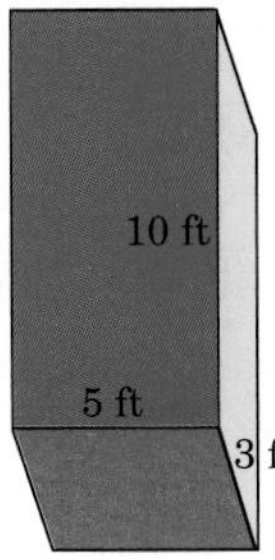

Independent Work

Part 8 **For each item, write the complete statement with one value on each side.**

a. $5\frac{7}{8}$ ■ $6 - \frac{1}{8}$

b. 11.01 ■ 10.985

c. $\frac{4}{5}$ ■ $\frac{5}{4}$

Part 9 **Work each item.**

a. Lisa earns $5.75 per hour. If she works for 3.4 hours, how much does she earn?

b. If each box holds $\frac{6}{10}$ of a pound, how many pounds do 7.3 boxes hold?

c. James earns $8.50 each time he paints a wall. So far, he has painted $2\frac{3}{10}$ walls. How much has he earned?

Part 10 **For each item, figure out the mystery number.**

a. ? ■ x 3 = ■

■ – 100 = 218

b. ? ■ ÷ 7 = ■

■ ÷ 2 = 140

Part 11 **Work each item.**

a. The ratio of fleas to dogs is 120 to 10. If there are 90 dogs, how many fleas are there?

b. In a mixture, there are 300 ounces of salt to every 100 ounces of carbon. If there are 16 ounces of carbon, how many ounces of salt are there?

c. If it takes 200 minutes to shear 50 sheep, how many sheep can be sheared in 40 minutes?

Part 12 **Copy and work each item.**

a. $41\overline{)3701}$ b. $48\overline{)392}$

c. $52\overline{)4682}$ d. $7\overline{)5302}$

Part 13 **Work each item.**

a. If a machine takes 36 minutes to cut out 5 patterns, how many patterns can the machine cut out in 12 minutes?

b. 8 bottles cost $68. How much does each bottle cost?

c. A farmer wants to divide a parcel of land that has 568 acres into 4 smaller parcels that are the same size. How many acres are in each parcel?

d. If a machine produces 6 buttons each second, how many buttons will the machine produce in 50 seconds?

Lesson 109

Part 1 **For each item, write two equations. Figure out the mystery number.**

a. You start with some number and subtract 18. Then you multiply by 5. You end up with 45. What's the mystery number?

b. You start with some number and multiply by 9. Then you add 15. You end up with 69. What's the mystery number?

c. You start with some number and subtract 20. Then you multiply by 4. You end up with 84. What's the mystery number?

d. You start with some number and multiply by 3. Then you multiply by 5. You end up with 105. What's the mystery number?

Part 2 **For each item, make a set of equivalent fractions. Answer each question.**

a. Which is longer, 33 feet or 10 yards?

b. Which is more, 72 pints or 10 gallons?

c. Which is more, 9 cups or 160 tablespoons?

Part 3 **For each item, make a fraction number family and a ratio table. Answer the questions the problem asks.**

a. 60% of the plates were chipped. There were 36 chipped plates.
   1. How many plates were not chipped?
   2. How many plates were there altogether?

b. The classroom was 20% shorter than the library. The classroom is 32 meters long.
   1. How long is the library?
   2. How much longer than the classroom is the library?

Part 4 **Find volume of the box.**

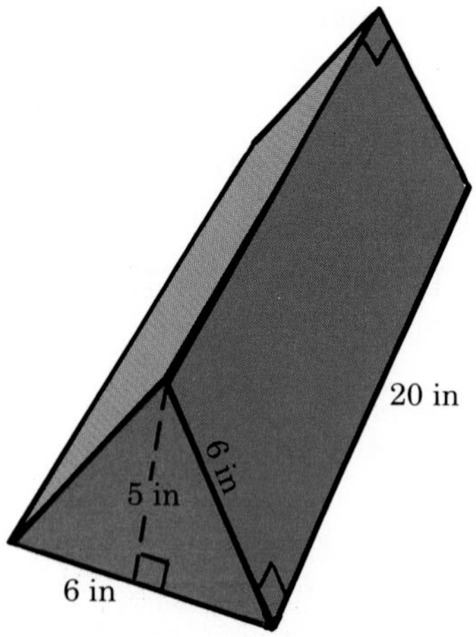

Part 5 **Answer each question.**

a. The high temperatures recorded on different days are as follows: 30°, 42°, 58°, 39°, 51°. What is the average high temperature?

b. Below are the number of airplanes sighted on different days of the week:

Day	Number of airplanes
Monday	24
Tuesday	17
Wednesday	0
Thursday	35

What is the average number of airplanes sighted each day?

Part 6 **Rewrite each value as dollars and cents.**

a. 120¢ b. 74¢ c. 85¢ d. 500¢ e. 1108¢

Independent Work

Remember to complete the problems for part 1 of your textbook.

Part 7 **Work each item.**

a. Divide the larger odd number between 85 and 90 by the first odd number after 1.

b. Multiply the second even number after 45 by 12.

c. Add the odd number that comes just before 13 to the second even number after 100.

Part 8 **For each item, figure out the mystery number.**

a. ■ (?) – 50 = ■
■ ÷ 5 = 19

b. ■ (?) x 12 = ■
■ ÷ 6 = 20

Part 9	Work each item.

a. Mr. Jones left all his money in equal shares to his children. He had $42,000. He had 4 children. How much did each child receive?

b. It takes 13 cups of milk to make 3 cakes. How many cups are needed for 7 cakes?

c. Each hat costs $13. How much do 65 hats cost?

d. If it takes 238 bricks to make 2 identical chimneys, how many bricks are in each chimney?

Part 10	Rewrite each value with the largest value on top.

a. 2.8
2.09
2.08

b. 12.003
12.100
12.2

c. .03
1.01
1.008

Part 11	Work each item.

a. John earns $3.50 for each job. How much does he earn for doing 8.3 jobs?

b. Each bag of flour weighs 3.5 pounds. How much do 7.5 bags of flour weigh?

c. If Hilda works for 3 hours, she earns $27. How much does she earn per hour?

d. It takes 350 bricks to make 10 steps. How many bricks are needed for 4 steps?

e. In 100 days, a shop builds 3000 bicycles. How many bicycles does the shop build in 20 days?

Part 12	Work each item. Show your answers in hundredths.

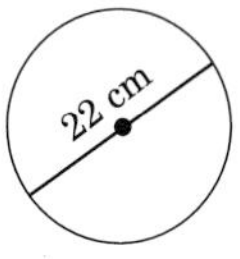

a. Find the circumference.

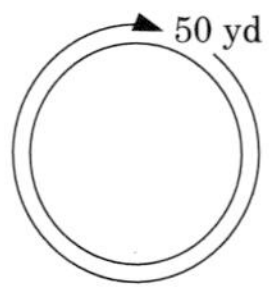

b. Find the diameter.

Part 13	Copy and work each problem.

a. 15 – 6.385   b. 11.05 + 105 + 8.3

Part J

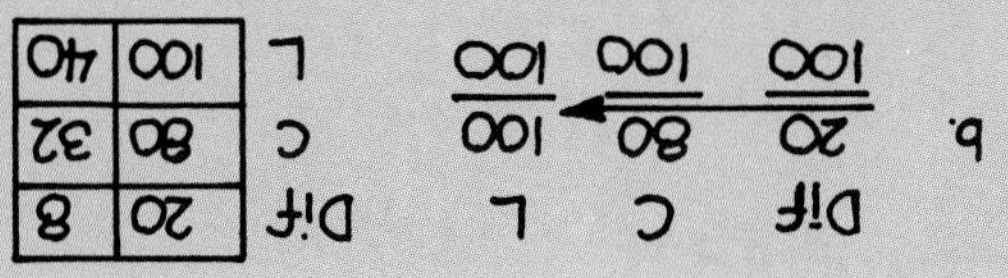

Lesson 110

Part 1

- Some percent problems tell about the difference. For those problems, you make number families with fractions.
- Here's a sentence:

  Sue had 25% more than Harry had.

- The sentence compares something to Harry. So **Harry** is 1 whole. That's $\frac{100}{100}$.

Dif	H	S
	$\frac{100}{100}$ →	

- The **difference** is 25%. That's $\frac{25}{100}$.

Dif	H	S
$\frac{25}{100}$	$\frac{100}{100}$ →	

- So **Sue** is 125%. That's $\frac{125}{100}$.

Dif	H	S
$\frac{25}{100}$	$\frac{100}{100}$ →	$\frac{125}{100}$

- Here's a different sentence:

  The price of the sweater was 140% the price of the pants.

- The **sweater** is 140%.

Dif	P	S
	→	$\frac{140}{100}$

- The **pants** are 1 whole. That's 100%.

Dif	P	S
	$\frac{100}{100}$ →	$\frac{140}{100}$

- So the **difference** is 40%.

Dif	P	S
$\frac{40}{100}$	$\frac{100}{100}$ →	$\frac{140}{100}$

Part 2

For each item, make a fraction number family and a ratio table. Answer the questions the problem asks.

a. Linda had 45% more stamps than Billy had. Linda had 290 stamps.
   1. How many stamps did Billy have?
   2. How many more stamps did Linda have than Billy had?

b. The regular price of bikes was 130% the sale price of bikes. The sale price was $190.
   1. What was the regular price?
   2. How much would you save if you bought a bike on sale?

c. 20% fewer boys than girls have joined the ski club. 60 more girls than boys have joined the club.
   1. How many girls joined the ski club?
   2. How many boys joined the ski club?

Part 3

For each item, write two equations. Figure out the mystery number.

a. You start with some number. You add 52. Then you multiply by 2. You end up with 678. What's the mystery number?

b. You start with some number. You divide by 7. Then you add 77. You end up with 84. What's the mystery number?

Test 11

Part 1

Figure out each mystery number.

a. ? ■ ÷ 20 = ■
■ x 9 = 45

b. ? ■ + 180 = ■
■ ÷ 4 = 50

Part 2 **For each item, make an equation and answer the question.**

Each yard is 3 feet.

a. Which is more, 7 yards or 20 feet?

b. Which is more, 57 feet or 18 yards?

Part 3 **Work the item. Show the answer as a decimal value.**

a. Fran earns $7.50 per hour. If she works for $\frac{6}{10}$ hour, how much does she earn?

Part 4 **For each item, write the complete equation.**

a. $\frac{8}{10} = \frac{\blacksquare}{100} = \blacksquare\%$

b. $\frac{5}{4} = \frac{\blacksquare}{100} = \blacksquare\%$

Part 5 **Work each item.**

a. If 50 crane buckets hold 300 tons of sand, how many tons do 4 crane buckets hold?

b. If it takes a machine 130 seconds to cut out 20 buttonholes, how long does it take the machine to cut out 50 buttonholes?

Part 6 **Copy and work each item.**

a. $\begin{array}{r} 3.02 \\ \underline{\times\ .04} \end{array}$

b. $\begin{array}{r} 5.09 \\ \underline{\times\ \ 1.6} \end{array}$

Part 7 **Work each item.**

a. Multiply the second odd number after 8 by the larger even number between 12 and 17.

b. Subtract 10 from the largest odd number that is less than 100.

Part 8 **Write each value as dollars and cents.**

a. 234¢ b. 50¢ c. 6021¢

Part 9 Work each item.

a. If each bucket holds 25 gallons, how many gallons do 7 buckets hold?

b. 16 biscuits weigh 3 pounds. How much does each biscuit weigh?

c. There are 180 chairs in the lunchroom. They are divided so the same number of chairs are in 12 groups. How many chairs are in each group?

d. If 16 biscuits weigh 3 pounds, how many biscuits weigh 7 pounds?

Part 10 Rewrite the decimal values with the largest value on top.

a. 5.099
5.1
5.09

Part 11 Write the complete statement with one value on each side and with the correct sign.

a. $\frac{3}{10} \times 4$ ■ 1.5

b. 4×12 ■ $\frac{76}{2}$

Part 12 Work each item.

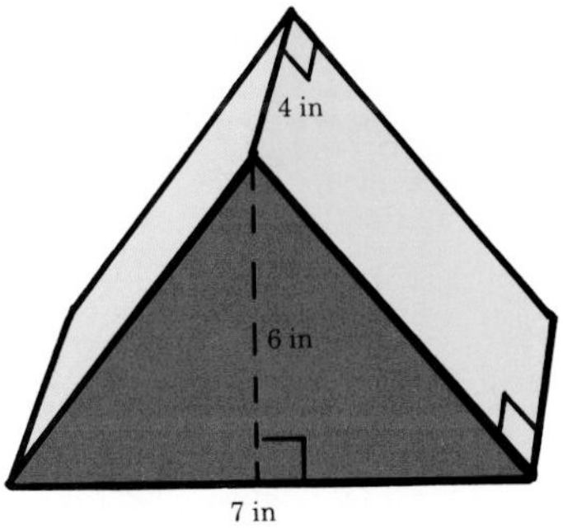

a. Find the volume of the box.

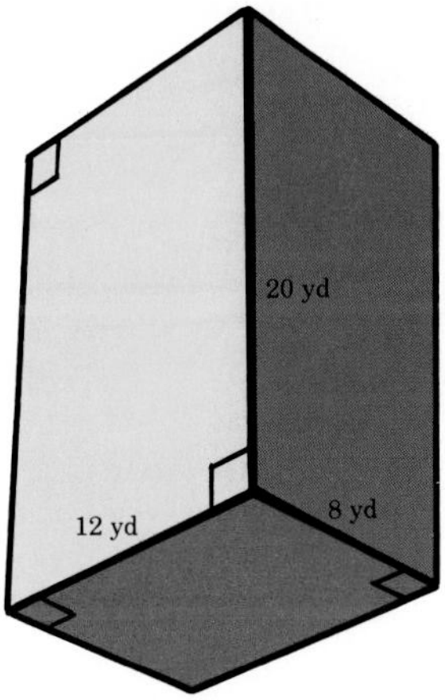

b. Find the surface area of the box.

Lesson 111

Part 1

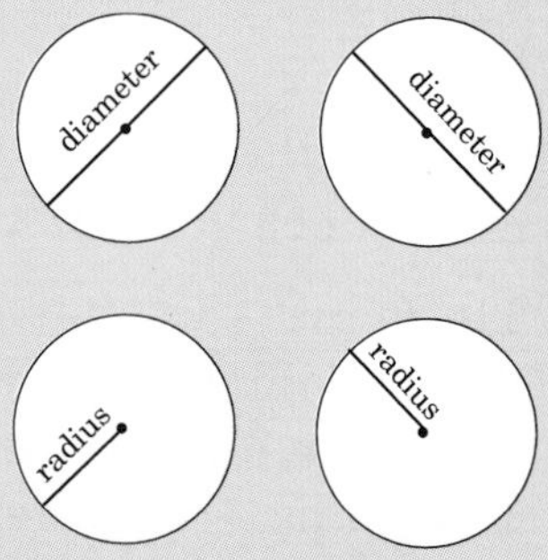

- The diameter is the distance through the center of a circle. The diameter goes from one side of the circle to the other side.
- Half the diameter is the **radius.** The radius goes to the center of the circle and then stops.
- Some circumference problems give information about the **radius** of the circle, not about the diameter.
- Here's a problem: **The radius is 3 feet. What's the circumference?**
- If the radius is 3 ft, the diameter is twice that length–6 ft.

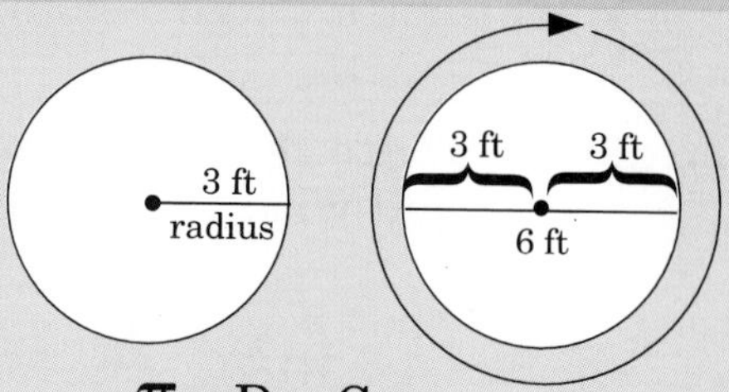

- So the circumference of the circle is π x 6. The answer is 18.84 ft.

π x D = C
3.14 x 6 = C
C = 18.84 ft

- If the problem gives the circumference and **asks** about the radius, the problem asks about half the diameter.
- You first figure out the diameter. Then you divide by 2 to find the radius.
- Here's a problem:

What's the radius?

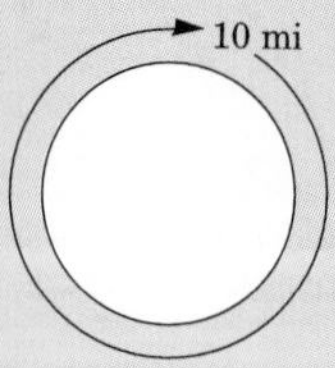

- You multiply 3.14 by some number to get 10. The fraction you multiply by is $\frac{10}{3.14}$.
- That's the diameter–3.18 mi.
- The radius is half that length–1.59 mi.

π x D = C
3.14 (   ) = 10
3.14 ($\frac{10}{3.14}$) = 10
D = 3.18 mi
r = 1.59 mi

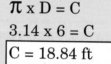

Part 2

Work each item. Round your answers to hundredths. Remember the unit name.

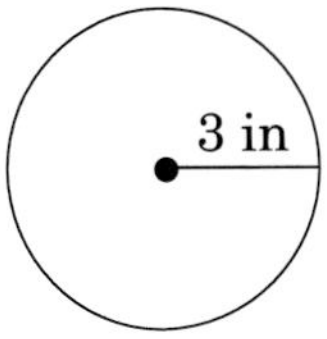

a. What's the circumference?

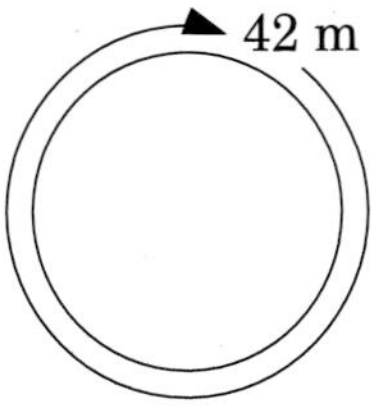

b. What's the radius?

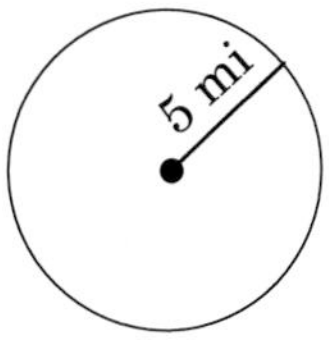

c. What's the circumference?

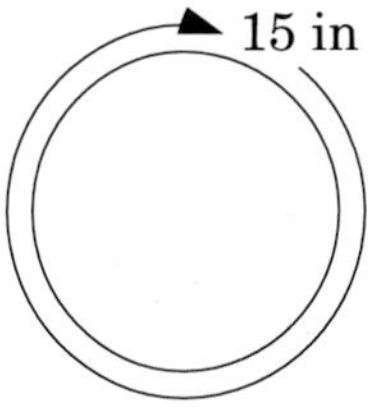

d. What's the radius?

Part 3

Make a set of equivalent fractions. Answer each question.

a. Which is more, 35 cups or 8 quarts?

b. Which is longer, 7 weeks or 49 days?

c. Which is heavier, 48 ounces or 2 pounds?

Part 4

- You can compare fractions by finding the lowest common denominator. When the denominators are the same, the fraction with the larger numerator is the larger fraction.
- Here's a problem: **Which is more, $\frac{3}{4}$ or $\frac{5}{8}$?**
- We write the fractions in a column and figure out the lowest common denominator.
- When both fractions have a denominator of 8, you can see that the larger fraction is $\frac{6}{8}$.

$$\frac{3}{4}\left(\frac{2}{2}\right) = \frac{6}{8}$$

$$\frac{5}{8} = \frac{5}{8}$$

$$\frac{6}{8} = \frac{3}{4} \text{ so: } \boxed{\frac{3}{4} > \frac{5}{8}}$$

Part 5

Work each item.

a. Which is more, $\frac{2}{3}$ or $\frac{3}{5}$?

b. Which is more, $\frac{9}{12}$ or $\frac{5}{6}$?

Part 6 **Answer each question.**

a. On the average, how many people are in each car?

b. What is the average weight of sand in each can?

Part 7 **For each item, write two equations. Figure out the mystery number.**

a. You start with a number and multiply by 7. Then you divide by 5. You end up with 14. What's the mystery number?

b. You start with a number. You divide by 3. Then you divide by 8. You end up with 72. What's the mystery number?

c. You start with a number. You add 100. Then you divide by 5. You end up with 35. What number did you start with?

Part 8 For each item, make a fraction number family and a ratio table. Answer the questions the problem asks.

a. The office complex is 50% taller than the apartment building. The apartment building is 120 feet tall.
   1. How many feet taller is the office complex than the apartment building?
   2. How many feet tall is the office complex?

b. 60% of the apples picked were used to make cider. The rest were sold in the store. There were 400 apples picked in all.
   1. How many apples were used to make cider?
   2. How many apples were sold in the store?

Independent Work

Part 9 For each item, make a ratio equation. Answer the question.

a. There are 30 eggs for every 20 robins. There are 240 eggs. How many robins are there?

b. A factory makes 900 buttons in 10 seconds. How many seconds does it take for the factory to make 100 buttons?

Part 10 Find the surface area and volume of the box.

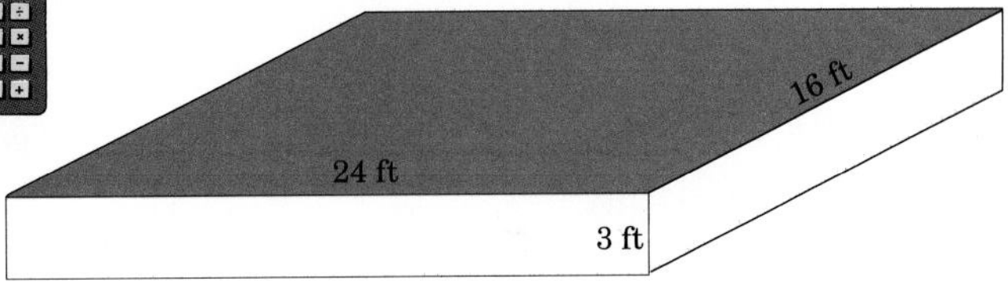

Part 11 Work each item.

a. What's $\frac{4}{3}$ of 90?

b. If each basket holds 11 eggs, how many eggs do 15 baskets hold?

c. A pile of sand is divided into 4 piles of equal weight. If the original pile weighs 460 tons, how much will each smaller pile weigh?

d. How many degrees are in $\frac{3}{5}$ of a circle?

e. The ratio of fish to worms is 15 to 4. If there are 40 fish, how many worms are there?

f. Mr. Wilson earns $96 each day. How much does he earn in 5 days?

Do the Independent Work for Lesson 111 of your workbook.

Lesson 112

Part 1

- Some fractions tell about what you expect to happen. These fractions don't tell what **will** happen, but what **probably** will happen.

- Here's a bag with Xs and circles in it:

- There are more Xs than circles. So if you reached into the bag without looking and pulled out one thing, it would **probably** be an X. Maybe it wouldn't be an X. But a smart bet would be that you would pull out an X.

- Here's a different bag with Xs and circles:
- There are more circles than Xs in the bag.

- Here are two bags with Xs and circles in them:
- Each bag has two Xs in it, but bag B has fewer circles in it than bag A. You'd have a better chance of pulling out an X from bag B.

a.

b.

- You can use fractions to tell about your chances of pulling out an X from a bag. For that fraction, the **denominator** tells the number of things that are in the bag. The **numerator** tells the number of Xs.

- In bag B, there are 5 things.
- There are 2 Xs.

b.

5

- So the fraction $\frac{2}{5}$ tells about your chances of pulling an X from bag B.

b.

$\frac{2}{5}$

- In bag A, there are 9 things.
- There are 2 Xs.
- The fraction that tells about the chances for bag A is $\frac{2}{9}$.

a.

$\frac{2}{9}$

- By comparing the fractions, you can figure out which bag gives the better chance.

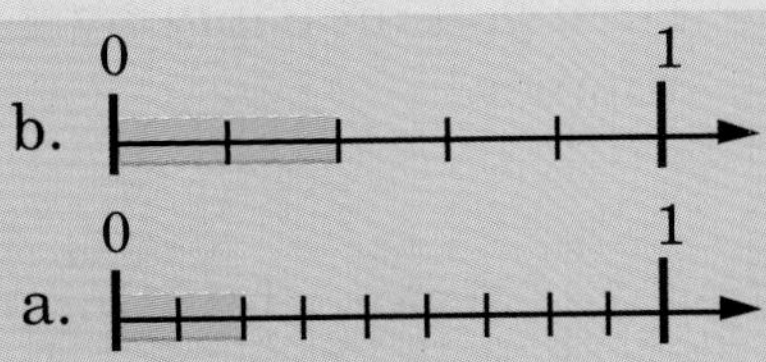

- Here's the rule: **The closer the fraction is to 1, the better your chance is of pulling out an X.**

Part 2 **Write the fraction that tells your chance of pulling an X from each bag.**

a.

b.

c.

d.

e. Fraction for best chance: [redacted]

f. Fraction for second best chance: [redacted]

g. Fraction for worst chance: [redacted]

Part 3 Work each item. Round your answers to hundredths. Remember the unit name.

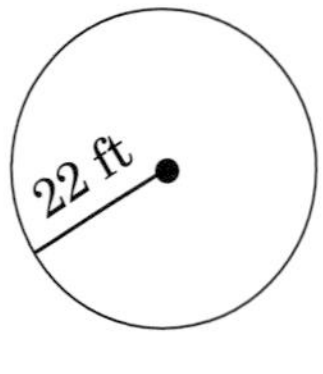

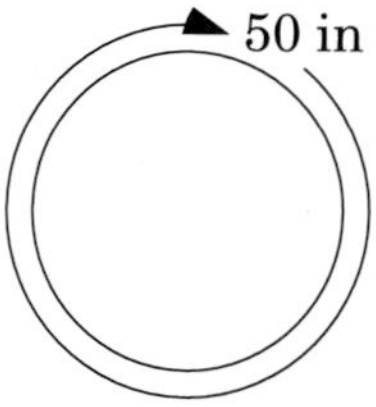

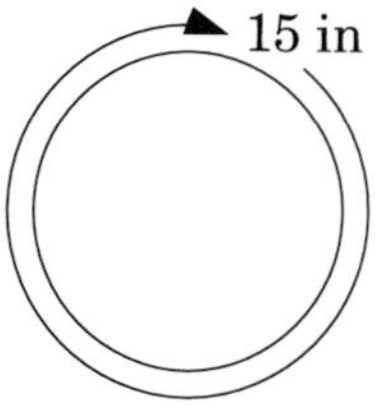

a. Figure out the circumference.

b. Figure out the radius.

c. Figure out the radius.

Part 4 For each item, write the equations. Figure out the mystery number.

a. You start with some number. Then you multiply by 5. Then you subtract 16. Then you add 11. Then you divide by 3. You end up with 30. What's the mystery number?

b. You start with a number. Then you divide by 3. Then you subtract 20. Then you multiply by 2. You end up with 8. What's the mystery number?

Part 5 Make a fraction number family for each item.

a. The sale price is 75% of the regular price.

b. Tim is 14% taller than Jim.

c. 9% of the people are sunburned.

d. $\frac{1}{7}$ of the trees fell down.

e. John is 40% heavier than his uncle.

f. The price of the shoes is $\frac{5}{4}$ the price of the jeans.

Part 6 Answer each question.

a. On the average, how much does a robot cost?

S b. The heights of different trees are: 14 feet, 10 feet, 18 feet, 9 feet, 14 feet, and 9 feet. What is the average height of these trees?

Part 7 Answer each question.

a. Which is larger, $\frac{6}{5}$ or $\frac{8}{7}$?

b. Which is larger, $\frac{3}{4}$ or $\frac{5}{6}$?

Independent Work

Part 8 Find the area and perimeter for each figure.

a.

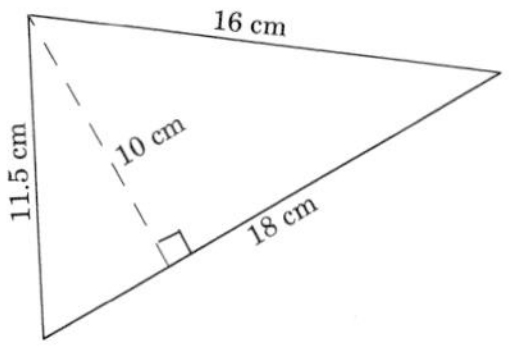

b.

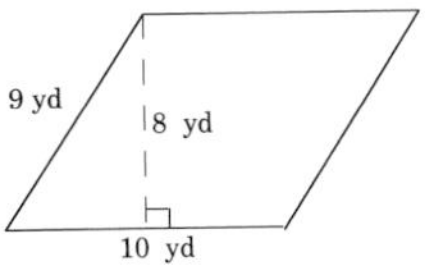

Part 9 Use the table of weights and measures. For each item, make a set of equivalent fractions with the larger quantity on top. Answer the question.

a. Which is more, 48 ounces or 3 pounds?

b. Which is more, 16 yards or 51 feet?

c. Which is more, 9 cups or 4 pints?

Do the Independent Work for Lesson 112 of your workbook.

Lesson 113

Part 1

- You've learned to find the circumference of a circle. That's the distance around the circle.

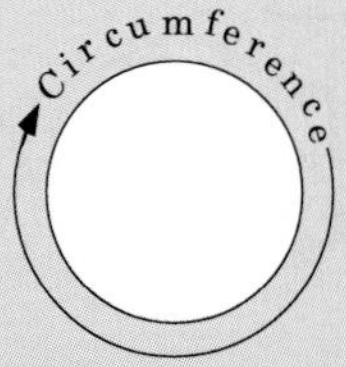

- You can also find the area of a circle. That's the number of square units that fill the circle.

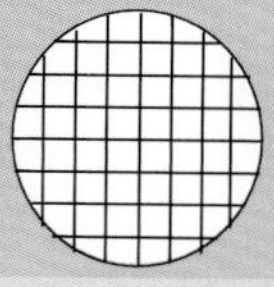

- Here's the equation for the area of a circle:

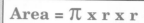

Area = π x r x r

- When you multiply the **radius** by the **radius,** you get a square that's as wide and as high as the radius.

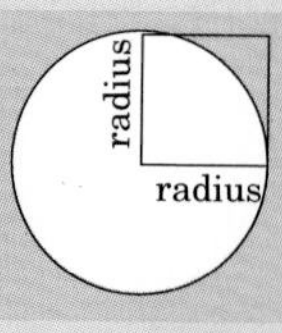

- When you multiply **that square** by π, you end up with a little more than 3 of those squares.

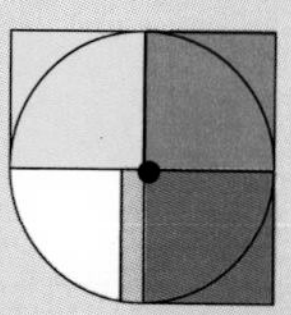

- Parts of each square are outside the circle. When you move those parts around, the entire circle is filled and there are no leftover parts.

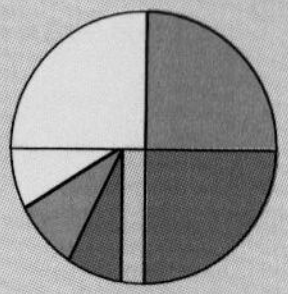

- Here's a circle:
  The diameter is 8 inches. So the radius is 4 inches.

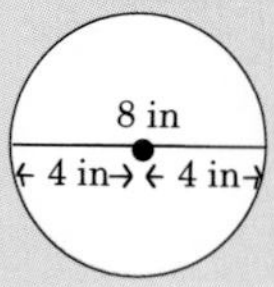

- Here's the problem you work:

A = π x r x r
A = 3.14 x 4 x 4

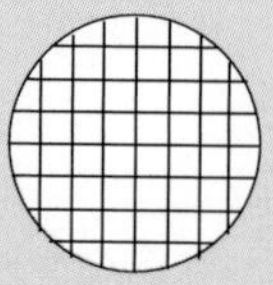

- There are 50.24 square inches in the circle.

A = 50.24 sq in

Part 2

Figure out the area of each circle.

$$A = \pi \times r \times r$$

a.
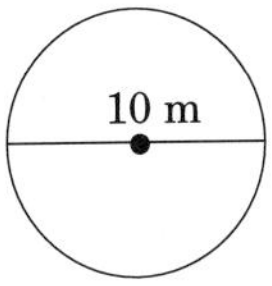

b.
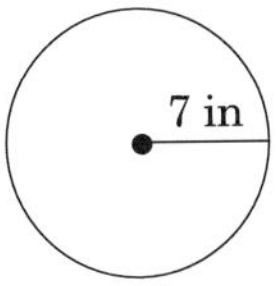

c.
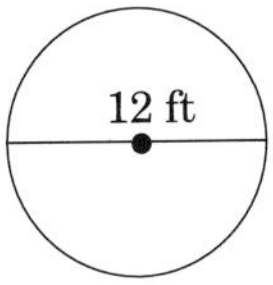

d.
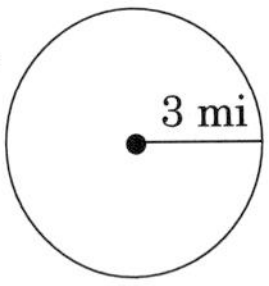

Part 3

Write the fraction that tells your chance of drawing an X from each bag. Then write the fractions for the best chance and the worst chance.

a.

b.

c.

d.

e. Fraction for best chance: [redacted]

f. Fraction for worst chance: [redacted]

Part 4

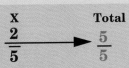

- You can make a **fraction number family** to tell about the chance of pulling an X from a bag.

X: $\frac{2}{5}$ ⟶

- If $\frac{2}{5}$ of the things in the bag are Xs, the fraction for **all** the things in the bag is $\frac{5}{5}$.

X: $\frac{2}{5}$ ⟶ Total: $\frac{5}{5}$

- $\frac{3}{5}$ of the things are not Xs.

X: $\frac{2}{5}$, Not X: $\frac{3}{5}$ ⟶ Total: $\frac{5}{5}$

Part 5

Make a number family for each item.

a.

b.
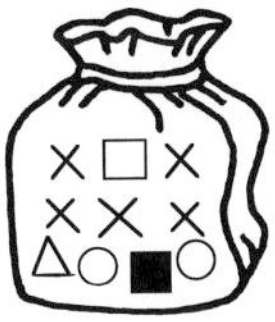

c.

Part 6 Make a fraction number family for each item.

a. The ball game took $\frac{5}{3}$ as much time as the lunch period.

b. Millie spent 35% more money than George spent.

c. 62% of the children wore shorts.

d. The number of people watching TV was $\frac{7}{5}$ the number of people walking in the woods.

e. The sale price was 80% of the regular price.

Part 7 For each item, make a picture of a bag based on the fraction.

a. $\frac{4}{7}$ of the things in the bag are Xs.

b. $\frac{3}{10}$ of the things in the bag are Xs.

c. $\frac{1}{5}$ of the things in the bag are Xs.

Part 8 Work each item. Round your answers to hundredths. Remember the unit name.

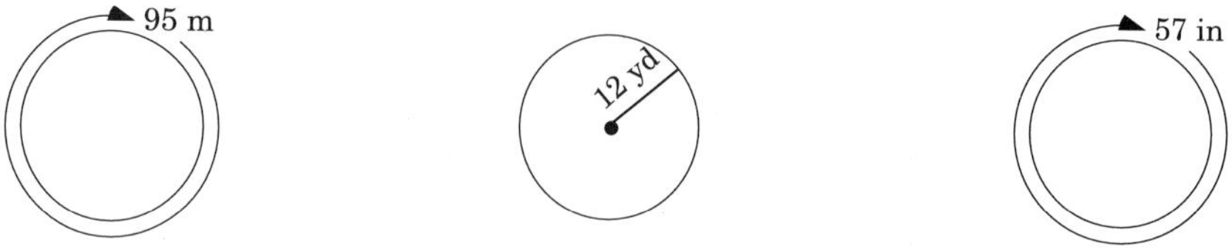

a. Find the radius.

b. Find the circumference.

c. Find the diameter.

By rolling this wheel around one time, we can find the circumference.
Yes, and by rolling this wheel around one time, we can also crack some walnuts.

Independent Work

Part 9 **Work each item.**

a. If each can weighs 15 ounces, how much do 20 cans weigh?

b. In a room, each row of desks has the same number of desks. If there are 36 desks in 4 rows, how many desks are in each row?

S c. A pie is cut into 6 pieces that are the same weight. If the whole pie weighs 800 grams, how much does each piece weigh?

d. A crew of workers can build 50 houses in 300 days. How many houses can the crew build in 70 days?

e. What is $\frac{3}{8}$ of 160?

Part 10 **Use the table of weights and measures. For each item, make a set of equivalent fractions. Answer the question.**

a. Which is more, 64 tablespoons or 2 cups?

b. Which is more, 42 inches or 3 feet?

c. Which is more, 4 cups or 3 pints?

Here's my table of weights and measures, but I couldn't find any liters.
Not that kind of table.
5 lb.
5 lb.

Lesson 114

Part 1

- You're going to work problems that refer to taking trials at pulling things from a bag.
- Here are the steps you would take for each trial:

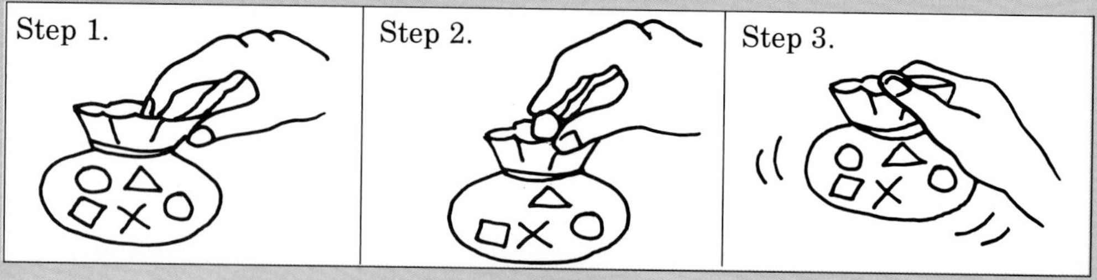

Step 1.
You'd reach into the bag without looking.

Step 2.
You'd pull out one thing and see if it's an X.

Step 3.
Then you'd return that thing to the bag and shake the bag so that all the things are mixed up.

- Those are the steps for one trial.
- If you took 50 trials, you'd do those steps 50 times, once for each trial.
- The total number of things in the bag tells the **number of trials** you would take to give each thing in the bag **one chance** to be pulled out.
- There are 7 things in bag A. If you took 7 trials, you'd expect each thing to be pulled out once.
- On 3 of those trials, you'd expect to pull out an X. That's because there are 3 Xs in the bag.
- On 4 of those trials, you'd expect to pull out something that is not an X. That's because 4 of the things in the bag are not Xs.

a. 

b. 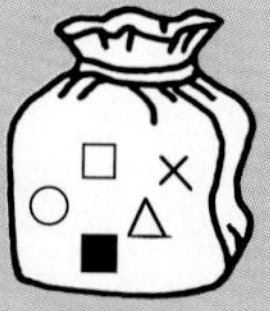

Part 2 For each bag, make a fraction number family. Answer the questions.

a. 

1. How many trials would you take to give each thing in the bag one chance of being pulled out?
2. On how many of those trials would you expect to pull out an X?
3. On how many of those trials would you expect to pull out something that is not an X?

b. 

1. How many trials would you take to give each thing in the bag one chance of being pulled out?
2. On how many of those trials would you expect to pull out an X?
3. On how many of those trials would you expect to pull out something that is not an X?

c. 

1. How many trials would you take to give each thing in the bag one chance of being pulled out?
2. On how many of those trials would you expect to pull out an X?
3. On how many of those trials would you expect to pull out something that is not an X?

Part 3 For each item, write the equations. Figure out the mystery number.

a. You start with some number and add 11. Then you multiply by 3. Then you add 33. Then you divide by 2. You end up with 33. What number did you start with?

b. You start with some number and divide by 2. Then you divide by 3. Then you add 50. You end up with 95. What number did you start with?

Part 4 Find the area of each circle. Use the equation: $A = \pi \times r \times r$.

a. 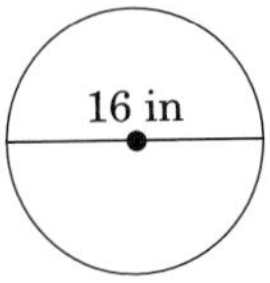

b. 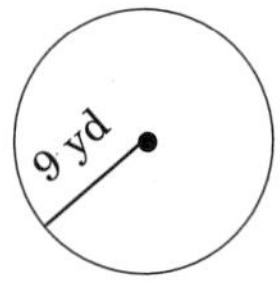

c. 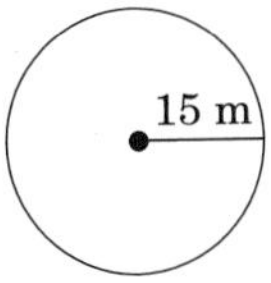

d. 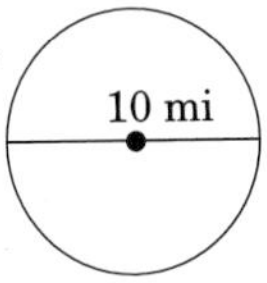

Part 5

- Straight lines can be drawn on a coordinate system. For each line there's a rule. The rule is called a **function.**
- The function tells about points on the line. The function tells how to go from any x value to the corresponding y value.

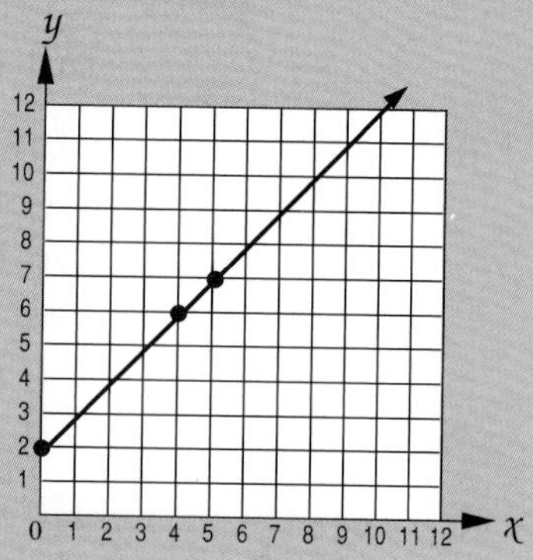

- Here's a line with points:
  The function for this line is x **+ 2.**
  That means you can start with an x value and add 2 to figure out the corresponding y value.

- Here's a table that shows the x values and corresponding y values for the points shown on the line:

x	Function $x + 2$	y
5	5 + 2	7
0	0 + 2	2
4	4 + 2	6

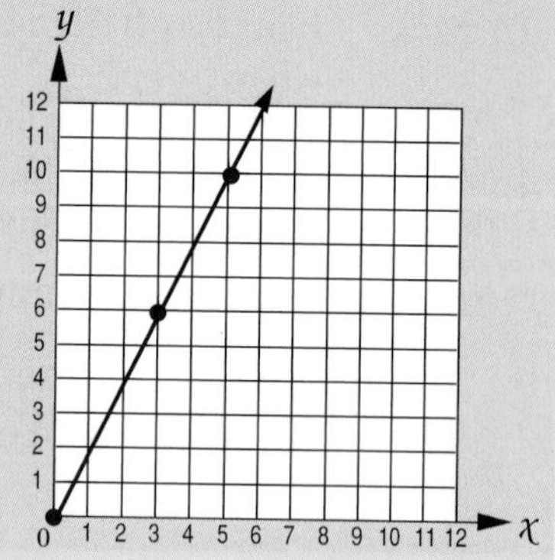

- This line is different:
  The function is $x \times 2$.

- That means each y value is 2 times the x value.

x	Function $x(2)$	y
5	5(2)	10
3	3(2)	6

Part 6 **For each item, make a picture of a bag based on the fraction.**

a. $\frac{1}{4}$ of the things in the bag are Xs.

b. $\frac{5}{9}$ of the things in the bag are Xs.

c. $\frac{1}{5}$ of the things in the bag are Xs.

Part 7 **Make a fraction number family and ratio table for each item. Answer the questions.**

a. The dog is 30% heavier than the cat. The cat weighs 60 ounces.
   1. How much does the dog weigh?
   2. How much more does the dog weigh than the cat weighs?

b. $\frac{4}{5}$ of the plants had flowers. There were 334 plants that did not have flowers.
   1. How many plants were there in all?
   2. How many of those plants had flowers?

c. The price of the socks on sale is 15% less than the socks at their regular price. The regular price of the socks is $2.
   1. What's the sale price of the socks?
   2. How much does a person save by buying socks on sale?

d. 2 out of every 7 bottles are full. There's a total of 140 bottles.
   1. How many bottles are full?
   2. How many bottles are not full?

Independent Work

Remember to complete the problems for parts 3 and 7 of your textbook.

Part 8 **Work the problem.**

Fran counted the number of birds she sighted on different days. On Monday, she sighted 42 birds. On Tuesday, she sighted 95 birds. On Wednesday, she sighted 80 birds. On Thursday, she sighted 44 birds. On Friday, she sighted 104 birds. What is the average number of birds she sighted per day?

Part 9 **Work the problems.**

a. Subtract the third odd number after 50 from the first odd number after 90.

b. Multiply the even number that comes just before 36 by the second even number after 10.

c. Divide the largest odd number between 200 and 208 by the odd number between 3 and 7.

Part 10 **Write an inequality statement to answer each question.**

a. Which is larger, $\frac{5}{7}$ or $\frac{4}{9}$?

b. Which is larger, $\frac{7}{6}$ or $\frac{10}{9}$?

Lesson 115

Part 1

- Some word problems involving division are tricky because they ask a question about things that cannot be divided into parts.
- The question may ask:

How many children are in each bus?

- The answer to the division problem may be $12\frac{1}{2}$.
- That's not the answer to the question because we can't put $\frac{1}{2}$ of a child on a bus. So you'd have either 12 or 13 children on the bus.
- Sometimes you have to round **up** to answer the question. Sometimes you have to round **down.**

Part 2 **Work each division problem. Answer each question.**

a. Bill wants to buy tapes. He has $37 to spend. Each tape costs $4. How many tapes can he buy?

b. The campers will take a bus trip. Each bus holds 16 campers. There are 102 campers. How many buses are needed for the trip?

c. The teacher wants to make as many teams as possible. Each team will have 6 students. There are 28 students in the class. How many complete teams can the teacher make?

d. Each can of paint covers 20 square yards. Molly wants to paint an area that is 110 square yards. How many cans of paint must she buy?

Part 3

- You've made number families that tell about the Xs in a bag and the number of **trials** you would take.
- You can also use these fraction number families to work ratio problems that involve **probability.** Those problems ask about what will **probably** happen.
- Here's a problem:

There are 8 things in a bag. 2 of them are Xs. If you took a total of 56 trials, on how many trials would you expect to pull out an X?

The first part tells you that there are 8 things in this bag. 2 of them are Xs.

- You make a fraction number family for the things in the bag. The family tells about the number of trials you would take to give each thing in the bag one chance.
- Here's the family:
There are 8 things in the bag. So you'd take 8 trials to give each thing one chance.

X	Not X		Total trials
$\frac{2}{8}$	$\frac{6}{8}$	→	$\frac{8}{8}$

- The problem asks: If you took a total of **56 trials,** on how many trials would you expect to pull out an X?
- For that problem, you're not giving each thing in the bag just one chance. You're giving it more than one chance.
- You work the problem by using the numerators of the fractions as ratio numbers. You put 56 as the total in the second column.
- Here's the ratio table:
The ratio numbers are 2 for Xs, 6 for not Xs, and 8 for total trials.

X	2	■
Not X	6	■
Total trials	8	56

- Now you make a ratio equation to figure out the number of Xs you'd expect to get in 56 trials.

$$\frac{\textbf{X}}{\textbf{trials}}\quad \frac{2}{8}\left(\frac{\blacksquare}{\blacksquare}\right) = \frac{\blacksquare}{56}$$

Part 4 Make a fraction number family and ratio table. Answer the question.

a. 

If you took trials until you pulled out 40 Xs, about how many trials would you take?

b. 

1.) If you took 30 trials, how many Xs would you expect to pull out?

2.) How many things that are not Xs would you expect to pull out?

Part 5 Figure out the circumference and the area of each circle.

a. 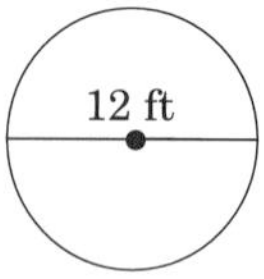

b. 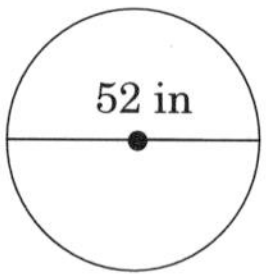

c. 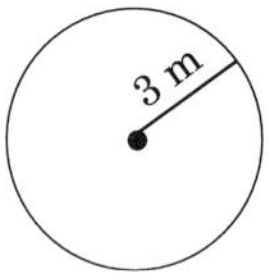

Independent Work

Part 6 For each item, make a picture of a bag based on the fraction.

a. $\frac{3}{5}$ of the things in the bag are Xs.

b. $\frac{2}{9}$ of the things in the bag are Xs.

Part 7 Figure out the missing number for each item.

a. Start with a number. Then divide by 7. Then add 15. Then you divide by 2. You end up with 10. What's the mystery number?

b. Start with a number. Then multiply by 20. Then subtract 19. You end up with 1. What's the mystery number?

Part 8 Use the table of weights and measures. For each item, make a set of equivalent fractions. Answer the question.

a. Which is more, 33 feet or 10 yards?

b. Which is more, 55 months or 5 years?

c. Which is more, 2 pounds or 32 ounces?

Part 9 Write an inequality statement to answer each question.

a. Which is more, $\frac{5}{12}$ or $\frac{4}{10}$?

b. Which is more, $\frac{13}{8}$ or $\frac{16}{12}$?

Part 10 Work each item.

a. The sale price of a phone is 60% of the regular price. If you bought a phone on sale, you would save $8. 1.) What is the regular price of the phone? 2.) What is the sale price of the phone?

b. The cost of the train fare is $\frac{7}{5}$ the cost of dinner. The train fare is $98. 1.) How much is dinner? 2.) How much more does the train fare cost than dinner costs?

c. The red truck can haul 120% the amount the yellow truck can haul. The yellow truck can haul 11 tons. 1.) How much can the red truck haul? 2.) How much more can the red truck haul than the yellow truck haul?

Part 11 **Work each item.**

a. At the beginning of the day, an automobile dealer had 56 vehicles. During the day, the dealership received a shipment of 14 cars. Later, the dealership received a shipment of 21 trucks. During the same day, the dealership sold 8 cars and 19 trucks. How many vehicles did the dealership have at the end of the day?

b. Kay's goal was to have a collection of 100 baseball cards. She has 41 old cards. She just bought 36 new cards. How many more cards does she need to reach her goal?

Part J

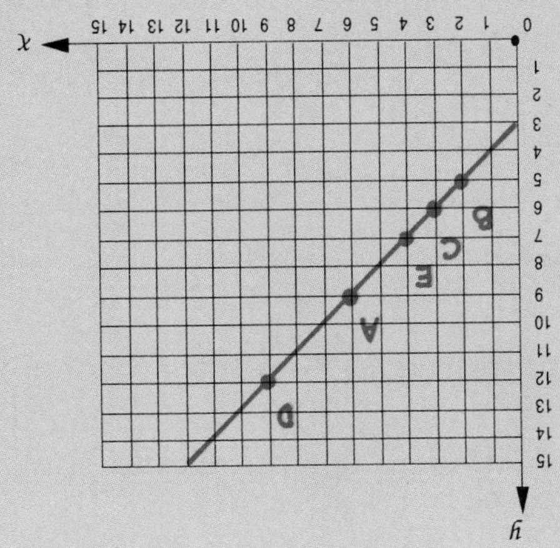

Part K

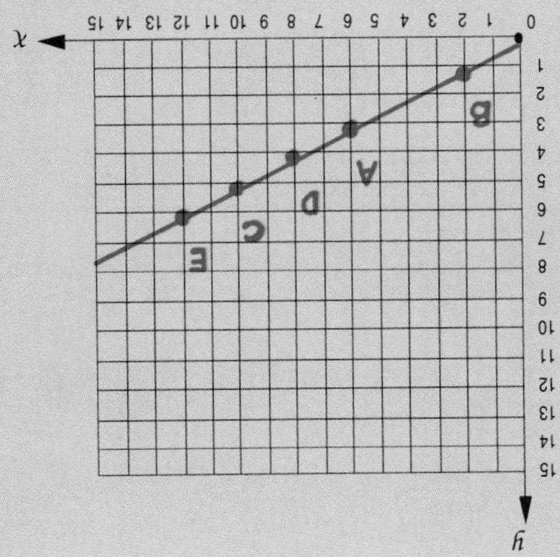

Lesson 116

Part 1

Work each division problem. Answer each question with a whole number and a unit name.

a. John will buy boards that are each 8 feet long. John needs 53 feet of wood. How many boards will John buy?

b. We need to make 5 equal-sized dog teams. We have 47 dogs. What's the largest number of dogs that can be on each team?

c. Donna wants to buy mugs that cost $3 each. She has $76 to spend. How many mugs can she buy?

Part 2

Work each item.

a. There are 5 marbles in a bag. 2 of them are red. The others are not red. How many red marbles would you expect to pull from the bag if you took 100 trials? How many marbles that are not red would you expect to pull out?

b. There are 4 marbles in a bag. 1 of them is blue. The others are not blue. If you take trials until you pull out 25 blue marbles, how many trials will you probably take? How many marbles that are not blue will you probably pull out?

Independent Work

Part 3

Use your weights and measures table. Write the equations. Answer the questions.

a. Which is more, 18 pints or 4 gallons?

b. Which is more 70 yards or 200 feet?

Part 4

Find the surface area and volume of the figure.

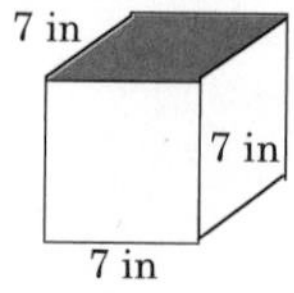

Part 5

Figure out the mystery number for each item.

a. You start with some number. Then you add 66 to the number. Then you triple the number. You end up with 198. What number did you start with?

b. You start with a number. Then you divide by 15. Then you add 200. You end up with 600. What number did you start with?

c. You start out with a number. Then you divide the number by 2. Then you subtract 98. You end up with 1. What number did you start with?

Part 6 **For each problem, make a fraction number family and a table. Answer the questions.**

a. 88% of the seeds sprouted. There were 1000 seeds. 1.) How many sprouted? 2.) How many did not sprout?

b. The regular price of gloves was 140% of the sale price. If you bought the gloves on sale you would save $6. 1.) What's the regular price? 2.) What's the sale price?

c. $\frac{3}{5}$ of the workers at Jones Factory played some type of team sport. 160 workers did not play a team sport. 1.) How many workers were in the factory? 2.) How many of them played team sports?

d. There are 8 things in a bag. 5 are Xs. You took 64 trials at pulling things from the bag. 1.) About how many Xs would you expect to pull out? 2.) About how many things that are not Xs would you expect to pull out?

Part 7 **Work each problem.**

a. Here are the heights of the basketball players on a high school team. Figure out the average height of the players.

Players	Height in Inches
Dan	72
Ed	66
J.T.	77
Mark	80
Lee	74

b. Here are the amounts of rainfall for 1990, 1991, and 1992 in River City. Figure out the average yearly rainfall for the 3-year period.

Years	Rainfall in Inches
1990	106
1991	92
1992	128

Part 8 **For each problem, make a number family and answer the question.**

a. At a store, you buy gloves for $11.50, socks for $3.75 and school supplies for $7.30. You give the clerk $30. How much change do you receive?

b. Herman's goal is to have 56 more baseball cards than he currently has. He currently has 88 minor league cards, 51 American League cards and 62 National League cards. When Herman reaches his goal, how many baseball cards will he have?

Lesson 117

Part 1 **Figure out the circumference and the area of each circle. If necessary, round your answers to hundredths.**

a. 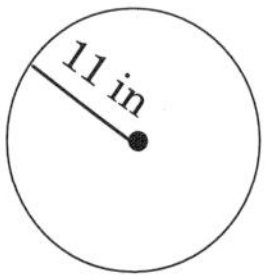

b. 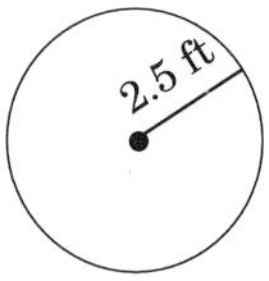

c. 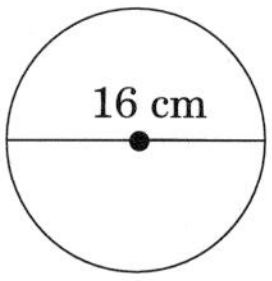

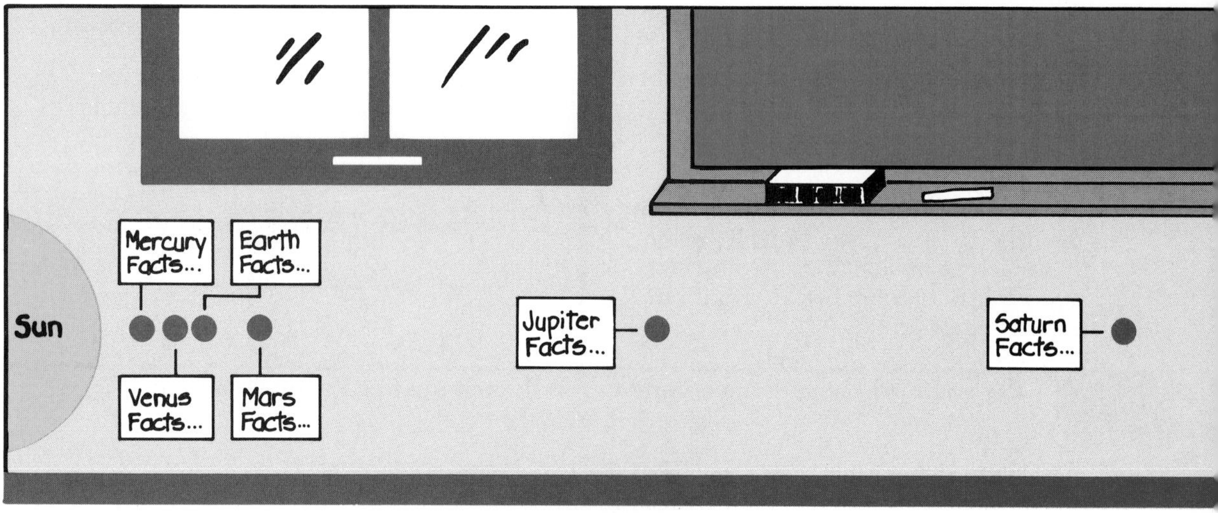

Independent Work

Part 3 **Figure out the mystery number for each item.**

a. You start out with a number. You triple the number. You add 25 to the number. You end up with 100. What number did you start out with?

b. You start with a number and divide by 50. Then you add 299. Then you double the amount. You end up with 600. What number did you start out with?

Part 4 **Figure out the answer to each question. Then write an inequality statement.**

a. Which is more, $\frac{5}{8}$ or $\frac{9}{12}$?

b. Which is more, $\frac{2}{5}$ or $\frac{9}{30}$?

Part 5 **Work each item.**

a. In Glennfork, the ratio of phones to houses is 7 to 3. There are 210 houses in Glennfork. How many phones are in these houses?

b. At Lincoln School, there were 96 students for every 3 teachers. There were 800 students in the school. How many teachers were there?

c. There are 4 things in a bag. 3 are Xs. You take trials until you pull 27 Xs from the bag. 1.) About how many trials would you expect to take? 2.) About how many things that are not Xs would you expect to pull out?

Part 2

- You're going to make a model of the sun and the planets. Your model will show the **correct proportions.** That means a planet that is twice as far from the sun in the solar system will be twice as far from the sun in your model.
- A planet that is $\frac{4}{10}$ as far from the sun in the solar system will be $\frac{4}{10}$ as far from the sun in your model.

Part 6

For each item, make a picture of a bag based on the fraction.

a. $\frac{3}{7}$ of the things in the bag are **triangles.**

b. $\frac{2}{5}$ of the things in the bag are **circles.**

Part 7

Write the fraction that tells your chance of pulling an X from each bag.

a. b. c.

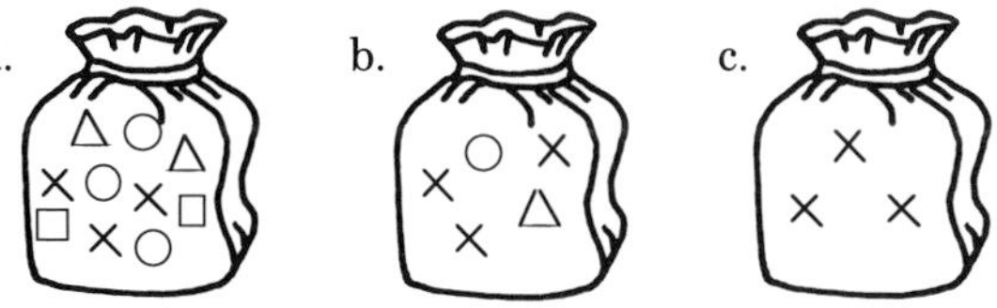

d. Which bag gives you the best chance?

e. Which bag gives you the worst chance?

Part 8

Work each item.

a. How many degrees are in $\frac{7}{9}$ of a circle?

b. If each container holds 14 ounces, how many ounces do 16 containers hold?

c. 7 identical flowers have a total of 98 petals. How many petals are on each flower?

S

d. A cake has 8 grams of fat. It is divided into 12 equal-sized pieces. How many grams of fat are in each piece?

e. If 6 containers hold 90 ounces, how many ounces do 4 containers hold?

f. What is $\frac{1}{2}$ of 196?

Lesson 118

Part 1 **Make a number family and a ratio table. Answer the question.**

a. In April, you can expect 1 sunny day for every 2 days that are not sunny. You go camping for 9 days in April. How many of those days would you expect to be sunny? How many of those days would you expect to be not sunny?

b. In a garden, there are 17 ripe tomatoes for every 6 tomatoes that are not ripe. A blindfolded person picks many tomatoes. 72 of them are not ripe. About how many total tomatoes did the person pick? About how many ripe tomatoes did the person pick?

Part 2 **Figure out the size of each angle.**

a.

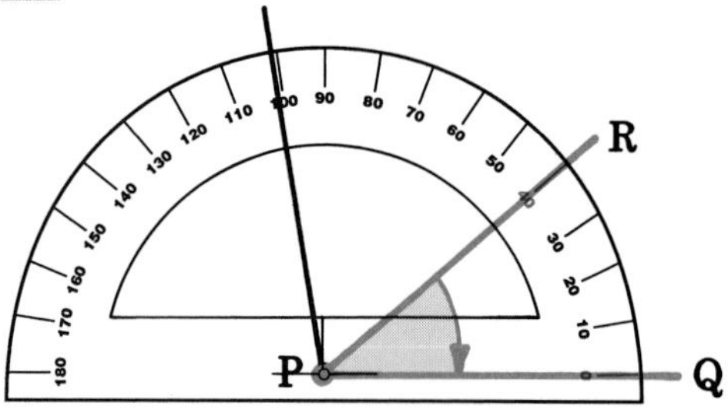

b.

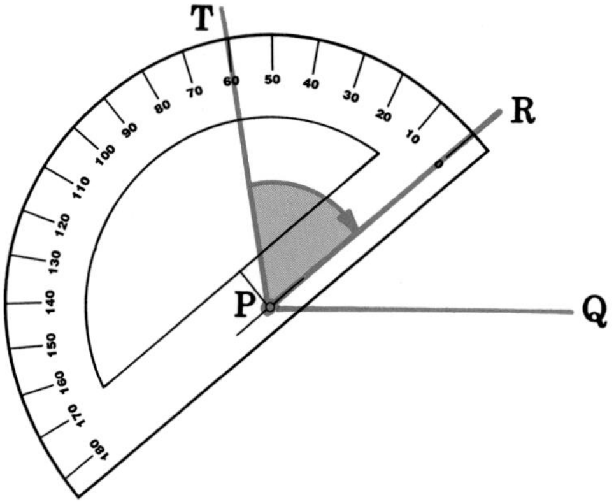

Part 3 **Use your protractor to measure each angle.**

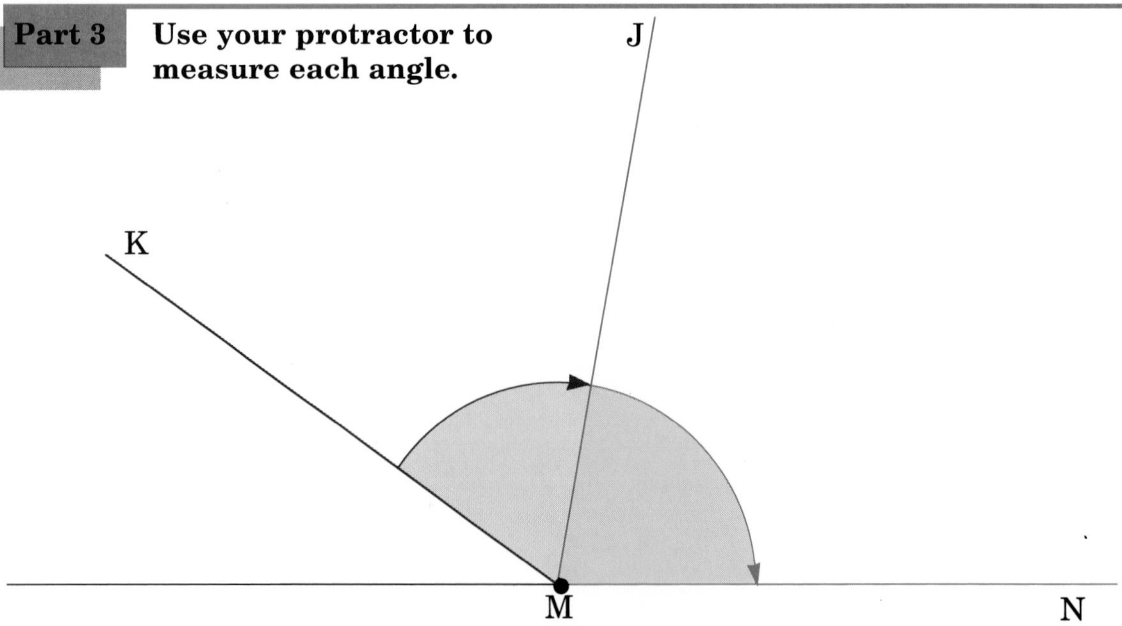

Part 4 Answer the questions your teacher asks.

a.

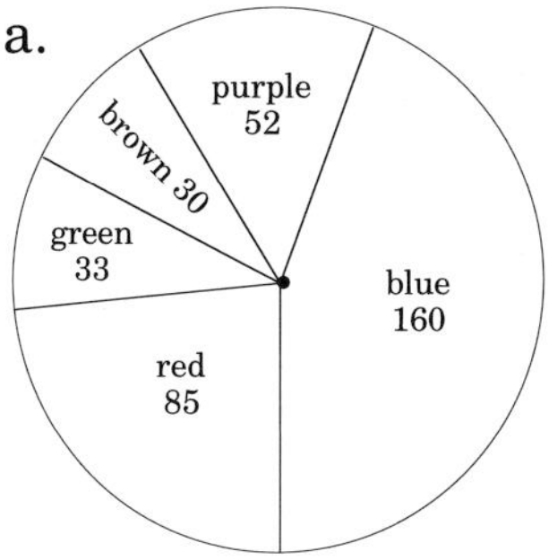

Favorite Colors

b.

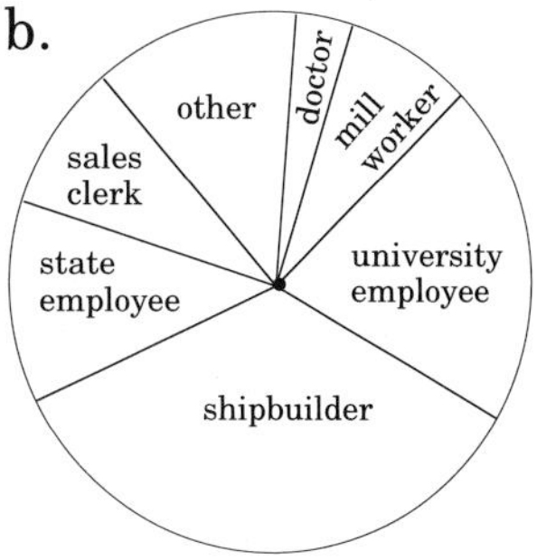

Occupations in Bay Shore Park

Independent Work

Part 5 Work each item. Write an inequality statement for each question.

a. Which is more, $\frac{2}{5}$ or $\frac{6}{15}$?

b. Which is more, $\frac{13}{4}$ or $\frac{20}{6}$?

c. Which is more, 17 cups or 32 pints?

d. Which is more, 50 cups or 12 gallons?

e. Which is more, 66 feet or 22 yards?

Part 7 For each item, make a number family and a table. Answer the questions.

a. Workers mixed sand and cement. 35% of the mixture was cement. The total mixture weighed 660 pounds. 1.) How much did the sand in the mixture weigh? 2.) How much did the cement weigh?

b. The length of the orchard was 130% the length of the barn. The barn was 45 feet shorter than the orchard. 1.) How long was the orchard? 2.) How long was the barn?

c. There are 9 things in a bag. 4 are Xs. You take trials until you pull 20 things that are not Xs from the bag. 1.) About how many trials would you expect to take? 2.) About how many Xs would you expect to pull from the bag?

Part 6 Work each item.

a. Vans are needed to transport the people to a picnic. Each van holds 8 people. 115 people are going to the picnic. How many vans are needed?

b. Construction paper is sold in pads of 12 sheets. A school project requires 100 sheets of construction paper. How many pads must be purchased for the project?

c. Basketball teams are made up of 5 players each. In an athletic program, there are 143 players. How many complete teams can be formed?

Part 8 Work each item.

a. Milly purchased socks for \$1.70, jeans for \$32.20, and sunglasses for \$11.98. She gave the cashier a check for \$50. How much change did she receive?

b. An elevator started out with 36 people in it. At the second floor, 4 more people got in. At the third floor, 21 people got in and some people got out. At the fourth floor, 5 people got in and some got out. At the top floor, the elevator had only 3 people in it. How many people got out before the top floor?

Part 9 Work each item.

a. Here are the number of people who used the tennis courts on 6 days. What was the average number of people who used the courts each day?

Days	People Using Tennis Courts
Monday	24
Tuesday	32
Wednesday	30
Thursday	28
Friday	38
Saturday	34

b. Here are the number of times a batter got on base during the months of April, May and June. What is the average number of times the player got on base each month?

Month	Times on Base
April	28
May	37
June	25

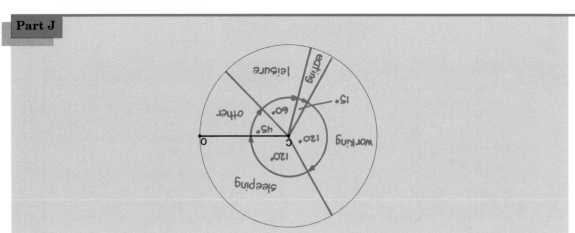

Part J

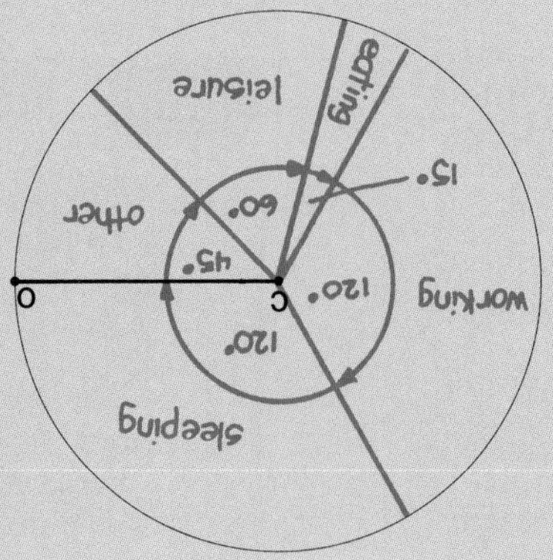

Lesson 119

Part 1 **Make a number family and a ratio table. Answer the question.**

a. Jane shoots baskets. For every 5 shots she takes, she makes 2 baskets. Her other shots are misses.
   1. If she takes 50 shots, about how many baskets would she make?
   2. How many shots would she probably miss?

b. There are 52 cards in a deck of cards. 4 of those cards are aces. A person took 13 trials at pulling cards from the deck.
   1. About how many aces would you expect the person to pull out?
   2. About how many cards that are not aces would you expect the person to pull out?

c. Another person took trials at pulling out cards until the person pulled out 6 aces.
   1. About how many trials did this person take?
   2. About how many cards that are not aces did the person pull out?

Independent Work

Part 2 **For each item, find the mystery number.**

a. You start out with a number. You divide the number by 15. You add 40. You triple the amount. You end up with 120. What number did you start out with?

b. You start out with a number. You add 50. You double the amount you have. You divide by 6. You end up with 100. What number did you start out with?

Part 3 **Draw a picture of a bag.**

a. $\frac{3}{5}$ of the things in the bag are black squares.

b. $\frac{2}{8}$ of the things in the bag are black squares.

Part 4 **Write the fractions that show your chances of pulling a black square from each bag.**

a.

b.
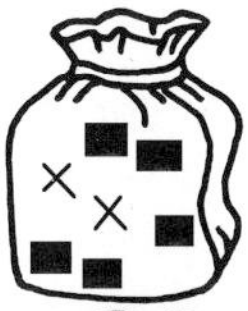

c.

d.

e. Which bag gives you the best chance?

f. Which bag gives you the worst chance?

Part 5 Work each item.

a. Bags of sand weighed different amounts. The table shows the weights for 6 bags. What was the average weight of the bags?

Bags	Pounds
1	47
2	51
3	50
4	46
5	49
6	52

b. The table shows the number of passengers in 5 different taxi cabs. Figure out the average number in each cab.

Cabs	Passengers
A	4
B	2
C	0
D	1
E	3

Part 6 Work each problem. Answer the question.

a. Each pair of shoes needs 2 shoelaces. How many complete pairs of shoes could be laced up with 345 shoelaces?

b. The tiles that John needs to cover his kitchen floor come in cartons of 24 tiles. John will need 210 tiles. How many cartons of tiles should he buy?

c. For the training course, runners rest every 7 miles. The training course is 46 miles long. How many times do the runners rest?

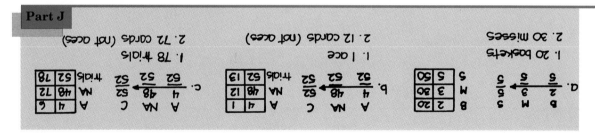

Part J

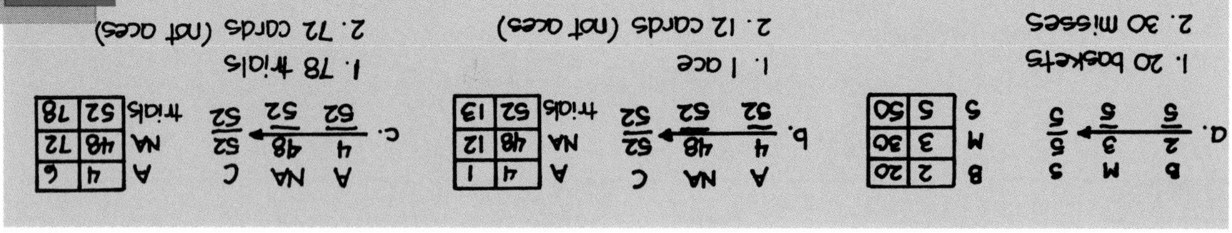

Test 12

Part 1 **Figure out the correct function. Copy and complete the table.**

x	Function $x \div 2$ or $x - 5$	y
10	[redacted]	5
18	[redacted]	9
6	[redacted]	[redacted]
2	[redacted]	[redacted]
12	[redacted]	[redacted]

Part 2 **Work each division problem, and answer the question.**

a. Mr. Franklin needs enough paint to cover his patio. The patio is 780 square feet. If one pint of paint covers 90 square feet, how many pints must Mr. Franklin buy to complete the work?

b. Donna has $200 to spend on rose bushes. If each bush costs $12, how many bushes can she buy?

Part 3 **Work each item. Write a statement (<, >, =).**

a. Which is more, $\frac{3}{8}$ or $\frac{5}{12}$?

b. Which is more, $\frac{6}{10}$ or $\frac{2}{5}$?

c. Which is more, $\frac{8}{16}$ or $\frac{3}{6}$?

Part 4 **Find the mystery number for each item.**

a. You start out with some number. You triple the number. Then you subtract 200. You end up with 1. What number did you start with?

b. You start with a number. You divide by 10. You multiply by 7. Then you subtract 2. You end up with 54. What number did you start with?

Part 5 **Write the fractions that show your chances of pulling a circle from each bag.**

a. 

b. 

c. 

d. Which bag gives you the worst chance?

e. Which bag gives you the best chance?

Part 6 Work each item.

a. Train A is 10% longer than train B. Train A is 550 yards long. 1.) How long is train B? 2.) How much shorter is train B than train A?

b. 15% of the flowers in Mrs. Anderson's garden were pink. 170 of her flowers were not pink. 1.) How many pink flowers did she have? 2.) How many flowers did she have in all?

c. The sale price of skis was 80% of the regular price. By purchasing skis on sale, you'd save $18. 1.) What was the regular price of skis? 2.) What was the sale price?

Part 7 Work the item.

a. Each day, the wildlife refuge at Glenn's Point captured birds, put rings on the legs, and then let them go. The table shows the number of birds the refuge ringed on five days.

Days	Birds Ringed
Thursday	152
Friday	91
Saturday	208
Sunday	0
Monday	84

Figure out the average number of birds ringed each day.

Part 8 Work the item.

a. There are 6 marbles in a bag. 5 of those marbles are blue. You take 48 trials, replacing the marble in the bag after each trial.

1.) On how many of those trials would you expect to pull out a blue marble?

2.) On how many of those trials would you expect to pull out a marble that is not blue?

Part 9 Work each item. Round answers to two decimal places.

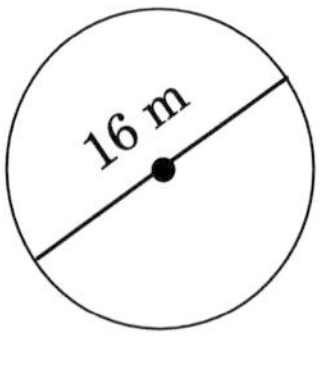

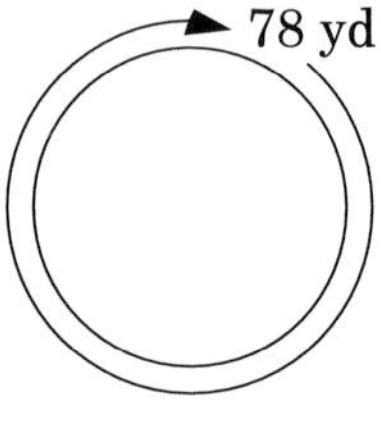

a. What's the circumference?

b. What's the area?

c. What's the radius?

Lesson 121

Part 1

- You've worked with problems that tell about 1 and ask about more than 1. You solve those problems by multiplying.
- Here's a problem you solve by multiplying:

> **A machine produces 16 boxes in 1 minute. How many boxes will the machine produce in 60 minutes?**

- You can solve the problem by multiplying because it tells about **1 minute** and gives another number for **minutes.** That number is **60.**

$$\begin{array}{r} \textbf{16} \\ \underline{\textbf{x 60}} \\ \boxed{\textbf{960 boxes}} \end{array}$$

- If the problem does not give **two numbers** for **minutes,** you cannot solve the problem by multiplying.
- Here's a problem you **cannot** solve by multiplying:

> **A machine produces 16 boxes in 1 minute. How many minutes will it take the machine to produce 60 boxes?**

- That's a ratio problem:

$$\frac{\textbf{boxes}}{\textbf{minutes}} \; \frac{16}{1}\left(\blacksquare\right) = \frac{60}{\blacksquare}$$

Part 2 Figure out whether you can solve each problem by multiplying.

a. A machine produces 16 boxes in 1 minute. How many minutes will it take the machine to produce 60 boxes?

b. A machine produces 16 boxes in 1 minute. How many boxes will the machine produce in 13 minutes?

c. A plane is traveling at the rate of 6 miles per minute. How many minutes will it take the plane to travel 400 miles?

Part 3 For each item, write answers to each question and work the problem.

If the problem tells about 1, you can find the name for 1. Then see if the problem gives another number for that name. If it does, you can solve the problem by multiplying. Otherwise, it's a ratio problem.

a. A conveyor belt moves 4 cans of fish in 1 second. How many cans of fish does the belt move in 20 seconds? (1.) What's the name for 1? (2.) Does the problem give another number for that name? (3.) Can you solve the problem by multiplying?

b. Alan saves $17 each week. How many weeks will it take Alan to save $51? (1.) What's the name for 1? (2.) Does the problem give another number for that name? (3.) Can you solve the problem by multiplying?

c. Each day, a mail carrier delivers 200 packages. How many packages does the carrier deliver in 5 days? (1.) What's the name for 1? (2.) Does the problem give another number for that name? (3.) Can you solve the problem by multiplying?

d. Billy earns $12 per hour. He earned $84. How many hours did he work? (1.) What's the name for 1? (2.) Does the problem give another number for that name? (3.) Can you solve the problem by multiplying?

Independent Work

Part 4 Figure out the mystery number for each item.

a. You start with a number and multiply by 9. Then you subtract 54. Then you divide by 3. You end up with 27. What number did you start with?

b. You start with a number and multiply by 6. Then you subtract 30. Then you add 2. You end up with 668. What number did you start with?

Part 5 Make a table. Answer the questions.

There were trucks and cars on a lot. The lots were A-1 and B-B. The total cars for both lots was 137. On A-1 there were 59 trucks. The total number of vehicles on B-B was 173. The total number of vehicles for both lots was 344.

a. How many trucks were on B-B lot?

b. How many cars were on A-1 lot?

c. What was the total number of trucks on both the lots?

d. Which lot had more trucks?

Part 6 Write whether each unit could be for the perimeter, area, or volume of a figure.

a. 78 meters
b. 12 cubic yards
c. 9 square feet
d. 47 feet

Part 7 Work each item.

a. Each carton holds 14 ounces. How many ounces do 11 cartons hold?

b. 10 pizzas cost $122. How much do 3 pizzas cost? (Write your answers as dollars and cents.)

c. A plot is 120 acres. It is divided into 6 equal-size plots. How many acres are in each plot?

d. 14 picture frames cost $36. How much does each frame cost?

Part 8 Work each item.

a. There are 26 students in Mrs. Brown's classroom. Each name is written on a slip of paper and placed in a bag. Somebody takes trials at drawing names from the bag until they have pulled the name Anthony Briggs from the bag 3 times. 1.) About how many trials would you expect the person to take? 2.) About how many times would you expect the person to draw a slip of paper that did not have the name Anthony Briggs on it?

b. The people working in an office are either secretaries or supervisors. The ratio of secretaries to supervisors is 10 to 3. You select the names of 52 people who work in the office. 1.) About how many of these people would you expect to be supervisors? 2.) About how many would you expect to be secretaries?

Part 9 Work each item.

a. If a machine can make 5 buttons in 11 seconds, how many seconds will it take the machine to make 30 buttons?

b. The ratio of dogs to cats at an animal hospital was 6 to 7. If there were 54 dogs, how many cats were there?

c. Figure out the average high temperature.

Day	High Temperature
Monday	57°
Tuesday	38°
Wednesday	46°
Thursday	44°

Part 10 Find the perimeter and area of each figure.

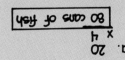

a.

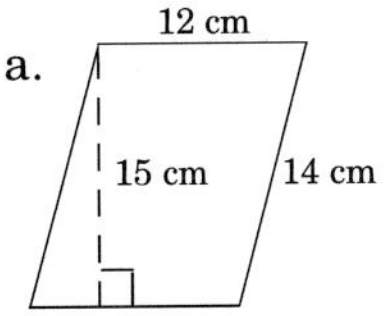

b.

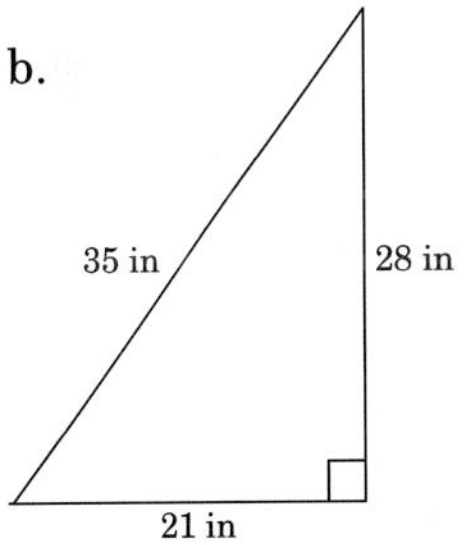

Part J

a. 20 × 4 = 80 cans of fish

b. $\frac{\$}{\text{weeks}}$ $\frac{17}{1}\left(\frac{51}{17}\right) = \frac{51}{17}$ 3 weeks

c. 200 × 5 = 1000 packages

d. $\frac{\$}{\text{hours}}$ $\frac{12}{1}\left(\frac{84}{12}\right) = \frac{84}{12}$ 7 hours

Lesson 122

Part 1

- Two box designers wanted to make efficient cubic containers. An efficient container would have a large volume compared to the surface area. You'd use less material to make the box, compared to the amount the box could hold.
- An inefficient container would have a small volume compared to the surface area.
- Box designer Al said, "Boxes that are smaller are more efficient."

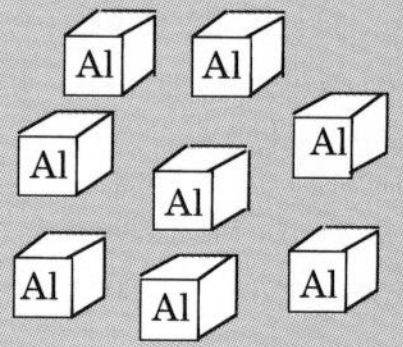

- Box designer Jean said, "No, boxes that are bigger are more efficient."

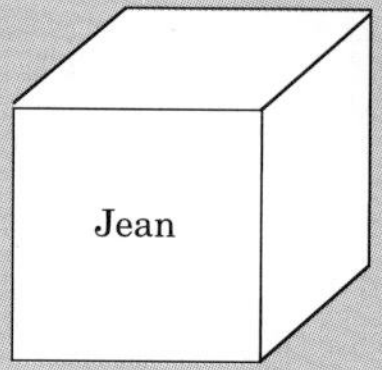

- Both designers finally agreed to settle their argument. Each made a box in the shape of a cube.
- Each designer figured out how much the box would hold and figured out the surface area of the box.
- Designer Al made a box that was 2 feet on each edge.

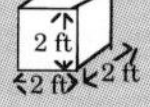

- Designer Jean made a box that was 10 feet on each edge.
- Then they figured out who had the best ratio for the volume of the box compared to the surface area.

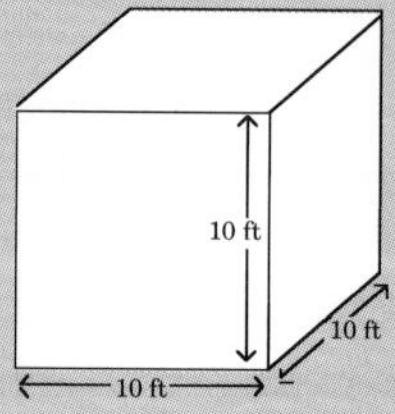

- Here's the ratio each designer used:
- The fraction that is larger is the most efficient because it gives more volume compared to the surface area.

$$\frac{\textbf{volume of cube}}{\textbf{surface area of cube}}$$

Part 2

- You've figured out that with a smaller cube, the number for the volume is less than the number for the surface area.
- With a larger cube, the number for the volume is more than the number for the surface area.
- For a cube with an edge of a certain length, the numbers are the same. The number for volume is the same as the number for surface area.
- Here are two edge lengths a person tried:

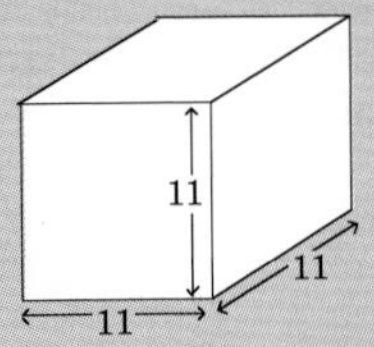

Volume number = 1331
Surface area number = 726
Difference number = 605

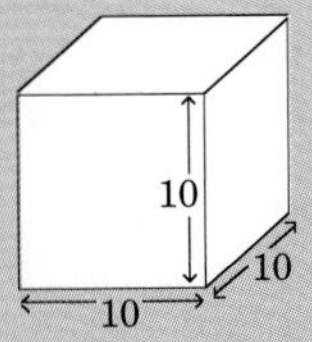

Volume number = 1000
Surface area number = 600
Difference number = 400

- The cube with an edge of 10 has a smaller difference. That means that an edge of 9 will give a difference that is even smaller. So the mystery edge is 9 or less than 9.
- You know that the mystery edge is more than 2, because when it **is** 2, the volume number is less than the surface area number. Remember Designer Al's cube? The number for volume is **8,** but the number for the surface area is 24.
- Somewhere between 9 and 2 is the mystery edge number.

Part 3 **First work each problem you can figure out by multiplying. Then work the other problems.**

a. 1 box holds 4 toys. How many toys do 15 boxes hold?
b. 1 box holds 4 toys. How many boxes are needed for 36 toys?
c. Each liter of material weighs 17 grams. How many liters of material weigh 200 grams?
d. Each liter of material weighs 17 grams. How many grams do 12 liters weigh?
e. If 1 bottle holds 9 ounces, how many ounces do 16 bottles hold?
f. If 1 bottle holds 9 ounces, how many bottles hold 144 ounces?

Independent Work

Part 4 **See part 2 of your textbook. Figure out the mystery edge of a cube. That's the edge length that gives the same number for the volume and surface area.**

Part 5 **Make a ratio equation and answer each question.**

a. If 4 buses have 88 seats, how many seats do 5 buses have?

b. A truck travels at the steady rate of 450 miles in 9 hours. How many miles does the truck travel in 1 hour?

Part 6 **Write whether each unit could be for the perimeter, area, or volume of a figure.**

a. 56 sq cm b. 80 m c. 48 sq in d. 9 cu yd

Part 7 **Figure out the mystery number for each item.**

a. You start with some number. You triple the number. Then you subtract 100. You end up with 1265. What number did you start with?

b. You start with some number. You divide by 14. Then you add 200. Then you double the number. You end up with 624. What number did you start with?

Part 8 **Find the area and perimeter of each figure.**

a.

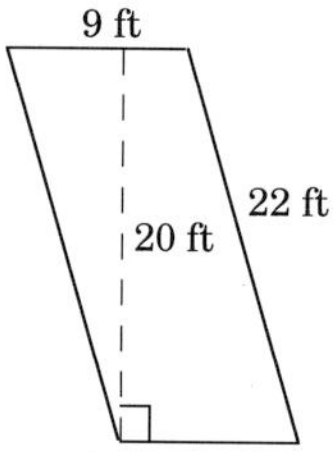

b.

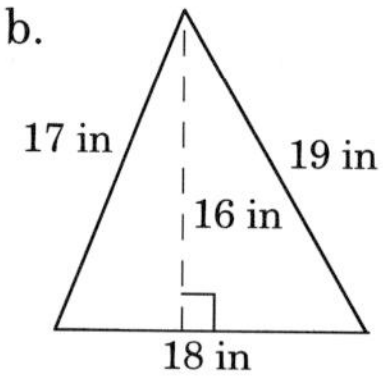

Part 9 **Start with the equation that has the symbol π. Work each item. Round your answers to hundredths.**

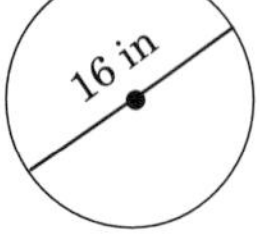

a. What is the circumference? What is the area?

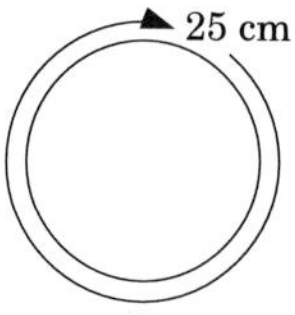

b. What is the diameter? What is the area?

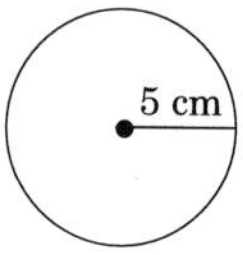

c. What is the circumference? What is the area?

Part 10 **Make a table. Answer the questions.**

There were children and adults at two picnics. The picnics were held at Grant's Park and View Park. The total number of children at the picnics was 254. There were 82 adults at the View Park picnic. There were 99 children at the Grant's Park picnic. The total number of people at the Grant's Park picnic was 176.

a. How many people were there at both picnics?

b. How many children were at the View Park picnic?

c. How many adults were at the Grant's Park picnic?

d. Which picnic had more children?

Part 11 **For each item, write the equivalent fraction and answer the questions.**

a. Which is more, 4 pounds or 130 ounces?

b. Which is more, 135 inches or 12 feet?

Lesson 123

Part 1 Copy and work each item.

Sample problem

$5\overline{)\dot{.}305}$

a. $7\overline{).455}$

b. $8\overline{)12.48}$

c. $4\overline{)6.00}$

d. $2\overline{)24.046}$

Part 2 Work each problem.

a. A car is traveling at the rate of 18 feet per second. How many seconds will it take for the car to travel 90 feet?

b. A car is traveling at the rate of 18 feet per second. How many feet will the car travel in 200 seconds?

c. If a machine makes garments at the rate of 4 garments in 1 minute, how many garments will the machine make in 30 minutes?

d. If a machine makes garments at the rate of 4 garments in 1 minute, how many minutes will it take for the machine to make 11 garments?

Part 3

- When you do experiments that involve probability, you don't often get the exact number you'd expect, but you get close to that number.
- Let's say there's a bag with 6 things in it. And let's say you'll take 42 trials and record how many times you pull an X from the bag.
- The more Xs there are in the bag, the more Xs you'd expect to pull out.

Part 4

- The ratio equations show the number of Xs you'd expect to pull out of different bags:

	Bag		Expected Xs for 42 trials
a.		$\frac{Xs}{total}\ \frac{0}{6}$	$= \frac{0}{42}$
b.		$\frac{Xs}{total}\ \frac{1}{6}$	$= \frac{7}{42}$
c.		$\frac{Xs}{total}\ \frac{2}{6}$	$= \frac{14}{42}$
d.		$\frac{Xs}{total}\ \frac{3}{6}$	$= \frac{21}{42}$
e.		$\frac{Xs}{total}\ \frac{4}{6}$	$= \frac{28}{42}$
f.		$\frac{Xs}{total}\ \frac{5}{6}$	$= \frac{35}{42}$
g.		$\frac{Xs}{total}\ \frac{6}{6}$	$= \frac{42}{42}$

Part 5 **Work each item.**

a. You take 42 trials, and you pull out 12 Xs.
   1. Which expected fraction is closest?
   2. Which bag did you use?

b. You take 42 trials, and you pull out 24 Xs.
   1. Which expected fraction is closest?
   2. Which bag did you use?

c. You take 42 trials, and you pull out 38 Xs.
   1. Which expected fraction is closest?
   2. Which bag did you use?

d. You take 42 trials, and you pull out 30 Xs.
   1. Which expected fraction is closest?
   2. Which bag did you use?

Independent Work

Part 6 **Make a table. Answer the questions.**

Two nurseries raised evergreen trees and deciduous trees. The nurseries were Moss Point Nursery and Clement Nursery. The total number of trees for both nurseries was 2674. The total number of trees at Moss Point Nursery was 1184. Clement Nursery had 700 deciduous trees. Moss Point Nursery had 200 fewer deciduous trees than Clement Nursery had.

a. What was the total number of deciduous trees for both nurseries?

b. What was the total number of evergreen trees?

c. Were there more evergreens or deciduous trees at Clement Nursery?

d. How many total trees did Clement Nursery have?

Part 7 **Work each item.**

a. The ratio of fish to waterbugs in a pond is 2 to 17. If there are 119 waterbugs in the pond, how many fish are there?

b. The ratio for the height of the triangle to the width of the triangle is 7 to 5. If the triangle is 46 units wide, how high is the triangle?

c. Figure out the average height of the dogs.

Dogs	Height in Inches
Rover	24
Spot	11
Ed	16
Herman	19
King	10

d. Some of the flowers had a ladybug on them. The ratio of flowers to ladybugs was 30 to 10. 1.) If you looked at 360 flowers, about how many ladybugs would you expect to find? 2.) About how many flowers would not have a ladybug on them?

Part 8 **Write whether each unit could be for the perimeter, area, or volume of a figure.**

a. 12 cu in　　b. 17 in　　c. 903 cu in　　d. 86 sq mi

Part J

a. $\frac{\text{feet}}{\text{seconds}} \quad \frac{18}{1}\left(\frac{\frac{90}{18}}{\frac{90}{18}}\right) = \frac{90}{\frac{90}{18}}$ 5 seconds

b. 200×18: 1600 + 2000 = 3600 feet

c. 30×4 = 120 garments

d. $\frac{\text{garments}}{\text{minutes}} \quad \frac{4}{1}\left(\frac{\frac{11}{4}}{\frac{11}{4}}\right) = \frac{11}{\frac{11}{4}}$ $2\frac{3}{4}$ minutes

Lesson 124

Part 1 **For each item, figure out the mystery number. Then answer the question.**

a. Jan had some money. She spent $41 on presents. She received $15 dollars from her parents. She doubled the amount of money she had by selling her stereo. She ended up with $200. How much did she start out with?

b. There was a gravel pile. Several truckloads of gravel were added to the pile to make the pile 3 times its original size. Then 200 tons of gravel were removed from the pile. Later, 49 tons were added to the pile. The pile now weighs 566 tons. How many tons were in the pile to begin with?

Part 2 **Work each item.**

Sample problem

If a person earns $10.60 in 4 hours, how much does the person earn each hour?

a. 9 buttons cost $.36. What does each button cost?

b. 8 nights at the campground cost $200.00. What is the cost per night?

c. If the total cost of 3 identical tents is $120.60, what does 1 tent cost?

Part 3

- Here's a problem that seems hard:

  Which of these two bags gives you the better chance of pulling out a circle?

$\frac{4}{6}$

$\frac{3}{4}$

- You know how to compare fractions. You rewrite them with a common denominator.

$$\frac{4}{6}\left(\frac{2}{2}\right) = \frac{8}{12}$$

- The bag in which $\frac{3}{4}$ of the objects are circles gives you the better chance.

$$\frac{3}{4}\left(\frac{3}{3}\right) = \frac{9}{12}$$

Part 4 Work each item.

a. In factory R, $\frac{3}{8}$ of the workers are women. In factory P, $\frac{2}{3}$ of the workers are women. In one factory, the chances are better that the first worker you meet will be a woman. Which factory is that?

b. In plot M, there are 3 doves for every 7 acres. In plot J, there are 2 doves for every 5 acres. At one of the plots, you'd have a better chance of seeing a dove. Which plot is that?

c. At Tiger Bend, 4 of every 10 spring days are sunny. At Moss Peak, $\frac{3}{8}$ of the days in the spring are sunny. Where would you go to stay if you wanted more sunny days?

Part 5

- If a square is very small, the number for the perimeter is larger than the number for the area.
- If the square is much larger, the number for the perimeter is smaller than the number for the area.

- Here's a square with sides that are 1 inch long:
- The number for the perimeter is 4, but the number for the area is only 1.

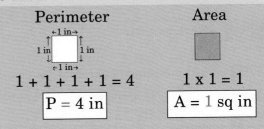

Perimeter

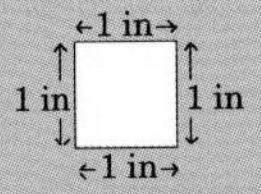

1 + 1 + 1 + 1 = 4

P = 4 in

Area

1 x 1 = 1

A = 1 sq in

- Here's a square with sides that are 10 inches long:
- The number for the perimeter is 40, but the number for the area is much larger than 40.

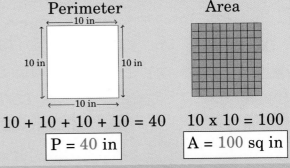

Perimeter

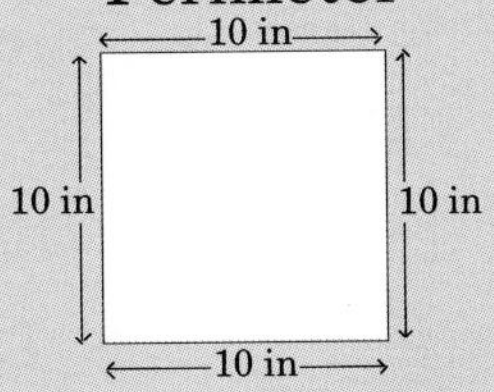

10 + 10 + 10 + 10 = 40

P = 40 in

Area

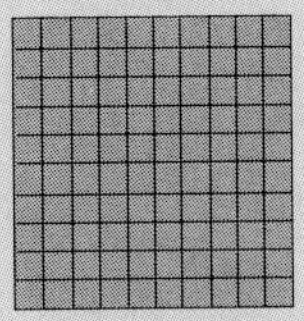

10 x 10 = 100

A = 100 sq in

- When the side of a square is a particular length, the number for the perimeter and the area are the same.
- Hint: When you find the correct edge length, you work the same problem for the perimeter and for the area.

Independent Work

Remember to complete the problems for part 1 of your textbook.

Part 6 **For each item, make a ratio equation and answer the questions.**

a. If 5 cartons hold 12 pounds, how many pounds do 4 cartons hold?

b. If each carton holds 16 ounces, how many ounces do 20 cartons hold?

c. If each carton holds 16 ounces, how many cartons are needed to hold 400 ounces?

Part 7 **Work each item.**

a. Which is more, 14 gallons or 56 quarts?

b. Which is more, 540 inches or 14 yards?

Part 8 **Make a table. Answer the questions.**

In February, the emergency rooms at Mercy Hospital and Hope Hospital treated patients. Some patients had serious injuries and others were not serious. At Mercy Hospital, 314 of the patients were not seriously injured. At Hope Hospital, 481 were seriously injured. The total number of patients treated at Mercy's emergency room was 491. The total number of patients treated at Hope was 150 more than the number treated at Mercy.

a. How many total patients were treated at Hope?

b. What was the total number of patients treated at both hospitals?

c. How many patients that were not seriously injured were treated at Hope?

d. Which hospital treated more patients that were seriously injured?

Part 9 **Work each item.**

a. 7 identical blocks weigh 44 pounds. How much do 6 blocks weigh?

b. 250 identical newspapers had 1000 pages. How many newspapers are needed for 1750 pages?

Lesson 125

Part 1 **For each item, figure out the mystery number. Then answer the question.**

a. John said, "If I add 3 to my age and then triple that amount, I end up with the number 57. How old am I?"

b. If you subtract 6 from my dog's age, then double the number, you get 18. How old is my dog?

c. A mail truck started out with bags of letters. The **number** of bags was divided by 4 when the truck delivered mail to the houses on Elm Street. At the end of the street, the truck picked up 6 bags. At the end of the next street the truck picked up another 14 bags. The truck ended up with 27 bags. How many bags did the truck start out with?

Independent Work

Part 2 **Copy and work each item.**

a. $29\overline{)560}$

b. $29\overline{)2006}$

c. $51\overline{)766}$

d. $\begin{array}{r} 150 \\ \underline{\text{x } .37} \end{array}$

e. $\begin{array}{r} 20.30 \\ \underline{\text{x } \quad .6} \end{array}$

Part 3 **Start with the equation that has the symbol π. Work each item. Round your answers to hundredths.**

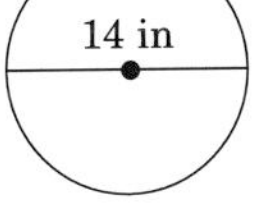

a. What is the circumference?
What is the area?

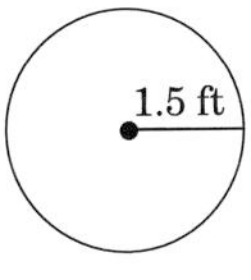

b. What is the diameter?
What is the circumference?
What is the area?

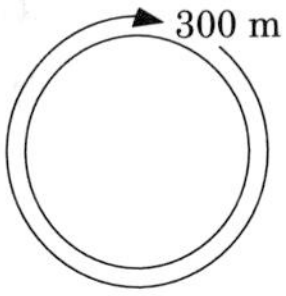

c. What is the diameter?
What is the radius?

Part 4 **Simplify each fraction and write the complete equation. Show your answer as a mixed number.**

a. $\frac{120}{100} = ■$

b. $\frac{32}{56} = ■$

Part 5 **For each item, write the equivalent fractions and answer the question.**

a. Which is more, 4 years or 46 months?

b. Which is more, 16 yards or 47 feet?

Part 6 **Find the area and perimeter of each figure.**

a. 

b. 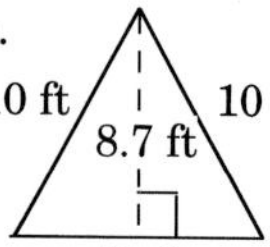

Part 7 **Work the item.**

S

Figure out the average number of chin-ups this group of people is able to do.

People	Chin-ups
Ms. Smith	3
Mr. Jones	0
Mr. Tony	5
Slim	21
George	2
Amy	1

Part 8 **Make a table. Answer the questions.**

James and Rita collected baseball cards and football cards. James had a total of 260 cards. Rita had 30 football cards. James had 110 more football cards than Rita had. Together both children had 501 baseball cards.

a. Who had more baseball cards?

b. How many baseball cards did James have?

c. How many football cards did the children have together?

d. What was the total number of cards the children had together?

31 Textbook

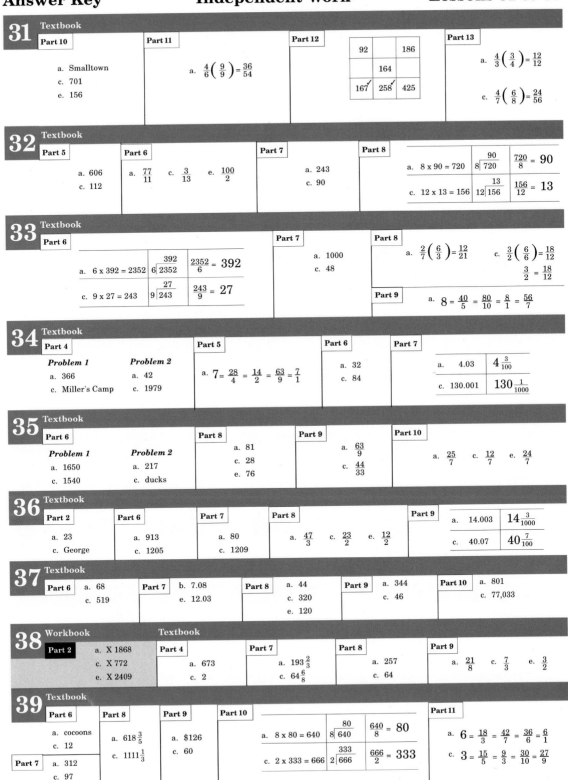

Part 10
a. Smalltown
c. 701
e. 156

Part 11
a. $\frac{4}{6}\left(\frac{9}{9}\right) = \frac{36}{54}$

Part 12

92		186
	164	
167✓	258✓	425

Part 13
a. $\frac{4}{3}\left(\frac{3}{4}\right) = \frac{12}{12}$
c. $\frac{4}{7}\left(\frac{6}{8}\right) = \frac{24}{56}$

32 Textbook

Part 5
a. 606
c. 112

Part 6
a. $\frac{77}{11}$ c. $\frac{3}{13}$ e. $\frac{100}{2}$

Part 7
a. 243
c. 90

Part 8

a. 8 x 90 = 720	$8\overline{)720}$ = 90	$\frac{720}{8} = 90$
c. 12 x 13 = 156	$12\overline{)156}$ = 13	$\frac{156}{12} = 13$

33 Textbook

Part 6

a. 6 x 392 = 2352	$6\overline{)2352}$ = 392	$\frac{2352}{6} = 392$
c. 9 x 27 = 243	$9\overline{)243}$ = 27	$\frac{243}{9} = 27$

Part 7
a. 1000
c. 48

Part 8
a. $\frac{2}{7}\left(\frac{6}{3}\right) = \frac{12}{21}$
c. $\frac{3}{2}\left(\frac{6}{6}\right) = \frac{18}{12}$
$\frac{3}{2} = \frac{18}{12}$

Part 9
a. $8 = \frac{40}{5} = \frac{80}{10} = \frac{8}{1} = \frac{56}{7}$

34 Textbook

Part 4

Problem 1
a. 366
c. Miller's Camp

Problem 2
a. 42
c. 1979

Part 5
a. $7 = \frac{28}{4} = \frac{14}{2} = \frac{63}{9} = \frac{7}{1}$

Part 6
a. 32
c. 84

Part 7

a. 4.03	$4\frac{3}{100}$
c. 130.001	$130\frac{1}{1000}$

35 Textbook

Part 6

Problem 1
a. 1650
c. 1540

Problem 2
a. 217
c. ducks

Part 8
a. 81
c. 28
e. 76

Part 9
a. $\frac{63}{9}$
c. $\frac{44}{33}$

Part 10
a. $\frac{25}{7}$ c. $\frac{12}{7}$ e. $\frac{24}{7}$

36 Textbook

Part 2
a. 23
c. George

Part 6
a. 913
c. 1205

Part 7
a. 80
c. 1209

Part 8
a. $\frac{47}{3}$ c. $\frac{23}{2}$ e. $\frac{12}{2}$

Part 9

a. 14.003	$14\frac{3}{1000}$
c. 40.07	$40\frac{7}{100}$

37 Textbook

Part 6
a. 68
c. 519

Part 7
b. 7.08
e. 12.03

Part 8
a. 44
c. 320
e. 120

Part 9
a. 344
c. 46

Part 10
a. 801
c. 77,033

38 Workbook

Part 2
a. X 1868
c. X 772
e. X 2409

Textbook

Part 4
a. 673
c. 2

Part 7
a. $193\frac{2}{3}$
c. $64\frac{6}{8}$

Part 8
a. 257
c. 64

Part 9
a. $\frac{21}{8}$ c. $\frac{7}{3}$ e. $\frac{3}{2}$

39 Textbook

Part 6
a. cocoons
c. 12

Part 7
a. 312
c. 97

Part 8
a. $618\frac{3}{5}$
c. $1111\frac{1}{3}$

Part 9
a. $126
c. 60

Part 10

a. 8 x 80 = 640	$8\overline{)640}$ = 80	$\frac{640}{8} = 80$
c. 2 x 333 = 666	$2\overline{)666}$ = 333	$\frac{666}{2} = 333$

Part 11
a. $6 = \frac{18}{3} = \frac{42}{7} = \frac{36}{6} = \frac{6}{1}$
c. $3 = \frac{15}{5} = \frac{9}{3} = \frac{30}{10} = \frac{27}{9}$

41 Textbook

Part 9

a. 53

Part 10

a. $5 = \frac{15}{3} = \frac{100}{20} = \frac{55}{11} = \frac{5}{1}$

Part 11

a. Kellys' wedding
c. 200 red roses

Part 12

a. $5\frac{3}{7}$ c. $9\frac{6}{7}$ e. $9\frac{7}{8}$

42 Textbook

Part 6

a. $\frac{4}{1} \times \frac{7}{8} = \frac{28}{8}$ ($\frac{4}{1}$ circled)
c. $\frac{1}{8} \times \frac{1}{8} = \frac{1}{64}$ (first $\frac{1}{8}$ circled)
e. $\frac{1}{8} \times \frac{12}{1} = \frac{12}{8}$ ($\frac{12}{8}$ circled)

Part 7

a. 14

Part 8

a. 4 x 15 = 60	$4\overline{)60}$ with quotient 15	$\frac{60}{4} = 15$

Part 9

a. 16 elm trees
c. 2800 gallons
e. 58 gallons

43 Textbook

Part 6

a. 128 drummers
c. Flint Town band

Part 7

a. 2.75
c. 2.25

Part 8

a. $638
c. 54 daisies

Part 9

a. $7\frac{2}{5}$ c. $4\frac{4}{5}$
e. $9\frac{1}{4}$ g. 6

Part 10

a. $10 = \frac{30}{3} = \frac{100}{10} = \frac{80}{8} = \frac{250}{25}$

44 Textbook

Part 5

a. 27 minutes
c. 165 miles per hour
e. 220 tapes

Part 6

a. $148\frac{2}{5}$
c. $36\frac{1}{9}$
e. $54\frac{5}{6}$

Part 7

a. $\frac{10}{18}$ c. $\frac{9}{9}$ e. $\frac{60}{81}$

Part 8

a. $2\frac{5}{6}$ c. $2\frac{1}{3}$

45 Textbook

Part 6

a. $6\frac{3}{10}$	6.3	$\frac{63}{10}$
c. $2\frac{5}{100}$	2.05	$\frac{205}{100}$

Part 7

a. 3 x 2 x **2 x 2 x 2** = 48
c. **2 x 7 x 2 x 2** = 56

Part 8

a. $\frac{95}{20}$ c. $\frac{105}{2}$

Part 9

a. $67.35
c. 6690 pounds

Part 10

a. $\frac{3}{4}\left(\frac{4}{5}\right) = \frac{12}{20}$
c. $\frac{5}{8}\left(\frac{4}{4}\right) = \frac{20}{32}$
$\frac{5}{8} = \frac{20}{32}$

46 Textbook

Part 5

a. $\frac{2}{3}\left(\frac{4}{4}\right) = \frac{8}{12}$
$\frac{2}{3} = \frac{8}{12}$
c. $\frac{2}{11}\left(\frac{4}{3}\right) = \frac{8}{33}$

Part 6

a. $1\frac{7}{12}$	$\frac{19}{12}$
c. $3\frac{3}{7}$	$\frac{24}{7}$

Part 7

a. 105 gallons
c. 7 boxes

Part 8

a. $\frac{7}{5}$
c. $\frac{4}{9}$
e. $\frac{13}{12}$

Part 9

a. 2165 pounds
c. 60 degrees

Part 10

a. $97\frac{1}{5}$ c. 53

47 Textbook

Part 6

a. 5.4
c. 6.8

Part 7

a. 36 = 2 x 2 x 3 x 3
c. 90 = 2 x 3 x 3 x 5
e. 20 = 2 x 2 x 5

Part 8

a. 122 students
c. 57 apple trees
e. 337 passengers

Part 9

a. 190 c. $118\frac{2}{5}$ e. 106

48 Textbook

Part 6

a. 64 fish
c. October

Part 7

a. .75
d. .003

Part 8

a. 193
c. $161\frac{1}{5}$

Part 9

a. $\frac{10}{12}$
c. $\frac{35}{36}$

Part 10

a. $\frac{13}{10}$	$1\frac{3}{10}$
c. $\frac{28}{25}$	$1\frac{3}{25}$

49 Textbook

Part 6

a. 0.75
e. 1.5

Part 7

a. $\frac{35}{15}$
c. $\frac{7}{7}$

Part 8

a. 7476
c. 4368

Part 9

a. 245 women
c. 1186 workers

Part 10

a. 3.75
c. 4.1

Part 11

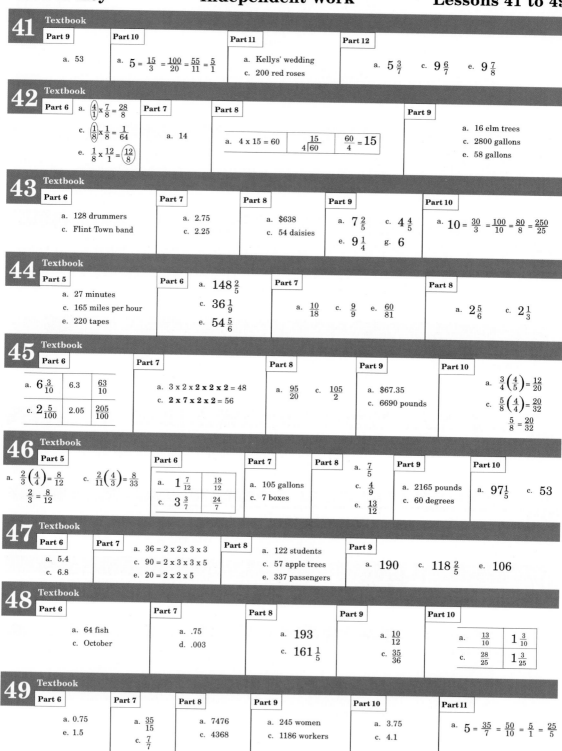

a. $5 = \frac{35}{7} = \frac{50}{10} = \frac{5}{1} = \frac{25}{5}$

51 Textbook

Part 5

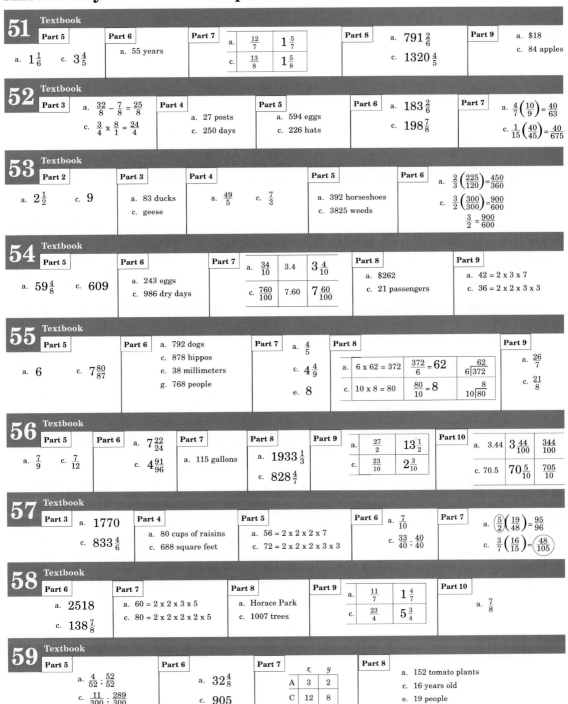

a. $1\frac{1}{6}$ c. $3\frac{4}{5}$

Part 6

a. 55 years

Part 7

a.	$\frac{12}{7}$	$1\frac{5}{7}$
c.	$\frac{13}{8}$	$1\frac{5}{8}$

Part 8

a. $791\frac{2}{6}$

c. $1320\frac{4}{5}$

Part 9

a. $18

c. 84 apples

52 Textbook

Part 3

a. $\frac{32}{8} - \frac{7}{8} = \frac{25}{8}$

c. $\frac{3}{4} \times \frac{8}{1} = \frac{24}{4}$

Part 4

a. 27 posts

c. 250 days

Part 5

a. 594 eggs

c. 226 hats

Part 6

a. $183\frac{2}{6}$

c. $198\frac{7}{8}$

Part 7

a. $\frac{4}{7}\left(\frac{10}{9}\right) = \frac{40}{63}$

c. $\frac{1}{15}\left(\frac{40}{45}\right) = \frac{40}{675}$

53 Textbook

Part 2

a. $2\frac{1}{2}$ c. 9

Part 3

a. 83 ducks

c. geese

Part 4

a. $\frac{49}{5}$ c. $\frac{7}{3}$

Part 5

a. 392 horseshoes

c. 3825 weeds

Part 6

a. $\frac{2}{3}\left(\frac{225}{120}\right) = \frac{450}{360}$

c. $\frac{3}{2}\left(\frac{300}{300}\right) = \frac{900}{600}$

$\frac{3}{2} = \frac{900}{600}$

54 Textbook

Part 5

a. $59\frac{4}{8}$ c. 609

Part 6

a. 243 eggs

c. 986 dry days

Part 7

a.	$\frac{34}{10}$	3.4	$3\frac{4}{10}$
c.	$\frac{760}{100}$	7.60	$7\frac{60}{100}$

Part 8

a. $262

c. 21 passengers

Part 9

a. 42 = 2 x 3 x 7

c. 36 = 2 x 2 x 3 x 3

55 Textbook

Part 5

a. 6 c. $7\frac{80}{87}$

Part 6

a. 792 dogs

c. 878 hippos

e. 38 millimeters

g. 768 people

Part 7

a. $\frac{4}{5}$

c. $4\frac{4}{9}$

e. 8

Part 8

a.	6 x 62 = 372	$\frac{372}{6} = 62$	$6\overline{)372}$ = 62
c.	10 x 8 = 80	$\frac{80}{10} = 8$	$10\overline{)80}$ = 8

Part 9

a. $\frac{26}{7}$

c. $\frac{21}{8}$

56 Textbook

Part 5

a. $\frac{7}{9}$ c. $\frac{7}{12}$

Part 6

a. $7\frac{22}{24}$

c. $4\frac{91}{96}$

Part 7

a. 115 gallons

Part 8

a. $1933\frac{1}{3}$

c. $828\frac{4}{7}$

Part 9

a.	$\frac{27}{2}$	$13\frac{1}{2}$
c.	$\frac{23}{10}$	$2\frac{3}{10}$

Part 10

a. 3.44	$3\frac{44}{100}$	$\frac{344}{100}$
c. 70.5	$70\frac{5}{10}$	$\frac{705}{10}$

57 Textbook

Part 3

a. 1770

c. $833\frac{4}{6}$

Part 4

a. 80 cups of raisins

c. 688 square feet

Part 5

a. 56 = 2 x 2 x 2 x 7

c. 72 = 2 x 2 x 2 x 3 x 3

Part 6

a. $\frac{7}{10}$

c. $\frac{33}{40}$; $\frac{40}{40}$

Part 7

a. $\left(\frac{5}{2}\right)\left(\frac{19}{48}\right) = \frac{95}{96}$

c. $\frac{3}{7}\left(\frac{16}{15}\right) = \frac{48}{105}$

58 Textbook

Part 6

a. 2518

c. $138\frac{7}{8}$

Part 7

a. 60 = 2 x 2 x 3 x 5

c. 80 = 2 x 2 x 2 x 2 x 5

Part 8

a. Horace Park

c. 1007 trees

Part 9

a.	$\frac{11}{7}$	$1\frac{4}{7}$
c.	$\frac{23}{4}$	$5\frac{3}{4}$

Part 10

a. $\frac{7}{8}$

59 Textbook

Part 5

a. $\frac{4}{52}$; $\frac{52}{52}$

c. $\frac{11}{300}$; $\frac{289}{300}$

Part 6

a. $32\frac{4}{8}$

c. 905

Part 7

	x	y
A	3	2
C	12	8

Part 8

a. 152 tomato plants

c. 16 years old

e. 19 people

61 Textbook

Part 5

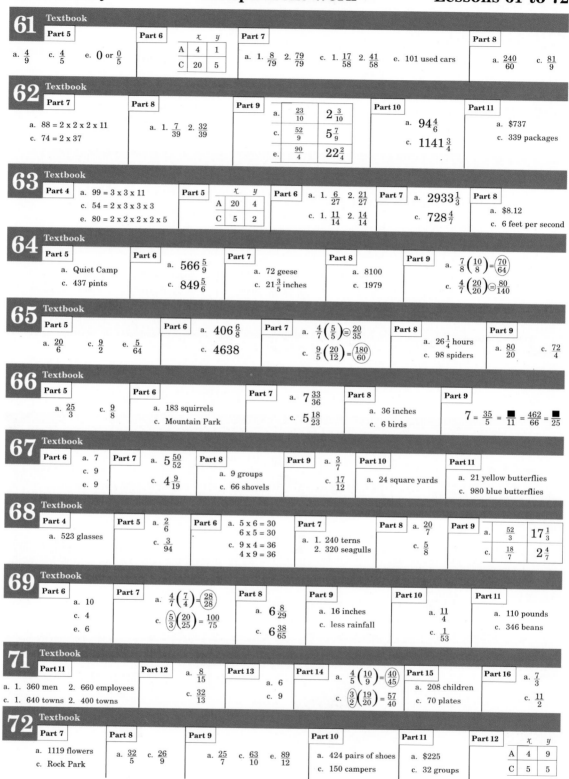

a. $\frac{4}{9}$ c. $\frac{4}{5}$ e. 0 or $\frac{0}{5}$

Part 6

	x	y
A	4	1
C	20	5

Part 7

a. 1. $\frac{8}{79}$ 2. $\frac{79}{79}$ c. 1. $\frac{17}{58}$ 2. $\frac{41}{58}$ e. 101 used cars

Part 8

a. $\frac{240}{60}$ c. $\frac{81}{9}$

62 Textbook

Part 7

a. 88 = 2 x 2 x 2 x 11
c. 74 = 2 x 37

Part 8

a. 1. $\frac{7}{39}$ 2. $\frac{32}{39}$

Part 9

a.	$\frac{23}{10}$	$2\frac{3}{10}$
c.	$\frac{52}{9}$	$5\frac{7}{9}$
e.	$\frac{90}{4}$	$22\frac{2}{4}$

Part 10

a. $94\frac{4}{6}$
c. $1141\frac{3}{4}$

Part 11

a. $737
c. 339 packages

63 Textbook

Part 4

a. 99 = 3 x 3 x 11
c. 54 = 2 x 3 x 3 x 3
e. 80 = 2 x 2 x 2 x 2 x 5

Part 5

	x	y
A	20	4
C	5	2

Part 6

a. 1. $\frac{6}{27}$ 2. $\frac{21}{27}$
c. 1. $\frac{11}{14}$ 2. $\frac{14}{14}$

Part 7

a. $2933\frac{1}{3}$
c. $728\frac{4}{7}$

Part 8

a. $8.12
c. 6 feet per second

64 Textbook

Part 5

a. Quiet Camp
c. 437 pints

Part 6

a. $566\frac{5}{9}$
c. $849\frac{5}{6}$

Part 7

a. 72 geese
c. $21\frac{3}{5}$ inches

Part 8

a. 8100
c. 1979

Part 9

a. $\frac{7}{8}\left(\frac{10}{8}\right) = \frac{70}{64}$
c. $\frac{4}{7}\left(\frac{20}{20}\right) = \frac{80}{140}$

65 Textbook

Part 5

a. $\frac{20}{6}$ c. $\frac{9}{2}$ e. $\frac{5}{64}$

Part 6

a. $406\frac{6}{8}$
c. 4638

Part 7

a. $\frac{4}{7}\left(\frac{5}{5}\right) = \frac{20}{35}$
c. $\frac{9}{5}\left(\frac{20}{12}\right) = \frac{180}{60}$

Part 8

a. $26\frac{1}{4}$ hours
c. 98 spiders

Part 9

a. $\frac{80}{20}$ c. $\frac{72}{4}$

66 Textbook

Part 5

a. $\frac{25}{3}$ c. $\frac{9}{8}$

Part 6

a. 183 squirrels
c. Mountain Park

Part 7

a. $7\frac{33}{36}$
c. $5\frac{18}{23}$

Part 8

a. 36 inches
c. 6 birds

Part 9

$7 = \frac{35}{5} = \frac{■}{11} = \frac{462}{66} = \frac{■}{25}$

67 Textbook

Part 6

a. 7
c. 9
e. 9

Part 7

a. $5\frac{50}{52}$
c. $4\frac{9}{19}$

Part 8

a. 9 groups
c. 66 shovels

Part 9

a. $\frac{3}{7}$
c. $\frac{17}{12}$

Part 10

a. 24 square yards

Part 11

a. 21 yellow butterflies
c. 980 blue butterflies

68 Textbook

Part 4

a. 523 glasses

Part 5

a. $\frac{2}{6}$
c. $\frac{3}{94}$

Part 6

a. 5 x 6 = 30
6 x 5 = 30
c. 9 x 4 = 36
4 x 9 = 36

Part 7

a. 1. 240 terns
2. 320 seagulls

Part 8

a. $\frac{20}{7}$
c. $\frac{5}{8}$

Part 9

a.	$\frac{52}{3}$	$17\frac{1}{3}$
c.	$\frac{18}{7}$	$2\frac{4}{7}$

69 Textbook

Part 6

a. 10
c. 4
e. 6

Part 7

a. $\frac{4}{7}\left(\frac{7}{4}\right) = \frac{28}{28}$
c. $\left(\frac{5}{3}\right)\left(\frac{20}{25}\right) = \frac{100}{75}$

Part 8

a. $6\frac{8}{29}$
c. $6\frac{38}{65}$

Part 9

a. 16 inches
c. less rainfall

Part 10

a. $\frac{11}{4}$
c. $\frac{1}{53}$

Part 11

a. 110 pounds
c. 346 beans

71 Textbook

Part 11

a. 1. 360 men 2. 660 employees
c. 1. 640 towns 2. 400 towns

Part 12

a. $\frac{8}{15}$
c. $\frac{32}{13}$

Part 13

a. 6
c. 9

Part 14

a. $\frac{4}{5}\left(\frac{10}{9}\right) = \frac{40}{45}$
c. $\left(\frac{3}{2}\right)\left(\frac{19}{20}\right) = \frac{57}{40}$

Part 15

a. 208 children
c. 70 plates

Part 16

a. $\frac{7}{3}$
c. $\frac{11}{2}$

72 Textbook

Part 7

a. 1119 flowers
c. Rock Park

Part 8

a. $\frac{32}{5}$ c. $\frac{26}{9}$

Part 9

a. $\frac{25}{7}$ c. $\frac{63}{10}$ e. $\frac{89}{12}$

Part 10

a. 424 pairs of shoes
c. 150 campers

Part 11

a. $225
c. 32 groups

Part 12

	x	y
A	4	9
C	5	5

73 Textbook

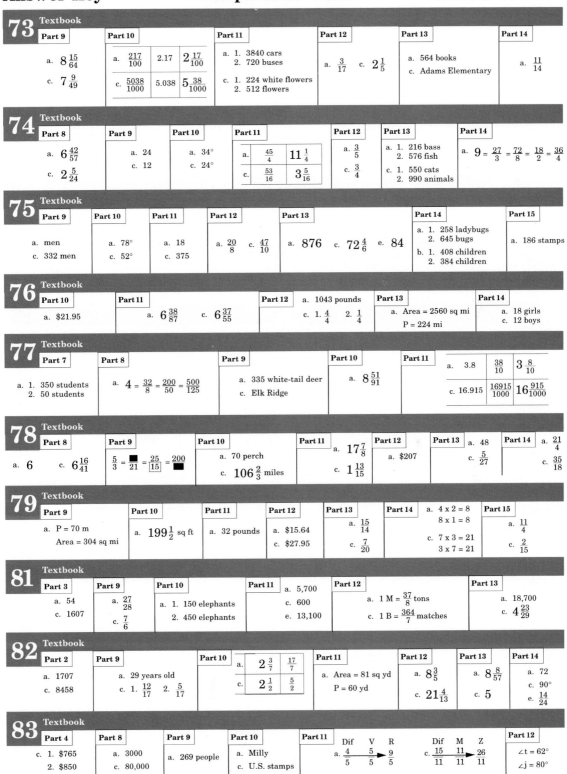

Part 9
a. $8\frac{15}{64}$
c. $7\frac{9}{49}$

Part 10

a.	$\frac{217}{100}$	2.17	$2\frac{17}{100}$
c.	$\frac{5038}{1000}$	5.038	$5\frac{38}{1000}$

Part 11
a. 1. 3840 cars
2. 720 buses
c. 1. 224 white flowers
2. 512 flowers

Part 12
a. $\frac{3}{17}$ c. $2\frac{1}{5}$

Part 13
a. 564 books
c. Adams Elementary

Part 14
a. $\frac{11}{14}$

74 Textbook

Part 8
a. $6\frac{42}{57}$
c. $2\frac{5}{24}$

Part 9
a. 24
c. 12

Part 10
a. 34°
c. 24°

Part 11

a.	$\frac{45}{4}$	$11\frac{1}{4}$
c.	$\frac{53}{16}$	$3\frac{5}{16}$

Part 12
a. $\frac{3}{5}$
c. $\frac{3}{4}$

Part 13
a. 1. 216 bass
2. 576 fish
c. 1. 550 cats
2. 990 animals

Part 14
a. $9 = \frac{27}{3} = \frac{72}{8} = \frac{18}{2} = \frac{36}{4}$

75 Textbook

Part 9
a. men
c. 332 men

Part 10
a. 78°
c. 52°

Part 11
a. 18
c. 375

Part 12
a. $\frac{20}{8}$ c. $\frac{47}{10}$

Part 13
a. 876 c. $72\frac{4}{6}$ e. 84

Part 14
a. 1. 258 ladybugs
2. 645 bugs
b. 1. 408 children
2. 384 children

Part 15
a. 186 stamps

76 Textbook

Part 10
a. $21.95

Part 11
a. $6\frac{38}{87}$ c. $6\frac{37}{55}$

Part 12
a. 1043 pounds
c. 1. $\frac{4}{4}$ 2. $\frac{1}{4}$

Part 13
a. Area = 2560 sq mi
P = 224 mi

Part 14
a. 18 girls
c. 12 boys

77 Textbook

Part 7
a. 1. 350 students
2. 50 students

Part 8
a. $4 = \frac{32}{8} = \frac{200}{50} = \frac{500}{125}$

Part 9
a. 335 white-tail deer
c. Elk Ridge

Part 10
a. $8\frac{51}{91}$

Part 11

a.	3.8	$\frac{38}{10}$	$3\frac{8}{10}$
c.	16.915	$\frac{16915}{1000}$	$16\frac{915}{1000}$

78 Textbook

Part 8
a. 6 c. $6\frac{16}{41}$

Part 9
$\frac{5}{3} = \frac{■}{21} = \frac{25}{\boxed{15}} = \frac{200}{■}$

Part 10
a. 70 perch
c. $106\frac{2}{3}$ miles

Part 11
a. $17\frac{7}{8}$
c. $1\frac{13}{15}$

Part 12
a. $207

Part 13
a. 48
c. $\frac{5}{27}$

Part 14
a. $\frac{21}{4}$
c. $\frac{35}{18}$

79 Textbook

Part 9
a. P = 70 m
Area = 304 sq mi

Part 10
a. $199\frac{1}{2}$ sq ft

Part 11
a. 32 pounds

Part 12
a. $15.64
c. $27.95

Part 13
a. $\frac{15}{14}$
c. $\frac{7}{20}$

Part 14
a. 4 x 2 = 8
8 x 1 = 8
c. 7 x 3 = 21
3 x 7 = 21

Part 15
a. $\frac{11}{4}$
c. $\frac{2}{15}$

81 Textbook

Part 3
a. 54
c. 1607

Part 9
a. $\frac{27}{28}$
c. $\frac{7}{6}$

Part 10
a. 1. 150 elephants
2. 450 elephants

Part 11
a. 5,700
c. 600
e. 13,100

Part 12
a. 1 M = $\frac{37}{8}$ tons
c. 1 B = $\frac{364}{7}$ matches

Part 13
a. 18,700
c. $4\frac{23}{29}$

82 Textbook

Part 2
a. 1707
c. 8458

Part 9
a. 29 years old
c. 1. $\frac{12}{17}$ 2. $\frac{5}{17}$

Part 10

a.	$2\frac{3}{7}$	$\frac{17}{7}$
c.	$2\frac{1}{2}$	$\frac{5}{2}$

Part 11
a. Area = 81 sq yd
P = 60 yd

Part 12
a. $8\frac{3}{5}$
c. $21\frac{4}{13}$

Part 13
a. $8\frac{8}{57}$
c. 5

Part 14
a. 72
c. 90°
e. $\frac{14}{24}$

83 Textbook

Part 4
c. 1. $765
2. $850

Part 8
a. 3000
c. 80,000

Part 9
a. 269 people

Part 10
a. Milly
c. U.S. stamps

Part 11

	Dif	V	R
a.	$\frac{4}{5}$	$\frac{5}{5}$ →	$\frac{9}{5}$

	Dif	M	Z
c.	$\frac{15}{11}$	$\frac{11}{11}$ →	$\frac{26}{11}$

Part 12
∠t = 62°
∠j = 80°

84 Textbook

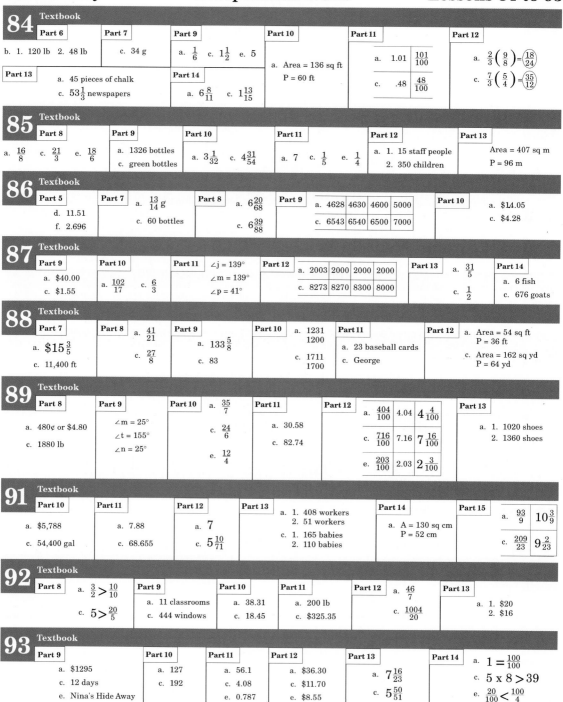

Part 6
b. 1. 120 lb 2. 48 lb

Part 7
c. 34 g

Part 9
a. $\frac{1}{6}$ c. $1\frac{1}{2}$ e. 5

Part 10
a. Area = 136 sq ft
P = 60 ft

Part 11

a.	1.01	$\frac{101}{100}$
c.	.48	$\frac{48}{100}$

Part 12
a. $\frac{2}{3}\left(\frac{9}{8}\right)=\frac{18}{24}$
c. $\frac{7}{3}\left(\frac{5}{4}\right)=\frac{35}{12}$

Part 13
a. 45 pieces of chalk
c. $53\frac{1}{3}$ newspapers

Part 14
a. $6\frac{8}{11}$ c. $1\frac{13}{15}$

85 Textbook

Part 8
a. $\frac{16}{8}$ c. $\frac{21}{3}$ e. $\frac{18}{6}$

Part 9
a. 1326 bottles
c. green bottles

Part 10
a. $3\frac{1}{32}$ c. $4\frac{31}{54}$

Part 11
a. 7 c. $\frac{1}{5}$ e. $\frac{1}{4}$

Part 12
a. 1. 15 staff people
2. 350 children

Part 13
Area = 407 sq m
P = 96 m

86 Textbook

Part 5
d. 11.51
f. 2.696

Part 7
a. $\frac{13}{14}$ g
c. 60 bottles

Part 8
a. $6\frac{20}{68}$
c. $6\frac{39}{88}$

Part 9

a.	4628	4630	4600	5000
c.	6543	6540	6500	7000

Part 10
a. $14.05
c. $4.28

87 Textbook

Part 9
a. $40.00
c. $1.55

Part 10
a. $\frac{102}{17}$ c. $\frac{6}{3}$

Part 11
∠j = 139°
∠m = 139°
∠p = 41°

Part 12

a.	2003	2000	2000	2000
c.	8273	8270	8300	8000

Part 13
a. $\frac{31}{5}$
c. $\frac{1}{2}$

Part 14
a. 6 fish
c. 676 goats

88 Textbook

Part 7
a. $\$15\frac{3}{5}$
c. 11,400 ft

Part 8
a. $\frac{41}{21}$
c. $\frac{27}{8}$

Part 9
a. $133\frac{5}{8}$
c. 83

Part 10
a. 1231
1200
c. 1711
1700

Part 11
a. 23 baseball cards
c. George

Part 12
a. Area = 54 sq ft
P = 36 ft
c. Area = 162 sq yd
P = 64 yd

89 Textbook

Part 8
a. 480¢ or $4.80
c. 1880 lb

Part 9
∠m = 25°
∠t = 155°
∠n = 25°

Part 10
a. $\frac{35}{7}$
c. $\frac{24}{6}$
e. $\frac{12}{4}$

Part 11
a. 30.58
c. 82.74

Part 12

a.	$\frac{404}{100}$	4.04	$4\frac{4}{100}$
c.	$\frac{716}{100}$	7.16	$7\frac{16}{100}$
e.	$\frac{203}{100}$	2.03	$2\frac{3}{100}$

Part 13
a. 1. 1020 shoes
2. 1360 shoes

91 Textbook

Part 10
a. $5,788
c. 54,400 gal

Part 11
a. 7.88
c. 68.655

Part 12
a. 7
c. $5\frac{10}{71}$

Part 13
a. 1. 408 workers
2. 51 workers
c. 1. 165 babies
2. 110 babies

Part 14
a. A = 130 sq cm
P = 52 cm

Part 15

a.	$\frac{93}{9}$	$10\frac{3}{9}$
c.	$\frac{209}{23}$	$9\frac{2}{23}$

92 Textbook

Part 8
a. $\frac{3}{2} > \frac{10}{10}$
c. $5 > \frac{20}{5}$

Part 9
a. 11 classrooms
c. 444 windows

Part 10
a. 38.31
c. 18.45

Part 11
a. 200 lb
c. $325.35

Part 12
a. $\frac{46}{7}$
c. $\frac{1004}{20}$

Part 13
a. 1. $20
2. $16

93 Textbook

Part 9
a. $1295
c. 12 days
e. Nina's Hide Away

Part 10
a. 127
c. 192

Part 11
a. 56.1
c. 4.08
e. 0.787

Part 12
a. $36.30
c. $11.70
e. $8.55

Part 13
a. $7\frac{16}{23}$
c. $5\frac{50}{51}$

Part 14
a. $1 = \frac{100}{100}$
c. $5 \times 8 > 39$
e. $\frac{20}{100} < \frac{100}{4}$

94 Textbook

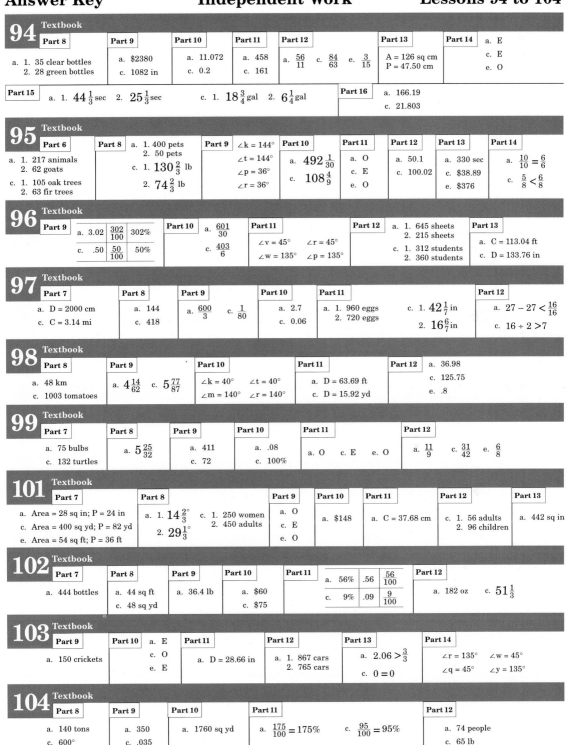

Part 8
a. 1. 35 clear bottles
2. 28 green bottles

Part 9
a. \$2380
c. 1082 in

Part 10
a. 11.072
c. 0.2

Part 11
a. 458
c. 161

Part 12
a. $\frac{56}{11}$ c. $\frac{84}{63}$ e. $\frac{3}{15}$

Part 13
A = 126 sq cm
P = 47.50 cm

Part 14
a. E
c. E
e. O

Part 15
a. 1. $44\frac{1}{3}$ sec 2. $25\frac{1}{3}$ sec
c. 1. $18\frac{3}{4}$ gal 2. $6\frac{1}{4}$ gal

Part 16
a. 166.19
c. 21.803

95 Textbook

Part 6
a. 1. 217 animals
2. 62 goats
c. 1. 105 oak trees
2. 63 fir trees

Part 8
a. 1. 400 pets
2. 50 pets
c. 1. $130\frac{2}{3}$ lb
2. $74\frac{2}{3}$ lb

Part 9
∠k = 144°
∠t = 144°
∠p = 36°
∠r = 36°

Part 10
a. $492\frac{1}{30}$
c. $108\frac{4}{9}$

Part 11
a. O
c. E
e. O

Part 12
a. 50.1
c. 100.02

Part 13
a. 330 sec
c. \$38.89
e. \$376

Part 14
a. $\frac{10}{10} = \frac{6}{6}$
c. $\frac{5}{8} < \frac{6}{8}$

96 Textbook

Part 9

a. 3.02	$\frac{302}{100}$	302%
c. .50	$\frac{50}{100}$	50%

Part 10
a. $\frac{601}{30}$
c. $\frac{403}{6}$

Part 11
∠v = 45° ∠r = 45°
∠w = 135° ∠p = 135°

Part 12
a. 1. 645 sheets
2. 215 sheets
c. 1. 312 students
2. 360 students

Part 13
a. C = 113.04 ft
c. D = 133.76 in

97 Textbook

Part 7
a. D = 2000 cm
c. C = 3.14 mi

Part 8
a. 144
c. 418

Part 9
a. $\frac{600}{3}$ c. $\frac{1}{80}$

Part 10
a. 2.7
c. 0.06

Part 11
a. 1. 960 eggs
2. 720 eggs
c. 1. $42\frac{1}{7}$ in
2. $16\frac{6}{7}$ in

Part 12
a. $27 - 27 < \frac{16}{16}$
c. $16 \div 2 > 7$

98 Textbook

Part 8
a. 48 km
c. 1003 tomatoes

Part 9
a. $4\frac{14}{62}$ c. $5\frac{77}{87}$

Part 10
∠k = 40° ∠t = 40°
∠m = 140° ∠r = 140°

Part 11
a. D = 63.69 ft
c. D = 15.92 yd

Part 12
a. 36.98
c. 125.75
e. .8

99 Textbook

Part 7
a. 75 bulbs
c. 132 turtles

Part 8
a. $5\frac{25}{32}$

Part 9
a. 411
c. 72

Part 10
a. .08
c. 100%

Part 11
a. O c. E e. O

Part 12
a. $\frac{11}{9}$ c. $\frac{31}{42}$ e. $\frac{6}{8}$

101 Textbook

Part 7
a. Area = 28 sq in; P = 24 in
c. Area = 400 sq yd; P = 82 yd
e. Area = 54 sq ft; P = 36 ft

Part 8
a. 1. $14\frac{2}{3}°$
2. $29\frac{1}{3}°$
c. 1. 250 women
2. 450 adults

Part 9
a. O
c. E
e. O

Part 10
a. \$148

Part 11
a. C = 37.68 cm

Part 12
c. 1. 56 adults
2. 96 children

Part 13
a. 442 sq in

102 Textbook

Part 7
a. 444 bottles

Part 8
a. 44 sq ft
c. 48 sq yd

Part 9
a. 36.4 lb

Part 10
a. \$60
c. \$75

Part 11

a. 56%	.56	$\frac{56}{100}$
c. 9%	.09	$\frac{9}{100}$

Part 12
a. 182 oz c. $51\frac{1}{3}$

103 Textbook

Part 9
a. 150 crickets

Part 10
a. E
c. O
e. E

Part 11
a. D = 28.66 in

Part 12
a. 1. 867 cars
2. 765 cars

Part 13
a. $2.06 > \frac{3}{3}$
c. $0 = 0$

Part 14
∠r = 135° ∠w = 45°
∠q = 45° ∠y = 135°

104 Textbook

Part 8
a. 140 tons
c. 600°

Part 9
a. 350
c. .035

Part 10
a. 1760 sq yd

Part 11
a. $\frac{175}{100} = 175\%$ c. $\frac{95}{100} = 95\%$

Part 12
a. 74 people
c. 65 lb

105 Textbook

Part 2
a. $25\frac{5}{7}$ sunny days
c. 360 fish

Part 9

a.	8%	.08	$\frac{8}{100}$
c.	103%	1.03	$\frac{103}{100}$

Part 10
a. 229 steers
c. 261 stamps

Part 11
a. 8.030, 3.080, .038
c. .410, .400, .041

Part 12
a. 49 loaves

Part 13
a. 66
c. 121

106 Textbook

Part 6
a. 110 days
c. 268 employees; 335 students

Part 8
a. 1155
c. 60

Part 9
a. $\frac{13}{7}$
c. $\frac{1}{9}$

Part 10
a. 126 oz
c. $73\frac{1}{3}$ oz

Part 11
a. 147°
c. 288°

Part 12
a. 2.1350
c. 69.0

Part 13
a. $\frac{175}{100} = 175\%$
c. $\frac{60}{100} = 60\%$

107 Textbook

Part 7
b. 1600 yd
d. 1. 48 oz
2. 12 oz

Part 8
a. 12.96
c. .0237

Part 9
a. .560, .555, .500
c. 6.10, 5.98, 5.90

Part 10
a. 184 tons
c. 7534 tons

Part 11
a. $8\frac{5}{8}$
c. 522

Part 12
a. 94

Part 13
a. $741\frac{3}{5}$
c. 6

Part 14
a. $\frac{100}{100} = 100\%$
c. $\frac{6}{100} = 6\%$

108 Textbook

Part 8
a. $5\frac{7}{8} = 5\frac{7}{8}$
c. $\frac{4}{5} < \frac{5}{4}$

Part 9
a. $19.55
c. $19.55

Part 10
a. 106

Part 11
a. 1080 fleas
c. 10 sheep

Part 12
a. $90\frac{11}{41}$
c. $90\frac{2}{52}$

Part 13
a. $1\frac{24}{36}$ patterns
c. 142 acres

109 Textbook

Part 1
a. 27
c. 41

Part 7
a. $29\frac{2}{3}$
c. 115

Part 8
a. 145

Part 9
a. $10,500
c. $845

Part 10
a. 2.80, 2.09, 2.08
c. 1.010, 1.008, .030

Part 11
a. $29.05
c. $9
e. 600 bicycles

Part 12
a. C = 69.08 cm

Part 13
a. 8.615

111 Workbook

Part 1
a. 32.973
c. 40.24

Part 2
a. 19

Part 3
a. 4.960, 4.600, 4.509
c. 1.700, 1.070, 1.007

Part 4
a. $\frac{70}{100} = 70\%$

Textbook

Part 9
a. 160 robins

Part 10
SA = 1008 sq ft
V = 1152 cu ft

Part 11
a. 120
c. 115 tons
e. $10\frac{10}{15}$ worms

112 Workbook

Part 1
a. $928\frac{5}{7}$
c. $1902\frac{2}{4}$

Part 2

A	6	9
C	3	6
E	0	3

Part 3
a. $3.64
c. $11.03

Part 4
$\angle r = 12°$
$\angle w = 168°$
$\angle y = 168°$

Part 5
a. $\frac{28}{100} = 28\%$

Textbook

Part 8
A = 90 sq cm
P = 45.5 cm

Part 9
a. They are equal.
c. 9 cups

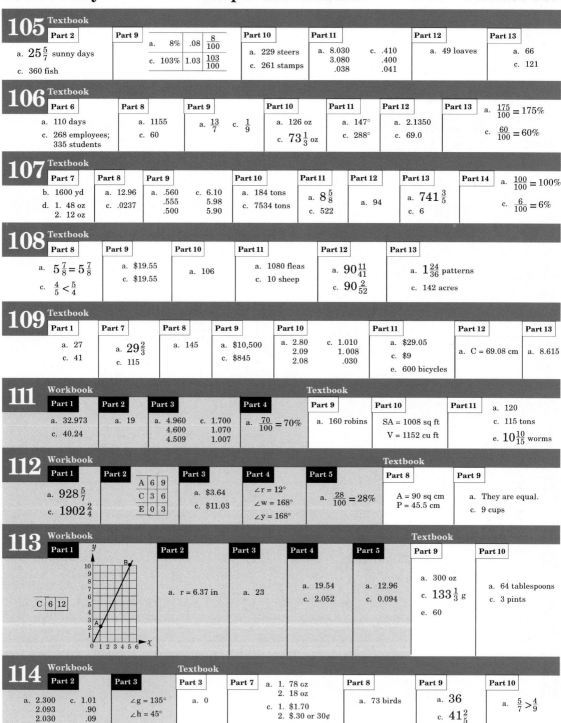

113 Workbook

Part 1

C	6	12

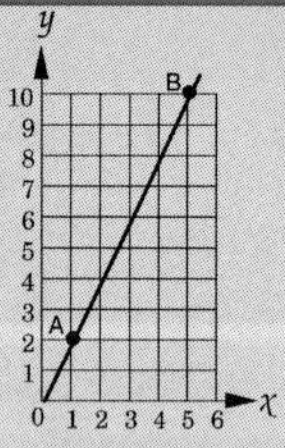

Part 2
a. r = 6.37 in

Part 3
a. 23

Part 4
a. 19.54
c. 2.052

Part 5
a. 12.96
c. 0.094

Textbook

Part 9
a. 300 oz
c. $133\frac{1}{3}$ g
e. 60

Part 10
a. 64 tablespoons
c. 3 pints

114 Workbook

Part 2
a. 2.300, 2.093, 2.030
c. 1.01, .90, .09

Part 3
$\angle g = 135°$
$\angle h = 45°$

Textbook

Part 3
a. 0

Part 7
a. 1. 78 oz
2. 18 oz
c. 1. $1.70
2. $.30 or 30¢

Part 8
a. 73 birds

Part 9
a. 36
c. $41\frac{2}{5}$

Part 10
a. $\frac{5}{7} > \frac{4}{9}$

115

Textbook

Part 6

Part 7
a. 35

Part 8
a. 33 ft
c. They are equal.

Part 9
a. $\frac{5}{12} > \frac{4}{10}$

Part 10
a. 1. $20 2. $12
c. 1. $13\frac{2}{10}$ tons 2. $2\frac{2}{10}$ tons

Part 11
a. 64 vehicles

116

Workbook

Part 2
a. $38\frac{6}{18}$
c. $9\frac{58}{60}$

Part 3
a. $\frac{60}{100} = 60\%$
c. $\frac{75}{100} = 75\%$

Part 4

a.	7	7 + 3	10
c.	1	1 + 3	4

Textbook

Part 3
a. 4 gallons

Part 4
SA = 294 sq in
V = 343 cu in

Part 5
a. 0
c. 198

Part 6
a. 1. 880 seeds
2. 120 seeds
c. 1. 400 workers
2. 240 workers

117

Workbook

Part 2
a. 27.4
c. .858

Part 3

a.	7%	$\frac{7}{100}$	.07
c.	152%	$\frac{152}{100}$	1.52

Part 4
a. 3.060
2.999
2.990

Part 5
a. $14\frac{12}{21}$

Textbook

Part 3
a. 25

Part 4
a. $\frac{5}{8} < \frac{9}{12}$

Part 5
a. 490 phones
c. 1. 36 trials
2. 9 not Xs

Part 6

Part 7
a. $\frac{3}{10}$
c. $\frac{3}{3}$
e. bag a

Part 8
a. 280°
c. 14 petals
e. 60 oz

118

Workbook

Part 3
a. r = 9.24 cm

Part 4
∠j = 144°
∠p = 144°

Textbook

Part 5
a. $\frac{2}{5} = \frac{6}{15}$
c. 32 pints
e. They are equal.

Part 6
a. 15 vans
c. 28 teams

Part 7
a. 1. 429 lb
2. 231 lb
c. 1. 36 trials
2. 16 Xs

Part 8
a. $4.12

Part 9
a. 31 people

119

Workbook

Part 3
Angles of slices equals same numbers in Degrees Column in part 2.

Part 4
a. 101.91 cm
c. 314 sq in

Part 5
a. $12\frac{16}{19}$
c. $248\frac{1}{6}$

Part 6
a. $\frac{48}{100} = 48\%$
c. $\frac{2}{100} = 2\%$

Part 7
a.

x	$x + 4$	y
2	2 + 4	6
0	0 + 4	4

Textbook

Part 2
a. 0

Part 3
a.

Part 4
a. $\frac{3}{7}$ c. $\frac{1}{7}$
e. bag b

Part 5
a. $49\frac{1}{6}$ lb.

Part 6
a. 172 pairs
c. 6 times

121

Workbook

Part 3
a. $4\frac{3}{5}$ c. $1\frac{2}{3}$

Part 4
a. $9\frac{3}{5}$
c. $\frac{1}{3}$

Part 5
a. 112.32
c. $45\frac{1}{13}$
e. $94\frac{24}{29}$

Textbook

Part 4 a. 15

Part 5
a. 148 trucks
c. 207 trucks

Part 6
a. perimeter
c. area

Part 7
a. 154 oz
c. 20 acres

Part 8
a. 1. 78 trials
2. 75 times

Part 9
a. 66 sec
c. $46\frac{1}{4}°$

Part 10
a. A= 180 sq cm
P = 52 cm

122

Workbook

Part 1

2	2 x 4	8
1	1 x 4	4

Part 2
a. .7308
c. .3996

Part 3

a.	$1\frac{9}{100}$	$\frac{109}{100}$	1.09
c.	$13\frac{28}{100}$	$\frac{1328}{1000}$	13.28

Part 4

a.	$\frac{6}{10}$	$\frac{60}{100}$	60%	.60
c.	$\frac{3}{25}$	$\frac{12}{100}$	12%	.12

Part 5
a. $1\frac{3}{5}$
c. $\frac{1}{2}$

Textbook

Part 4 mystery edge length = 6 units

Part 5
a. 110 seats

Part 6
a. area
c. area

Part 7
a. 455

Part 8 A = 180 sq ft; P = 62 ft

Part 11 a. 130 oz

Part 9
a. C = 50.24 in
A = 200.96 sq in
c. C = 31.4 cm
A = 78.5 sq cm

Part 10
a. 413 people
c. 77 adults

123

Workbook

Part 2
a. 1.6821
c. 72
e. 1725

Part 3
a. $9\frac{1}{2}$
c. $\frac{14}{15}$

Part 4
a. $\frac{1}{20}$
c. $1\frac{1}{2}$

Textbook

Part 6
a. 1200 trees
c. evergreen trees

Part 7
a. 14 fish
c. 16 in

Part 8
a. volume
c. volume

124

Workbook

Part 1
a. .4544
c. 1.0016
e. $14\frac{5}{11}$

Part 2
a. $\frac{13}{20}$
c. $\frac{1}{24}$

Textbook

Part 1
a. $126

Part 6
a. $9\frac{3}{5}$ lb
c. 25 cartons

Part 7
a. They are equal.

Part 8
a. 641 patients
c. 160 patients

Part 9
a. $37\frac{5}{7}$ lb

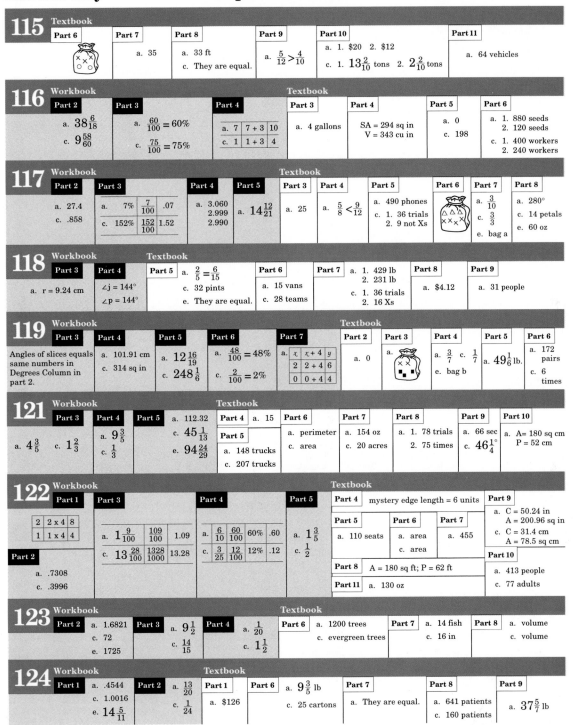

125

Workbook

Part 3

a.	$3\frac{1}{1000}$	$\frac{3001}{1000}$	3.001
c.	$5\frac{9}{100}$	$\frac{509}{100}$	5.09

Part 4

3	3 x 7	21
2	2 x 7	14
1	1 x 7	7

Textbook

Part 2

a. $19\frac{9}{29}$
c. $15\frac{1}{51}$
e. 12.180

Part 3

a. C = 43.96 in
A = 153.86 sq in
c. D = 95.54 m
r = 47.77 m

Part 4

a. $1\frac{1}{5}$

Part 5

a. 4 years

Part 6

a. A = 360 sq in
P = 98 in

Part 7

a. $5\frac{1}{3}$ chinups

Part 8

a. Rita
c. 170 football cards

ABBREVIATIONS

U.S. SYSTEM | **METRIC SYSTEM**

CAPACITY

teaspoons = tsp	milliliters = ml
tablespoons = tbsp	centiliters = cl
cups = c	liters = l
pints = pt	kiloliter = kl
quarts = qt	
gallons = gal	

LENGTH

inches = in	centimeters = cm
feet = ft	meters = m
yards = yd	kilometers = km
miles = mi	

WEIGHT

ounces = oz	grams = g
pounds = lb	kilograms = kg

RATE

miles per hour = mph

TIME

seconds = sec
minutes = min
hours = hr
weeks = wk
months = mo
years = yr

MONEY

dollar = $
cents = ¢

AREA

square inches = sq in
square centimeter = sq cm

VOLUME

cubic feet = cu ft
cubic meters = cu m